ONE WE

Dealing with Death

Dealing with Death

A Handbook of Practices, Procedures and Law

Second Edition

Jennifer Green and Michael Green

Jessica Kingsley Publishers
London and Philadelphia

First published in 2006
by Jessica Kingsley Publishers
116 Pentonville Road
London N1 9JB, UK
and
400 Market Street, Suite 400
Philadelphia, PA 19106, USA

www.jkp.com

Library of Congress Cataloging in Publication Data

Green, Jennifer, 1938-
  Dealing with death : a handbook of practices, procedures and law / Jennifer Green and
Michael Green. -- 2nd ed.
    p. cm.
  Includes bibliographical references and index.
  ISBN-13: 978-1-84310-381-3 (pbk. : alk. paper)
  ISBN-10: 1-84310-381-8 (pbk. : alk. paper) 1. Death. 2. Burial laws--Great Britain. 3.
Death--Religious aspects. I. Green, Michael, 1938- II. Title.
  RA1063.G74 2006
  614'.1--dc22

                    2006009678

British Library Cataloguing in Publication Data
A CIP catalogue record for this book is available from the British Library

ISBN-13: 978 1 84310 381 3
ISBN-10: 1 84310 381 8

Printed and bound in Great Britain by
Athenaeum Press, Gateshead, Tyne and Wear

For Tana and Maia and their families

'Grandma, where's your mortuary?'
'Oh – we haven't got one, Darling.'
'Well – what do you do with your dead people then?'

The authors' daughter, aged 4

Contents

PREFACE   15

A NOTE ON THE TEXT   17

ACKNOWLEDGEMENTS   19

LIST OF ABBREVIATIONS   21

Part 1. Legal and Technical Aspects

Chapter 1. Customs and Laws   25

Introduction 25; Development of funeral practices in the UK
26; Cremation – the modern favoured option 27; Development of formal
registration of death 28; What is death? Definition and diagnosis 28; Life
support and its discontinuation 29; Changes after death 31; The general
legal requirements relating to death 31; What to do when someone dies –
an overview 32; Burial at sea 35; Export of bodies 36; References 36

Chapter 2. Medical Certification of Cause of Death   38

History 38; The Medical Certificate of Cause of Death 42; Accuracy of
death certification 43; Referral of a death to the Coroner by the Registrar
44; References 45

Chapter 3. Registration of Death   47

History of the office of Registrar 47; Responsibility for registration –
'qualified informants' 49; Registration without reference to the Coroner
49; Disposal in special circumstances 50; Reference to the Coroner by the
Registrar 51; Registration of deaths at sea, or overseas (HM Forces)
52; Stillbirth and neonatal death certification and registration 53; Certificate
of no liability to register 53; Missing persons – presumption of death
53; Registration of deaths occurring in Scotland and Northern Ireland
54; References 54

Chapter 4. Coroners and Coroner's Inquiries   56

History of coronership 56; The present-day office of Coroner
58; Reportable deaths 59; Coroner's certificates A, B and E 61; Removal of
bodies out of England 62; The coronial autopsy, consent, and retention of
material 62; Objections to autopsy and tissue retention 64; The Coroner's
inquest 66; Verdicts and 'findings' 66; Verdicts – the need for change
70; Neglect 70; Judicial review – when things go wrong 71; Scotland – the
Procurator Fiscal 71; The Coroner – proposals for change 73; The Home
Office Fundamental Review 74; The Shipman Inquiry 75; References 76

Chapter 5. Fetal Loss, Stillbirth, Neonatal Death
and Sudden Death in Infancy   78

History of legislation and recent changes in law and terminology
78; Definitions 80; Stillbirth certification and registration 81; Certification of
perinatal and neonatal death 83; Sudden and unexpected death in infancy –
SIDS (cot death) 86; Proposed improvements in the investigation of sudden
infant death 87; References 88

Chapter 6. The Autopsy and Mortuary Practice   89

History of the autopsy 89; The autopsy in decline 91; The reasons for
autopsy 91; When may an autopsy be performed? 92; Unauthorised
retention of organs and tissues – the Alder Hey Inquiry 93; The Coroner's
autopsy 95; Autopsy technique 95; Mortuary design and administration
98; Documentation 99; References 100

Chapter 7. Funeral Direction and Disposal by Burial   102

Modern funeral direction 102; The role of the funeral director 103; The
practice of embalming 104; Disposal by burial 105; Churchyard burials
106; Burials in municipal and private cemeteries107; Registration of burials
108; 'Green' garden and woodland burial 108; Burial at sea
110; References 110

Chapter 8. Disposal by Cremation   112

History and principles of cremation 112; Cremation legislation and
certification 113; Forms required for cremation 114; Cremation of body
parts removed at post mortem 117; Cremation of stillborn infants and fetal
remains 118; Arrangements for cremation 119; References 119

Chapter 9. Organ and Tissue Donation and Transplantation   121

Retention and disposal of specimens, organs and tissues from living patients 121; History 122; The Human Tissue Act (2004) 123; The Human Tissue Authority (HTA) 125; Who can give consent? 125; Implementation of the Human Tissue Act (2004) 126; Organ donation: practical considerations 126; Brainstem death and selection of donors 127; Donation when the Coroner is involved 128; Live donors and commercial issues 129; The transplant coordinator 129; 'Leaving my body to science': donation to an anatomy department 129; References 130

Chapter 10. The Law and Practice of Exhumation   132

History 132; Exhumation under the authority of the Secretary of State (Home Office) 133; Exhumation by order of the Coroner 134; The practice of exhumation 134; Health and safety aspects of exhumation 136; References 136

Chapter 11. Deaths in Major Disasters   137

What constitutes a major disaster? 137; Planning for large-scale disasters 138; The role of the pathologist 139; Facilities required 140; References 143

Part 2. Considerations for the Living, Care of the Dying, and Death with Dignity

Chapter 12. Palliative Care   147

Department of Health guidance 148; The delivery of palliative care 151; Symptom control 153; Diagnosing dying 155; Care of the dying child 156; Quality in palliative care157; References 158

Chapter 13. Medico-legal Issues at the End of Life   161

Confidentiality 160; Consent 161; The persistent or permanent vegetative state 162; Advance directives or living wills 167; Resuscitation 169; Elective ventilation of potential organ donors 175; Euthanasia 175; Suicide 176; The treatment of pain 177; Terminal sedation 177; Human Rights Act (1998) 177; Mental Capacity Act (2005) 178; References 180

Chapter 14. Last Offices   182

When not to perform Last Offices 183; When to perform Last Offices
183; Equipment for Last Offices 184; Procedure 184; Care of orifices
185; General toilet 186; Jewellery and religious emblems 186; Labelling the
body 186; Shrouding the body 187; Additional information required
187; Clearing up and checking property 188; Helping the bereaved
188; 'Limited laying out' 189; Procedure following an alleged assault
189; Corneal transplant donors 189; References 190

Chapter 15. Bereavement   191

Grief 191; The pattern of grief 192; Complicated grief 192; What is
counselling? 194; The principles of bereavement counselling 194; Support
organisations 195; References 195

Chapter 16. The Control of Infection in Life and in Death   196

The routes of infection 196; The law and infectious disease
197; Classification of infective organisms 199; Place of treatment of
infectious disease 200; Standard infection control precautions
200; Antibiotic-resistant organisms 202; Ward practice for infectious
disease deaths 204; Mortuary practice for infectious disease deaths
205; Post mortem examinations 205; Special situations 206; Stillbirth
211; Infection and bereaved contacts 211; Sources of local advice
211; References 212

Part 3. Religious, Ethnic and Cultural Aspects of Dying and Death

Chapter 17. Christianity and the Sacraments   217

Christianity 217; Reference 218

**Chapter 18. The Anglican Church (The Church in Wales,
the Church in Ireland, the Episcopalian Church in Scotland)**   219

Baptism 219; Anointing 220; Post mortem examinations 221; Donation of
the body for research and teaching 221; Blood transfusion 221; Organ
transplantation 221; Abortion 221; Stillbirths 221; Suicide 222; Euthanasia
222; Funerals 222

Chapter 19. The Roman Catholic Church 223

The Sacraments 223; Diet 224; The dying Roman Catholic 224; Last Offices 225; Post mortems 225; Blood transfusion 225; Organ donation 225; Abortion 225; Miscarriage or stillbirth 225; Euthanasia 225; Suicide 225; Funerals 226; References 226

Chapter 20. Free Churches and Other Churches 227

Last Offices 228; Post mortems 228; Blood transfusion and organ transplantation 228; Donation of the body 228; Funerals 228; References 228

Chapter 21. Jehovah's Witnesses 229

Jehovah's Witnesses and the question of blood 229; Bloodless medicine and surgery 230; Religious ceremonies (the Sacraments) 231; Jehovah's Witnesses in hospital 232; At death 233; Post mortem examination and body donation 233; Organ transplantation 233; Abortion 234; Euthanasia 234; Suicide 234; Funerals 234; Evangelising 234; References 235

Chapter 22. The Mormon Church 236

The Sacraments 237; The Mormon patient in hospital 238; The dying Mormon 238; At death 238; Post mortem examinations 238; Blood transfusion 238; Organ transplantation 239; Donation of the body 239; Abortion 239; Euthanasia 239; Suicide 239; Funerals 239

Chapter 23. Christian Science 241

The Christian Scientist in hospital 242; The Sacraments 243; The dying Christian Scientist 243; At death 244; Post mortem examinations 244; Blood transfusion 244; Organ transplantation 244; Donation of the body 244; Abortion 244; Suicide 245; Euthanasia 245; Funerals 245

Chapter 24. The African-Caribbean Community 246

African-Caribbean patients in hospital 247; At death 247; Post mortem 247; Blood transfusion 248; Organ transplantation 248; Donation of the body 248; Abortion 248; Suicide 248; Euthanasia 248; Funerals 248

Chapter 25. Rastafarianism 250

The Rastafarian patient in hospital 251; Diet 252; The dying patient 252; At death 252; Post mortem and donation of the body 252; Blood transfusion 253; Organ transplantation 253; Abortion 253; Suicide and euthanasia 253; Funerals 253; References 253

Chapter 26. The Jewish Faith 254

Jews in Britain 254; Religious principles of medical treatment 254; The Jewish patient in hospital 255; Dietary laws 256; The dying patient 256; At death 257; Post mortem examinations 258; Blood transfusion 258; Organ transplantation 258; Donation of the body 259; Abortion and miscarriage 259; Suicide and euthanasia 259; Disposal of body parts 260; Preparation of the body for disposal 260; Funerals 262; Mourning 262; For advice 262; References 263

Chapter 27. Buddhism 264

Buddhists in Britain 264; The Buddhist patient in hospital 265; The dying Buddhist patient 265; At death 265; Post mortem 266; Blood transfusion and organ transplant 266; Donation of the body 266; Abortion and euthanasia 266; Suicide 266; Funerals 266; Buddhist Hospice Trust 267; Reference 267

Chapter 28. The Bahá'i Faith 268

The Bahá'i patient in hospital 269; The dying patient 269; At death 269; Post mortem, transfusion, transplant and research 269; Suicide 270; Euthanasia 270; Funerals 270; Reference 271

Chapter 29. Islam 272

The Muslim patient in hospital 273; Diet 273; The dying patient 274; At death 274; Post mortem examinations 276; Blood transfusion 276; Organ transplantation 276; Donation of the body 276; Abortion 277; Euthanasia and suicide 277; Preparation of the body for the funeral 277; Funerals 277; References 278

Chapter 30. Hinduism 279

The Hindu patient in hospital 280; Diet 280; The dying patient 281; At death 281; Post mortem examinations 282; Blood transfusion 282; Organ transplantation 282; Donation of the body 282; Abortion 282; Suicide 283; Euthanasia 283; Funerals 283; References 284

Chapter 31. Sikhism 285

The Sikh patient in hospital 286; Diet 286; The dying patient 287; At death 287; Post mortem examinations 288; Blood transfusion 288; Organ transplantation 288; Donation of the body 288; Suicide 288; Euthanasia 288; Abortion 289; Funerals 289; References 290

Chapter 32. Zoroastrians (Parsees)   291

The Zoroastrian patient in hospital 292; The dying patient 292; At death 292; Post mortem examinations 293; Blood transfusion 293; Organ transplantation and donation of the body 293; Abortion and euthanasia 293; Suicide 293; Funerals 294; References 295

Chapter 33. The Chinese Community   296

The Chinese patient in hospital 297; The dying Chinese patient 298; At death 299; Blood transfusion 299; Post mortem examinations 299; Organ transplantation 299; Abortion 300; Suicide 300; Euthanasia 300; Funerals 300; References 302

Chapter 34. The Japanese Community   303

The Japanese patient in hospital 304; The dying Japanese patient 304; At death 304; Post mortem and body donation 304; Blood transfusion 305; Organ transplantation 305; Suicide 305; Euthanasia 306; Abortion 307; Funerals 307; References 308

Chapter 35. HIV/AIDS   310

The changing picture 310; Counselling 312; Treatment 312; The dedicated AIDS unit 312; The dying patient 313; The Civil Partnership Act (2004) 313; References 314

APPENDIX A. ORGANISATIONS WHICH MAY BE ABLE TO OFFER
HELP WITH VARIOUS ASPECTS OF DYING AND DEATH   315

APPENDIX B. SOURCES OF ADVICE ON FORENSIC PATHOLOGY   337

APPENDIX C. FURTHER READING   340

SUBJECT INDEX   346

AUTHOR INDEX   352

PREFACE

At the beginning of the 20th century, the population of the United Kingdom was almost entirely white, Anglo-Saxon and Christian. Medicine and surgery were, by today's standards, primitive; 90 per cent of deaths occurred at home, many in young people; and less than 5 per cent were the subject of coronial inquiry. Earth burial was the rule. Families were close both geographically and socially; dying, death, disposal and bereavement were part of everyday life.

Today, we are a long-lived multi-ethnic society; a substantial majority of deaths occur in institutions; cremation is by far the commonest method of disposal; and a Coroner is involved in the investigation of more than one-third of all deaths. If proposed new legislation is introduced (unlikely before 2010), all deaths will be referred to the coronial service in the first instance. The average adult, however, has had little personal experience with the social, legal and technical aspects of death.

Since the first edition of this book was published in 1992, several major events have occurred which have changed public attitudes to the investigation of death, in particular to autopsy and tissue retention. These in turn have led to major legislative changes, notably the Human Tissue Act (2004), proposed changes in death and cremation certification and in the respective roles of the Registrar and Coroner. We had hoped that these changes would have been fully implemented during the preparation of this book. This was not to be, although registration procedures have been simplified. We have tried to anticipate as accurately as possible the nature of the proposed changes and the approximate timetable for their introduction.

Health care professionals, funeral directors, police officers, Coroners and Registrars have to deal with clients from numerous religious and ethnic minorities, in circumstances where grief may easily be increased and offence be unwittingly inflicted.

This book aims to provide a brief but comprehensive guide to the current laws controlling, and the customs surrounding, the disposal of the dead. It is intended to complement, rather than supplant, the many authoritative texts already available, reducing a vast body of knowledge to a manageable size, and providing access to organisations and sources of information.

We hope that medical and nursing staff, and others who deal with death in their professional lives, will find it a concise and readable reference work. Part 1 deals with historical background and current legal and medical practice. Part 2 gives a brief overview of current medico-legal issues surrounding dying and death, modern palliative care, Last Offices, bereavement, and infection control. Part 3 considers the practical aspects of dying and death in the major Christian denominations and other ethnic and religious groups in the UK.

We have provided a modest number of references at the end of each chapter, but have increasingly resorted to websites, which we have also included, along with their accession dates.

A more extensive reading list and a directory of caring organisations are provided as appendices. We extend our thanks to all those who have helped us to give an accurate account; we accept full responsibility for any errors and omissions, but hope that these are few.

Michael and Jennifer Green
(April 2006)

A NOTE ON THE TEXT

This book follows the Interpretation Act 1978 Section 6, in that, unless contrary intention appears, words reporting the masculine gender include the feminine, and words reporting the feminine gender include the masculine.

A NOTE ON THE TEXT

ACKNOWLEDGEMENTS

Many people have helped us with both editions of this book. Our friends, colleagues and total strangers have given time to share their thoughts with us. Every one had a truly valuable contribution to make and we wish to thank them publicly for their expertise and their kindness.

Part I

Mr J. Tempest of Dodgson's Funeral Services, Leeds. Mr D.A. Gibbon, Manager of Leeds Public Mortuary. Dr S.L. Popper, HM Coroner for S. Yorkshire Western District. Mr N. Thompson, Coroner's Officer for S. Yorkshire Western District. Mrs P. Brewster, Librarian at St James's University Hospital, Leeds. Miss J. Birkenshaw, Assistant Registrar, Calderdale District Council. Mr C. P. Dorries, HM Coroner for South Yorkshire Western District. Mr D. Hinchliff, HM Coroner for West Yorkshire Eastern District. Mr J. S. Coupe, Chief Superintendent Registrar of Births, Marriages and Deaths, Leeds. Numerous other medical colleagues, Coroners' Officers and Coroners have also given helpful comments and advice.

Part 2

Many medical and nursing colleagues from relevant disciplines have contributed greatly to this section. In particular, we would like to thank: Noreen Young, Roy Freeman, Dr Nigel Sykes, Hazel Pinfield, Dr Sally Pearson, Dr Graham Sutton, Dr Martin Schweiger, Dr Nigel Peel and Barbara Goodall. Mrs Alison Cox, Senior Mortuary Technician at St James's Hospital, Leeds (also for help with Part 1). Dr Martin Schweiger, Consultant in Communicable Disease Control and Local Director of Health Protection (West Yorkshire). Mrs Jean Lawrence, Director of Infection Prevention and Control, Leeds Mental Health NHS Teaching Trust; Current Chairperson of the Infection Control Nurses Association. Dr Keith Budd, Emeritus Consultant in Pain Management. Alison Smith, Assistant Chief Nurse, Sheffield Teaching Hospitals NHS Trust, and her committee for 'Last Offices'– the Nursing Executive Policy Sub-Group. Lucy Sutton, Palliative Care Policy Lead, and Eve Richardson, Chief Executive, from National Council of Palliative Care.

Part 3

We have been greatly privileged with the help we have received from many contributors for this section. For the first edition we would like to thank: Rev. Philip Clarke, Rev. Helen Mace and Rev. Jeff King (Anglican Church). Monsignor P. Maguire (Roman Catholic Church). Rev. D. Whitehall (Methodist Church). Mr Christopher Brown and the Medical Desk of Jehovah's Witnesses. President Robison and the Public Communications/Special Affairs Department of the Church of Jesus Christ of Latter-Day Saints. Mr G. Phaup and the Christian Science Committee on Publications. Mrs M. Sadler and members of the Afro-Caribbean Community. Ms E. Blair and her Rastafarian colleagues. Mr David Evans (Buddhism). Dr S. Fathe'Azam and Mr Hugh Adamson, Secretary General of the National Spiritual Assembly of the Bahá'is of the United Kingdom. Mrs Hazel Broch and Dayan Berkovits (Judaism). Mr K. Ansari, Mrs K. Knight and the IQRA Trust (Islam). Mr M. Patel and Dr Sunil Minocha (Hinduism). Mr H. Singh Sagoo and Dr B. Singh (Sikhism). Mr Ervad Zal N. Sethna, President, the Zoroastrian Trust Funds of Europe.

For this second edition, our thanks go to Rabbi Daniel Levy, United Hebrew Congregation, Leeds, and Mr David Frei (Registrar) and Dayan Binstock of the London Beth Din (Jewish Faith). Mr Dennis Sibley and the Buddhist Hospice Trust (Buddhism). President James Woodward of the Mormon Church, England (Leeds) Mission. Mr Tony Lobl (District Manager) and Rosemary Castle of the Christian Science Committee on Publications. Mr John Barnabas Leith, Secretary for External Affairs of the National Spiritual Assembly of the Bahá'is of the UK. Canon Jeff King, Vicar of St Peter's Church, Thorner, and Ecumenical Officer for the Diocese of Ripon and Leeds (Anglican Church). Mr Paul Wade, Coordinator of the Hospital Information Services of Jehovah's Witnesses. Father Michael Anthony Kelly, Parish Priest of St Augustine's Roman Catholic Church, Leeds. Dr Hassan Alkatib, Assistant Imam at the Leeds Grand Mosque and Muslim Chaplain to Leeds University. Dr S. Sivaloganathan, retired Forensic Pathologist (Hinduism). Pastor Gloria Hanley of the Wesleyan Holiness (Pentecostal) Church, Leeds (African-Caribbean Community). Mr Surrinder Singh (Sikhism). Dr Tana Green, Consultant in Sexual Health Medicine at the Josephine Butler Centre for Sexual Health, Wakefield. Dr Jeanne Fay, Hospice Practitioner, Singapore; Kim Y F Chan; Lai Fong Chiu, Senior Health Promotion Officer, Leeds; Liza Poon, Health Visitor, Leeds; and Mr Chua Chin Karr, undertaker, Singapore (Chinese Community); Dr Hiroko Harada, Department of Science of Living, Tokushima University, Japan; Noriaki Ikeda, M.D. Professor and Chairman, Department of Legal Medicine, Hirosaki University School of Medicine, Japan; Naofumi Yoshioka, M.D. and Ph.D. Professor of Forensic medicine, Akita University School of Medicine, Japan (Japanese Community).

Secretarial assistance for the first edition was cheerfully provided by Miss Catherine Piper, Ms Pauline Whitaker and Mrs Julie Rodger.

A special thank-you goes to Mrs Mary De Jager, Senior Nurse (Commissioning and Planning) at the General Infirmary at Leeds, for commissioning the first operational policies for ethnic minority deaths in Leeds Western District. The first edition of this book was a direct result of that exercise.

LIST OF ABBREVIATIONS

ACD PAdvisory Committee on Dangerous Pathogens

AHA American Heart Association

AllER All England Law Reports

AP Advanced Practitioner

APT Anatomical Pathology Technician

BMA British Medical Association

BMLR Butterworths medico-legal reports

BSE Bovine spongiform encephalopathy

CAB Citizen's Advice Bureau

CJD Creutzfeldt–Jakob disease

CCRC Criminal Cases Review Commission

Cmnd/Cmn/Cm 'Command document' (a government publication)

CMO Chief Medical Officer

CMV Cytomegalovirus

CO Coroner's Officer

CPA Clinical Pathology Accreditation UK Ltd

CPR Cardiopulmonary resuscitation

CT scan Computerised tomography scan

DCA Department for Constitutional Affairs

DEFRA Department for Environment, Food and Rural Affairs

DNA Deoxyribonucleic acid

DoH Department of Health

EEG Electroencephalogram

ERC European Resuscitation Council

FME Forensic Medical Examiner

FSID Foundation for the Study of Infant Deaths

GMC General Medical Council

HMSO Her Majesty's Stationery Office (now TSO)

HO Home Office

HOTA Human Organ Transplant Act

HPA Health Protection Agency

HSAC Health Services Advisory Committee

HSE Health and Safety Executive

HTA Human Tissue Authority, Human Tissue Act

IBCA Institute of Burial and Cremation Administration

IMCA Independent Mental Capacity Advocate

LPA Lasting Power of Attorney

MAJAX Major accident plan

MCCD Medical certificate of cause of death

MRI Magnetic resonance imaging

MRSA Methicillin-resistant *Staphylococcus aureus*

NCEPOD National confidential enquiry into peri-operative deaths

NCHPCS National Council for Hospices and Palliative Care Services

ONS Office for National Statistics

OPCS Office of Population, Censuses and Surveys (now ONS)

PABFP Policy Advisory Board for Forensic Pathology

PACE Police and Criminal Evidence Act 1984

PCP *Pneumocystis carinii* pneumonia

PRHO Pre-registration house officer (junior doctor)

QBD Queen's Bench Division

RCN Royal College of Nursing

RCOG Royal College of Obstetricians and Gynaecologists

RCP Royal College of Physicians

RCPath Royal College of Pathologists

RCUK Resuscitation Council UK

SANDS Stillbirth and Neonatal Death Society

SIDS Sudden infant death syndrome

SMA Statutory Medical Advisor

SUDI Sudden unexpected death in infancy

TB Tuberculosis

TSO The Stationery Office

UK United Kingdom

ULTRA Unrelated Live Donor Transplant Registration Authority

USA United States of America

USS Ultrasound scan

VES Voluntary Euthanasia Society

WRVS Women's Royal Voluntary Service

PART I
Legal and Technical Aspects

CHAPTER I

CUSTOMS AND LAWS

Introduction

From time immemorial, the disposal of the dead has been a ritual of great importance, usually accompanied by some form of preparation for an afterlife. Disposal by burial has overall been the commonest method adopted. Special techniques, such as vault inhumation or mummification, were reserved for the eminent, as was cremation in Western society until fairly recently. Some societies and religions, for example Orthodox Jewry, have always opposed cremation; in others, it has always been the favoured method.

Perhaps disposal by exposure was first employed, as early man had few tools for digging, and the available caves were needed to shelter the living. In 1994, at Boxgrove in Sussex, a tooth and shinbone were found, along with bones from a variety of other animals (Jupp and Gittings 2000). This site has been estimated to be 500,000 years old. Exposure is still practised by a declining number of Australian aboriginal tribes (Elkin 1968) and by some Tibetans. In India, some Zoroastrians (Parsees) still expose bodies within 'Towers of Silence' until destruction by predators, such as vultures, is complete (Polson and Marshall 1975). Unfortunately the vulture population has undergone dramatic decline in recent years, due the widespread use of non-steroidal anti-inflammatory drugs (NSAIDS) in both human and veterinary practice. These drugs are extremely toxic to the birds of prey, and their disappearance is a major concern to conservationists (Shultz *et al.* 2004). Disposal by cremation has, in consequence, become more common.

The earliest known graves in the UK are in caves at Pont Newydd, in Wales, and date from 225,000 BCE (Jupp and Gittings 2000). Throughout history the purposes of burial were threefold: to remove the corpse from society; to protect it from the elements and from animals; and to prepare it, and often to also supply provisions, for a future life. The form and wealth of provision in burial chambers and graves varies widely between cultures, but modern practice tends towards relative simplicity. Very little property is buried with the corpse in Western societies, although there is no prohibition upon the placing of some treasured object in the coffin – a piece of jewellery for example, or, in the case of a child, a favourite toy. Clothing, also, is simpler than it was. In the UK some form of shroud is most commonly used, although in some countries the corpse is clad in everyday attire. Note that, contrary to popular belief, the use of a coffin is not mandatory in the UK. Many, but not all, local authorities give a dispensation to Muslims, who may be interred in a shroud alone. In the USA, funeral practices often tend towards the ostentatious and are satirised in works by Evelyn Waugh (1993) and Jessica Mitford (1980).

Development of funeral practices in the UK

Funeral practices in the UK have their roots in Judaeo-Christian culture. To the Jewish people, seemly and immediate disposal of the dead has always been, and remains, a 'mitzva' – a solemn obligation. The Christians adopted these customs and attitudes. In early Christian times the Church exercised control over all aspects of disposal and the established (Anglican) Church still retains, in theory at least, absolute control over all interments in its consecrated grounds. Church officials were appointed to organise funerals. A similar practice still persists in the Jewish Community, where responsibility is usually assumed by the local synagogues and voluntary burial societies (the Chevra Kadisha or 'Holy Society'). In early Christian societies, everyone, even the poorest, was entitled to minimum standards. For example, every body had to be followed to the grave by 'a cross bearer, eight monks, and three acolytes' (Polson and Marshall 1975).

Through the 13th to the 15th centuries the Guilds and Craft Companies organised the obsequies for their members and every parish had to provide a bier and a sufficiency of candles. After the late 18th century Industrial Revolution, the role of the Guilds was taken over by burial clubs and friendly societies, which, in return for a small weekly subscription, provided a form of 'death insurance'. Unfortunately, the ease with which such insurance could be obtained through membership of multiple burial clubs is thought to have made a significant contribution to infant mortality in Victorian England. Chadwick (1843) told of a man who had insured a child with no less than 19 such organisations – with a pay-out of £5 per time, a handsome profit! This widespread epidemic of infanticide by poisoning and other methods, such as smothering, provided a major impetus towards a national system of death certification and registration. It was suspected that many deaths from diarrhoea and vomiting, in a society where enteric infections were common, were due to homicidal poisoning by arsenic or antimony, both of which were readily available. Controls upon the sale of these poisons were not introduced until the Arsenic Act of the late 19th century.

Until the 18th century, burial took place in the deceased's local parish churchyard. Following the growth of non-conformism, numerous small private graveyards were established. These were subject to no form of control and many were situated close to water supplies, then thought to be a potential health hazard. Water authorities still impose distance restrictions today, although the grounds for these fears are dubious. City parish churchyards became over-full, and the shallow multiple burials caused both hygienic and aesthetic problems. The 'graveyard stench', consequent upon bodies lying near or upon the surface, was part of Victorian life.

The rich landed gentry retreated behind their estate walls, establishing private mausoleums. Vault inhumation became fashionable among the *nouveaux riches* also. By the middle of the 19th century control of earth burial and restrictions upon vault burial became essential for the maintenance of the public health, and following reports such as that by Chadwick, appropriate legislation was laid before Parliament. This restricted vault burial and burial within churches, and regulated the licensing and management of church and municipal cemeteries.

Cremation – the modern favoured option

Cremation is a relatively new phenomenon in Western society. Held by some to be proscribed in the Old Testament, and still anathema to orthodox Jews and Muslims, it was accepted by mainstream Christian communities only in the closing years of the 19th century. The first efficient crematorium ovens were designed in Italy, independently, by Gorini and Poli in 1872. Brunetti exhibited a furnace in Vienna in 1873. In England, the Cremation Society was founded by Sir Henry Thompson in 1874. Other founder members included the surgeon Spencer Wells, the artist Millais, and the novelist (and ex-Postmaster General) Anthony Trollope. The first crematorium was built at Woking in 1879: a horse was cremated within a few weeks thereafter. There was an enormous public outcry; the then Home Secretary refused to license the cremation of human remains and the crematorium remained unused for six years (Jupp and Gittings 2000; Polson and Marshall 1975). The Bishop of Lincoln, Dr Wordsworth, spoke for many when he described cremation as a 'barbarous and unnatural heathen practice' (cited in Jupp and Gittings 2000).

In 1883 Dr William Price of Llantrisant, Glamorgan, attempted the disposal by burning of his infant son (*R v Price* 1884). He had refused to register the death and in consequence an inquest would have been necessary before permission to inter could be given. The immolation was prevented by the police, who arrested Price. He was charged with attempting to burn the body and attempting to prevent the holding of an inquest. He was subsequently acquitted of both charges.

The view of the trial judge was that no offence was committed in attempting to burn a body, providing that no public nuisance was created. This legal decision was a breakthrough for the Cremation Society, and the first cremation was performed at Woking on 26 March 1885. The Society laid down its own regulations for the conduct of cremations. After vigorous campaigning, and despite widespread public opposition, the first Cremation Act, which incorporated the Society's practices, was passed in 1902.

Cremation remained a minority choice until the late 1950s. Since then, partly due to a change in public and religious attitudes and partly on economic grounds, it has now gained wide acceptance and, in 2005, accounted for over 70 per cent of all disposals in England and Wales. There are now over 200 crematoria, and over 400,000 bodies are cremated annually (Cremation Society of Great Britain 2004).

Development of formal registration of death

The history of registration of both the fact and cause of death is also relatively recent. Until 1836 there was no national system for death registration. The only records were the local 'Bills of Mortality' and parish records. Dissenting chapels and private graveyards were numerous, and records of these interments, maintained on a voluntary basis, were haphazard and incomplete. Each parish appointed two 'searchers', usually elderly women, whose duty it was to inspect dead bodies for signs of infectious disease and to record the numbers of deaths. The system was inefficient and inaccurate. It has been estimated that, so ill-kept were the records, that almost one-third of burials were unaccounted for (Registrar-General's Office 1839). Conversely, the numbers of deaths due to epidemic illness were frequently exaggerated. Other deaths due to infectious diseases with external signs, for example smallpox, were not reported at all, because the family bribed the searchers not to inspect the bodies. Coronial history and the obligation to deal with sudden unexpected, or violent, deaths are dealt with in Chapter 4.

In 1842 the first attempt to obtain *medical* certification of cause of death was made. The Registrar General distributed books of death certificates to the 10,000 medical practitioners licensed by the Medical Royal Colleges and the Society of Apothecaries (medical registration was not introduced until 1858). He invited them to return certificates for those patients whom they had attended before death. Obligatory certification of the cause of death came only with the Births and Deaths Registration Act of 1874 (see Chapter 2).

What is death? Definition and diagnosis

Sigmund Freud defined death as 'an abstract concept with a negative content for which no unconscious co-relative can be found' (cited in Enright 1987). We find this difficult to understand, but in the opinion of Enright (1987) 'it puts the subject in its non-place'. There is no legal definition of death, but Dorries (2004), though not himself a doctor, offers a medical definition in his book *Coroners' Courts*.

The medical profession was remarkably unconcerned with the problem until the development of techniques for organ transplantation created a demand for warm-blooded donors. Techniques for life support created a requirement for agreed criteria for the definition and diagnosis of 'brain death', and the Harvard Definitions (Special Communication 1961) were universally accepted. Since 1976 (*British Medical Journal* 1976) decision-making in the UK has been based on the agreed tests laid down by the Royal Colleges of Physicians and Surgeons. The most recent updated advice was given by the Royal College of Physicians in 1995 (Royal College of Physicians 1995). Dorries goes on to state 'problems normally only arise when a patient is ventilated on a life-support machine due to irreversible coma', but Charlton (1996) pointed out that an increasing number of deaths occur in the community and therefore those involved in primary care need guidance so that opportunities for resuscitation would not be missed.

The criteria for a diagnosis of brainstem death are more fully discussed in Chapter 9, but it seems appropriate here, at the outset, to discuss the basic facts of physical death. Its metaphysical aspects shall be left to others.

THE SIGNS OF DEATH

Two phases of death are generally recognised. Somatic death is the extinction of personality, which is the immediate sign of secession of the vital processes. The eyes glaze, the jaw drops, heartbeat and respiration cease. This state is potentially reversible by cardiopulmonary resuscitation, but a brain deprived of oxygen for as short a time as three minutes is usually irreversibly damaged. Severe hypothermia may lengthen this time. The brains of children under the age of five years seem to be able to withstand hypoxia for longer periods.

Molecular death, the progressive disintegration of the body's tissues, is irreversible, and proceeds through pallor and rigor mortis (stiffening) to decomposition and ultimate dissolution.

THE DIAGNOSIS OF DEATH

The diagnosis of death outside hospital usually becomes clear within a matter of minutes, if no resuscitation is attempted. A complete physical examination should be rapidly undertaken, preferably in private, though these conditions are often difficult to achieve when one is confronted with sudden and unexpected collapse. The major pulses should be palpated and auscultation of the heart and breath sounds, with adequate exposure of the chest, should take place over a period of at least five minutes. The eyes should be examined; not merely for the pupil reflexes. Ophthalmoscopic confirmation of the cessation of blood flow in the retinal vessels should be undertaken if possible. Even when these rules are fully observed, problems can occasionally arise. Those situations in which death has been prematurely assumed include hypothermia, especially in the elderly, and with bodies recovered from cold water, especially those of young children. Overdoses of sedatives and anti-depressants, electric shock and lightning strike have also led to misdiagnoses.

Life support and its discontinuation

The situation on the intensive care unit when a patient is respirator dependent poses much more difficult problems, and there is still widespread debate on the adequacy and reliability of the Joint College criteria referred to above. In general, UK practice is to carry out tests for brainstem function on at least two occasions separated by at least three hours. (The brainstem, situated between the brain proper and the base of the skull, contains the vital centres which control heartbeat and respiration.) The two senior doctors carrying out these tests must be satisfied that there are no drugs within the body which might suppress vital functions, that the reversible causes of coma have been excluded and that the basic blood chemistry is within normal limits.

These tests are intended to demonstrate the absence of fundamental reflexes and are also discussed in Chapter 9. Brainstem death is presumed if the corneal, gag and vestibulo-ocular reflexes cannot be elicited, the pupils are fixed and dilated and there are no spontaneous efforts to breathe when ventilation is suspended. This end-of-life decision has to be taken with increasing frequency and not just when organ harvesting is being considered. With adequate support a patient with no higher brain functions can be kept alive with mechanical assistance for months or even years; surely an undesirable situation for all concerned.

PERSISTENT VEGETATIVE STATE

In some circumstances, the 'thinking' part of the brain has been destroyed but the brainstem continues to function, so that unassisted respiration and heartbeat are maintained for so long as nutrition and fluids are supplied (see also p.162). To withdraw administration of basic hydration, glucose and electrolytes in such a situation is regarded by many as unlawful killing, but in 1993 the case of Tony Bland (*Airedale NHS Trust ex parte Bland* 1993) attempted to clarify the situation (see p.163) and, for many years thereafter, practice was based upon the High Court's determination of that case. Subsequent decisions also took into account the various decisions of the European Court, notably *Glass v UK* (2004). The Court ruled that, save in rare emergency situations, a court must be involved in the decision-making process in the event of parental or other objections to a proposed management plan founded upon 'medical best interests'.

Currently, policy is based upon the case of *Burke v GMC* (2004) and the subsequent reversal of the judge's guidance by the Court of Appeal (2005). Leslie Burke was suffering from a progressive degenerative disease of the nervous system, which would eventually result in loss of movement, requiring artificial feeding. He was concerned that such treatment might be withdrawn, despite his expressed wish to receive life-maintaining therapy (Artificial Nutrition and Hydration, ANH) even after he had lost the ability to communicate and so would be aware of being starved to death. He argued, through his lawyers, that the GMC's guidance in these matters was unclear. *Munby J* (2004) ruled in favour of Burke; the main points of his judgment were:

1. The GMC guidelines failed to recognise the presumption of a right to require treatment.

2. The guidelines failed to recognise a natural presumption in favour of life-prolonging treatment.

3. If at any time the patient has expressed a positive wish for life-prolonging treatment, that treatment must be continued, or the patient must be transferred to the care of those willing to continue it.

The GMC appealed against Mr Justice Munby's judgment, and the Court of Appeal's rulings (2005) form the basis of current practice, although hotly debated at the time of writing by doctors, lawyers and ethical committees. Their Lordships criticised

Munby's extension of the relevant issues beyond Mr Burke's situation into wider areas of concern. Mr Burke's condition was unlikely to affect his competence; he would be able to communicate his wishes until very shortly before death. They held that 'the Courts should not be used as general advice centres. They might enunciate propositions of principle without a full appreciation of the implications which these might have in practice…particularly where there are ethical considerations which the courts should be reluctant to address.'

The Appeal Court goes on to respond in detail to more than ten areas of the initial judgment, and confirms the legality of the GMC End of Life Guidelines. The most up-to-date version of these was published in February 2006. Mr Burke, and others, may rest assured that they will receive the treatment that they need, including artificial hydration and nutrition. The duty to provide ANH is not absolute, but any doctor who withholds such treatment against the patient's previously expressed wishes will be open to a charge of murder. At the extreme end of life, when ANH will not prolong life, the decision to withhold it will depend upon the clinical assessment of the best interests of the patient. The GMC's guidance is therefore in compliance with common law and the Mental Capacity Act (2005). This is a complex area, under constant discussion, and the reader is referred to the relevant areas of the Appeal judgment, and to the GMC End of Life Guidelines. These are constantly reviewed and may be accessed through the Council's and other relevant websites.

THE CORONER AND THE DECISION TO END LIFE

The Coroner has no legal right to consent to the switching off of a ventilator, nor to the withdrawal of other means of life support. His office is concerned only with the investigation of death; nor can he consent to the removal of organs or tissues for donation: that is a matter for the relatives. However, as a matter of courtesy, he should be consulted in any case which is likely to come within his remit, for example before the discontinuation of life support for victims of assault, to ensure that the removal of the organs will not in any way compromise subsequent medico-legal issues.

Changes after death

The changes immediately consequent upon death are dealt with in greater detail in Chapter 13. The progressive disintegration of the tissues in the days after death is covered extensively in standard textbooks of forensic medicine and pathology and is touched upon briefly in the section on embalming in Chapter 7.

The general legal requirements relating to death

All aspects of death and disposal are now regulated by law, to a greater or lesser extent. The principal matters so controlled include:

1. Registration of the death.
2. Authority for disposal.

3. Funeral arrangements – including financial responsibilities.

4. Burial – including maintenance of graveyards, relatives' rights and other matters.

5. Cremation – including certification and regulation of crematoria.

6. Disposal at sea.

7. Removal of bodies out of the UK.

These will be briefly reviewed here. Detailed information on registration, cremation and referral to the Coroner will be found in the appropriate chapters of this book. It will perhaps simplify consideration of these matters if the practical requirements following a death are considered chronologically.

What to do when someone dies – an overview

If the death occurs anywhere other than in hospital, whoever discovers the body should contact the family doctor, if known, the nearest relative and also the police if the circumstances are obviously 'suspicious'. If the death occurs in hospital, the ward staff will notify the nearest relative and, in certain circumstances, the Coroner's Office. In NHS hospitals, some of these duties may be undertaken by a special Bereavement Counselling Office, whose specially trained staff will comfort the relatives and guide them through the procedures.

The relatives should quickly find out if a will has been made (see also 'Advance directives', p.167). The deceased may have expressed wishes concerning organ donation, anatomical dissection, or disposal. Plans for donation of any organ, other than the cornea, must be made before death (see Chapters 9 and 10). The doctor who is the usual medical attendant of the deceased will issue a Medical Certificate of Cause of Death (MCCD) if the cause is natural, is known, and if the deceased had been seen, by him or by a colleague, in the previous 14 days (see Chapter 3). Otherwise he will inform the Coroner of the circumstances (see Chapter 4). Note that, although the various Registration Acts apparently oblige the doctor to issue a certificate in every case, in practice the doctor seldom issues if the case is to be referred to the Coroner.

Authority to dispose of the body, after certification, is granted by the local Registrar of Births, Marriages and Deaths (hereafter referred to as 'the Registrar'). This is known as a 'Certificate for Disposal'. If cremation is desired, additional certificates are required (see Chapter 8).

The Coroner's authority to permit disposal takes one of three forms. He may issue 'pink form A', which is taken to the Registrar, along with the MCCD, who then authorises disposal in the usual way. After an autopsy (without inquest necessary) he issues form B for presentation to the Registrar. If cremation is desired, he also issues Coroner's form E, which replaces the other cremation certificates and is presented to the Medical Referee for Cremations (see Chapter 4). If an inquest is necessary, the

Coroner will usually issue a document after the inquest has been opened and adjourned, for presentation to the Registrar, so that disposal may proceed. In cases of undetected homicide where no person has been charged, the Coroner may refuse to release the body, or may forbid cremation, but these are nowadays rare occurrences. The Coroner will usually permit disposal after a few weeks have passed, provided that a second autopsy has been performed by an independent pathologist, and the report has been lodged with him for disclosure to the Defence, should a trial ensue.

The funeral arrangements are usually placed in the hands of a firm of funeral directors, who are experienced in the complex processes involved. Relatives and others concerned with disposal should remember that funeral direction is a business like any other, and the person who opens negotiation will be held liable in law for the debts incurred. One is not obliged to employ a funeral director. An executor can take the arrangements upon himself, but they may prove complex and time-consuming. Private funerals, arranged directly by the relatives and executors, are now increasingly common. Various organisations produce literature and give advice to those who require it. (For details of 'green' woodland and garden burials see Chapter 7; cremation is dealt with in Chapter 8.)

Disposal by burial requires purchase of a grave space. This should preferably be done during life. Not everyone has an automatic right to interment in a particular parish churchyard. Only residents of the parish in question have such a right, and this may be overturned if the graveyard is full or has been made redundant by the authorities. The UK is currently running out of grave space. Older graveyards are literally full to overflowing, and skeletal remains frequently come to the surface. Numerous proposals are being considered: these have included re-opening and re-using graves after a period of 7–10 years, but a recent survey (Department of Constitutional Affairs 2004) revealed that more than 50 per cent of the population were opposed this suggestion.

Where cremation is desired, the funeral director will arrange for the completion of the various medical certificates (see Chapter 8) and will book the crematorium. He will also arrange any religious or secular ceremony, the publicity, transport, catering and so forth and will advise on disposal of the ashes. The costs of any funeral, even a simple one, can be considerable and are currently about £2000 for the simplest obsequies. The obligation to dispose of a body falls upon the nearest relative or upon the deceased's estate. The State may, through the Department of Social Security, make interim arrangements for paying of funeral expenses, but can legally recover these charges from the estate of the deceased in due course.

If there are no near relatives, anyone close to the deceased, for example a co-habitee (Civil Partnership Act 2005), can undertake this responsibility. If there is dispute over the arrangements between relatives or friends, the funeral director will normally give precedence to the wishes of the nearest relative or the named executor. If there are no relatives, or they are unwilling to organise disposal, the hospital authorities can arrange the funeral of an inpatient. The Local Authority will arrange the funeral of a person who died at home, if no relative or friend is able or willing to shoulder the responsibility. Such disposal will always be by cremation, unless the deceased has left specific instructions forbidding this. For Local Authority disposal by burial an unmarked common grave will be used, with no memorial rights. A contract funeral director is employed. The service used is usually that of the Anglican Church, if the religion of the deceased is unknown. It is a simple and dignified procedure, of the same basic standard as the cheapest privately arranged funeral. The Local Authority or the Health Authority can recover costs from the estate of the deceased, or from anyone who had a legal liability to honour the deceased's debts, for example a spouse, son, daughter, parent, or other close relative.

A funeral director should be chosen with great care, either through personal knowledge or local reputation. It is advisable to use a funeral director who is able to provide an arbitration service in case of complaint (see National Association of Funeral Directors in Appendix A). Some Local Authorities run their own funeral direction schemes. A basic funeral will include the provision of a plain lined coffin, transport for a distance of up to 16 km (10 miles), basic preparation of the body (but embalming, also called 'sanitisation', often carries an extra charge) and the provision of a hearse and one following car. All other services, for example publicity and flowers, are extras. The financial responsibility for funeral arrangements falls primarily upon the person who made the arrangement with the funeral director and who is held to be contractually liable. If the deceased leaves no estate, the personal representative, executor, or nearest relative is liable for the costs incurred. Help may be available from the Department of Social Security's Social Fund if the deceased was in receipt of Family Income Supplement or Housing Benefit. The relatives of ex-service personnel may be entitled to a grant from the Ministry of Defence. The Soldiers, Sailors and Airforce Association (SSAFA) will give advice and help in these cases. In a few cases of industrial disease, an additional payment may also be obtainable from the Department of Social Security.

There is no specified time limit within which a funeral must take place, but if the local Health Protection Officer or Consultant in Communicable Disease Control feels that the body presents a health hazard, he can order immediate disposal. There are special techniques required for the disposal of those bodies which may be infected by high risk pathogens. These are outlined in Chapter 16.

Burial is permitted in a churchyard (subject to the constraints of Ecclesiastical Law, and the prior purchase of a grave space), in a local authority cemetery, or in a private burial ground. All churchyards are consecrated ground, as are parts of both local authority and private cemeteries. The two latter may have dedicated plots for members of different faiths. Once a plot has been so allocated, members of other faiths may not be interred within them. Permission to bury on private land should be requested from the local Health Protection Agency. Until recently permission was rarely given, even in rural areas, and never in built-up areas, but these attitudes are now more relaxed and several organisations will assist in making such arrangements.

There are basically two types of grave. A so-called 'lawn grave' has no integral support. A 'bricked grave' is often reserved for the use of a particular family, and can accommodate four or more bodies. Modern municipal cemeteries are purpose built, with concrete-lined grave spaces – so-called reticulation. Multiple interments in any type of grave are permitted provided that the topmost coffin is more than 90 cm (36 in) below ground in local authority cemeteries and 75 cm (30 in) in all others. Obtaining a 'faculty' from the appropriate officer of the Church of England, known as the Diocesan Registrar, for interment in a churchyard takes six weeks or more, so application should be made during life when planning one's funeral arrangements. Similarly, permission for the re-opening of a family grave should be sought in advance. Burial within a church is nowadays permitted only in a few of those which were built before 1848. A few rural churches fall into this category, as do certain 'national institutions', for example Westminster Abbey and the Chapel Royal of Windsor Castle. Burial within these national monuments is a privilege accorded only to a few members of the immediate royal family and to even fewer distinguished statesmen.

Maintenance of graves and the provision of monuments and gravestones are not regulated by statute, but the ecclesiastical and local authorities impose their own regulations, which must be observed. Any monument whose design does not conform to the standards laid down by the governing body in question can be removed. Many churches, dioceses, and local cemeteries impose restrictions upon overall size and design. There are usually restrictions upon the wording of the inscription also, and advice should always be sought from the monumental mason, and the authorities, before a particular memorial is chosen. Further restrictions upon both new and existing gravestones have been imposed recently. A child was killed whilst playing in a cemetery, when a large tombstone fell upon him and crushed him. Although the parents' action for damages was unsuccessful, many local authorities are now clearing and laying flat existing monuments, and severely restricting the size and height of new ones. They rely on the provisions of the Health and Safety at Work Act (1974) and consequent regulations for their right to do this.

Commemoration of the cremated is simpler. Most commonly the only formal record is an entry in a 'Book of Remembrance'. A few relatives pay for the placing of a tablet in a lawned area or columbarium.

Gravestones are usually erected within a few weeks of death, as soon as the earth has settled, and with no ceremony. In the Jewish community, the 'stone setting' is an important occasion, which takes place at or near the first anniversary of the death. In Islam, graves are often unmarked.

Burial at sea

For an account of the procedures to be followed for burial at sea, see Chapter 7. There are, so far as we can determine, no restrictions upon the scattering of cremation ashes on land, lake, stream or sea – apart from the considerations of good neighbourliness! In 2005, HM Coroner for the Isle of Wight called for the abandonment of sea burial, following the stranding of seven bodies upon beaches within his jurisdiction within the space of six months.

Export of bodies

It is not lawful to remove a body out of England and Wales without the Coroner's authority. Notice must be given to the Coroner in prescribed form and he must be allowed four clear working days to complete his enquiries. Usually the application is dealt with much more speedily than this. The application must be accompanied by the Registrar's 'authority for disposal after registry'. The Coroner then returns this to the Registrar, and issues his acknowledgement of receipt of 'the notice of intention to remove the body from England', which has been submitted to him by the applicant. This acknowledgement is usually referred to as the 'Out of England' certificate. Cremation ashes for export should be accompanied by a certificate from the crematorium, which confirms the fact of cremation and gives details of the appropriate disposal and cremation certificates.

AIR AND SEA EXPORT OF BODIES FROM THE UK

The transport of uncremated human remains by sea or air is a complex and expensive procedure. Carriers impose strict specifications for the material and dimensions of the coffin to be employed, and demand certificates of freedom from infection and fever. In addition, a certificate of embalming is almost always required. The persons arranging export will also need to provide the 'out of England' certificate, a certified copy of the death register entry, and a declaration that the coffin contains only a body. Further advice on this subject can be obtained from the National Association of Funeral Directors (see Appendix A). It must be appreciated that the export of a body is an expensive undertaking. Detailed advice and estimates of cost should be sought before embarking upon it. Repatriation of bodies is frequently desired within the Muslim communities of Pakistani and Bangladeshi origin. Local mosques will often assist in the provision of this service, and should be consulted as soon as possible after the death has occurred.

References

Airedale NHS Trust v Bland (1993) 1 AllER 821.

Births and Deaths Registration Act (1874) 37 and 38 Vict.

British Medical Journal (1976) 'Conference of Medical Royal Colleges and their Faculties in the United Kingdom. Criteria for the diagnosis of brain death.' *British Medical Journal 2*, 1187–1188.

Burke v General Medical Council (2004) EWHC 1879 (Admin).

Chadwick, E. (1843) *The Practice of Interment in Towns.* London: Clowes.

Charlton, C.A.R. (1996) 'Diagnosing death.' *British Medical Journal 313*, 956–957.

Civil Partnership Act (2005) Chapter 33. London: The Stationery Office.

Cremation Society of Great Britain (2004) www.srgw.demon.co.uk/CremSoc/ (accessed August 2005).

Department of Constitutional Affairs (2004) Burial Law and Policy in the 21st Century: the need for a sensitive and sustainable approach. London: Department of Constitutional Affairs.

Dorries, C.P. (2004) Coroners' Courts, 2nd edn. Oxford: Oxford University Press.

Elkin, A.P. (1968) The Australian Aboriginal, 4th edn. Sydney: Angus and Robertson.

England and Wales Court of Appeal (Civil Decisions) website: www.bailili.org/ew/cases /EWCA/Civ/2005/1003.html

Enright, D.J. (1987) The Oxford Book of Death. Oxford: Oxford University Press.

General Medical Council website: www.gmc-uk.org (accessed 12 March 2006).

Glass v UK (2004) European Court of Human Rights, Chamber Judgement 61827/00.

Health and Safety at Work Act (1974) all sections.

Jupp, P.C. and Gittings, C. (2000) Death in England: An Illustrated History. New Jersey: Rutgers University Press.

Mental Capacity Act (2005).

Mitford, J. (1980) The American Way of Death. London: Quartet Books.

Polson, C.J. and Marshall, T.K. (1975) The Disposal of the Dead, 3rd edn. London: English Universities Press.

R v Price (1884) 12 QBD 187.

Registrar-General's Office (1839) 1st Annual Report (187) XVII 8–10 London.

Royal College of Physicians (1995) 'Criteria for the diagnosis of brain stem death.' Journal of the Royal College of Physicians 29, 381–382.

Shultz, S., Baral, H.S., Charman, S., Cunningham, A.A., Das, D., Ghalsasi, G.R. et al. (2004) 'Diclofenac poisoning is widespread in declining vulture populations across the Indian subcontinent.' Proceedings of the Royal Society of London B (suppl) 04BL120, s.3.

Special Communication (1961) 'Guidelines for the determination of death.' Journal of the American Medical Association 246, 2184.

Waugh, E. (1993) The Loved One. London: The Folio Society.

CHAPTER 2

MEDICAL CERTIFICATION OF CAUSE OF DEATH

History

Before 1836 there was no certification of the cause of death, and only incomplete recording of the fact of death (Births and Deaths Registration Act 1836). Records of burials were poorly maintained, particularly in overcrowded urban graveyards or when many funerals took place within a relatively short time and often during epidemics. Many small private burial grounds maintained poor records; these were often lost or deliberately destroyed.

The Births and Deaths Registration Act 1836 had three principal aims: to facilitate legal proof of death, to prevent the concealment of crime, and to produce accurate mortality statistics. The Registers were kept in a prescribed form, with a space provided for the cause of death, but completion of this was based upon information volunteered by the informant, i.e. the person registering the death, or by the Coroner – who at that time seldom had access to autopsy findings. Even in those cases where doctors tried to provide information, there were wide variations in terminology, which resulted in the recording of irrelevant detail, which was valueless for statistical purposes.

The provision of a registration service fell upon the newly constituted Boards of Guardians (Poor Law Act 1834). This was in addition to their other duties. The office of registrar was poorly paid. It was therefore frequently undertaken with reluctance and extremely badly executed. Furthermore, although registration was supposedly compulsory under the above Acts, there were no penalties for failure to do so.

The deficiencies of the system were quickly identified. In 1842, the Registrar General asked doctors to provide informants with a written cause of death, and in the following year produced a 'statistical nosology'. This was the first attempt to produce standardised classified lists of causes of death. In 1845, 10,000 licensed doctors received books of death certificates which they were invited to complete 'to the best of their knowledge and belief', but in 1858, over 11 per cent of deaths were still registered without any medical information. The 5000 medical practitioners not registered with the General Medical Council, which came into existence that same year, were not initially included in the death certification exercise.

The Births and Deaths Registration Act (1874) attempted to improve matters. Penalties for failure to register were introduced, and the 'invitation' to the doctor to provide information became a 'duty'. The Registrar was instructed to refer unexpected deaths and those of unknown cause to the Coroner, as well as those deaths which were frankly suspicious. In such cases, final registration could not take place until the Coroner's inquiry had been completed. The Act also introduced registration of stillbirth for the first time, because there was a suspicion that the crime of infanticide was increasing. Unregistered 'medical practitioners' could still issue certificates. They only lost this right in 1885.

In 1893, a Parliamentary Select Committee on Death Certification was established, in response to fears that homicide was passing undetected. It placed great emphasis on ascertaining the cause of death and recommended that every dead body should be viewed by a registered medical practitioner. It also suggested that disposal should be monitored by the introduction of a written 'order for burial'. However, none of these recommendations were implemented until 1926, when a further Births and Deaths Registration Act, along with a contemporaneous Coroners (Amendment) Act (see Chapter 4), made some of them legal requirements. These Acts also standardised the Death Certificate Form, and forbade disposal before registration. The Coroners Act (1887) gave the Coroner the power to order an autopsy and inquest in other than non-violent deaths. The 1926 Coroners (Amendment) Act abolished the need for an inquest in every case; where autopsy showed the death was due to natural causes the inquest could be dispensed with.

In the 1980s and 1990s various working parties drawn from the medical and legal professions, and the Office of Population, Censuses and Surveys (OPCS) (now the Office for National Statistics (ONS)), considered major reviews of death certificate design and of registration procedure. In 1989, a Green Paper entitled *Registration: A Modern Service* was published. This was followed in 1990, by a White Paper: *Registration: Proposals for Change*. It was hoped that the proposals contained therein would have been implemented within a very short time, but nothing happened until the arrest and conviction of Dr Harold Shipman, a general practitioner in Cheshire, for the murder of a large number of his patients. A Public Inquiry was established under the chairmanship of a High Court Judge, Dame Janet Smith, who has made sweeping recommendations for reform of both death certification and the whole structure of the Coroners' service. During the same period, the Home Office instituted a *Fundamental Review* (2000) chaired by Mr Tom Luce, which examined the same areas, but offered different solutions to some of the problems which both studies had identified. All of these recommendations are currently under review. They are examined more fully in Chapters 3 and 4.

The current procedures and the laws relating to death and cremation certification will be briefly outlined below, and in Chapters 3 and 8. This chapter deals only with routine death certification. Stillbirths and neonatal deaths are discussed in Chapter 5.

Figure 2.1a Medical certificate of cause of death (MCCD) (front). Crown copyright.

Complete where applicable

PERSONS QUALIFIED AND LIABLE TO ACT AS INFORMANTS

The following persons are designated by the Births and Deaths Registration Act 1953 as qualified to give information concerning a death:—

DEATHS IN HOUSES AND PUBLIC INSTITUTIONS

(1) A relative of the deceased, present at the death.

(2) A relative of the deceased, in attendance during the last illness.

(3) A relative of the deceased, residing or being in the sub-district where the death occurred.

(4) A person present at the death.

(5) The occupier* if he knew of the happening of the death.

(6) Any inmate if he knew of the happening of the death.

(7) The person causing the disposal of the body.

DEATHS NOT IN HOUSES OR DEAD BODIES FOUND

(1) Any relative of the deceased having knowledge of any of the particulars required to be registered.

(2) Any person present at the death.

(3) Any person who found the body.

(4) Any person in charge of the body.

(5) The person causing the disposal of the body.

*"Occupier" in relation to a public institution includes the governor, keeper, master, matron, superintendent, or other chief resident officer.

A

I have reported this death to the Coroner for further action.

Initials of certifying medical practitioner.

The Coroner needs to consider all cases where:

  The death might have been due to or contributed to by a violent or unnatural cause (including an accident);

or the cause of death cannot be identified;

or the death might have been due to or contributed to by drugs, medicine, abortion or poison.

B

I may be in a position later to give, on application by the Registrar General, additional information as to the cause of death for the purpose of more precise statistical classification.

Initials of certifying medical practitioner.

or there is reason to believe that the death occurred during an operation or under or prior to complete recovery from an anaesthetic or arising subsequently out of an incident during an operation or an anaesthetic;

or the death might have been due to or contributed to by the employment followed at some time by the deceased.

LIST OF SOME OF THE CATEGORIES OF DEATH WHICH MAY BE OF INDUSTRIAL ORIGIN

MALIGNANT DISEASES

Causes include:

(a) Skin — radiation and sunlight
       — pitch or tar
       — mineral oils

(b) Nasal — wood or leather work
       — nickel

(c) Lung — asbestos
      — nickel
      — radiation

(d) Pleura — asbestos

(e) Urinary Tract — benzidine
       — dyestuff
       — chemicals in rubbers

(f) Liver — PVC manufacture

(g) Bone — radiation

(h) Lymphatics and haematopoietic — radiation
       — benzene

POISONING

(a) Metals — e.g. arsenics, cadmium, lead

(b) Chemicals — e.g. chlorine, benzene

(c) Solvents — e.g. trichlorethylene

INFECTIOUS DISEASES

Causes include:

(a) Anthrax — imported bone, bonemeal, hide or fur

(b) Brucellosis — farming or veterinary

(c) Tuberculosis — contact at work

(d) Leptospirosis — farming, sewer or underground workers.

(e) Tetanus — farming or gardening

(f) Rabies — animal handling

(g) Viral hepatitis — contact at work

BRONCHIAL ASTHMA AND PNEUMONITIS

(a) Occupational asthma — sensitising agent at work

(b) Allergic Alveolitis — farming

PNEUMOCONIOSIS

— mining and quarrying pumices, asbestos

NOTE:—The Practitioner, on signing the certificate, should complete, sign and date the Notice to the Informant, which should be detached and handed to the Informant. The Practitioner should then, without delay, deliver the certificate itself to the Registrar of Births and Deaths for the sub-district in which the death occurred. Envelopes for enclosing the certificates are supplied by the Registrar.

Figure 2.1b Medical certificate of cause of death (MCCD) (back). Crown copyright.

The Medical Certificate of Cause of Death

The certificate (Medical Certificate of Cause of Death, MCCD) currently in use has changed little since 1953, apart from a modification in 1985 which specifically requires the declaration of any possibility of employment related disease (see Figs. 2.1a and 2.1b).

Books of death certificates are supplied by the local registrar only to registered medical practitioners and hospitals. They contain detailed advice for completion of the certificate, but no longer list the 'non-specific and undesirable terms' given in earlier editions. The design of the certificate itself conforms to an internationally agreed pattern. It is divided into three parts: the notice to the informant, the certificate proper, and the counterfoil.

THE NOTICE TO THE INFORMANT

This is a tear-off slip, which is completed by the certifying medical practitioner and handed to the prospective informant. It sets out the informant's duties and the information which must be supplied to the Registrar. On the back it lists the designated persons 'who have a duty to register the death under the 1953 Act'. There is no notice to the informant on Scottish death certificates, which are otherwise similar in content to that used in England and Wales, although different in lay-out.

THE MEDICAL CERTIFICATE

This lays down stringent requirements for its completion. It may be completed only by the registered medical practitioner *who has been in attendance* during the deceased's last illness, and charges him or her with the duty of delivery to the Registrar. In practice the doctor may send a certificate by mail (Registrars provide franked addressed envelopes) but most commonly the doctor hands it, in a closed envelope, to the informant, for delivery to the Registrar.

The MCCD requires the name, the stated age, the stated date of death, and the place of death. The date when last seen alive by the certifying practitioner must also be given. Appropriate numbers and letters must be ringed to indicate whether a post mortem has been, or will be, held and whether the body was seen after death by the signatory, by another doctor, or not by any doctor. There is as yet no legal requirement for the body to be seen after death by a doctor, but in practice the Registrar is most unlikely to accept a certificate if this is the case.

The space for cause of death is enclosed within a box. The chain of events is listed serially backwards from the immediate fatal incident. For example, a certificate issued in the case of a heart attack following a long history of angina (*chest pain*) might read:

Ia.   Myocardial infarction 24 hours (*heart attack*) due to

Ib.   Coronary occlusion 2 days (*blocking of an artery*) due to

Ic.   Coronary atheroma 2 years (*degenerative arterial disease*).

This is known as the 'underlying cause of death' and is that which is recorded for statistical purposes by the Office of National Statistics (ONS; previously the Office of Population Censuses and Surveys (OPCS)).

Contributory causes, such as diabetes mellitus or chronic bronchitis, are recorded on a separate line numbered II.

Accuracy of death certification

The cause of death given by the doctor 'is correct to the best of his knowledge and belief'. Obviously, in many cases, the cause of death is known beyond doubt, and the increasing number of deaths in hospital, where sophisticated diagnostic techniques have been applied during life, has led to increased accuracy. However, the decline of the 'hospital' or 'academic' autopsy must leave a group of cases where the diagnosis given is a 'best guess'. We cannot know for certain how large this group is; studies in the UK and the USA have produced different estimates (see Chapter 6). In some Eastern European countries an autopsy is performed upon every case. This has never been the case in the UK and never will be so. Such an imposition would be undesirable on religious and social grounds, as well as creating a major charge upon the health service. However, hospital doctors in particular should bear in mind the continuing value of the autopsy, both for statistical and educational purposes. The autopsy is in decline. The public backlash against the so-called 'retained organs scandal' at the Royal Liverpool Children's Hospital (Redfearn 2001) has resulted in an even greater reduction in the number of permission or academic autopsies – and these are now performed in less than 10 per cent of all hospital deaths (see Chapters 6 and 9). Likewise, many Coroners now more readily conclude their death investigation without autopsy; a so-called A pass (see Chapter 4). Many younger doctors are satisfied that the extent and accuracy of investigation in life has rendered autopsy redundant. There have been some trials of magnetic resonance imaging (MRI), but subsequent autopsy examinations have shown this technique to be of limited value (Bissett et al. 2002); however, some Coroners will accept this form of post mortem examination, in conjunction with detailed inquiry into the surrounding circumstance, as sufficient grounds for issuing an A pass for deaths within an orthodox Jewish or Muslim community. It is our view that autopsy retains an important place in the investigation of sudden and unexpected deaths within the community. The proposals currently being examined suggest, inter alia, the creation of a system of legal and medical Coroners, who will scrutinise every death (HO Fundamental Review 2000; Shipman Inquiry 2003). These suggestions, if implemented, may introduce added safeguards against some cases of covert homicide, but a few unnatural deaths will always slip through the net.

The doctor must enquire into the deceased's occupational history (common occupational diseases are listed on the back of the certificate) and tick the box provided if appropriate. Normally, when the death may be due to industrial disease, the doctor will not issue a certificate but will report the death directly to the Coroner. It should be noted that there is as yet no legal obligation upon a doctor to report any death to the Coroner. He is supposed to issue the certificate and pass it on to the Registrar, who assumes the legal responsibility for notification. In practice, however, most doctors do not issue a death certificate if the case is to be reported to the Coroner. They merely advise the relatives that referral to the Coroner is necessary, and inform the Coroner's Office by telephone.

The information printed upon the certificate (MCCD) thus serves as an *aide-memoire*, reminding the doctor of the circumstances in which he should report the death to the Coroner, rather than issuing the MCCD.

Finally, the certificate is signed, the doctor enters his registered qualifications and gives his registered address and date (note that if the death occurs in hospital, the name of the consultant in charge of the case must also be given). The doctor should only give qualifications registered with the General Medical Council; additional diplomas etc. should not be used.

On the back of the certificate are two boxes. Box A, 'I have reported this case to the Coroner', is seldom used, for reasons given above (see also Chapter 4). Box B indicates that further information, for example the microscopic identification of a type of cancer, may be available for statistical purposes at some later time. If box B has been completed, the doctor will receive, in due course, a further certificate for completion from the Office for National Statistics. This requests more detailed information, if possible, for example the cell type of a malignant tumour. The completion of this form is not a statutory obligation, but obviously any concerned and conscientious doctor will provide the relevant information whenever possible. This information cannot be used to change the cause of death as given in the Register.

THE COUNTERFOIL

The counterfoil is a summary record of all the information given on the certificate. It must always be completed (failure to do so is a grave and potentially litigious dereliction of a doctor's duty). The completed counterfoils should be retained in the hospital or medical practice for a minimum of ten years.

The 'death certificate' proper, which serves as the legal authority for disposal, and for settlement of the deceased's estate, is supplied to the relatives by the Registrar when they take the MCCD to him. It is 'a certified copy of an entry in the Register of Deaths' and must record the medical cause of death exactly as given by the doctor – spelling mistakes and all!

Referral of a death to the Coroner by the Registrar

The Registrar is required to report certain deaths to the Coroner. The circumstances of these are laid down by Regulation 51 of the Registration of Births, Marriages and Deaths Regulations 1968, and are reproduced at the front of each book of death certificates for the guidance of medical practitioners. These are, briefly:

1. Where the deceased was not medically attended in his last illness.

2. Where a certificate is incomplete.

3. Where the deceased was seen neither in the 14 days before, nor after, death by the certifying doctor.

4. Where the cause appears to be unknown.

5. Where the Registrar has reason to believe that the death may be unnatural.

6. Where the death may be related to an operation, investigative procedure or anaesthetic.

7. Where a death may be due to industrial disease.

In the majority of these cases, the doctor will have decided to report anyway, and the Registrar will not be involved until the coronial inquiry is complete.

In practice, the Registrar acts as a 'long stop'. During the interview with the informant, facts or allegations may emerge which were not known to the certifying doctor, for example the widow may recall that the husband worked for a short time in a 'dangerous occupation' many years previously.

The doctor should also remember that 'words mean what words say'. If, for example, an accidental injury such as a fracture is shown as contributing to death, the Registrar has no alternative but to withhold registration and refer the matter to the Coroner. Junior hospital doctors in particular often fall into this trap. Relatives are most displeased when the funeral arrangements are disrupted at short notice, and even more distressed when told that a *coronial* autopsy has become necessary. Doctors should carefully read the advisory note 'dealing with multiple pathology' in the Death Certificate book. It has been suggested that a third 'boxed' category for 'other morbid conditions present, but *not* contributing to death' should be incorporated into any redesigned certificate, and this proposal is being considered by the ONS.

A death certificate therefore should only be issued after careful study of the circumstances and the history. If there is any doubt, the case should be discussed with the Coroner or his officer at an early stage, before the certificate is completed.

References

Births and Deaths Registration Act (1836) Chaps 6 and 7 William IV.

Births and Deaths Registration Act (1874) Chaps 37 and 38 Victoria c 88 s 20.

Births and Deaths Registration Act (1926) Chaps 16 and 17 George V Regulation 49(3) s 1.

Bissett, R.A.L., Thomas, B., Turnbull, I.W. and Lee, S. (2002) 'Post mortem examination using magnetic resonance imaging: a four-year review of a working service.' *British Medical Journal 324*, 1423–1424.

Coroners Act (1887).

Coroners Amendment Act (1926) Chaps 16 and 17 George V cap 59 ss 1, 12, 21, 23.

Home Office (2000) *The Report of the Fundamental Review of Death Certification and the Coroners Services.* Cm 58/31. London: The Stationery Office.

Poor Law Act (1834) Chaps 4 and 5 William IV.

Redfearn, H.C. (ed) (2001) *Royal Liverpool Children's Hospital Inquiry Report.* London: The Stationery Office.

Registration of Births, Marriages and Deaths Act (1968) s 51. London: HMSO.

Registration: A Modern Service (1989) Cm 531. London: The Stationery Office (Green Paper).

Registration: Proposals for Change (1990) Cm 939. London: The Stationery Office (White Paper).

The Shipman Inquiry's 3 Reports (2003) Cm 58/34. London: The Stationery Office.

CHAPTER 3

REGISTRATION OF DEATH

History of the office of Registrar

Local registration of the fact of death was introduced during the reign of Henry VIII (1538) as a revenue-gathering exercise. The church authorities were required to record every burial, and to charge a fee, payable to the Crown, for each interment. A further Act in 1597 required deposition of a second copy of the local register in the office of the appropriate diocese. The Crown's fiscal interest in the disposal of the dead was further enhanced by the taxes levied under the Wool Acts of 1667 and 1668. The requirement to bury every person, irrespective of rank or wealth, in woollen grave clothes resulted in a form of registration as a by-product of taxation. The diligence with which these registers were maintained varied greatly between districts. With the rise of non-conformist religion and the resulting proliferation of private graveyards, the records became increasingly incomplete (Smale 2002).

National registration of the fact of death in England and Wales was first introduced in 1836 and was originally the responsibility of the Poor Law Guardians, whose Boards had been established two years previously (Births and Deaths Registration Act 1836; Poor Law Act 1834). The quality and accuracy of registration were poor. Many Guardians' clerks approached the task with only limited enthusiasm and, as there were no sanctions against those members of the public who failed to register, the statistics remained incomplete. After the Births and Deaths Registration Act of 1874 and the Coroners Act of 1887, there was a progressive improvement, which was assisted by the introduction of the requirement for certification of cause of death by a *registered* medical practitioner. There is now a national network of Registrars at Local Authority District and Sub-District level, administered by the Office for National Statistics (ONS) through the National Registration Service. All aspects of registration are now regulated by the Births and Deaths Registration Act (1953) and the amended 'consolidated regulations' (1987).

CURRENT PROPOSALS FOR CHANGE
Proposals for major reforms of the National Registration Service were published in a Green Paper in 1989 and were re-emphasised in the White Paper *Civil Registration: Vital Changes*, published in 2002 (ONS 2002). Their implementation is in progress, and many may well be introduced by 2007. These imminent changes should be borne in mind when reading this chapter. They include:

- Registration on-line or by telephone. The legislative framework for this was introduced in 2004, under the Regulatory Reform Act (2001).
- Registration at any registration office – not just that for the sub-district where death occurred.
- Qualified informants will include executors and life partners, whose relationships are recognised in the provisions of the Civil Partnership Act (2004).
- Commonality of information in the register for both men and women, i.e. details of occupation, marital status for the deceased and for the partner in every case.

All of these proposed changes will be affected by the implementation of the recommendations of the Home Office Fundamental Review of Death Certification and the Coroner Service, the recommendations in the reports of the Shipman Inquiry, or a compromise solution drawing upon both of these. These proposals are more fully discussed in Chapters 2 and 4.

Under the 1953 Act, every death in England and Wales must be registered in the sub-district in which it occurred or, failing that, in that where the body was found (Section 15) within five days of its occurrence. There is no charge for registration (Section 20), but certified copies of the entry in the register (commonly called the 'death certificate') are charged for (currently £3.50 per copy if requested within 28 days of registration; £7.00 thereafter). Registration serves three purposes: to prevent the concealment of crime by illicit disposal; to provide accurate mortality statistics; and to provide evidence of death for insurance or pension purposes, or as evidence of freedom to re-marry.

There are several categories of Registrar and many only undertake the duty on a part-time basis. There is no compulsory formal training programme, nor is there at present any professional qualification. Although usually employed within, and salaried by, a Local Authority, they can only be dismissed by the Registrar General. Proposals for a national hierarchical structure within local authorities are being considered at present. The Registrar General issues guidelines to Registrars, which are regularly updated. These are contained in the *Handbook for Registration Officers*. In addition, his office publishes a booklet, *The Proper Officer's Manual*, intended for the use of local authorities. These books are not available to the general public.

The qualified informant (see below) must attend the Registrar's office during normal working hours (although many offices offer a limited weekend service, primarily for the registration of ethnic minority deaths). A medical certificate of cause of death (MCCD) (Chapter 2) and the appropriate Coroner's certificate, where necessary (Chapter 4), must be presented to the Registrar, along with the deceased's National Health Service medical card and any state or public service pension documents. Production of the deceased's birth certificate is also helpful but not mandatory.

Responsibility for registration – 'qualified informants'

The persons qualified to act as informants are specified in the Births and Deaths Registration Act 1953, Sections 16 and 17. They are also set out on the 'Notice to Informant', which forms a tear-off part of the MCCD (Chapter 2), and which is handed to the next of kin or other potential informant by the certifying medical practitioner, or by the staff of the hospital's bereavement services office.

When a death occurs in a house or its gardens, the responsibility for registration falls successively upon a relative present at the death, one present during the deceased's last illness, or one 'residing or being in the sub-district where death occurred'. If no relative is available, liability is transferred to any person present at the death or residing at the same address. As a last resort the duty falls upon the person who has assumed responsibility for arranging disposal. It is proposed in the recent White Paper (Cm 939; ONS 1990) (see Chapter 2) that 'the deceased's executor' be added to the list of qualified informants.

Deaths at other locations are dealt with similarly. The first obligation falls upon a relative. If none is available any person present at the death, finding the body, or who is to arrange the disposal, has the obligation to register. For deaths occurring in hospitals or similar institutions, the category 'Senior Administrator' will also be added to the list, in place of the present non-specific 'occupier'.

At the present time, all the registration documents are completed in longhand and processed manually. The government's new proposals will permit 'the sensible use of modern technology', improving the initial service to the public, and facilitating access to past records of cause and fact of death (see *Civil Registration: Vital Changes* Cm 5355, referred to above). Computers are already being introduced in parallel with the existing system, and eventually 'loose-leaf' computer generated entries will replace the handwritten registers.

Registration without reference to the Coroner

(See also Chapter 4.)

Approximately three-fifths of all deaths in England and Wales are dealt with in this way. In 2003, 210,700 deaths were referred to the Coroner, and 303,550 were registered upon MCCD alone. The informant must attend the Registrar's Office within five days of the death (Births and Deaths Registration Act, 1953), and produce the medical certificate, the deceased's NHS medical card, and be able to furnish the other particulars required by the Registrar (Births and Deaths Registration Act, 1953; Registration of Births, Deaths and Marriages Regulations, 1968 – the so-called 'consolidated regulations', as amended in 1985).

The informant must be able to supply:

1. the date and place of death
2. the name and address of the deceased (including a woman's maiden name)
3. the date and place of birth

4.   the usual address

5.   the occupation (or last known occupation). In the case of a woman, the occupation of the husband also

6.   details of any state pension or allowance from public funds

7.   the date of birth of the surviving spouse

8.   the deceased's marital status.

In the case of a woman, her marital status and the name and occupation of her husband (surviving or late) are also required. A single woman's last known occupation must be recorded. At present, details of marital status are required under the provision of the various Population (Statistics) Acts and regulations, and do not appear in the register or upon the certificate. These details are used only for statistical purposes, and are confidential. However, it is now recognised that they may be relevant to medical or sociological research, and it is proposed that in future they will appear in the England and Wales death entry (they already do in Scotland and Northern Ireland).

If the date and/or place of death are unknown, the entry on the register and the certificate (form 9) will read, 'Dead body found at .... on or about ....'.

The informant checks and signs the register entry in the presence of the Registrar. The Registrar then copies exactly the cause of death as given by the certifying medical practitioner and adds the doctor's name and qualifications.

Finally the Registrar issues his 'Certificate for Burial or Cremation after Registration'. This incorporates a form of notification of disposal, which must be completed and returned to the Registrar by the person who disposed of the body, usually the cemetery superintendent or, in the case of churchyards, the incumbent of the parish. He will also issue a Certificate of Registration of Death (form BD 8) to send off in respect of pension and any other state benefits which the deceased was receiving.

Registration of garden burials is covered in Chapter 7. Note that additional medical certificate forms are required before disposal by cremation can proceed. These are dealt with fully in Chapter 8.

Disposal in special circumstances

Occasionally, where immediate disposal is required (for example, for religious reasons) but all the information is not readily available, the Registrar may issue a document which permits disposal before formal registration. This may only be used when burial is desired. It cannot be used in cases of cremation. If the Coroner's enquiries are proceeding, the Registrar may permit disposal if he is assured in writing by the Coroner that all specimens for pathological and toxicological examinations have been retained, and that no further examination of the body is required. If registration has not been completed within 14 days, the Registrar may issue written notice to any qualified informant to attend at his office on a specified date. Failure to do so may attract legal proceedings. The Registrar may register a death for up to 12 months after its occurrence, or within 12 months of the date when the body was found. After 12 months have elapsed, only the Registrar General can authorise registration (Consolidated Regulations, 1968, Regulation 56, paras 1–3).

Reference to the Coroner by the Registrar

The Registrar has a statutory duty to report to the Coroner any death which he believes to be unnatural or of uncertain cause. Such causes of death are itemised in the Consolidated Regulations 1968, Regulation 51. Indeed, were the requirements of the various Registration and Coroners Acts strictly applied, doctors would always issue an MCCD, and the Registrar would initiate the reporting procedure. In practice this rule is honoured in the breach. Its observance would waste time and would often cause inconvenience and distress to relatives. It would also, in some cases, hamper police inquiries. Normally the Coroner is informed by telephone of a sudden or unnatural death, directly or through his officer, by the doctor or the police (see Chapter 4).

The Registrar, however, serves a valuable supervisory function. Conversation with the relatives, who have attended to register an apparently straightforward death, may reveal a need for coronial enquiry. For example, the death certificate may be incomplete, or the cause of death not sufficiently specific; the relatives may vouchsafe information relating to the deceased's previous occupation, or may mention some illness or accident of which the certifying doctor was unaware. In all the above circumstances the Registrar will notify the Coroner and suspend the registration process forthwith. Occasionally, after consultation with the Coroner and the certifying medical practitioner, registration may proceed on the basis of the MCCD. More commonly, the Coroner will assume jurisdiction.

If no coronial post mortem is deemed necessary, the Coroner will issue 'pink form A' and the death will be registered on the basis of the information supplied on this, along with the cause of death as given on the MCCD. If a coronial autopsy has been performed but no inquest held, the Coroner's pink form B, which states the cause of death, will be issued and registration details will be taken from this. After an inquest the precise details of the Coroner's 'Certificate after Inquest' must be transcribed.

Where a person has been charged with murder, manslaughter or infanticide, so that the inquest has been adjourned under Section 16 of the Coroners Act 1988, pending the outcome of criminal proceedings, the verdict of the criminal court ('unlawfully killed') will be recorded, but the name of any accused person will be omitted.

For many years, it has been appreciated that the process of registration after referral to the Coroner is inconvenient and often distressing for the relatives. They have to return to the Registrar's office, with the appropriate Coroner's certificate (see Chapter 4), to obtain the authority for disposal. It is now proposed that the Coroner should assume the duty to issue the appropriate disposal order, rather than maintaining the present situation where either he or the Registrar may do so. With the advent of modern computer technology and proposed on-line registration, it might even be reasonable to impose the registration function upon the Coroner also, so that relatives would obtain the certified copy of the Death Register entry ('death certificate') at his office, rather than from the Registrar. However, this proposal has been rejected for the time being.

The requirement to register the death in the sub-district where it occurred also greatly inconvenienced relatives who lived a considerable distance away. It is now possible to register 'by declaration' before a more conveniently located Registrar.

Registration of deaths at sea, or overseas (HM Forces)

Deaths which occur on board Royal Naval ships and UK registered merchant vessels are reported by the Captain or Master on arrival at any UK port. The body may be disposed of at sea, this being regarded as part of the 'normal working' of the ship. If the death is thought to be unnatural or 'suspicious', the Master nowadays usually preserves the body by refrigeration, until arrival at the first convenient port, where the police and Coroner take over the investigation. A copy of the relevant logbook entry is sent to the Registrar General of Shipping and Seamen, Board of Trade. This is forwarded, duly certified, to the appropriate Registrar General for England and Wales, Scotland or Northern Ireland, and the information is then recorded in the Marine Register of the Office of National Statistics (ONS).

Deaths aboard merchant ships registered in the UK are finally registered in the usual way. However, the death must first be investigated by either the Coroner for the appropriate port of entry, or by the Board of Trade, under the appropriate sections of the Merchant Shipping Acts of 1894 and 1970 (Merchant Shipping Regulations 1979). Masters of ships not registered in the UK are only required to report the deaths of UK citizens aboard their vessels.

The regulations covering the deaths of passengers aboard civil aircraft registered in the UK are similar in content, and are embodied in the Civil Aviation Acts of 1947 and 1971. Usually, the body is removed from the aircraft on arrival at a UK airport, the local Coroner assumes jurisdiction, and conducts the inquiry (see Chapter 4).

The situation for the registration of deaths abroad of serving members of the Armed Forces, their dependants or civilian forces employees is complex, with variations depending upon the branch of the services.

The position with bodies recovered from the sea or river is at present anomalous, for it may not be clear whether the death occurred in the sub-district (the boundary of which extends to the low-water mark) or elsewhere. In practice the local Registrar usually makes an entry in the register, on the assumption that the death occurred 'close to these shores', but there is no legal basis for this. It is proposed to amend the law, so that such bodies may be properly registered in the sub-district where they were found.

Stillbirth and neonatal death certification and registration

In the case of death within the first 28 days of life, a special certificate of neonatal death must be produced (see Chapter 5). There are also special requirements for the disposal of stillbirths and of non-viable fetal remains (see Chapter 5). The name and occupation of the father (and/or mother) must be supplied for all deaths occurring under the age of 15 years.

Certificate of no liability to register

In cases where a death has occurred overseas and the body is being returned to England and Wales for disposal, the Registrar is permitted under present legislation to issue a certificate stating that formal registration is not necessary. A fee is payable for this service. These bodies must be accompanied by a certificate of registration from the country in which the death occurred (this is also required by HM Customs and Excise). Deaths occurring outside the British Commonwealth also require verification of any registration certificate by the local British Consul. Now, however, bodies brought into England and Wales automatically become the subject of a coronial inquiry, especially since the death in Jeddah of Helen Smith in 1979. Smith's father was not satisfied with the conduct of the Saudi inquiry. He pressed for an inquest, and won his case against the West Yorkshire Coroner in the Divisional Court, setting a precedent which has remained unchallenged.

Missing persons – presumption of death

British law requires that seven years elapse before relatives of a missing person can obtain a certificate of presumed death for registration purposes and gain access to their assets and estate. On 26 December 2004 a massive tidal wave or tsunami devastated the coasts of Indonesia, Thailand and Sri Lanka. Within days it was confirmed that over 300 British nationals were dead. By the end of January 2005, more than 300 others were still missing, presumed dead. The then Foreign Office Minister, Mr Douglas Alexander, announced to Parliament that special regulations would be enacted so that families could settle their affairs. Although the process was going to be slow and was expected to take several months, it was agreed that if British police were satisfied that four criteria had been met the Foreign Office would issue certificates of presumed death so that registration could proceed.

These four tests were as follows:

1. that evidence existed beyond reasonable doubt that the person concerned had travelled to the region

2. that, on the balance of probabilities, they were in the area at the time that the tsunami struck

3.   that there was no reasonable evidence of life after 26 December 2004

4.   that there was no reason to believe that the person would want to disappear.

Similar measures were adopted in the USA following the Twin Towers terrorist attack of 11 September 2001. They apparently worked successfully. It remains to be seen if, following the success of these emergency provisions, the law is relaxed further for other cases where there is a strong presumption of the death of an individual or of small groups of missing persons.

Registration of deaths occurring in Scotland and Northern Ireland

The principles and practice of death registration in Scotland are essentially the same as those obtaining in England and Wales. The investigation of unexplained and unnatural death is the responsibility of the Procurator Fiscal, whose office is, in most matters, similar to that of the Coroner. The Scottish equivalent of the Coroner's certificate is the 'Schedule of Result of Precognition'. The role and powers of the Procurator Fiscal are briefly dealt with in Chapter 4. Scottish cremation procedure is dealt with in Chapter 8.

The registration procedures employed in Northern Ireland are similar to those in England and Wales, but several important differences should be noted. There is no 'Notice to Informant' on a Northern Ireland MCCD, and the period during which the deceased must have been seen alive is extended to 28 days, not 14. The Coroner's forms, although similar in purpose to those used on the mainland, have different identifying titles. Form 14 is similar to form A, and form 17 replaces form B. Bound registers are not maintained. The registrable particulars are entered on an A4 sized form, copies of which are retained loose-leaf, locally, and centrally in the Belfast General Register Office. The Registrar's certificate does not incorporate a certificate for disposal. Burial can proceed without it. He therefore has no direct knowledge of whether or not, when, or where the burial has taken place. In those cases where burial takes place without a Coroner's or Registrar's certificate, the celebrant or other person performing the burial must notify the Registrar within seven days. Cremation legislation, and the certificates required, is essentially similar to that in England and Wales.

References

Births and Deaths Registration Act (1836) 6 and 7 William IV c 86.

Births and Deaths Registration Act (1874) 37 and 38 Victoria. Chap 88.

Births and Deaths Registration Act (1953) 2 and 3 Elizabeth II ss 16, 17.

Birth and Death Registration Consolidated Regulations (1968) reg 56 (1–3).

Birth and Death Consolidatory Regulations (1968) s 56, paras 1–3.

Civil Aviation Act (1971) Chap 77 s 114.

Civil Partnership Act (2004).

Coroners Act (1887).

Merchant Shipping Regulations (Return of Births and Deaths) (1979) No 1577.

Office for National Statistics (1990) *Registration: Proposals for Change.* Cm 939. London: The Stationery Office.

Office for National Statistics (2002) *Civil Registration: Vital Changes.* Cm 5355. London: The Stationery Office.

Poor Law Act (1834) 5 and 6 William IV s 2.

R v West Yorkshire Coroner (1983) *ex parte* Smith QBD 335.

Registration of Births, Deaths and Marriages Regulations (amendment no.2) (1985) S.I. 1985/1333. London: HMSO.

Registration of Births, Deaths and Marriages Regulations (1987) S.I. 1987/2088. London: HMSO.

Regulatory Reform Act (2001) s 3 (2) (b).

Smale, D.A. (2002) *Davies' Law of Burial, Cremation and Exhumation,* 7th edn. Crayford: Shaw and Sons.

CHAPTER 4

CORONERS AND CORONER'S INQUIRIES

History of coronership

The appointment, powers and duties of Coroners are currently controlled by the Coroners Act 1988. This repeals all the previous Acts referred to in the introductory account below, but they are still referred to in this chapter because of their significance as milestones in the development of modern coronership. The 1988 Act was not greeted with universal acclaim. Many Coroners feel that it enshrines numerous anachronisms (for example, the power to direct a general practitioner to conduct an autopsy), and that an opportunity to introduce non-controversial reforms, such as streamlining the procedure for death registration, was lost.

In England and Wales, 39 per cent (210,000) of all deaths were referred to the Coroner in 2004 (Home Office 2004). In 57 per cent of cases, an autopsy (necropsy, post mortem examination) was performed. Over the last 20 years, Coroners have become increasingly willing to close their investigation without autopsy (A Pass). Currently, the autopsy rate is falling by approximately 1 per cent per year. This trend has accelerated even more sharply since the public disquiet raised by the revelations of autopsy practices and human organ retentions at the Royal Liverpool Children's Hospital in 1999 (Redfearn 2002) (see Chapters 6 and 9). In only a small number (13%) of referred cases is an inquest held, and in even fewer (3%) is this a full, or jury, inquest. In 2004, 24,000 inquests were held and, of these, only 690 were held in the presence of a jury.

There is much ignorance amongst the general public about the reasons for coronial investigation, which often carries an undeserved stigma. There is also a degree of ignorance, fear and defensive suspicion amongst some members of the caring professions. These reactions are understandable, but unjustified. The Coroner's obligation is to inquire into any sudden unexpected death, any death whose cause is uncertain and, of course, any death which may be unnatural. His investigation is limited to ascertaining the identity of the person who has died, how, when and where the death occurred, and the details required for registration. He is not a judge in the commonly accepted sense, as he cannot preside over criminal trials or civil disputes, but he is a member of the mainstream judiciary appointed by the Lord Chancellor, dismissible only by him, through the Department of Constitutional Affairs, and accorded all the rights and privileges of a High Court judge. An inquest is sometimes referred to as an inquisition, and he is specifically forbidden to imply guilt, or apportion blame (Coroners Rules 1984, r.42). These are tasks for the criminal or civil courts. If he suspects any criminal involvement, he must adjourn the inquest and refer the investigation to the Crown Prosecution Service.

The office of Coroner was established in 1194, in the Articles of Eyre of Richard I. The Coroner's position was further re-inforced by the Assizes Act (1228). The Statute of Westminster (1275) clarified his role in the investigation of death (Hill 1990).

Until recently, the Coroner's duties and powers were much wider than they are today, but they now face challenges and restrictions. Before the introduction of the Criminal Law Act (1977) he could still commit a named person directly to the Crown Court on a charge of unlawful killing, although this power was seldom used. The last occasion was in 1975, when the Jury in the inquest upon Lord Lucan's nanny returned a verdict of unlawful killing against him. He has never been apprehended, and is presumed by most authorities to be dead.

Immediately before and after the Norman Conquest (11th century), the Coroner was largely concerned with matters financial, ensuring that the Crown and the State received their share of the property accruing from any unnatural death, hence the word Coroner, which derives from 'custos placitorum coronae' – 'the keeper of the Crown's pleas'. By the time of Magna Carta (1215), he had lost many of his fiscal duties and, as the years went by, his powers were further eroded. By the 19th century, he was an elected local officer concerned only with the investigation of deaths and adjudication upon the ownership of buried hoards (treasure trove). He was subject to the direction of circuit judges, and able only to inquire into 'manifestly felonious' deaths. He was unable to recover any fees or expenses for so doing.

His current rise in status began in 1860, when the first County Coroners Act made provision for the payment of a salary. About this time, there was a perceived though unproven rapid rise in the incidence of homicidal poisoning, both in adults and in children, which prompted not only the rejuvenation of the coronial system, but the establishment of forensic medicine as a specialist discipline in the UK (see also Chapter 10).

The Coroners Act of 1887 extended the Coroner's powers, conferring upon him the right to investigate all sudden or unexplained deaths. An inquest was mandatory in every case so referred, until the Coroners (Amendment) Act of 1926. An autopsy was not, and payment of a nationally agreed fee for the doctor performing it was established only in 1927. Since the 1926 Act, the Coroner is permitted, after initial inquiry, to refer a death back to the reporting doctor, recording the fact that no further action is needed. Alternatively, he may refer the case to the Registrar without inquest, if he is satisfied that the death was due to natural causes, as is the case with the vast majority. If no autopsy is held, Coroner's form A is used, but the reporting doctor must supply a medical certificate of cause of death (MCCD). After autopsy, the coroner issues form B (see below). This replaces the MCCD.

Election by popular vote was abolished in 1888 and the Coroner became an independent officer, paid by the Local Authority but not subject to their control or discipline. He is confirmed in his office by the Lord Chancellor's Department (now the Department for Constitutional Affairs (DCA)) and can only be dismissed by him/them. The future of the Office of Lord Chancellor is currently uncertain. If it is abolished, we presume that his powers will be assumed by the DCA.

Until the 1926 Act, any freeholder could become a Coroner. The first 'Coroners Rules' were also published in 1926. Note that, despite their title, they are advisory, not mandatory, and are open to differing interpretations by individual Coroners. Even after these reforms, there was widespread discontent with the varying quality of coronership, and in 1936 the Wright Committee (Home Office 1936) made sweeping recommendations for the imposition of basic standards and procedures, none of which were implemented until revision of the Coroners Rules in 1953. (These were most recently further amended in 1984 and again in 2005.)

The Brodrick Committee made further recommendations in 1971 (Home Office 1971). Some of these were belatedly incorporated into revised Coroners Rules, which came into force in 1984.

The requirement to personally view every body subject to his inquiry was finally abolished in 1980. There is currently a Working Party within the Home Office examining some coronial practices. Their *Fundamental Review of Coroners*, overseen by Mr Tom Luce, was published in 2004 (Home Office 2004) and its recommendations are incorporated into a position paper *Reforming the Coroner and Death Certification Service* (Home Office 2004). Also, following the inquiry into the activities of Dr Harold Frederick Shipman (see below), Dame Janet Smith, a senior High Court judge, has made sweeping recommendations for reform of the Service, although there is some considerable divergence of opinion between her conclusions and those embodied in the Luce report (see below). It is widely accepted that reform is long overdue (Pounder 1999) and the proposals have been subjected to wide scrutiny by the medical profession (Milroy and Whitwell 2003) and by Coroners themselves (Forrest 2003).

The present-day office of Coroner

A present-day Coroner must be either a doctor or a lawyer of more than five years' professional standing. Some Coroners are doubly qualified. Legally qualified Coroners heavily outnumber medical ones. At the time of writing, 27 are whole-time salaried officials, whose salaries and expenses are met by the Local Authority. Others, about 90 in all, hold part-time appointments, combining their duties with their ordinary legal or medical practice. Each Coroner must nominate a deputy and at least one assistant deputy, so that someone is always available. The Coroner is independent of the judiciary, and of local and central government. In larger jurisdictions, he has a full-time officer or officers (the Coroner's Officer) who undertakes initial routine enquiries on his behalf. The costs of this support are, in theory, borne by the employing

Local Authority, but the level of support varies, and many part-time Coroners say that their legal practice subsidises their coronial duties. The support staff were, until recently, usually serving or ex-police officers. In some rural areas the police officer first involved in the death still assumes the functions of Coroner's Officer (CO). There is now an increasing tendency to 'civilianise' the CO post. Although many officers are ex-police, the majority are now drawn from a wide variety of professions, particularly nursing and the social services. They are praised by many for their more sympathetic approach to the newly bereaved, but some of those concerned with the investigation of crime feel that these officers lack the high index of suspicion and 'nose for the irregular' possessed by those with a police background.

In normal circumstances the Coroner can only investigate the death of a person whose body lies within his jurisdiction. He sometimes has occasion to hold an inquest without a body. Home Office approval is needed for him to do so. This may take place in cases of presumed drowning, where the body has not been recovered within a reasonable period. Since 1988, he has been able to maintain his jurisdiction even when the patient dies in a hospital beyond the area where the injury was sustained, or the body has been removed for a specialised post mortem examination, but this decision is taken on a case-by-case basis, and there must be agreement in writing between the Coroners involved.

Reportable deaths

As stated above, the Coroner may investigate any death where there is uncertainty about the circumstances or its cause. The deaths which should be reported to the Coroner are specified in the Instructions to Registrars (see Chapter 3) and in the advice given to medical practitioners by their professional and defence bodies (Coleman 1996; Day 2001; Start et al. 1995). Registrars are legally obliged to report certain types of death to the Coroner. Medical practitioners confirming the fact of death are merely advised to report. The legal obligation remains with the Registrar. This is expected to change in the near future, if the recommendations of the Fundamental Review are implemented. If the Shipman Inquiry's (2004) recommendations are fully implemented, every death will be referred for preliminary screening by the Medical Coroner (see below). The principal categories reportable at present are as follows:

1. The doctor has not been in attendance upon the patient during his last illness.

2. The doctor has not seen the patient during the 14 days immediately prior to death (28 days in Northern Ireland), or no doctor has seen the body after death.

3. The death may have been caused by an industrial disease or injury (no time limits).

4. Any sudden or unexplained death.

5. Any death in suspicious circumstances.

6.   Any death which an accident may have caused or even contributed to. There is no time limit upon this requirement.

7.   Any suggestion that the death may be due to neglect (individual or corporate, and including self-neglect), poisoning, misuse of drugs, or abortion (whether spontaneous or induced).

8.   Any death in police custody (note that custody now begins at the very moment of the arrest or application of physical restraint). All prison and custodial institutional deaths must be reported. There is, at present, no formal obligation to report the death of those voluntarily detained in mental hospitals, but it is wise to do so. The death of a patient in a psychiatric hospital, who is compulsorily detained, must be reported.

9.   Any death which may be related to an operation or anaesthetic. There is no formal time limit laid down. It is also mandatory to report any death during or related to minor procedures such as endoscopic examination or X-rays involving the use of injected contrast medium. Doctors who do not report such cases are at risk of General Medical Council disciplinary procedures.

10. In some circumstances a natural disease is reportable. For example, a death due to HIV or hepatitis B, where the infection was transmitted by blood transfusion; new variant Creutzfeldt–Jakob disease (the human form of BSE) from the consumption of infected meat; or where neglect or mishap might have contributed to the death. The case of *Touche* (2001), where death from a brain haemorrhage due to eclampsia in a newly delivered woman followed a failure to monitor her blood pressure, is a good illustration of this category. The obligation to report this type of case was resolved only after the intervention of the Divisional and the Appeal Courts, and is worthy of more detailed study (*Touche* 2001).

From the above list it will be obvious that most investigations are initiated by the medical profession. In addition to the above well-defined circumstances, there are many 'grey areas', where a doctor would be well advised to discuss the circumstances informally with the Coroner or his officer, before deciding whether to issue the MCCD or formally report the case. These include many deaths of psychiatric hospital inpatients, patients who die several days after an operation where surgery or the anaesthetic might conceivably have played a part, and even some deaths where there is a history of accident, no matter how many years previously it occurred. For example, consider the case of an elderly woman who dies after a fall, in which she fractures the neck of her femur. Some Coroners would hold this to be an accidental death. Others would argue that osteoporosis (fragility of the bones) is part of the ageing process, and that this is a natural death, which requires no coronial investigation. In the case of postoperative deep vein thrombosis, some Coroners take the view that this is misadventure, but an increasing number hold thrombosis to be an unfortunate natural response of the body to surgery, and so permit the issue of a death certificate, or issue form B (see below), after an autopsy.

In law, the Registrar is the principal reporter of deaths to the Coroner (Births and Deaths Registration Act 1953), when presented with an incomplete MCCD or one with an initialled 'box A' on its reverse (see Chapter 3). In practice, most doctors will report the case directly and not complete a death certificate. Most deaths in the community are reported by the police, who are notified by the ambulance services when they attend the scene of a sudden death. They also notify when crime is suspected, a serious accident has occurred, or a body or remains, thought to be human, have been found. Any member of the public, who feels unease about a death, may convey his disquiet to the Coroner. Indeed, there is a common law obligation to do so, although the foundation for this is so far back in time that some authorities express a doubt as to its continued applicability (Leadbeater and Knight 1993). Crime need not necessarily be suspected. It may be a civil matter, for example a suspicion of medical negligence, which prompts such an action, often by a relative or friend of the deceased. The obligation to report a death remains, even if the body is 'destroyed or irrecoverable'. A relative or other person may receive information of concern after the deceased has been cremated. Under these circumstances, as no body remains, the authority of the Secretary of State is required before the Coroner can assume jurisdiction.

Coroner's certificates A, B and E

When a death is reported to a Coroner, four possible courses of action are open to him. The Coroner may advise the doctor that an ordinary medical certificate of cause of death may be issued. The Registrar receives the MCCD completed by the reporting doctor and registers the death in the usual way. The Coroner records that he is taking no further action. Alternatively, the Coroner may assume jurisdiction over the case and decide, after discussion with the doctors and others involved, that no post mortem is necessary. He will then issue pink form A (form 14 in Northern Ireland). This certifies that no autopsy is needed and gives the cause of death in Ia, Ib, Ic format, as does a death certificate (see Chapter 2), and therefore in a form appropriate for registration and statistical record.

The relative or other informant takes form A to the Registrar along with the MCCD, and a death certificate is issued.

Whichever method is used, some confusion and delay may result, and the informant has to make at least two journeys, one to the Coroner's office and one to that of the Registrar. The same usually applies following the issue of forms B or E, and in inquest cases (see below). Consideration is therefore being given to the proposal that the Coroner should take on the functions of the Registrar in all cases referred to him and assume the obligation to issue the appropriate disposal order and the authority to complete registration. This will require parliamentary legislation. In the meantime, the recent introduction of 'on-line' registration has simplified the procedure.

Coroners vary in the frequency with which they permit disposal and registration without autopsy. In some jurisdictions the 'A pass' rate is as high as 50–60 per cent.

In many others it is considerably lower. In England and Wales overall, approximately 55 per cent of reported cases come to autopsy.

Removal of bodies out of England

From time to time relatives desire the return of a body to the country of birth or ethnic origin. Permission must be sought from the Coroner in every case, even if the death is natural and the doctor is willing to issue an MCCD. Application is made on form 104 (rev). The Coroner will then initiate inquiries in the usual way and, if satisfied that no autopsy is necessary, he will issue an 'out of England' certificate (form 103) which will confirm either that his inquiry is complete, and the body may be moved forthwith, or that the body must be held for four clear days whilst further inquiries and, if necessary, a post mortem are made. It is preferable for statistical purposes that the death be then registered in the usual way, although there is no legal requirement to do this.

OTHER MATTERS

For the Coroner's involvement in decisions relating to organ donation and transplantation, see Chapter 9. For exhumations ordered by the Coroner, see Chapter 10.

The coronial autopsy, consent, and retention of material

When the Coroner orders an autopsy (see Chapter 6), it is performed by a pathologist (a doctor who has made a special study of the naked eye and microscopical changes in disease). Up to 20 years ago, it was not uncommon for general practitioners, with no special training in pathology, to undertake these examinations. A full examination of the body must be made. There are no legally binding rules for the conduct of such examinations, but the Royal College of Pathologists (2004a) and the Home Office (2004) have both issued detailed guidelines and codes of practice. Failure to observe them incurs no legal sanction, but the practitioner would be at risk of falling foul of the GMC's Fitness to Practice Directorate. An appendix to the Coroners Rules, setting out the recommended format for the pathologist's report (Coroners Rules 1984), also makes it clear that a detailed examination is required. The pathologist's report must be similarly detailed. A full description of the external appearances of the body must be given; this should include height, weight, and any distinguishing features. Mere 'positive reporting' with a description of abnormalities is not sufficient; if an organ or system is normal, this must be stated also. The costs of the autopsy, the transport to, and storage of, the body at a suitable mortuary, and the cost of the post mortem are the responsibility of the Coroner, not the relatives.

The Coroner's autopsy report is confidential to him and may not be disclosed to any other person without his consent. Persons desiring a copy of the report must apply to the Coroner, not the pathologist or hospital authority. In practice, most Coroners allow the pathologist to send a copy of his report to the general practitioner or hospital consultant, without formal prior authority being sought. It is now recommended that relatives should be offered a copy of the report also.

The pathologist is also obliged, under the various Coroners Rules (1984), in particular Rule 9, to retain any tissue or organ which *may* have a bearing upon the cause of death. He may retain nothing else. He can only undertake further special examinations (e.g. microscopy, X-ray, toxicology) with the Coroner's specific permission, except in the case of road traffic accidents, where estimation of blood or urine alcohol levels, although not mandatory, is strongly advisable. Rule 9 was further amended in June 2005 (Coroners (Amendment) Rules 2005). The pathologist must notify the Coroner in writing of all material retained. He can advise the Coroner on the probable period for which retention might be necessary. Under no circumstances may such material be retained once the Coroner has discharged his function. The Coroner must contact the relatives and inform them that his examination is complete, and offer them the opportunity to dispose of the retained material, for example by a second burial or cremation. If the relatives decline the offer, the pathologist and the Coroner must both keep details of how, when and by whom the material was disposed of. This latest amendment has caused grave concern amongst pathologists and Coroners alike, many of whom believe that the loss of this material could compromise investigation of subsequent deaths, the causation of which might possibly be connected in some way. Those relatives who have reason to fear future re-examination of retained material will be the most likely to seek its return and disposal, creating an alarming potential for miscarriages of justice. Despite representations to Government by both Coroners and the Royal College of Pathologists, the Government is not at present minded to modify its stance. For a full discussion of the provisions of the Human Tissue Act (2004) and related legislation see Chapter 9.

The Coroner's Officer obtains the appropriate medical history from the relatives and the doctors involved. This information is passed to the pathologist by the Coroner's office. The Coroner can choose his pathologist. Certain guidelines are followed. A pathologist specialising in respiratory disease might be invited to examine a case of alleged pneumoconiosis; a paediatric pathologist will examine infant deaths; a specialist whole time forensic pathologist or hospital pathologist on the 'Home Office List' will investigate suspicious deaths. In suspicious deaths in infants and young children, it is recommended in the Kennedy Report (Royal College of Pathologists 2004b) that the examination be performed jointly by a paediatric and a forensic pathologist, or a forensic pathologist who has undertaken an approved period of special training in paediatric pathology. In these latter cases, the Coroners Rules (1984) recommend that, when choosing the appropriate pathologist, the Coroner should take the advice of the senior investigating police officer.

After the post mortem is completed, the pathologist transmits the cause of death, in writing, to the Coroner. Very few Coroners will accept a verbal report, but facsimile transmission, although not strictly an 'original document', is gaining increasing acceptance. If the death is natural, the Coroner then issues pink form B (form 17 in Northern Ireland). This certifies that, after post mortem examination, the cause of death was 'Ia, Ib, Ic', exactly like a medical certificate of cause of death (see Chapter 2), and this is accepted by the Registrar. If cremation is desired, the Coroner issues yellow form 100E in addition to forms A or B. This is accepted for cremation by the appropriate authorities, and replaces the medical certificates B and C for cremation, which are described in Chapter 8. The relatives must still register the death, although form E is an authority for disposal. The Coroner's certificate does not replace form F. The medical referee's authority is still required.

If the cause of death cannot be immediately ascertained, or is unnatural, some delay is inevitable, but attempts are made to keep this to a minimum. If, for example, samples are submitted for analysis in a case of suspected drug overdose, the Coroner will usually open an inquest to take formal identification. If he is assured, in writing by the pathologist, that the appropriate samples have been retained and that no further examination of the body is necessary, he will issue an order for disposal. He may sometimes be reluctant to permit cremation in these circumstances, particularly if homicide is suspected. When the tests are completed, the Coroner will permit the completion of registration if the death proves to be natural, and complete the inquest (see below). Where a long delay is anticipated, the Coroner will issue an interim document in lieu of the Registrar's certificate, which, although it has no legal standing, may assist the family in their settlement of the deceased's affairs.

The Coroner's Officer must inform the next of kin (or partner) and the family doctor of the time and place of the post mortem, so that a medical representative may attend on their behalf, although this right is seldom claimed. The Coroner must also inform any other interested party, for example the Health and Safety Inspectorate or the police, in cases of industrial accidents, deaths upon the railway and similar incidents which may be a matter of public concern.

Objections to autopsy and tissue retention

The law is quite clear in this regard; if no doctor is prepared to issue a medical certificate of cause of death, an autopsy must be carried out. Many people have strong personal objections to autopsy, particularly if the patient is a child. These attitudes were reinforced following the revelations relating to autopsies and to the retention of tissues at the Royal Liverpool Children's Hospital throughout the last two decades of the 20th century (Redfearn 2002). Furthermore autopsy is anathema to some religions, notably Orthodox Jewry and Islam.

The Royal Liverpool Children's Hospital Report by Michael Redfearn QC, published in 2002, recognised the rights of families to information about autopsy and tissue retention. The report resulted in the passage of the Human Tissue Act (2004) and the publication by the Home Office of the Coroner's Model Charter (Home Office 2003). Detailed guidelines for best practice by pathologists were also published at the same time.

These documents indicate that the relatives should receive an explanation of the need for the autopsy and notice of the arrangements, so that they can organise a doctor's attendance, if they wish, and take up the offer of a copy of the report if they so desire. The limitations of the Coroner's autopsy, which is restricted to ascertaining the cause of death, should also be explained to them. If they require more detailed investigation of other medical conditions which might be present, then their written consent for retention of diagnostic material should be obtained in accordance with the Human Tissue Act (2004).

If the relatives object strongly, the reasons for autopsy should be clearly set out, either by a hospital bereavement counselling officer or by a member of the Coroner's staff. In some cases, it might be possible to determine an adequate cause of death by some other means, for example a blood test or by magnetic resonance imaging (MRI) (Bissett *et al.* 2002). If the relatives remain adamant in their opposition, the autopsy should be delayed for a short period to give them the opportunity to seek legal advice. Relatives rarely take the matter to judicial review, if matters have been clearly explained to them. Such a review nearly always gives a decision which upholds the Coroner's authority. The authors know of no recent case where such objections have been upheld.

Following the recommendations of the Redfearn Report (2002), when it is necessary for tissues, organs or fluids to be retained, the Coroner should, at the time of the examination, explain the need for retention, specify what has been retained and say for how long such retention might be necessary. The relatives or partner should be informed of their rights relating to the return and disposal of the material. Indefinite retention of items, such as slides and paraffin blocks, is no longer permitted under any circumstances, unless the relatives give specific consent in accordance with the requirements of the Human Tissue Act (2004). Pathologists must inform the Coroner, in writing, of the nature of any such samples retained, and the reasons for retention. They must give an estimate of the probable length of time for which retention might be necessary. In criminal cases, the minimum periods set for retention prior to the passage of the Act were three years after conviction, or until the outcome of any appeal was determined. However, many feel that retention in some criminal cases should be for much longer periods. The Criminal Cases Review Commission (CCRC) increasingly refers cases back for a second appeal, sometimes several years after the first was rejected. Many pathologists and Coroners are concerned that the new requirement to surrender or dispose of material, may lead to miscarriages of justice.

If the relatives are dissatisfied with the cause of death as given by the pathologist, they can request a second autopsy by an independent pathologist. This should normally be arranged through a solicitor and is relatively expensive (£500–£1500). The solicitors representing a person or persons charged with unlawful killing will usually request an independent autopsy. The cost of this is met through the Legal Aid Fund. It is now normal practice, in the investigation of any potentially contentious hospital death, for the Coroner to nominate a pathologist from another NHS trust or University department of pathology to perform the examination (Coroners Rules 1984, Rule 6).

Occasionally the post mortem, toxicological analysis and microscopical examination fail to reveal the cause of death. The cause is then formally given as 'not ascertained'. It is now recommended that this term should not be used in cases of deaths of children under the age of 12 months. 'Sudden unexpected death in infancy (SUDI)' is less stigmatising, and is less distressing to the relatives, and no inquest is necessary. In cases where 'not ascertained' has been given as the cause of death, an inquest, usually without a jury, is held. The pathologist states his belief that the death was not due to any unnatural cause. The Coroner gives the relatives an opportunity to ask questions of the pathologist and 'clear the air', and an open verdict is returned.

The Coroner's inquest

The purpose of an inquest is to answer four questions, and four questions only: who, where, when and how. It is not a forum for the establishment of responsibility for a death, nor of civil liability (Coroners Rules 1984, Rule 42). However, the proceedings are sometimes used by lawyers to explore the possibility of a subsequent civil action; rarely, if evidence emerges suggesting that a crime may have been committed, the Coroner will adjourn the inquest and refer the case to the Director of Public Prosecutions.

Under the terms of the Coroners Act 1988, the Coroner may hold an inquest only when a post mortem has revealed a death to be unnatural. However, if there is a possibility that human failing or a culpable lack of care may have contributed to an otherwise natural death, an inquest is now mandatory (see *Touche* 2001).

An inquest must be held on deaths due to unlawful killing, those occurring in custody, during arrest by a police officer, in a transportation accident, or those resulting from any industrial incident. Inquests are also held in cases of drug overdose or chronic misuse, suspected suicide, therapeutic misadventure, alleged negligence, and death due to neglect. There is no longer an obligation to hold an inquest upon a death in which chronic alcohol abuse played a part, but acute alcohol poisoning is treated in the same way as any other acute drug overdose.

A jury *must* be empanelled where the death needs to be notified to a government department, i.e. all deaths in custody, all deaths resulting from air, sea and rail transportation accidents, and all industrial accidents. The Coroner may empanel a jury in any other hearing in which he thinks it appropriate.

Verdicts and 'findings'

A jury consists of 7 to 11 persons, who are randomly chosen from the electoral roll of the district in which the death occurred. If not more than two of them disagree, they may return a majority verdict. The Coroner merely gives directions on the verdicts available, and on points of law. It is the jury that returns the verdict. There is an increasing tendency for verdicts to be given in narrative form. This trend follows the current practice in certain states of Australia to replace the 'verdict', with its judgemental overtones, with the more neutral 'finding'. This is also becoming common when the Coroner is sitting without a jury, the narrative being more in accordance with Article 2 of the European Convention on Human Rights. For a full discussion of this complex area see Dorries, Chapter 4 (2004), and his discussions of the case of *Middleton* (see also *R (Middleton) v W Somerset Coroner* 2002).

The most commonly used verdicts available to a Coroner sitting alone, or to a jury, are:

1. Natural causes.

2. Unlawful killing – this encompasses murder, manslaughter, infanticide, and assisting suicide. The verdict that is returned is simply recorded as 'unlawfully killed'. The assailant is not named, even if he has been convicted in a criminal court.

3. Suicide. This, since 1984, has replaced the old style verdict 'Did kill himself'. It is now uncommon for the supplementary statement 'Whilst the balance of mind was disturbed' to be added. This was used only as a convenience, in an era when the attitude of the major religions to suicide was less sympathetic than it is now. There is an increasing tendency, particularly following drug overdose and drowning, to return a narrative finding, in which it is stated that evidence of intent is unclear. In recent years, many verdicts of suicide have been overturned on judicial review, because clear evidence of intent was not available. Therefore the tendency now is to return an open verdict, unless the deceased left a note, a tape recording, had clearly stated to others his intention to kill himself, or in circumstances where the observation of witnesses (e.g. precipitation from a height or under a train) leave no room for reasonable doubt.

4. Accidental death or misadventure. The fine distinction between these two categories sometimes causes confusion. A simple illustration will help to clarify this. If a person falls into a lake whilst returning home from work drunk this is an accident. If a drunken person goes to the same lake, removes his clothes, tells his comrades that he is going for a swim, enters the water and then drowns, this is misadventure. In other words, the misadventure verdict is reserved for those who voluntarily put themselves into the situation which led to death. A misadventure verdict is therefore usually returned, for example, following therapeutic mishaps in the operating theatre.

5. Drug dependence. This is self-explanatory, but note that a verdict of chronic alcoholism has not been permitted since the Coroners Rules were amended in 1984. It is no longer necessary to report deaths due to chronic alcohol abuse to the Coroner.

6. Certain industrial diseases, for example pneumoconiosis in ex-coal miners.

7. Neglect (formerly 'lack of care' or 'system neglect' (see below).

8. Want of attention at birth.

9. An open verdict. The open verdict is used in several circumstances. It may be used where the cause of death has not been ascertained. It may be returned in a death due to an overdose of drugs, where there is insufficient evidence as to intent. It may also be returned in a case where a child has died of head injuries, for example, and there is insufficient evidence to show whether the injuries were deliberately inflicted, or the result of an accident. These verdicts are often unsatisfactory in that the other persons involved in the death may be left carrying a certain stigma. The consequences are rather similar to the old Scottish criminal verdict of 'not proven'. For this reason, in some countries (for example, in some Australian States) the 'open verdict' option is no longer available, and is replaced by a narrative setting out of the circumstances as best they can be ascertained.

Most inquests are now held in purpose-built courts, but they may be held in a town hall or any other local authority owned premises. They may not be held in licensed premises. They are not held on Sundays or public holidays, and are usually held only in normal working hours. An inquest is, by its nature, public. It may only be held *in camera* where national security may be threatened; interested parties may challenge even this decision. The Coroner may, however, ask the media representatives present to handle a particular case with appropriate sensitivity, and this request is usually honoured. Conversely the Coroner sometimes enlists the aid of the media to highlight a particular hazard, for example solvent abuse, the dangers of 'designer drugs', or trespassing upon the railway, although the formal 'rider' added by the jury was abolished many years ago.

The Coroner must inform the following 'interested parties' of the time and place of an inquest:

- The married partner (or a co-habitee of longstanding under the Civil Partnerships Act 2004).
- The nearest relative.
- The personal representative or executor.
- Any person who has asked to be notified of the time and place of the inquest.
- Any person who has an interest in life insurance on the deceased.
- The trade union representative in any case where death may be due to industrial disease or accident.
- Any person, or his representative, who may have caused the death or contributed to it.
- The Chief Officer of Police, or his nominee.
- Any other person who the Coroner has reason to believe may be an interested party.

Traditionally, an inquest is opened by the Coroner's Officer reading a proclamation which summons 'All manner of persons' to attend and give evidence. Many Coroners now dispense with this and the opening is a less formal affair. The Coroner wears no wig, although a few Coroners wear a formal dark green gown for high-profile cases. When he enters, all in the court rise and return his bow. When everyone is seated the Coroner introduces himself, administers the jury oath (though his officer may do this) if one has been empanelled, and then outlines the background to the case. He indicates who the witnesses will be and in what order he will call them. At this stage he only explains the possible verdicts to the jury in the most general terms. The witnesses are then called.

The Coroner is addressed as 'Sir/Madam'. A witness may give evidence on oath or on affirmation. The first witness called is usually someone who has formally identified the body. The order of witnesses varies. The most common practice is to call them so that a progressive narrative of the events leading up to, and following, the death is established. Lay witnesses are usually called before the police. After the lay evidence and police evidence has been heard, the professional witnesses, for example the pathologist who carried out the autopsy, or the toxicologist, will be called to give their evidence. A witness must attend an inquest, although the summons is usually informally given over the telephone rather than in writing. Witnesses who fail to attend are issued with a written summons by the Coroner. If they still refuse to attend they may be fined. In extreme cases, where a duly warned witness fails to attend a hearing, which has been adjourned to permit his attendance, this may be held to be contempt in the face of the court, and imprisonment may result. Families and 'other properly interested persons' are entitled to legal representation; they are not at present entitled to legal aid. Pressure groups such as 'Inquest' (2002) have campaigned for many years to obtain this entitlement. Lawyers in a Coroner's court, be they barristers or solicitors, can only question witnesses. They are not allowed to address the court.

Each witness is first examined by the Coroner, and the deposition is recorded either by the Coroner, his secretary or, increasingly these days, by means of a tape-recorder. The witness is then cross-examined. He may be cross-examined by the lawyer representing any interested party, by any interested party directly, and by the jury, usually through the foreman. When all the questions have been put, the witness is re-examined by the Coroner and is then discharged. The rules of evidence in Coroners' courts are not so strict as they are in other English courts. Hearsay evidence is frequently admitted, and 'leading questions' are not expressly forbidden, as they are in other courts.

When all the evidence has been heard, the Coroner sums up the facts as they have been given in court, and directs the jury as to what verdicts are available to them. The jury then retire and consider their verdict in private. They may ask the Coroner, through the foreman, for guidance, either verbal or written, at any time during their deliberations.

After the inquest is over the Coroner, and jurors if present, sign the 'Certificate after Inquisition'. This permits registration formalities to be completed and allows the disposal of the body to proceed, if this has not already taken place after the opening of the inquest. The relatives may ask for material evidence, for example suicide notes, clothing or weapons, to be returned to them. If no such request is made, non-paper evidence may be destroyed. The Coroner's Register, which is a record of all inquest verdicts, is kept indefinitely. Associated documents are destroyed after 15 years. County Archive Departments usually hold Coroners' records. Only properly interested persons (see above) may inspect the Coroner's records of the inquest. They are made available for public inspection after 75 years. Unfortunately, many older inquest records consisted only of a very brief résumé of the facts and the verdict, and yield little information of value.

Verdicts – the need for change

It has long been recognised that the very term 'verdict' carries adversarial overtones, which are at odds with the whole purpose of the inquisitorial process. Short form verdicts, such as those described above, seldom tell the whole story, hence the trend towards the use of discursive or narrative verdicts. There is no definition in law of the terms 'misadventure' or 'accident'. Individual Coroners, therefore, have scope to modify their forms of verdicts. The Coroners Rules 1984 suggest a list of specimen verdicts, but no Coroner is bound to abide by this. The Fundamental Review (Home Office 2004) recommends abolition of the short form verdict and its replacement by an 'outcome label'. It suggests that the outcome should be a factual account of the circumstances and of the cause of death, with recognition of any failures identified and suggestions for their future remedy. Whatever changes are implemented, the requirement for the cause of death to be recorded in a form appropriate for statistical classification, national and international, will remain.

Although the standard of proof required in Coroners' records is not usually so rigorously set 'beyond reasonable doubt' as in criminal proceedings, there are circumstances, for example following a large dose of an anti-depressant tablets, where the criminal standard must be applied. Unless there is absolute proof of intent to commit suicide, an open verdict or a narrative account of the circumstances will be recorded.

The restrictions on the apportionment of blame or culpability imposed by Rule 42 are increasingly a source of conflict between the court's duty to fully inquire into the circumstances surrounding the death and the need to return a neutral verdict. This is particularly evident in the contentious area of neglect.

Neglect

'Neglect' is now a well-defined term, after many years of evolution. The term and its application have been clarified by the case of *Middleton* (2002). Middleton was a prisoner who hanged himself in his cell. He had been identified as a suicide risk, but the prison authorities had not put the proper safeguards in place. The jury, whilst returning a suicide verdict (the only course placed before them), made it clear in a note to the Coroner that the prison service had failed in their duty to care for the deceased. This case continues to exercise legal authorities, involving issues of care, human rights, and the limitations of the Coroner's powers to allocate culpability under the restrictions of Rule 42 of the Coroners Rules 1998. These deliberations are still ongoing at the time of writing, in both the English legal system and the European Court of Human Rights.

Negligence is a broad term, which is clearly understood and is applied in civil law to a failure to provide general and non-specific reasonable care. Neglect, originally 'a lack of care', is applied to a much narrower circumstance, for example failure of an individual prison officer to regularly supervise an inmate, who he was aware had previously exhibited disturbed behaviour, or to nursing staff who failed to maintain adequate observations of a patient or his life support equipment on an intensive care unit. For a detailed discussion of this complex area, which is far beyond the scope of this book, the reader is referred to Dorries (2004, pp.278–283).

Judicial review – when things go wrong

There is no right of appeal against the verdict of a Coroner's court. Further consideration of procedures or verdicts is obtained by judicial review. Review may be achieved by pursuing one of two routes. Section 13 of the Coroners Act 1988 gives the High Court power to act if the Coroner has refused to hold an inquest, if the conduct of the inquest was seriously flawed, or because new evidence has come to light. There is no time limit upon these applications. More commonly, under the provisions of the Supreme Court Act 1981, the High Court can make orders to review any aspect or outcome of the coronial inquiry if it considers it 'just and convenient' to do so. The processes of judicial review are complex and beyond the scope of this book. Readers should consult Dorries (2002) for more detailed discussion. Those seeking specific advice should contact the organisation 'Inquest' whose address is given in Appendix A.

The Legal Aid Act (1974) provided that legal aid should be available for persons 'who might be adversely affected' by an inquest. These recommendations remain unimplemented, despite pressure from organisations such as 'Justice' (Stone 1986).

Scotland – the Procurator Fiscal

The basic procedures for the registration of natural and expected death in Scotland parallel those in use in England and Wales. The only major difference is that any doctor can issue an MCCD, even if he has not been in attendance during the last illness. The investigation of sudden and unnatural death differs considerably.

The Scottish legal system is entirely distinct from that of the rest of the UK. It developed separately, unaffected by the Norman Conquest, and its roots are embedded deep in Roman and European law, largely in consequence of the close historical ties which existed between Scotland and France ('The Auld Alliance'). Criminal law is administered by a network of Public Prosecutors. The most senior, the Lord Advocate, appoints Procurators Fiscal in each Sheriffdom. The Fiscal prosecutes in the lower courts, but also carries out the initial investigation of any death reported to him.

His main concern is to establish whether there has been any criminality or negligence associated with the death, rather than establishing the medical cause thereof. He cannot issue a death certificate; the equivalent of Coroner's forms A and B do not exist in Scotland. The 'Fiscal's Certificate' is, in fact, issued either by the forensic medical examiner (formerly known as the 'police surgeon') or the pathologist. The Fiscal does not hold inquests. He takes informal, unsworn statements, so-called 'precognitions' from those involved. These may be used as a basis for a fatal accident enquiry or subsequent court proceedings.

Deaths are reported to the Fiscal by the Registrar, who has a statutory duty to report certain types of death. The categories of reportable deaths are similar to those laid down in England and Wales. Doctors, police officers and members of the public may also report as to the Coroner. The Fiscal does not have a dedicated equivalent of the 'Coroner's Officer', but the police carry out the initial investigations on his behalf. After these have been completed, the Fiscal has two courses open to him. If he is satisfied that the death is natural, he may require a doctor to examine the body externally and issue a 'View and Grant' certificate. If the cause of death is not known, or is thought to be unnatural, he must apply to the Sheriff for an authority for an autopsy. After autopsy, the certified cause of death is given by the pathologist, as stated above.

If the death was unnatural, the Fiscal must report the circumstances to the Crown Office. If the Lord Advocate, acting through Crown Counsel, feels that no further investigation is necessary, the matter is closed. In cases where a criminal act or negligence may be a factor, a fatal accident enquiry is held. These are regulated by the Fatal Accident and Sudden Death Enquiry (Scotland) Act 1976. They are held in public and must be advertised. No jury is empanelled. No verdict is returned; the Sheriff's 'determination' is the formal conclusion of the proceedings. This may apportion blame or highlight deficient safety procedures.

In Scotland all evidence must be corroborated, so whenever a death may be the subject of civil or criminal litigation, two doctors carry out the autopsy. The autopsy rate is much lower in Scotland than in the rest of the United Kingdom because of the relative ease of 'View and Grant' certification. Such a system, however, has an adverse effect on the accuracy of mortality statistics. Consent for an 'academic autopsy' following a death in hospital is obtained from the relatives, applying the same criteria for validity as obtained in England and Wales (see Chapter 6).

The Coroner – proposals for change

Dr Harold Frederick Shipman, a general practitioner in Hyde, Greater Manchester, was arrested in 1998 and charged with the murder of 15 patients. He was convicted in January 2000. It is believed, at the time of writing, that the total number of patients killed, all by the injection of morphine or heroin, is well in excess of 200, extending back to his early career as a junior resident at a Yorkshire hospital, where he is now known to have killed at least 15 patients, and to have perhaps accelerated to the death of more than 30 others. Shipman hanged himself in prison in January 2003, and so his secrets die with him.

In response to the widespread public concern which followed the revelations of the ease with which Shipman had concealed his crimes, two separate and wide-ranging investigations into the processes of certification, registration and disposal of the dead were established. The first, a Home Office study coordinated by Mr Thomas Luce, published its findings in a report entitled 'The Fundamental Review of Coroners' (Home Office 2004). As its name implies, it was concerned mainly with the role of the Coroner in the investigation of sudden and unexpected deaths. The second, a public inquiry chaired by a High Court judge, Dame Janet Smith (The Shipman Inquiry Reports 2004), was much more extensive in its remit. Five reports have been issued, examining and identifying defects in the systems of death and cremation certification, registration of death, the supervision of doctors' prescriptions for controlled drugs, and the role of the General Medical Council in the regulation of doctors' fitness to practise. Dame Janet also made detailed recommendations on reforms in the reporting of, and coronial involvement in, the investigation of deaths in the community.

The Shipman Inquiry's recommendations are in broad agreement with those set out in the Home Office Review. These reforms will require a radical rewriting of primary legislation relating to the registration of death, its medical certification, and applications for cremation. They will also completely supersede the Coroners Act 1988, the Coroners Rules 1984 and previous laws going back as far as the Coroners Act 1878 (Dyer 2004).

Further reforms, in particular relating to the use and retention of organs and tissues after autopsy, are being introduced following the so-called retained organs scandal at the Royal Liverpool Children's Hospital in 1988 and Mr Michael Redfearn's subsequent report (2002). Originally, the timetable laid down for these reforms would have seen their full implementation in June 2006. There has been considerable delay, and although a white paper and enabling legislation is expected in the 2005–6 parliamentary session, full implementation of a scheme incorporating selected Luce and Smith proposals is now not expected before 2007 at the earliest. The Coroners' Society is already making plans for their implementation, organising training courses for its members and their staff. A Coroners' Officers Association has also been established, which is introducing training courses and a range of professional development initiatives. Teesside University in the Northeast of England now runs an intensive course for Coroners' Officers, and a diploma is awarded to candidates upon successful completion of the period of study.

The Home Office Fundamental Review

This report was published in June 2003. Its remit was to modernise the Coroner system; to make it fit to meet the demands of modern society and to satisfy the public's expectations for speedy and effective investigation. These are now greater than Coroners can deliver under the present system, which has remained fundamentally unchanged since the reign of Queen Victoria. In its introductory paragraphs, the review stated that 'neither the certification (of death) nor the investigation system is "fit for purpose" in a modern society. Both need fundamental and substantial reform.'

Amongst the proposals of the review, the most significant are as follows. The current locally based system, in which every Coroner enjoys unique authority and is *primus inter pares*, will be replaced with a national jurisdiction, under the auspices of the Lord Chancellor's Department (although this office itself is currently being replaced by that of Department for Constitutional Affairs; the actual post of Lord Chancellor remains for the present). A Chief Coroner, assisted by an Inspectorate, will set and maintain standards throughout England and Wales (and Northern Ireland). The current number of jurisdictions will be reduced from 128 to 60, the boundaries of which will be based upon police authority areas.

A rigorous mandatory training programme for Coroners, with a requirement for continuing education, will be introduced. A statutory medical assessor (SMA) will be appointed in each area. SMAs will greatly increase the medical expertise of the service. They will also take part in the audit and certification of natural deaths, advise the legally qualified Coroners in their investigations, choose medically qualified 'second certificants' under the proposed new death and cremation procedures, and liaise with public health and statutory safety services. Relatives will be entitled to financial assistance under the Legal Aid scheme, a reform which is particularly welcome. At present, only those who might be 'adversely affected' by an inquiry qualify for this assistance (Legal Aid Act 1974).

These recommendations will take several years to implement. Currently, transitional arrangements are being progressively introduced. The Coroners Rules are also under review, particularly those appertaining to the conduct and outcomes of inquests. Designated doctors, working within the National Health Service, are to assist Coroners and begin the process of pilot audits of routine death certification. The frequency and use of autopsies is under review, and advice upon the appropriate circumstances for such examinations is being prepared by the Home Office, the National Registration Service and the Chief Medical Officer for England and Wales.

An informal Coronial Council, recruited mainly from among the members of the Coroners' Society, will be established to oversee implementation of these changes, but this will require legislation. The Coroners' Society is currently offering a supervisory and advisory service to its members, but this is purely voluntary.

The Shipman Inquiry

This inquiry, chaired by Dame Janet Smith, has issued five reports. The second, published in July 2003, examined death and cremation certification and the role of the Coroner in the investigation of sudden and unexpected deaths. Although Dame Janet is in broad agreement with the proposals for change contained in the Fundamental Review, the report differs in several important regards. The inquiry rejects the proposal for the advisory SMA system in favour of a network of Medical Coroners, who will operate in parallel with their judicial colleagues. The Medical Coroners will receive reports of all deaths, 'filtering out' those which, as at present, may proceed directly to registration with no coronial involvement.

The judicial Coroners will no longer be responsible for the collection of evidence. They will undertake the direction of more complex inquiries, even when no inquest is envisaged, and will work together with the Medical Coroners in appropriate cases, although conduct of the actual inquests will remain their responsibility.

The Inquiry's transitional proposals, briefly stated, include the following. Like the Fundamental Review, it is proposed that a proper centrally organised training programme be introduced. Relations between Coroners' departments and bereaved families should be made less formal and more open. The pathologists who perform the coronial autopsies, and who are frequently expected to give opinions well beyond the limits of their expertise, should have a more limited remit. Advice upon complex medical matters should be sought from clinicians practising in the appropriate field. The funding of the pathology services should be considerably increased, so that ancillary investigations like microscopy, microbiology and toxicology are more appropriately and frequently employed. The Inquiry and the Review both agree upon the need for ongoing training of Coroners' Officers.

At present, there are no reliable indications as to which of the above recommendations will be introduced, nor when the appropriate legislation will be enacted. It is unlikely that any major changes will take place before late 2007. Some Coroners say, in private, that it could be 2010 before any real changes take place.

The Government's most likely course of action was set out in a Home Office Position Paper (June 2004) and has been confirmed in a recent Briefing Note from the DCA (Department of Constitutional Affairs 2006). This recommends a meld of the Shipman and Review proposals, which can be briefly set out as follows:

- The national service will be overseen by a Chief Coroner, a management board and a Coronial Council.

- There will be 40–60 full time Coroners, each assisted by a medical examiner's inquiry team.

- These medically qualified examiners will advise the Coroner on medical matters, and also act as 'second certifier' for *every* death.

- The document gives no detail of proposed changes to the Inquiry and Inquest system.

- The proposed timetable for reform aims to have new legislation in place by 2007, but adds that this is 'subject to the availability of parliamentary time' and 2010 is regarded by many as a more realistic date.

References

Births and Deaths Registration Act (1953) ss 15, 16.

Bissett, R.A.L., Thomas, N.B., Turnbull, I.W. and Lees, J. (2002) 'Post mortem examination using magnetic resonance imaging: a 4 year review of a working service.' *British Medical Journal 324*, 1423–1424.

Civil Partnerships Act (2004).

Coleman, P. (1996) *Death Certification and the Coroner.* Newsletter 1 July 1996. London: Office for National Statistics.

Coroners Act (1988) c 13 all sections.

Coroners (Amendment) Act (1926) c 59 s 21.

The Coroners (Amendment) Rules (2005) si no 420 r 3.

The Coroners Rules (1984) r 42.

Criminal Law Act (1977) s 56 (1).

Day, A. (2001) 'Medico-legal aspects of sudden death.' *Case Book.* Winter 2001 16, 10–12. London: Medical Protection Society.

Department of Constitutional Affairs (2006) *Coroners Service Reform – Briefing Note.* London: Department of Constitutional Affairs.

Dorries, C.P. (2004). *Coroners Courts,* 2nd edn. Oxford: Oxford University Press.

Dyer, C. (2004) 'New coroner's system will require two people to verify cause of death.' *British Medical Journal 328,* 727.

Fatal Accident and Sudden Death Enquiry (Scotland) Act (1976).

Forrest, A.R.W. (2003) 'Coroners: What next for death investigation in England and Wales?' *Science and Justice 43,* 3, 125–126.

Hill, I.R. (1990) 'The Coroner: 12th and 13th century development of the office.' *Medicine, Science and the Law 30,* 2, 133–137.

Home Office (1936) *Departmental Committee on Coroners* ('The Wright Committee'). Cmnd 507. London: HMSO.

Home Office (1971) *Report of the Committee on Death Certification and Coroners* ('The Brodrick Report'). Cmnd 4810. London: HMSO.

Home Office (2003) *Death Certification in England, Wales and Northern Ireland: Report of a Fundamental Review.* Cm 5831. London: HMSO.

Home Office (2004) *Reforming the Coroner and Death Certification Service: A Position Paper.* Cm 6159. London: The Stationery Office.

Human Tissue Act (2004) s 1 part 2.

Inquest (2002) *How the Inquest System Fails Bereaved People.* London: 'Inquest'.

Leadbeater, S. and Knight, B. (1993) 'Reporting deaths to the coroner – all the legal aspects of dying need re-examining.' *British Medical Journal 306,* 1018.

Legal Aid Act (1974).

Milroy, C.M. and Whitwell, H.L. (2003) 'Reforming the coroner service: major necessary reforms would mean an integrated service and more medical input.' *British Medical Journal 327*, 175–176.

Pounder, D.J. (1999) 'The Coroner Service. A relic in need of reform.' *British Medical Journal 318*, 1502–1503.

Redfearn, M. (2002) *The Royal Liverpool Children's Hospital Inquiry Report.* London: The Stationery Office.

R. (Middleton) v W Somerset Coroner (2002) 3 WLR 505 and 4 All ER 336.

R v N. London Coroner ex parte Touche (2001) QBD 1206.

R v N. London Coroner ex parte Touche (2001) All ER 752.

Royal College of Pathologists (2004a) *Code of Practice and Performance Standards for Forensic Pathologists.* (Published jointly with the Home Office Policy Advisory Board for Forensic Pathology.) London: RCPath.

Royal College of Pathologists (2004b) *Sudden Unexpected Death in Infancy ('The Kennedy Report'). The Report of a Working Party of the Royal College of Pathologists and the Royal College of Paediatrics and Child Health.* www.rcpath.org/index.asp?pageID=286 (accessed 12 March 2006).

The Shipman Inquiry (2004) 3rd Report. www.the-shipman-inquiry.org.uk (accessed 27 July 2005).

Start, R.D., Usherwood, T.P., Carter, N., Dorries, C.P., Cotton, D.K. (1995) 'General Practitioners' knowledge of when to refer a death to the coroner'. *British Journal of General Practice 45*, 191–193.

Stone, E. (1986) *Coroners' Courts in England and Wales.* London: 'Justice'.

CHAPTER 5

FETAL LOSS, STILLBIRTH, NEONATAL DEATH AND SUDDEN DEATH IN INFANCY

History of legislation and recent changes in law and terminology

Until the closing years of the 20th century, the legal procedures surrounding the loss of a fetus in early pregnancy or a stillbirth received a somewhat unsympathetic approach from government departments, such as the Home Office and the Department of Health, and from the caring professions. The gestational age at which a fetus was deemed capable of a separate existence was fixed at 28 weeks, by the Offences against the Person Act (1861), and remained unchanged until 1992. The remains of a child born before 28 weeks' gestation were regarded as clinical waste, rather than as a potential human being. Disposal was usually by incineration, along with other laboratory detritus. Even after 28 weeks, when the registration of stillbirth and disposal by burial or cremation became mandatory, the involvement of the parent or parents was relatively uncommon. Disposal was usually effected by the hospital through the good offices of a funeral director or local crematorium. The infant was placed in an already open grave, or cremated informally at the end of the day's funerals.

The last 30 years have seen rapid changes in law, custom and practice. Advances in neonatal resuscitation and intensive care led to the recognition that infants of less than 28 weeks' maturity are potentially capable of separate existence. The Human Fertilisation and Embryology Act (1990) reduced the age of viability to 24 weeks' gestation. This created a legal conflict, as the statutory definitions of viability and stillbirth under the Infant Life Preservation Act (1929) and the Births and Deaths Registration Act (1953) remained at 28 weeks until the Stillbirth (Definition) Act of 1992 removed the anomaly.

Similarly, until the various organ retention scandals of the late 1990s in Liverpool and Bristol (see Chapters 6 and 9), autopsies upon fetal remains and stillbirths were regarded as routine examinations of clinical material, rather than major and potentially distressing procedures for which the mothers' informed consent should be obtained. The Human Tissue Act (2004) has clarified the position and has also imposed stringent controls upon the retention of tissues and organs (although the status of the placenta as a part of the fetus for disposal purposes has not been clarified).

The Stillbirth and Neonatal Deaths Society (SANDS) was established in the early 1980s and quickly instigated a more sympathetic approach. The majority of disposals of stillbirths are now organised by the parents, often with some form of ceremony, which provides an opportunity to say goodbye, and assists the process of grieving (Kohner 1995).

The screening techniques now routinely employed in the early weeks of pregnancy have also led to changes in the attitudes of the caring professions towards second and third trimester intra-uterine deaths, be they spontaneous or surgically induced in response to the discovery of some major fetal abnormality. Ultrasound scans (USS) are now part of routine antenatal care. The first, at 12 weeks, detects neural tube abnormalities. Those most commonly encountered are hydrocephalus and spina bifida. The second examination at 18 weeks concentrates upon the appearance of the region of the nape of the neck (a nuchal scan) and is used, in conjunction with blood tests, for the diagnosis of Down's syndrome. If termination of pregnancy is elected for in consequence of such examinations, the fetus is accorded disposal in accordance with the mother's wishes. Only a minority request a formal funeral. In most cases the hospital arranges disposal, usually by cremation, but at all times the fetus is accorded due respect as a separate entity, and a detailed record is kept of the time and place and the method of disposal. Late termination, near to the age of legal viability (i.e. 24 weeks), may pose a problem if the dead fetus is retained *in utero* beyond that date. In law, such a delivery should be regarded as a stillbirth and registered accordingly, but special arrangements are now in place for such cases, so that the remains are treated as those of a non-viable fetus, with no necessity to register the stillbirth nor to organise a conventional funeral with registration of disposal.

Deaths in the first year of life receive particularly detailed pathological investigation. Two out of three of these deaths occur within the first seven days after delivery (Royal College of Obstetricians and Gynaecologists 2005a). For this reason, a neonatal death certificate was introduced in 1986 to better enable the compilation of statistics. Deaths under the age of 12 months are certified in the usual form (see Chapter 2), but are investigated with particular rigour in an endeavour to detect the rare instances of unnatural death, whilst causing a minimum of embarrassment and distress to those innocent and grief-stricken families who form the vast majority.

Historically the detection of feticide and infanticide has always been a matter of concern to the authorities, and this has influenced the legal processes surrounding registration and disposal. As early as 1843, Chadwick expressed concern that infanticide was passing undetected, but it was not until 1927 (Births and Deaths Registration Act 1926) that the registration of stillbirths was introduced, in an attempt to address this problem. It had been known for many years that there was a higher incidence of stillbirth amongst unmarried mothers, and until 1984 the Office of Population Censuses and surveys (OPCS) (now the Office for National Statistics or ONS) maintained separate records. This is no longer the case. The numbers of stillbirths annually fell progressively from 3855 in 1993 to 3203 in 2000, but there was a sharp rise (to 3327) in 2002. At the time of writing no more recent figures are available and, although a Working Party has been established to examine the reasons for this rise, no firm conclusions have been reached as to its cause or causes. The increase cannot be due simply to the change in the law reducing the age of viability to 24 weeks. Were this the cause, the increase would have occurred in 1990 (ONS 2003, *Health Statistics Quarterly*).

Definitions

ABORTION ('MISCARRIAGE')
Abortion ('miscarriage') is the death and expulsion of the fetus at any stage of pregnancy prior to the age of viability (24 weeks). The word 'abortion' implies no surgical or criminal intervention. Spontaneous abortion, the classical 'miscarriage', is common in the first trimester. It is estimated that one in every five conceptions ends in this way, usually within a few weeks of fertilisation.

STILLBIRTH
Stillbirth occurs when a fetus is delivered after 24 weeks' gestation, and there are no signs of life (gasping, heartbeat, or limb movements) after its complete expulsion from the birth canal. A fresh stillbirth has usually died during labour; less commonly the fetus shows signs of decomposition (maceration) with peeling of the skin and collapse of the skull bones (Spalding's sign). It is very difficult to estimate the time of intra-uterine death by examination of the fetus. One must rely upon the mother having noted the time of cessation of movement. Occasionally, following spontaneous death in the third trimester, or after feticide induced following the 18 week ultrasound detection of a grave abnormality, the fetus is retained beyond 24 weeks, and is therefore a stillbirth were the law to be strictly applied. It has now been agreed by the National Registration Service that, providing a certificate is issued by the attending doctors giving the estimated date of intra-uterine death, formal registration will not be required. A generic certificate was designed by the Stillbirth and Neonatal Death Society (SANDS) in 1995, and this is now in general use.

PERINATAL DEATH
A perinatal death occurs within seven days of birth, and a neonatal death certificate is used. This special form of medical certificate (MCCD) is used for any death which occurs within 28 days of delivery, irrespective of the stage of pregnancy (see reproduction on p.80–81). It is very similar to the normal death certificate, but space is provided to record relevant maternal conditions as well as those within the infant itself.

SUDDEN UNEXPECTED DEATH IN INFANCY
Sudden unexpected death in infancy (SUDI) is any sudden death occurring between one week and one year of age. In about one-fifth of these cases, a sufficient cause of

death, for example meningitis, is found at autopsy. The remainder, approximately 400 per year in England and Wales, are classified as sudden infant death syndrome.

SUDDEN INFANT DEATH SYNDROME

Sudden infant death syndrome (SIDS, cot death) was defined by Bergman, Beckwith and Rae (1969) as 'any sudden unexpected death in an infant under one year, where a full autopsy and a range of appropriate investigations fails to reveal a cause of death'. This definition was subsequently adopted by the World Health Organization (WHO) and is internationally recognised.

Stillbirth certification and registration

Stillbirth registration was introduced in 1927 (Births and Deaths Registration Act 1926) in response to the suspicion that some newborn infants were being deliberately killed and their deaths passed off as stillbirths. The disposal procedures currently in use combine the features of both birth and death registration. The qualified informants, i.e. mother, father or a person present at the birth, are the same as those for a live birth. The medical certificate of stillbirth is required before registration can be completed (Fig. 5.1). This certificate has changed but little since 1927, although the amount of detail was increased in 1986, when the section devoted to the cause of death was changed from the Ia, Ib, Ic format of the adult certificate (see Chapter 2) to a three-tier layout, which permits accurate description of the fetal, maternal and other conditions contributing to the death. This amendment brought UK practice into line with the internationally employed recommendations of the World Health Organization.

A stillbirth certificate can be completed either by a doctor or a midwife but, if both were present at the birth, the doctor should sign. The signatory need not be present at the birth; the certificate may be completed merely on the basis of subsequent external examination. This practice is not entirely satisfactory. The proof of stillbirth, and the establishment of its cause, are often difficult even after a detailed post mortem examination. Any opinion based upon external inspection alone must be pure speculation. It therefore follows that any deaths resulting from an unsupervised delivery, or the finding of the body of a newborn infant, should be reported to the Coroner, so that a full pathological investigation can be performed; that is unless the mother, having been admitted to hospital after the delivery, gives consent to an academic autopsy. It should be noted that the Coroner has no legal jurisdiction over stillbirth. Obviously, until it is established that the case is indeed a stillbirth, the Coroner must investigate. Once the diagnosis of stillbirth is established, or is presumed on the basis of a negative autopsy, the Coroner may surrender jurisdiction, and refer the case back for routine registration. The pathologist who performed the autopsy then completes the stillbirth certificate. The death is registered and the appropriate order for disposal is issued. In practice, most Coroners will issue form B, or form E if cremation is desired.

MEDICAL CERTIFICATE OF STILL-BIRTH SPECIMEN

(Births and Deaths Registration Act 1953, S 11(1), as amended by the Population (Statistics) Act 1960)
(Form prescribed by the Registration of Births and Deaths Regulations 1987)

SB 801446

To be given only in respect of a child which has issued forth from its mother after the 24th week of pregnancy and which did not at any time after being completely expelled from its mother breathe or show any other signs of life.

Registered at
Entry No.

*I was present at the still-birth of a *male / *female child born

*I have examined the body of a *male / *female child which I am informed and believe was born

on................................day of.................................19........ to ....
                                                                                    (NAME OF MOTHER)

at ....
        (PLACE OF BIRTH)

†{ 1 The certified cause of death has been confirmed by post-mortem.
    2 Post-mortem information may be available later.
    3 Post-mortem not being held.

Weight of fetus..................grams
Estimated duration of pregnancy
State (a) the number of weeks of delivery..................
       (b) When the child died

*Strike out the words which do not apply.
†Ring appropriate digit.

(i) before labour*
(ii) during labour*
(iii) not known*

CAUSE OF DEATH

a. Main diseases or conditions in fetus ....

b. Other diseases or conditions in fetus ....

c. Main maternal diseases or conditions affecting fetus ....

d. Other maternal diseases or conditions affecting fetus ....

e. Other relevant causes ....

I hereby certify that (i) the child was not born alive, and
                     (ii) to the best of my knowledge and belief the cause of death and the estimated duration of
                          pregnancy of the mother were as stated above.

Signature...   Date ....

Qualification as registered by General Medical Council, or }
Registered No. as Registered Midwife.   } ....

Address ....

For still-births in hospital: please give the name of the consultant responsible for the care of the mother ....

THIS IS NOT AN AUTHORITY FOR BURIAL OR CREMATION [SEE OVER]

NOTE TO INFORMANT

Under Section 11(1) of the Births and Deaths Registration Act 1953, this certificate must be delivered to the Registrar of Births and Deaths by the person attending to give information of the particulars required to be registered concerning the still-birth. The persons qualified and liable to give such information include:

(1) the mother;

(2) the father (of a legitimate child only);

(3) the occupier of the house in which to the knowledge of that occupier the still-birth occurred;*

(4) any person present at the still-birth;

(5) any person in charge of the still-born child;

(6) in the case of a still-born child found exposed, the person who found the child.

The still-birth is required to be registered within 42 days of its occurrence.

*Occupier in relation to a public institution includes the governor, keeper, master, matron, superintendent, or other chief resident officer.

Figure 5.1 Medical Certificate of Stillbirth. Crown copyright.

The stillbirth certificate requires the name of the mother, the date of birth, the sex of the child, and an estimate of the duration of the pregnancy. In hospital cases, the name of the consultant responsible for the care of the mother must be given. The attached counterfoil should be completed by the certifying doctor in every case. Unlike the death certificate, there is no 'notice to the informant' attached to a stillbirth certificate. Registration must take place within 42 days of the birth or the finding of the body. It is not possible to register a stillbirth if more than three months have elapsed.

There is at present no obligation to register the birth of a fetus of less than 24 weeks' gestation period; likewise there is no requirement for its disposal by formal burial or cremation. It is now required of hospitals that they should have an arrangement with a local funeral director or crematorium, so that every fetus is respectfully disposed of. A record must be kept of the place and method of each disposal and next of kin must be informed. Most hospitals now ensure that written consent is obtained from the mother before products of conception are disposed of. Mass disposal by incineration or maceration as 'clinical waste' is no longer permitted. It is now recognised that many parents would value some form of obsequy as a means of closure and as part of the grieving process, irrespective of the gestational age of the fetus. Facilities for this are now available in most areas. The Stillbirth and Neonatal Death Society (SANDS) provide leaflets and have a very informative website. Many funeral directors and hospital authorities provide leaflets and advice.

After a stillbirth of more than 24 weeks' gestation has been registered, the body must be disposed of by formal burial or cremation. A specific 'application for cremation' document, similar to form A (see Chapter 8), has now been introduced. It is most unusual for the parent or parents to refuse to assume this responsibility but, should they do so, the obligation to dispose falls upon the local health authority. A hospital-funded disposal may be by burial or cremation, but the ceremony and facilities will be basic. Earth burial may take place in a common grave in the unconsecrated part of the cemetery, and may be delayed until three or four stillborn infants await burial. Each fetus is accorded a separate casket, but the grave may be unmarked.

Disposal arranged by parents must attract charges like any other funeral, but the majority of funeral directors, cemeteries and crematoria authorities now provide heavily subsidised, or even free, services. Chaplains of the major religious faiths also give their services readily, and usually without charge. They will give advice on the most appropriate rituals to be performed.

Certification of perinatal and neonatal death

The registration of infant deaths generally takes exactly the same form as that for adult deaths. In 1986 a new certificate of neonatal death (Fig. 5.2) was introduced for use within the first 28 days (Registration of Births, Deaths and Marriages Regulations 1985). This takes the same form as the standard death certificate, with a notice to informant, a counterfoil, and boxes A and B on the reverse. However, the space de-

MED B 120326
1

(Form prescribed by the Registration of Births, Deaths and Marriages Regulations 1968)

NOTICE TO INFORMANT

I hereby give notice that I have this day signed a medical certificate of cause of death of

....

Signature ....

Date ....

This notice is to be delivered by the informant to the registrar of births and deaths of the sub-district in which the death occurred.

The certifying medical practitioner must give this notice to the person who is qualified and liable to act as informant for the registration of death (see list overleaf).

SPECIMEN

DUTIES OF INFORMANT

Failure to deliver this notice to the registrar renders the informant liable to prosecution. The death cannot be registered until the medical certificate has reached the registrar.

When the death is registered the informant must be prepared to give to the registrar the following particulars relating to the deceased:

1. The date and place of death.
2. The full name and surname.
3. The date and place of birth.
4. The names and occupations of the parents.
5. The usual address.

IF THE CHILD WAS ISSUED WITH A MEDICAL CARD, THE CARD SHOULD BE DELIVERED TO THE REGISTRAR.

MED B 120326
1

Register to enter No. of Death Entry

BIRTHS AND DEATHS REGISTRATION ACT 1953

(Form prescribed by the Registration of Births, Deaths and Marriages (Amendment) (No. 2) Regulations 1985)

MEDICAL CERTIFICATE OF CAUSE OF DEATH OF A LIVE-BORN CHILD DYING WITHIN THE FIRST TWENTY-EIGHT DAYS OF LIFE

For use only by a Registered Medical Practitioner WHO HAS BEEN IN ATTENDANCE during the deceased's last illness, and to be delivered by him forthwith to the Registrar of Births and Deaths.

Name of child ....

Date of death .... day of .... 19 ....

Age at death .... days (complete period of 24 hours) .... hours

Place of death ....

Place of birth ....

Last seen alive by me .... day of .... 19 ....

1 The certified cause of death has been confirmed by post-mortem.
2 Information from post-mortem may be available later.
3 Post-mortem not being held.
4 I have reported this death to the Coroner for further action.

[See overleaf]

Please ring appropriate digit and letter.

a   Seen after death by me.
b   Seen after death by another medical practitioner but not by me.
c   Not seen after death by a medical practitioner.

SPECIMEN

CAUSE OF DEATH

a. Main diseases or conditions in infant.

b. Other diseases or conditions in infant.

c. Main maternal diseases or conditions affecting infant

d. Other maternal diseases or conditions affecting infant

e. Other relevant causes ....

I hereby certify that I was in medical attendance during the above-named deceased's last illness, and that the particulars and cause of death above written are true to the best of my knowledge and belief.

Signature ....   Qualifications as registered by General Medical Council

Address ....   Date ....

For deaths in hospital: Please give the name of the consultant responsible for the above-named as a patient.

Figure 5.2 Neonatal death certificate. Crown copyright.

PERSONS QUALIFIED AND LIABLE TO ACT AS INFORMANTS

The following persons are designated by the Births and Deaths Registration Act 1953 as qualified to give information concerning a death:—

DEATHS IN HOUSES AND PUBLIC INSTITUTIONS

(1) A relative of the deceased, present at the death.
(2) A relative of the deceased, in attendance during the last illness.
(3) A relative of the deceased, residing or being in the sub-district where the death occurred.
(4) A person present at the death.
(5) The occupier* if he knew of the happening of the death.
(6) Any inmate if he knew of the happening of the death.
(7) The person causing the disposal of the body.

DEATHS NOT IN HOUSES OR DEAD BODIES FOUND

(1) Any relative of the deceased having knowledge of any of the particulars required to be registered.
(2) Any person present at the death.
(3) Any person who found the body.
(4) Any person in charge of the body.
(5) The person causing the disposal of the body.

**"Occupier" in relation to a public institution includes the governor, keeper, master, matron, superintendent, or other chief resident officer.

Complete where applicable

A	B
I have reported this death to the Coroner for further action.	I may be in a position later to give, on application by the Registrar General, additional information as to the cause of death for the purpose of more precise statistical classification.
Initials of certifying medical practitioner. _____	Initials of certifying medical practitioner. _____

The Coroner needs to consider all cases where:

The death might have been due to or contributed to by a violent or unnatural cause (including an accident);
or the cause of death cannot be identified;
or the death might have been due to or contributed to by drugs, medicine, abortion or poison;

or there is reason to believe that the death occurred during an operation or under or prior to complete recovery from an anaesthetic or arising subsequently out of an incident during an operation or an anaesthetic.

NOTE:—The Practitioner, on signing the certificate, should complete, sign and date the Notice to the Informant, which should be detached and handed to the Informant. The Practitioner should then, without delay, deliver the certificate itself to the Registrar of Births and Deaths for the sub-district in which the death occurred. Envelopes for enclosing the certificates are supplied by the Registrar.

Figure 5.2 cont.

voted to cause of death is in similar format to that of the stillbirth certificate, in that it requires conditions in the infant, maternal conditions and other conditions to be specified rather than the simple Ia, Ib, Ic classification used on the standard MCDC (see Chapter 2). If the death occurred in hospital, the name of the consultant in charge must be given. Once 28 days have elapsed, the procedures followed are exactly the same as those for older persons (see Chapter 2). When a child's death occurs in the community, the circumstances are nearly always sudden and unexpected, and demand that the Coroner be informed.

Sudden and unexpected death in infancy – SIDS (cot death)

Every year, approximately 400 infants under the age of 12 months die suddenly and unexpectedly. There has been a dramatic reduction in numbers over the last 40 years. There were over 2000 such deaths annually in the early 1960s. There was a steady decrease over the next 20 years, and in the 1980s the numbers had stabilised at around a thousand per year. At the beginning of the 1990s a dramatic breakthrough occurred. For many years, mothers throughout the English-speaking world had been told that their babies should sleep face down, or on their sides. The 'back to sleep' campaign was introduced in New Zealand and Australia in the late 1980s. Mothers were advised to put the infant to sleep on its back, and this resulted in a dramatic reduction in the number of cases. Take-up was slow at first in the UK, but following the death of the son of a well-known television presenter, the scheme received widespread publicity; within 12 months the annual number of deaths had reached its present level of about 400 yearly (Alexander and Radisch 2005). In about one-fifth of these cases, detailed post mortem examination, with a wide range of ancillary tests, establishes a cause of death or identifies a significant pathological condition that might have predisposed to death. In the majority of cases, even the most comprehensive examination fails to reveal any significant abnormality; these are cases of sudden infant death syndrome (otherwise known as 'cot death').

Unfortunately, a small minority of these infants will have died in consequence of some criminal act, or neglect may be a contributing factor (Hogan 1995). Subtle forms of infant abuse, such as a deliberate obstruction of the airway or poisoning by the administration of sodium chloride (common salt) or methadone, leave no obvious signs. It is therefore essential that every case, even if it occurs in an apparently ideal social environment, be thoroughly investigated from the outset. This cautious and, of necessity, inquisitorial approach is often deeply distressing to the parents or carers, who feel that they are being subjected to a criminal investigation. The Coroner is involved from the outset, the police are notified by the ambulance authorities as soon as death is confirmed, and the parent(s) are questioned in depth, not only by a succession of doctors, but by the police. The death scene is visited by a senior paediatrician. He is usually accompanied by the police or the Coroner's Officer. Their presence makes the meeting seem more like a formal interview under PACE (Police and Criminal Evidence Act 1984) rules rather than a medical consultation. The police will also take videos and photographs and they may remove items of furniture, clothing, bedding etc. as potential evidence. A post mortem examination is always made, ideally within 24 hours, but only rarely is a diagnosis immediately available. Several weeks may elapse before all the tests are completed and their results are usually negative. All of this is unsatisfactory. The parents feel that they are not only being kept in the dark, but also that they are under continuing suspicion. This may not be completely allayed when they are eventually told that their child has died of SIDS – a diagnosis of exclusion.

Proposed improvements in the investigation of sudden infant death

Major changes in the way in which these deaths are investigated are now being introduced. In 2003, three major cases, in which mothers were convicted of killing their children, were overturned on appeal. At the instigation of the Department of Health, a Working Party, chaired by Baroness Helena Kennedy QC, was established by the College of Pathologists and the College of Paediatrics and Child Health (Royal College of Pathologists 2004). Its recommendations were far-reaching. They included training for Coroners and their Officers, ambulance personnel, and for the staffs of accident and emergency and paediatric departments. Most importantly, the report sets out mandatory criteria for the pathological investigations. Autopsies must be carried out only by those trained in paediatric pathology. If there are any suspicious circumstances, an accredited forensic pathologist should assume the role of lead investigator, but a paediatric pathologist should be involved both at the post mortem and throughout the subsequent investigations. They should then submit an agreed report.

The Working Group's report sets out a detailed mandatory list of the investigations which must be performed. It provides a list of the questions to be asked by the designated SUDI paediatrician at the first home visit, and provides a flow chart for the subsequent interviews, consultations and the eventual counselling of the bereaved family. It is now recommended that if the criteria for a diagnosis of SIDS are not fulfilled, then the diagnosis 'not ascertained' should no longer be used. Such a diagnosis always renders an inquest inevitable, and carries undertones of suspicion. It is now recommended that the diagnosis in these cases should be simply recorded as SUDI, which is a death from natural causes. Unfortunately, there are at present severe shortages of both paediatric and forensic pathologists, throughout the UK. The majority of Coroners and NHS trusts are using their best endeavours to implement the Report's recommendations as quickly as possible.

There is now excellent support and information available for those families who have suffered a SIDS bereavement. The Foundation for the Study of Infant Deaths (FSID) provides a range of leaflets, a website and individual counselling. There are also numerous local support groups, and a large amount of published material, both in print and on the Web (see Appendix A).

References

Alexander, R.T. and Radisch, D. (2005) 'Sudden Infant Death Syndrome risk factors with regard to sleep position, sleep surface, and co-sleeping.' *Journal of the Forensic Science Society 50*, 1, 147–151.

Bergman, A.B., Beckwith, R.E. and Rae, C.O. (eds) (1969) *Sudden Infant Death Syndrome: Proceedings of the Second International Conference, Seattle.* Seattle: Washington University Press.

Births and Deaths Registration Act (1926) 17 & 18 George 5 s.12.

Births and Deaths Registration Act (1953) 1 & 2 Elizabeth 2 ch 20 s.41.

Chadwick, E. (1843) *The Practice of Interment in Towns.* London: Clowes.

Hogan, J. (1995) 'The mystery of Sudden Infant Death: a murder conviction raises questions about infant death.' *Scientific American 273*, 22–24.

Human Fertilisation and Embryology Act (1990) 38 & 39 Elizabeth 2 ch 37 s.37.

Human Tissue Act (2004) 52 & 53 Elizabeth 2, all sections.

Infant Life Preservation Act (1929) 19 & 20 George 5 ch 34 ss.1 & 2.

Kohner, N. (1995) *Guidelines for Professionals: Pregnancy Loss and Death of a Baby.* London: Stillbirth and Neonatal Death Society (SANDS).

Offences against the Person Act (1861) 24 & 25 Victoria Ch 100 s.60.

Office for National Statistics (2003) Table 1 'Live births, stillbirths and infant deaths 1976–2000.' *Health Statistics Quarterly 23.* London: The Stationery Office.

Registration of Births, Deaths and Marriages (amendment no.2) (1985) S.I. 1985/1133.

Royal College of Obstetricians and Gynaecologists (2005a) *Confidential Enquiry into Maternal and Child Health; Stillbirth, Neonatal and Perinatal Mortality.* London: RCOG Press.

Royal College of Obstetricians and Gynaecologists (2005b) *Good Practice Leaflet No 4. Registration of Stillbirths and Certification of Pregnancy Loss Before 24 Weeks of Gestation.* London: RCOG Press.

Royal College of Pathologists (2004) *Sudden Unexpected Death in Infancy: The Report of a Working Group Chaired by the Baroness Helena Kennedy QC.* London: The Royal College of Pathology (published jointly with the Royal College of Paediatrics and Child Health).

Stillbirth (Definition) Act (1992) 40 & 41 Elizabeth 2.

CHAPTER 6

THE AUTOPSY AND MORTUARY PRACTICE

History of the autopsy

Autopsy (also known as necropsy or post mortem examination) – the examination of the organs and tissues after death – has been practised for many thousands of years. The embalmers of Pharaonic Egypt possessed considerable anatomical skills. Roman and Greek army surgeons developed their clinical skills through the dissection of battlefield casualties. There are also references to the practice in the early records of Indian and Chinese civilisations (Inglis 1965).

Unfortunately, the public in general has never been particularly sympathetic to the procedure. Autopsy is still absolutely forbidden in many religions (for example Orthodox Judaism), and many people who profess no deep religious belief display a marked aversion to its performance upon their relatives or themselves (Bradfield 1994). These antipathies have been hardened recently by the publicity surrounding the retention of organs, which occurred at the Royal Liverpool Children's Hospital in the 1990s (Redfearn 2003), and by the public exhibitions of human dissection specimens by Professor Gunther von Hagens (Tuffs 2003), some of which were screened on a commercial television channel in 2004.

This has always been so. During the so-called Dark Ages in Christian Europe, autopsy was almost unheard of; to dissect a body, even in part, was to deprive the deceased of subsequent corporeal resurrection (Editorial, *London Medical Gazette* 1825). Those convicted of capital crimes were subjected to dissection; this was a greater deterrent than death itself, and in the 18th century an Act of Parliament firmly established the practice of anatomisation following execution 'to add more greatly to the horror' (Bradfield 1994). The consequences for medical and scientific knowledge were dire. The small store of facts acquired during the Graeco-Roman period was quickly forgotten, distorted or discarded. Medicine became a mixture of quackery, superstition and misinterpreted external observation, coupled with an overweening professional superiority amongst its practitioners, which reduced the status of surgeons and bonesetters to that of tradesmen of the lowest rank; childbirth was left in the hands of the village grandmothers.

By the 16th century, change was becoming apparent throughout Britain and Europe. In 1538, The College of Surgeons successfully petitioned King Henry VIII for possession of the bodies of four convicted criminals every year for anatomical dissection (Richardson 1987).

The practice of dissection became increasingly common over the next three centuries, but the antipathy of the public persisted, and is well exhibited in the works of the 18th century artists Gilray, Rowlandson and Hogarth (Haslam 1996). The supply of subjects was totally inadequate until the passage of the Anatomy Act in 1832 (see Chapter 9), and so surgeons throughout the country were almost entirely dependent upon the activities of the body-snatchers or 'resurrection men' (Wise 2004). It should be emphasised that dissection then was concerned entirely with structure; function was often misinterpreted and the physiological significance of 'morbid changes' in diseased organs was not generally appreciated.

During the late 18th century, the pathological autopsy became a specialised procedure, and searches for the causes of disease, as opposed to anatomical dissection, began. Doctors attempted to co-relate altered appearances of organs to symptoms and signs which the patient had exhibited during life. However, there were no standardised methods of examination and no specialists in the subject. Any interested doctor might undertake a limited examination of a patient who had been under his care. For example, if the diagnosis in life had been heart disease, only the heart would be examined; the same would apply to 'inflammation of the liver'; the contents of the skull were rarely examined.

A few practitioners, such as John Hunter (Moore 2005), made enormous contributions to our knowledge. Credit, for the standardisation of autopsy techniques and the development of morbid anatomy (anatomical pathology) as a speciality, must be given to German physicians, notably Rokitanski and Virchow. In the mid-19th century they laid down dissection protocols, which are still used throughout the world, with only minor local variations (Virchow 1876).

Autopsy sometimes made a contribution to the investigation of sudden and suspicious death but, until the beginning of the 20th century, the vast majority of Coroners' inquiries were conducted solely upon 'view of the body'. If an autopsy was called for, it was undertaken by any local doctor; the lack of skilled observation and the errors of interpretation must have resulted in numerous miscarriages of justice over the years!

The golden age of the autopsy spanned a hundred years from the mid-19th century to the early 1950s. Since then, its reputation and use have declined everywhere. In England and Wales the 'academic' autopsy rate seldom exceeds 10 per cent, even in teaching hospitals (O'Grady 2003; Underwood 2003). In peripheral hospitals it is even less common. The vast majority of autopsies are now performed on behalf of the Coroner (see Chapter 4). In 2003, 119,700 Coroners' autopsies were carried out (less than one-third of all registered deaths but nearly 90 per cent of all autopsies).

The autopsy in decline

There is an increasingly common belief amongst clinicians that investigation during life is now so thorough that autopsy is seldom necessary; an accurate ante mortem diagnosis can almost always be made. Particular reliance is placed upon magnetic resonance imaging (MRI) and, in some areas, Coroners will accept the results of an MRI as sufficient confirmation of cause of death in patients from those communities (for example Jewish and Muslim) who wish to avoid the performance of a conventional autopsy (Bissett *et al.* 2002; Eustace and Nelson 2004). This confidence in non-invasive investigation, sometimes referred to as 'virtual autopsy', is not entirely supported by the facts. Surveys undertaken over many years have repeatedly shown discrepancies between the clinical and autopsy diagnoses (see Chapter 2). The majority of these are relatively minor, but it is not uncommon for the autopsy diagnosis to be completely different from that made during life, no matter how intensive and wide-ranging the clinical observations and investigations (Royal College of Pathologists of Australasia 2004).

The autopsy is losing ground as a method of medical undergraduate and nurse teaching. An overcrowded curriculum and an increasing emphasis on the biosciences at cellular level have stripped the autopsy room of its sacerdotal status. In postgraduate teaching, the attendance of junior medical staff (let alone the consultant) at an autopsy is now a rare event, and regular clinico-pathological conferences are held in only a limited number of centres (O'Grady 2003). Candidates for the membership examination in histopathology of the Royal College of Pathologists can now elect to obtain membership without having to perform an autopsy.

The authors regret this decline. We are of the opinion that viewing and physical handling of diseased organs is invaluable to the understanding of pathology; frequently the abnormalities observed can be correlated with the symptoms and signs present during life. Furthermore, when the post mortem findings are at variance with the clinical diagnosis, it concentrates the clinicians' minds wonderfully, and the lesson is long remembered.

The reasons for autopsy

The principal aim of the clinician requesting, and the pathologist performing, a hospital autopsy is to confirm or establish the cause of death and to correlate the findings with the results of clinical investigations during life. The purpose of an autopsy ordered by the Coroner is to establish the cause of sudden or unexpected death, and to ensure that homicide, suicide and other unnatural deaths are detected. That is its sole function – the examination must not be used as a source of material for treatment, teaching or research purposes, without the express consent of the next-of-kin. These 'Coroner's autopsies' are performed in a mortuary attached to a hospital, or a public mortuary provided by the Local Authority. In many places, the local hospital trust leases mortuary facilities to the Coroner.

The hospital, or 'academic', autopsy serves several purposes. Obviously, the cause of death must be confirmed as accurately as possible. We have already referred to studies showing that there is an element of 'guess-work' in ante mortem diagnosis. Additionally, other contributory conditions may be found, and the extent of their relevance can be assessed. Third, some other disease may be found which played no part in the death, but which is of statistical significance. For example, an early cancer of the lung, as yet producing no symptoms, may be found in a middle-aged man who has died suddenly of coronary heart disease.

The hospital autopsy has a place in medical audit; it acts as a form of quality assurance. Additionally, it plays an essential part in the teaching of medical students, of doctors – both physicians and surgeons – in training, and occasionally rekindles humility in the most senior consultant! Finally, it is an essential part of the investigation of alleged medical mishap, and early discussion of its findings with the relatives may nip threatened legal action in the bud, to the mutual benefit of all parties. The process of confidential enquiry into perioperative outcomes and deaths (NCEPOD) which was introduced into all NHS hospitals in the mid-1980s (Buck, Devlin and Lunn 1988), with all-round improvements in service quality assessment, depends heavily upon autopsy findings.

When may an autopsy be performed?

(See also Chapters 4 and 9.)

A hospital autopsy may not be performed without the written consent of the relatives, nor may any organs or tissues be retained without such consent (Human Tissue Act 2004). This Act supersedes the Act of 1961, the Anatomy Act 1984, and the Human Organ Transplant Act 1989. It incorporates the recommendations of the Redfearn Inquiry into the retention of organs at the Royal Liverpool Children's Hospital in the 1990s (Redfearn 2003) and the similar inquiry into events in the Bristol hospitals. The relatives should be interviewed as soon as possible after the death has occurred, ideally by a member of the medical 'firm' which was responsible for the care of the patient (McDermott 2003). This is often difficult to arrange in large and busy hospitals, so an administrator, often with a nursing background, may assume the role of bereavement liaison officer or counsellor.

It is wise to ascertain the deceased's religion at the outset, before any question of autopsy is raised. Remember that many religions expressly forbid any interference with the body (some require that Last Offices should be performed only by a co-religionist, or that those performing them should wear gloves) (see Part 3). To ask permission of such relatives will not only result in a flat refusal; it will cause distress and may give grave offence. If it is decided to request permission for an autopsy, the relatives should be told the reasons for the request, and given reassurances as to the subsequent aesthetic reconstruction of the body. A full explanation of what an autopsy is should be given. It is folly to obfuscate, telling relatives that, for example, 'the doctor will make some small cuts and just have a quick look inside'. The Royal College of

Pathologists has produced a short and clearly written explanatory booklet (2003) which has proved invaluable. Particularly detailed and helpful guidance is contained in a handbook produced by the Northern Ireland Department of Health, Social Services and Public Safety in 2004.

If it is desirable that tissues or organs should be retained, specific written consent, coupled with further explanation, should be sought (Department of Health 2003). The relatives should be assured that, if an organ, for example the brain, is to be retained, it will be returned to them for disposal, if they so wish. They should be assured that, otherwise, the material will be respectfully treated and stored, and that the hospital will, in the fullness of time, dispose of it. Organs, tissues and the paraffin waxed blocks used in the preparation of microscope slides will be buried or cremated, usually by arrangement with a local crematorium or funeral director. The family should also be given some indication of the likely period for which retention might be necessary. Under no circumstances should this issue be fudged, or material illicitly retained; such actions invite, at best, serious complaint or censure and, at worst, litigation, under the provisions of the Human Rights Act relating to the right to family life (YourRights.org.uk 2005).

When the Human Tissue Act is fully implemented in June 2006, any such covert retention, or the exceeding of the consent obtained, will become criminal offences, punishable by a fine or imprisonment.

Unauthorised retention of organs and tissues – the Alder Hey Inquiry

In 1998, in the course of an inquiry into the mortality rates for cardiac surgery at the Bristol Royal Infirmary and the Bristol Children's Hospital (Department of Health 2001), it emerged that organs had been retained from both hospital and Coroners' autopsies without the relatives' knowledge or consent. This was quickly followed by revelations that other children's hospitals, notably the Royal Liverpool at Alder Hey, possessed collections of organs and tissues removed during autopsies. Further investigation led to the discovery of large numbers of entire sets of organs from both hospital and Coroners' autopsies, fixed in formalin, which had undergone not even the most superficial examination, although the written autopsy reports gave the impression that detailed dissections had been performed. Many specimens had deteriorated to such an extent that belated attempts at examination failed.

The then Secretary of State for Health, Alan Milburn, appointed an inquiry, under the chairmanship of Michael Redfearn QC (Redfearn 2003). The report, published in 2003, was a damning indictment of the conduct of the then Head of the Department of Pathology, Dr Dick van Velzen. It also exposed unacceptably lax procedures in the obtaining of informed consent by clinicians, and deplorably low standards of performance of the majority of paediatric autopsies. Professor van Velzen was dismissed from his post, and his name was subsequently erased from the Register of the General Medical Council. The relatives and others, whose children's organs had been retained in many other hospitals, received unreserved apologies, financial compensation and, for those who desired it, the return of their children's organs, tissues, blocks and slides for formal disposal by burial or cremation. Over the next three years, at the direction of the Department of Health, every NHS hospital had to conduct an audit of retained organs, contact the next of kin, offer appropriate financial recompense, and make arrangements for disposal by burial or cremation where desired. The Human Tissue Act (1961), the inadequacies of which had been known but ignored for many years previously, was replaced by the Human Tissue Act (2004), which came into force in early 2005 and is due for full implementation in June 2006.

The new Act lays down detailed mandatory procedures for the obtaining of informed consent for retention of organs, for their storage, record keeping, the time normally acceptable for retention, and for their ultimate disposal. Most importantly, it is now a criminal offence, punishable by a fine and/or imprisonment, to breach any of these requirements. Detailed instructions and standard operating procedures are set out in the Royal College of Pathologists' (2002) guidance booklet, published in anticipation of the Act's implementation, but most of its requirements have already been put into practice. For further discussion of the provisions of the Act and its codes of practice, see Chapter 9. Although broadly welcomed by all parties, both clinicians and patients' groups, one aspect of the Act has given rise to concerns, which are still unresolved. It has already been explained that Rule 9 of the Coroners Rules 1984 obliges the pathologist to retain any material which may have a bearing on the cause of death. The Act now requires that any such retention be undertaken only with the Coroner's consent in writing, and that detailed records be kept. The Act then goes on to permit retention only for the duration of the Coroner's interest in the case.

The concurrently introduced Coroners (Amendment) Rules 2005, which came into force in June 2005, impose further restrictions, which give rise to serious concerns. Once the Coroner has completed his inquiry (*functus officio*), the relatives must be offered the opportunity to dispose (or demand the disposal) of all the organs, tissues, blocks and slides (some authorities go so far as to advise the inclusion of post mortem photographs within this remit). This has given rise to grave concerns amongst Coroners and pathologists. After all, if someone has been deliberately but cleverly harmed or killed by the next of kin (for example, poisoning an infant by salt administration, or deliberately obstructing the airway) the correct diagnosis may be missed. The guilty party will be first in the queue to request the return of, and to organise the complete destruction of, any material which might be of crucial evidential value in the future. Unfortunately, the Government has so far remained adamant in its refusal to countenance these protests from the Coroners' Society and the Royal College of Pathologists. Fuller discussion of the wider implications of the Human Tissue Act may be found in Chapters 4 and 9.

The Coroner's autopsy

If the autopsy is ordered by the Coroner, consent by the relatives is of no relevance. The body, once the Coroner has assumed jurisdiction over the case, is his property until the investigation is completed and he has formally authorised its release (see Chapter 4). Relatives have, on a few occasions, challenged the Coroner's direction for autopsy in a higher court. To the best of our knowledge, in no case as yet has such a challenge been successful.

When a Coroner's autopsy is to be performed, the relatives should be informed as soon as possible, preferably in the course of a face-to-face discussion.

Many people, when told that the death has been reported to the Coroner, assume that 'something has gone wrong' and that there will be an inquest as well as an autopsy (many people need to have the difference explained to them) or that there is some suspicion or stigma surrounding the death. They usually believe that the inquiry will attract widespread publicity and that there will be a long delay before disposal is permitted. Such fears should be allayed as soon as possible, by the doctor, nurse or bereavement counsellor. When death occurs outside hospital, the Coroner's Officer or one of his office administrators (see Chapter 4) will interview the relatives and explain the reasons for his involvement, but additional and early reassurance by the doctor, or another health care professional involved in the treatment of the deceased, will always be welcomed.

Autopsy technique

An autopsy is performed by a pathologist. Pathology is now a very wide field, and includes the specialities of haematology, microbiology, chemical pathology and histopathology. Histopathologists (sometimes called morbid anatomists or anatomical pathologists, although both these terms are now obsolete) are doctors who have specialised in the study of the naked eye and microscopic appearances of diseased organs and tissues. They are usually Members or Fellows of the Royal College of Pathologists, which supervises higher professional training and accreditation. They usually carry out autopsies both for the hospital and the Coroner. In some jurisdictions, a forensic pathologist, who has made a speciality of the study of unnatural and violent death, carries out all the coronial autopsies.

In England and Wales, forensic pathologists are accredited by the Home Office, hence their commonly used designation ('Home Office pathologist'). In some coronial jurisdictions (mainly in central London), the body is removed from the hospital to a public mortuary. This is not entirely satisfactory, because the clinicians who treated the patient during life are often unable to attend the autopsy, and so opportunities to share information are lost; furthermore, although forensic pathologists are extremely competent generalists, they do not always possess the specialised knowledge required for the investigation of death following some highly specialised surgical procedures, nor in esoteric areas such as neuropathology or paediatric pathology. It is for this reason that the Kennedy Working Party (see p.87) has recommended that all autopsies in cases of sudden and unexpected death in infancy (SUDI) should be performed jointly by a paediatric and a forensic pathologist working together. Relatives should be reassured that the involvement of a forensic pathologist does not necessarily imply that crime is suspected.

The pathologist first studies the hospital case notes or information provided by the general practitioner and/or the police. He may also discuss the case further with the clinicians involved. Occasionally, particularly in forensic cases, it is desirable that X-rays, MRI or CT scans should be performed before the examination commences.

A careful external examination of the body is then made. The height and weight are noted, along with any identifying marks, tattoos, abnormalities and deformities. Photographs may be taken, either for teaching purposes (informed consent is required for their use, and anonymisation should be undertaken wherever possible), or by the attending police officers (in Coroners' cases) as a permanent record of injuries.

The body is then opened. This may be done by the pathologist or by a trained assistant (anatomical pathology technician, APT) who holds either the certificate or the diploma of the Royal Institute of Health. In some hospitals, technicians are trained to an even higher level, and may carry out some preliminary dissection of the organs, as well as the initial evisceration. Discussions are currently taking place within the NHS about the establishment of the grade 'Advanced Practitioner' in recognition of the skills possessed by these persons holding higher qualifications. The pathologist himself should always be present if the responsibility for evisceration is delegated to others, in case an unusual or subtle abnormality is encountered.

In a hospital autopsy, the body is usually opened through an incision from the level of the voice box to the pubis. In forensic cases a 'Y cut' from behind the ears to the top of the breastbone may be used. There is an increasing tendency to use a T-shaped incision, which runs across the upper chest from shoulder to shoulder just below the level of the collar-bones. The neck structures can be readily approached by upward dissection from here, and there is no sutured wound visible above the collar-line.

Once the rib cage has been exposed, it is cut through with shears or a saw so that the sternum (breastbone) can be removed, exposing the heart and lungs. The internal organs are inspected and any abnormalities, or accumulations of fluid, are recorded.

The organs are next removed, either as a single block (known as the Letulle or Rokitanski method) or in groups, from the chest, abdomen and pelvis (the Virchow or Ghon method). Each organ is closely examined, weighed and dissected. Small pieces (about 1 cm cube) may be taken from the diseased organs and placed in formaldehyde solution for subsequent microscopical examination. This may only be done in hospital cases if prior express consent has been obtained. In Coroners' cases, the pathologist is obliged to retain specimens of tissue or organs which he believes may be relevant to the cause of death, but nothing else may be taken. Occasionally an organ may be retained as a teaching or museum specimen. Specific consent as required under the provisions of the Human Tissue Act must have been obtained for this. Tissue removed for research or treatment purposes (for example, a heart valve) is also subject to prior consent (see Chapter 9). It must be emphasised that such consent must also be obtained if the requirement to take material for research or treatment arises during a Coroner's autopsy.

The scalp is incised, across the crown, from ear to ear. Care is taken to preserve the head hair as intact as possible. The flaps of skin are folded back and the skull is inspected. It is then opened circumferentially with a saw, the skull 'cap' lifted off, and the brain removed. This is weighed, dissected and returned to the body along with the other organs. Only very limited examination can be performed upon a fresh brain, especially if it is more swollen and softer than the ordinary brain due to injury or disease. Detailed dissection, with no artifactual damage, can only be performed if the brain is first fixed (hardened) in formalin solution, ideally for up to 12 weeks. This process may be reduced to as little as two weeks, particularly with an infant's brain. The fact of retention must be recorded, and the Coroner's written permission obtained. In due course the relatives must be contacted, either by the hospital authorities or by the Coroner, to arrange appropriate disposal. If they do not wish to arrange interment or cremation, the hospital will make appropriate arrangements. The Cremation Acts have been amended (see Chapter 9) to permit disposal of isolated human organs and tissues.

At the end of the examination, the body is washed out, and the orifices are packed with cotton wool or cellulose wadding. The organs are drained of blood and fluids, washed, and replaced in the chest and abdominal cavities. The skin incision is sewn up with strong twine. Particular attention is paid to the head. In cases of head and facial injury an attempt at restoration is made (although any final cosmetic improvements will be made by the funeral director subsequently). The body is washed and shrouded, and then returned to the refrigerator to await collection. Identification labels are never removed during an autopsy.

The pathologist writes up the rough notes and dictates a report (Royal College of Pathologists 2004). The results of microscopy, microbiological studies, toxicology and any other tests can be added later. Sometimes, a provisional 'cause of death' form is completed as an interim document and the extended report is prepared later, when all the subsequent tests and analyses have been completed. Occasionally, other tests, such as X-rays, may be performed also. The Royal College of Pathologists has laid down minimum standards for the performance of hospital autopsies and the content of reports.

Procedure is rather different in some coronial autopsies, particularly in cases of suspicious or violent death. Much more extensive dissection (for example, in neck or genital injury) may be necessary. The pathologist is also strongly advised to examine *every* organ (although this is not a mandatory requirement, the specimen autopsy report pro-forma, attached as an appendix to the Coroners Rules, makes it clear that this is expected of him) and to retain any organ, tissue or fluid that may have a bearing on the cause of death. Such material must be retained until the legal process is completed. It must then be returned to the relatives, if they so wish. The recommended periods vary according to the case. Advice on what may be retained, and for how long, should be sought from the Coroner concerned. Difficulties may arise when there is a significant external injury, such as a gunshot wound or patterned abrasion. Until recently, it was considered good practice to retain these wounds along with the surrounding skin, in case the pathologist retained by the Defence wished to order their own examination. This practice is now increasingly uncommon; photographs and diagrams are usually entirely adequate. It must be emphasised that, in cases where portions of skin with injuries are removed, every effort is made to reconstruct the body as accurately and aesthetically as possible.

In those cases where someone has been charged with homicide, the defending lawyers usually request a second autopsy by an independent pathologist. This is highly desirable from the point of view of the defendant(s) but has only dubious foundation in law. The Coroner has the authority to order the first autopsy; it is not certain that he can permit a second autopsy, not ordered by him, once the cause of death has been determined to his satisfaction. The view of some Coroners is that the defence pathologist should limit the examination to an external inspection, or should attempt to obtain consent from the victim's relatives. This, not surprisingly, is often refused.

A well-conducted autopsy should be like any other surgical or medical procedure: clean, tidy and carefully performed. The atmosphere should be one of sober and diligent inquiry, rather than irreverence or tasteless hilarity; and the surroundings should – and usually do – resemble an operating theatre rather than Dr Frankenstein's laboratory, or the gloomy ill-lit morgues depicted in some television series.

Mortuary design and administration

A mortuary, whether it is provided by the hospital or a Local Authority, must fulfil several functions. First, it is a place for storage of the dead in suitable conditions. Second, it should provide facilities for the cleansing and preparation of bodies, for viewing by relatives, in appropriate surroundings. It should provide facilities for autopsy, with provision for such ancillary techniques as X-ray, and with special provision for the examination and storage of decomposing or foul bodies; and it should then have suitable facilities for storage of the body until it is claimed by the funeral director or the relatives. There should also be appropriate storage and autopsy suite accommodation for 'high risk' (categories 3 and 4) infectious cases (see Chapter 16).

The design of a modern mortuary is a complex matter. Gone are the days of cheap conversion of stables and garages. The requirements of the Health and Safety at Work Act (1974) and the HSE publication *Safe Working and the Prevention of Infection in the Mortuary and Post Mortem Room* (2003) must be complied with. Building and design notes are issued by the Department of Health from time to time and these should be consulted. Only mortuaries whose standards are validated by Clinical Pathology Accreditation (CPA) Ltd, and are subjected to regular inspections, may now be used.

The building must be easy to clean and disinfect. Ventilation and containment of working and dissection areas must be adequate, and there must be suitable separation between the 'working' and 'public' areas, so that relatives are not distressed by sights, sounds or smells. There should also be a separate viewing area (preferably glass-screened) overlooking the autopsy suite, so that visiting medical or other personnel are not exposed to air-borne infection hazards. The actual working numbers should be reduced to pathologist, tableside assistant and 'runner'. Specialist advice on the design of mortuaries, and advice on hygiene and prevention of infection, may be obtained from the Department for Health's Hospital Building Directorate.

Documentation

The mislabelling and release of a wrong body is the greatest humiliation that can befall a mortuary and its staff. The distress caused to relatives by autopsy upon, or the release of, the wrong body is incalculable, especially if burial or cremation takes place before the mistake is discovered. Therefore, the documentation, both on admission and release, must be absolutely foolproof. Details of procedure vary, but in broad outline the following method should be followed. The body is labelled by the ward staff (or the funeral director if the death occurs outside hospital) as soon as possible after death. The label should be difficult to remove, for example a plastic identity wristband of the type used in operating theatres. The labelling should always be duplicated. In many mortuaries the name and unique identification number are written in indelible ink on the shin and the sole of a foot also.

Although most mortuaries are now equipped with computers, a paper register with a unique serial numbering system should be filled in on reception and countersigned by the person accompanying the body. Full details of the name, date of birth, date and time of death, age, address, religion, etc., should be entered. Clothing and property should be recorded in a separate duplicate receipt book. Valuables should be placed in a safety deposit box under the eyes of a witness, and a signed receipt obtained.

When the body is released the checking process is repeated. The body should only be released, to a funeral director or relative, on production of the appropriate authority to dispose and/or cremate (see Chapters 8 and 9). Wristbands and labels should be checked against the register and the disposal documents, and any discrepancy should be immediately questioned. Most hospital and public mortuary staff insist upon production of the Registrar's disposal order, but there is no legal requirement for this. The person collecting the body should sign the discharge register in the presence of the attendant. Receipts should also be obtained for clothing, property and valuables. All the records should be retained for at least ten years and preferably longer.

Health care professionals seeking further information upon autopsy and mortuary practice should speak to their local consultant pathologist in the first instance. Most pathologists and anatomical pathology technicians are always willing to discuss problems, explain their local policies, and in most cases will permit attendance at an autopsy by those with a bona fide interest, subject to an undertaking that confidentiality will be maintained.

References

Bissett, R.A.L., Thomas, N.B., Turnbull, I.W., Lee, S. (2002) 'Post mortem examinations using magnetic resonance imaging: a 4-year review of a working service.' *British Medical Journal 324*, 1423–1424.

Bradfield, J.B. (1994) *Green Burial*, 2nd edn. London: The Natural Death Centre.

Buck, N., Devlin, H.B. and Lunn, J.N. (1988) *The Report of a Confidential Inquiry into Peri-operative Deaths.* London: Nuffield Provincial Hospitals Trust.

Coroners (Amendment) Rules (2005) s.i 420 rule 3.

Coroners Rules (1984) s.i 552 rule 9.

Department of Health (2001) *The inquiry into the Management and Care of Children Receiving Complex Heart Surgery at Bristol Royal Infirmary.* Cm 5207. London: The Stationery Office.

Department of Health (2003) *Families and Post Mortems: A Code of Practice.* London: DOH Publications.

Department of Health, Social Services and Public Safety (N.I.) (2004) *Post Mortem Examinations: Good Practice in Consent and the Care of the Bereaved.* Belfast: DHSSPS.

Editorial (1825) *London Medical Gazette 31*, 5, 792–794.

Eustace, S.J. and Nelson, E. (2004) 'Whole body resonance imaging: a valuable adjunct to clinical examination.' *British Medical Journal 328*, 387–388.

Haslam, F. (1996) *From Hogarth to Rowlandson: Medicine in Art in Eighteenth Century Britain.* Liverpool: Liverpool University Press.

Health and Safety at Work Act (1974) c 37 all sections.

Health and Safety Executive (2003) *Safe Working and the Prevention of Infection in the Mortuary and Post Mortem Room.* Sudbury: HSE Books.

Human Tissue Act (2004) c 30 ss.1, 2, 5.

Inglis, B.A. (1965) *History of Medicine.* London: Weidenfeld and Nicolson.

McDermott, M.B. (2003) 'Obtaining consent for autopsy.' *British Medical Journal 327*, 804–806.

Moore, W. (2005) *The Knife Man: The Extraordinary Life of John Hunter, Father of Modern Surgery.* London: Bantam.

O'Grady, G. (2003) 'Death of the teaching autopsy.' *British Medical Journal 327*, 802–803.

Redfearn, M. (2003) *The Royal Liverpool Children's Hospital Inquiry Report.* London: The Stationery Office.

Richardson, R. (1987) *Death, Dissection and the Destitute.* London: Routledge and Kegan Paul.

Royal College of Pathologists (2002) *Guidelines for Post Mortem Reports.* London: RCPath.

Royal College of Pathologists (2003) *Examination of the Body after Death: Information about Post Mortem Examinations for Relatives.* London: RCPath.

Royal College of Pathologists (2004) *Sudden Unexpected Death in Infancy: The Report of a Working Group Chaired by the Baroness Helena Kennedy QC.* London: The Royal College of Pathologists (jointly with the Royal College of Paediatrics and Child Health).

Royal College of Pathologists of Australasia Autopsy Working Party (2004) 'The decline of the hospital autopsy: a safety and quality issue for health care in Australia.' *Medical Journal of Australasia 180*, 6, 281–285.

Tuffs, A. (2003) 'Von Hagens faces investigation over use of bodies without consent.' *British Medical Journal 237*, 1068.

Underwood, J.C.E. (2003) 'Resuscitating the teaching autopsy.' *British Medical Journal 327*, 803–804.

Virchow, R. (1876) *Post Mortem Examinations* [anonymous translation from the German]. London: J and A Churchill.

Wise, S. (2004) *The Italian Boy: Murder and Grave Robbery in the 1830s*. London: Jonathan Cape.

YourRights.org.uk (2005) *The Liberty Guide to Human Rights*. www.YourRights.org.uk (accessed 1 August 2005).

CHAPTER 7

FUNERAL DIRECTION AND DISPOSAL BY BURIAL

Modern funeral direction

Modern funeral direction is a complex subject. Its practitioners require a wide knowledge of disposal procedures and regulations, both for the UK and overseas, and considerable anatomical knowledge and skills, particularly if embalming is to be performed. In addition, the funeral director has at his disposal a range of cosmetic techniques, and an extensive choice of funeral furnishings. He must also be aware of differing customs in our present-day multi-ethnic society and be able to deal sympathetically with the bereaved, at a time when they greatly need support and counsel.

Health and safety requirements demand properly designed premises with facilities for body reception, preparation, viewing and storage; hearses and other vehicles are also needed. It follows, therefore, that provision of such services and employment of appropriate staff is a costly business. For these reasons, the 'small undertaker', who was often the local carpenter and joiner, is rapidly disappearing. Most funeral direction in the UK is now controlled by a handful of large companies, some of which have international links. A few firms offer highly specialised services, such as mass disaster disposal, the handling of 'high risk infection' cases, and the repatriation of bodies to other countries. The cost of these services has to be passed on to the clients; funeral direction is a business like any other. Those retaining the services of a funeral director are entering into a contract, for which they incur legal liability. It behoves relatives and executors to obtain several estimates beforehand and to select a reputable firm. The National Association of Funeral Directors maintains a list of its members, and offers an arbitration service when disputes arise (see Appendix A).

Basic funeral practice varies but little between burial and cremation. Therefore, most of this account is applicable whichever method of disposal is selected.

When a death occurs in hospital, 'laying out' procedures ('Last Offices') are performed by the nursing staff (see Chapter 14). The body is then removed to the hospital mortuary and is collected by the funeral director, when registration certification or the Coroner's inquiry is completed. Sudden deaths outside hospital, which become the subject of coronial investigation, are also taken to a public or hospital mortuary and the bodies are released upon production of the Registrar's authority to dispose, when the investigations are complete.

The role of the funeral director

When a natural death occurs at home and the doctor is prepared to issue a death certificate, the funeral director is involved at an early stage. It is his responsibility to remove the body to his premises. Only rarely do the relatives now keep the body at home. The body should be laid out as soon as possible after death before rigor mortis (stiffening) develops. The eyes are closed, the jaw lightly bandaged or supported, and the limbs composed. The body is then usually shrouded and removed on a covered stretcher or in a lightweight temporary 'shell'.

As soon as possible thereafter, the funeral director meets the relatives or executors to discuss the disposal arrangements. He obtains the full name, age and religion of the deceased, enquires as to the preferred method and place of disposal and discusses such matters as press notices, floral tributes, charitable donations and the 'funeral tea', or similar gathering for relatives and friends. He explains the procedures for registration, and will arrange for completion of the necessary medical certificates if cremation is chosen.

The nature of the ceremony, religious or secular, is discussed and the celebrant selected. If the deceased has not actively practised his religion, the funeral director will find a minister of the appropriate denomination. Cemeteries and crematoria maintain lists of retained chaplains of all denominations, who are available for such cases. If the burial is to take place in a churchyard, the permission of the incumbent is required (see p.35). This should have been sought during life. The incumbent will usually also agree to the service being conducted by another clergyman.

Burial authorities usually require two to four days' notice of intended interment. Crematoria may require a longer period of notice, particularly in winter when their workloads are increased. Jewish and Muslim funerals are arranged much more speedily (see Part 3, Chapters 26 and 29).

The funeral director takes instruction on such requirements as embalming (often called 'sanitisation'), the style and cost of the coffin, and the number of following cars required. Finally, he offers an estimate, preferably in writing. If the family or executors accept this, a binding contract is made.

Over the next few days, the funeral director assists the relatives with the registration procedures (see Chapter 3). If cremation is desired, he arranges completion of the application and other forms required (see Chapter 8). After the funeral is over, the funeral director advises on the provision of a gravestone, or the form of commemoration acceptable to the cremation authority concerned.

Funeral furnishings, coffins, shrouds etc. are supplied to the profession by specialist firms. These will supply such items direct to the public but sometimes charge much higher prices to do so (see 'Green burial' below). Many small businesses do not possess their own vehicles. A specialist 'carriage master' hires hearses and following cars, according to need.

The practice of embalming

The process of embalming is undertaken to retard, if not prevent, the changes which take place after death. It is an ancient practice. Joseph's body was embalmed in Egypt (Exodus 1, v.26). It is today widely practised in the USA, and is increasingly common in the UK, where it is often known as 'sanitisation'.

The changes which occur after death are complex. They are described only briefly here, and more detailed information should be sought from standard textbooks of forensic medicine, for example Saukko and Knight (2004).

CHANGES AFTER DEATH

In the period immediately after death, the body gradually cools. In average conditions, it takes 12 to 18 hours to reach ambient temperature. The blood settles into the dependent parts under the influence of gravity. This process is known as post mortem hypostasis or lividity, and becomes 'fixed' after 6 to 12 hours. Its presence is of no matter if the body is left lying on its back, but those who die face down and are left in that position show empurpling of the face, which can be quite disfiguring, especially if a considerable period of time has elapsed and the face has become swollen due to the accumulation of tissue fluid. The body becomes stiff (rigor mortis). This process begins in the facial muscles and the hands within a few hours of death and becomes complete within 12 to 18 hours. It then gradually passes off, and usually has disappeared within 48 hours.

In temperate conditions, the first signs of putrefaction appear in about 36 hours (more rapidly if infection, for example bronchopneumonia, was present at the time of death). A greenish hue develops in the skin of the right lower quadrant of the abdomen. Abdominal distension begins to appear, surface veins on the trunk and limbs become discoloured ('marbling'), and gas forms in the lungs and the chest cavity, so that offensive fluid may be expelled from the mouth ('lung purge'). Blisters appear on the skin, which then discolours and peels ('skin slip'), allowing widespread seepage of fluid. The body has, by now, a most unpleasant smell. As the putrefactive process continues, generalised bloating occurs. The body then gradually starts to dry out, the skin becomes leathery ('black putrefaction'), and, from about the 20th day, dissolution is a slow process.

These changes are accelerated by the activities of insects, notably bluebottles, and their larvae. Small animals, such as mice or domestic pets, may attack the corpse. Fungal growth occurs on exposed surfaces and this may continue, even when the body is refrigerated. For a full account of these changes, refer to a standard textbook of forensic pathology, for example Saukko and Knight (2004).

Embalming aims to retard these processes. Refrigeration, if properly maintained, will delay their onset for several days, but such storage facilities are often limited. Some ethnic and religious groups wish the deceased to be readily available for viewing. The pressure upon crematoria and funeral direction services may delay the funeral for several days. A secondary advantage is the cosmetic improvement which may be obtained.

METHODS OF EMBALMING

The principles of embalming are simple (Hanzlick 1994). The blood is washed out of the circulatory system and replaced with a preservative fluid which is usually formalin based. A pink dye (eosin) is commonly added. As this is instilled under pressure, it permeates the soft tissues and organs, and 'fills out' the face.

If no post mortem has been performed, an artery, usually in the upper arm, is opened, and approximately 8–10 litres (2 gallons) of embalming fluid is allowed to flow through the circulation, either under hydrostatic pressure from a raised reservoir, or assisted by some form of hand or electric pump. The blood, eventually admixed with the embalming fluid, is simultaneously withdrawn via a suitable vein.

The body cavities require separate treatment. A small incision is made in the upper abdomen, and any free fluid is sucked out of the abdominal and chest cavities. A sharp-ended hollow tube (a 'trocar') is then inserted. This is directed so as to puncture the heart, lungs and the bowels, and a more concentrated embalming solution ('cavity fluid') is introduced. Before this process is commenced, the lips and face are smeared with petroleum jelly or massage cream to prevent damage by gastric acid contents should regurgitation ('purging') occur. Finally, the body is carefully inspected, and any areas of skin which have not been adequately perfused with embalming fluid are directly injected by means of a syringe and needle. The associated cosmetic practices are straightforward. Any prominent areas of lividity (for example on the face or hands) are massaged to drain the capillaries before injection commences. After injection is complete, the hair, eyebrows and beard are trimmed, shaped 'shells' are placed beneath the eyelids and make-up is applied lightly to the face and lips.

If an autopsy has been performed, the body must be re-opened. The organs are removed and washed, and then immersed in cavity fluid. The cut ends of the major arteries and veins to the head, arms and legs are identified, cannulated, and regional injection is carried out. This is the so-called 'six point technique'. The organs are then replaced, the body sewn up, and final cosmetic treatment is applied.

Disposal by burial

Burial now accounts for less than 20 per cent of disposals within the UK. Some faiths (e.g. Orthodox Judaism and Islam) insist upon it. Others have gradually withdrawn their objections to cremation, with a consequent reduction in the total number of burials.

There is no legal requirement that burials should take place in approved cemeteries or churchyards. An increasing number of interments now take place in private lands (see 'green' and 'garden' burials, below). The establishment and maintenance of cemeteries has been rigorously controlled since the early 19th century (see Chapter 1). The first parliamentary regulation was the Kensal Green Cemetery Act 1832; subsequent legislation was modelled upon it. The Burial Acts of 1852 and 1853 made provision for the establishment of municipal cemeteries throughout the country. Numerous other Acts followed throughout the Victorian era. For a comprehensive review of this complex subject the reader should consult *Davies' Law of Burial, Cremation and Exhumation*, 7th edition. (Smale 2002).

Churchyard burials

An Anglican churchyard is consecrated ground. It is normally adjacent to the church and its prime purpose is to serve as a burial ground for the parishioners. The incumbent may have rights of herbage (for example the right to graze sheep) but he may not remove soil, or fell timber. The ground is consecrated by the written authority of a Bishop; once consecrated it may not be used for any secular purpose, except under the authority of a specific Act of Parliament.

Common Law bestows the right of churchyard burial upon every parishioner, every inhabitant of the parish, and any person dying within its boundaries. The incumbent's permission is required for the burial of a 'stranger'. Burial is not restricted to members of the Church of England. Full rights are accorded to members of other Christian denominations. Since 1882, suicides have also received Christian burial, and their right to interment was confirmed by the Suicide Act (1961). The unbaptised may be denied the full service ritual; the decision is the incumbent's. It is seldom refused in the case of infants. Attitudes to the burial rites accorded to unbaptised adults vary considerably amongst the clergy.

Although the right of burial within the churchyard is automatic, the site of burial is at the incumbent's discretion. Once a churchyard has been closed by an Order in Council (for example because it is full, or the church has become redundant), all rights of burial are extinguished. It is now lawful to inter cremated remains; the ban upon the burial of stillborn infants has now been removed (see Chapter 5).

The right of burial extends only to interment 'in an orderly manner'. The definition of this is loose, and is determined by the incumbent. A special fee must be paid if the body is to be enclosed in an indestructible (e.g. metal) coffin. There is no legal prohibition upon the use of such a coffin, but many church authorities forbid their use; nor is there any automatic right to erect a monument, or even to place flowers upon a grave.

Permission for burial within the church itself must be obtained from the ecclesiastical authorities and is rarely given. It is expressly forbidden in urban areas (unless the remains have been first cremated) and in any church built after 1848. Burial within Westminster Abbey or St Paul's Cathedral is permitted only upon the written authority of the Sovereign. Cremation must precede it.

The erection of monuments is sanctioned by the incumbent. He, and the Parish Council, may impose restrictions upon the size, materials, and form of inscription used. The incumbent's power is in fact founded in tradition, rather than law. The only legal authority for erection of a monument is a faculty granted by a senior church official, the Registrar of the Diocese. Each Diocese provides an Advisory Committee, who will assist intending applicants in the preparation of their petition.

If a faculty is refused, the relatives may appeal to the Arches Court of Canterbury, but this court seldom overturns a local refusal. The memorial remains the property of those who commissioned it, but the church authorities may obtain a faculty for its re-siting. Repairs to monuments are the responsibility of the erectors, not the church. Memorial windows and furnishings become the property of the church.

When advice is required on any of the above matters, the family or executors should first approach the incumbent, either through their funeral director, or personally. Disputes should be taken to the local Diocese Advisory Committee.

Burials in municipal and private cemeteries

The regulation of municipal cemeteries has, since 1974, been controlled by the Local Government Act (1972). They are also subject to regulation by the Health and Safety at Work Act (1974) and subsequent Statutory Instruments and Orders. Before that, a welter of individual Acts and regulations created numerous anomalies and local differences in practice. Management was further consolidated by the Local Authorities' Cemeteries Orders (1974, 1977) and various Church of England Provisions Orders (1976–1992). These comprehensive documents lay down standards of maintenance, protect the interests of various religious denominations, make provisions for chapels and mortuary accommodation where necessary, and even ensure that biers are provided. All the responsibilities of the diocese and incumbent for churchyard burials are clearly set out in the above Acts and Orders; the type of grave, depth of interment, design and size of memorials are also controlled. Following recent accidents to children resulting in injuries caused by unstable gravestones, many churches and municipal authorities have embarked upon a 'lay flat' policy. Most municipal cemeteries provide consecrated denominational plots, and also a general section. The Act and Orders specify certain offences. No game or sport may be played in a cemetery; neither may any grave, monument or floral tribute be interfered with.

Private burial grounds are less common. Many belong to religious sects, for example Jewish communities or the Society of Friends, commonly known as Quakers. Others are still in the hands of private companies. The general regulations for the preservation of public health, and the health and safety requirements, are the same as those for municipal cemeteries. Specific matters, such as standards for coffins, memorials and inscriptions, are in the hands of the appropriate religious authority, or Board of Management.

There is no obligation upon the owners of a cemetery, private or municipal, to maintain the ownership indefinitely. In 1989 Westminster Council sold three of its graveyards to private developers for 15 p each. The developers failed to maintain the cemeteries to the standards demanded by the relatives of many of those interred. Following widespread publicity, which included parliamentary questions and a prolonged campaign by the media, the Council regained possession of the cemeteries, and they are now fully restored to their former good condition.

Registration of burials

This should not be confused with registration of the fact and cause of death. It is a separate statutory duty, and the registers are maintained by the parochial or local burial authorities, not the Registrar of Births, Marriages and Deaths.

Every burial must be registered, whether it takes place in a churchyard, private or municipal cemetery. For burials in gardens and on private land, see below. Registration of churchyard burials is controlled by the Parochial Registers Act 1812, and by subsequent Acts. The form and material of the records is controlled, as is provision for their secure storage. Completed registers may be lodged at the appropriate Diocesan Record Office, rather than kept in the parish, if it is the opinion of the Bishop that they may be more securely retained there.

The registers are open to public search 'at all reasonable times', conditional upon the payment of a fee, which is determined and varied from time to time by the Bishop. Alternatively the incumbent or diocesan registrar may be willing to supply a certified copy of an entry by post. A higher fee is charged for this. A certified copy of the register entry may be produced in court in matters of proof of pedigree, inheritance etc. It follows that heavy penalties may be imposed upon those who deface, alter or destroy these important documents. Likewise, forgery or alteration of a certified copy of entry is a serious criminal offence.

Similar provisions are made for the maintenance and storage of Registers of Burials in private and local authority cemeteries. A named officer is designated as registrar. The obligation to register, store the records and to make them available for inspection falls upon him. Such registers have evidential value equivalent to those of a parish; the penalties for destruction, damage or forgery are equally severe.

'Green' garden and woodland burial

This is a subject which requires a full-length textbook in itself. When the first edition of this book was published in 1990, permission to bury on private ground, in a garden or meadow was rarely given. Local authorities and departments of environmental health created numerous obstacles. Crematoria and cemeteries were positively obstructive to those who wished to effect disposal without employing a funeral director. The few suppliers who would sell funeral furnishings directly to the public discouraged private initiative by charging exorbitantly high prices.

The natural death and 'green' burial movement gathered impetus throughout the 1990s. The first edition of *The Natural Death Handbook* was published in 1993. It is now into its 4th edition (Wienrick and Speyer 2003). The law has been clarified and frequently challenged, notably by John Bradfield of the AB Wildlife Trust. The latest edition of *Davies' Law of Burial, Cremation and Exhumation* (Smale 2002) lucidly sets out the current legal situation. There are now more than 200 natural burial grounds in mainland UK. Over 200 municipal cemeteries and a similar number of crematoria will accept funerals arranged by family or friends, without the use of an intermediary funeral director. There are specialist firms who will provide biodegradable woollen shrouds and coffins made of fibreboard, cardboard or wicker.

GARDEN BURIAL

The laws relating to garden or other privately owned land interment are now clear. There is no rule requiring the use of a coffin, there are no requirements for a minimum grave depth, and there is no stipulated minimum distance from other properties. However, local water authorities will forbid interment within 50 yards of any spring, borehole or other domestic supply. A burial authorisation (or Coroner's burial order) must be obtained from the Registrar (of Births, Marriages and Deaths), and notification of the date and place of burial must be returned to him within 96 hours. The Registration of Burials Act (1864) requires that a land burial register be kept for all graves in England. The format of the register, and the conditions of its storage, are also specified. It would appear that the practical solution for those undertaking a garden burial should be to register the date of interment, and the exact location of the site, in the deeds of the property. Note that all authorities giving advice on this topic warn those intending to perform or permit a garden burial that the value of the property may be considerably reduced. Also, all the potential beneficiaries of such a sale should have agreed in writing to the burial in the first place, lest there be subsequent dispute over any losses incurred in the subsequent sale of the property.

The legality of a do-it-yourself funeral pyre has yet to be challenged, although anecdotal and unsubstantiated accounts of its performance appear from time to time. In 2004, a man appeared before magistrates after he admitted to having burned his mother's body in the back yard. No death certificate had been issued, and the death had not been registered. He was convicted of the registration offences and received a conditional discharge. There was no mention of the burning in the charge sheet (*R v Wrigglesworth* 2005).

WOODLAND BURIALS

Numerous Local Authority and privately owned sites now exist. Many funeral directors willingly undertake collection, preparation and encoffining of the body. They will also meet the relatives' wishes for the supply of 'green' biodegradable burial garments and coffins. Lists of approved funeral directors and suppliers of funeral furnishings are available from the Natural Death Centre (Bradfield 1994; see Appendix A) and from many local Citizens' Advice Bureaux. It is possible to hire a light van for the transport of the body, or even a motorcycle combination; plans and materials for the construction of a chipboard coffin are also readily available through internet sites.

Many people do not regard cremation as 'green' because of the greenhouse gases which it creates, but for those who wish to arrange disposal by direct negotiations, the majority of crematoria will readily provide facilities. There is no legal restriction upon the place or method of disposal of cremation ashes. At least one firm makes provision for their incorporation into a firework display. There is no requirement for any form of religious ceremony. A family may devise their own committal ritual; there are also professional celebrants who will conduct humanist, atheist or even pagan obsequies. Whatever arrangements for disposal are desired, it is prudent to plan them well in advance, particularly if the requirements of the deceased and the family are out of the ordinary.

Burial at sea

Burial at sea requires a licence (free in England and Wales) from the Department for the Environment, Food and Rural Affairs (DEFRA). But there are only about 20 such burials a year because of technical and financial considerations. The practice is discouraged in the busy sea-lanes around the British Isles, because every year bodies are washed up on the shore, or brought to the surface by a trawler. For these reasons, licences are only granted for disposal at three sites: off Newhaven, near the Isle of White and in a small sea area nine miles off the mouth of the River Tyne. Sea burial can be expensive – funeral directors may charge up to £5000, especially if a commercial vessel is chartered. A private vessel may be used, provided it is equipped with global positioning satellite equipment, and the skipper holds a master's certificate.

The coffin must be made of biodegradable softwood, such as pine. It must be weighted with 200 kg of ballast and the body itself must be wrapped in chain. Only shrouds made of cotton or a paper base may be used. Holes must be drilled in the coffin to permit the ready ingress of seawater. The body must be labelled with a securely attached indelible plastic tag which bears its name, and the name and telephone number of the person holding the DEFRA licence. A freedom from infection certificate and an out of England certificate must be obtained. If the committal is delayed, for example by bad weather, DEFRA must be notified, at least verbally, and they will amend the licence accordingly.

Contact information for DEFRA is given in Appendix A.

References

Bradfield, J.B. (1994) *Green Burial; The d-i-y Guide to Law and Practice.* London: The Natural Death Centre.

Burial Act (1852) 15 & 16 Victoria c 85 ss.202–213.

Burial Act (1853) 16 & 17 Victoria c 134 ss.202–239.

Hanzlick, R. (1994) 'Embalming, body preparation, burial and disinterment. An overview for forensic pathologists.' *American Journal of Forensic Medicine and Pathology 15*, 2, 122–131.

Health and Safety at Work Act (1974) and subsequent Statutory Instruments and Orders, cited in Smale, D.A. (2002) pp.109–111.

Kensal Green Cemetery Company Act (1832) 2 & 3 William 4 c 10 s.201.

Local Government Act (1972) 20 & 21 Elizabeth 2 c 70 ss.214 et seq.

Registration of Burials Act (1864) 27 & 28 Victoria c 97 ss.239, 240, 245.

R v Wrigglesworth (2005) Leeds Crown Court. *The Yorkshire Post* 22 Jan 2005.

Saukko, P. and Knight, B. (2004) *Knight's Forensic Pathology*, 3rd edn. London: Arnold.

Smale, D.A. (2002) *Davies' Law of Burial, Cremation and Exhumation*, 7th edn. Crayford: Shaw and Sons.

Suicide Act (1961) 9 & 10 Elizabeth 2 c 6 s.210.

Wienrick, S. and Speyer, J. (eds) (2003) *The Natural Death Handbook*, 4th edn. London: Rider.

CHAPTER 8

DISPOSAL BY CREMATION

History and principles of cremation

The history of disposal by cremation has already been briefly touched upon in Chapter 1. Because of the finality of this destructive method, and the opportunities for concealment of crime, it has been carefully regulated since its introduction by increasingly stringent acts and regulations.

The principle of cremation is simple. The human body contains approximately 80 per cent water; the balance is made up of bone (mainly calcium phosphate) and the soft tissues. The aim is to achieve rapid high temperature oxidation, with a minimum of smoke emission, producing ash and friable fragments of bone, which are then pulverised in a cremulator. Usually approximately 2 kilograms (5 lb) of ash remains. The coffin burns away. The heat, which is produced by this, assists in the cremation process. Screws and other metallic fragments are removed before the ashes are placed in the urn. Artificial hip joints and other 'spare parts' present no problems. They are readily identified, and removed by hand. The exception is the cardiac pacemaker unit. The batteries contained within the unit may explode with sufficient force to cause serious damage to the cremation oven and to crematorium staff. For this reason a document certifying the absence of such an appliance is required before any cremation can proceed. Crematoria restrict the size of coffin and the material used therein to reduce the amount of smoke emitted. The Federation of British Cremation Authorities publishes detailed instructions for funeral directors (see Appendix A).

Increased concern for the environment has led to continuous improvements in the efficiency of combustion in UK crematoria. The view of the Department for the Environment, Food and Rural Affairs (DEFRA) is that emissions generally are now maintained at an acceptable level. However, the populations of developed countries are now living longer: they are keeping their own teeth, which until recently were filled, as the need arose, with a mercury and silver amalgam. Concerns about the potential hazards of rising mercury levels, due to crematoria emissions, were expressed as long ago as 1990. Since 1991, crematoria emissions in the UK have been controlled under the provisions of Part 1 of the Environmental Protection Act (1990), but reduction in levels of mercury were not addressed until recently.

In 2003, DEFRA initiated a consultation process, and received a large number of responses from crematoria operators, environmental groups and the public. They concluded that, for the time being, a cautious approach was all that was needed. No crematoria should be closed, but a rolling programme of emission reduction should be initiated. All new crematoria should be required to install mercury abatement equipment.

Contrary to some media stories, there should be no requirement to remove teeth from bodies prior to cremation, as has been proposed by some, for example a Senator in Maine, USA. Conservative dentistry is improving: fewer fillings are needed, and the use of mercury amalgam has been discontinued. So, after an initial rise in levels up to about 2020, it is expected that cremation generated emissions will fall rapidly thereafter.

Crematoria follow a fairly standard design. On the public side there is a waiting area, a non-denominational 'service room', and a committal area, into which the coffin passes at the appropriate moment in the ceremony. In some crematoria the body remains in the 'service room' itself, a curtain being closed at the moment of committal. Most authorities now provide rooms with no religious symbols; in others, care is taken to cover crosses and other religious artefacts before a secular or non-Christian funeral takes place.

Over 70 per cent of disposals in the mainland UK are now by cremation. It is less common in Northern Ireland. The majority of foreign countries now offer cremation facilities. Under Muslim Shariah Law, cremation is forbidden, but some Arab countries (e.g. Saudi Arabia) provide crematorium facilities for their expatriate populations. Information on facilities available abroad can be obtained from the International Cremation Federation (see Appendix A). A directory of these establishments is also provided in an appendix to Smale's 'Law of Burial Cremation, and Exhumation' (Smale 2002).

Cremation legislation and certification

Cremation is controlled by the Cremation Acts of 1902 and 1952 and by various regulatory instruments, principally those of 1930, which have been amended from time to time. The most recent amendments were made in 2000. Cremation is only permitted in a purpose built facility, approved by the Home Secretary. The legality of 'garden cremation' has recently been questioned. In a case heard at Leeds Crown Court in 2005 (*R v Wrigglesworth*) the accused, whose mother had died of lung cancer, left her body in the bedroom for eight weeks before setting fire to it in the garden. He then continued to claim her pension (and his late father's) for two years. The learned judge (James Stewart QC) held, citing *R v Price* (1884), that no offence had been committed in respect of the burning of the body, as no public nuisance had been complained of. Nor was he guilty of attempting to obstruct the Coroner from holding an inquest, as the cause of his mother's death (lung cancer) was not disputed, even though a medical certificate of cause of death (MCCD) had not been issued. However, Wrigglesworth was convicted of the fraud charges, and was sentenced to 12 months' community service (*R v Wrigglesworth* 2005).

Cremation may not take place until the death has been properly registered (and Coroner's form E has been issued), except where the body has been brought from overseas, and there is no liability to register; however, following the decision in *R v W. Yorks Coroner ex parte Smith* (see Chapter 4) such cases now usually pass through the coronial system. Cremation is permitted without the deceased's express consent; a declaration by the applicant that no objection was made is sufficient.

Forms required for cremation

There are eight forms in common use; their minimum content and format are laid down in the regulations. Those most commonly used are A, B, C and F. D is required only if a post mortem has been ordered by the Medical Referee. Form E is issued by a Coroner who has initially assumed jurisdiction and has completed his inquiry. The Cremation (Amendment) Regulations 2000 add forms AA, DD, FF and GG to provide for the cremation of body parts removed at autopsy (see also Chapter 6).

Form A is a one-page application for cremation. Forms B, C and F (the medical certificate) are supplied as a single four-page document; form B is completed by the attending doctor; form C by a second doctor, who has no close association or partnership with the first signatory; and form F by a third doctor (the Medical Referee to the crematorium). Form E, the Coroner's authority for cremation, replaces forms B and C, but the Medical Referee's certificate on form F is always required. Form G is the Registration of Cremation; forms D and H are rarely used, but their functions are explained below.

FORM A – APPLICATION FOR CREMATION

This single sided A4 document is completed by a near relative or an executor. If any other person (e.g. a hospital administrator or Local Authority official) completes the application, he must explain his right to do so.

The applicant must state whether the deceased left any written instructions for the disposal of his remains and, particularly, must affirm that no objection to cremation was ever expressed. If any near relative objects to cremation, this must be stated. The applicant must declare that he is satisfied that the death was not due to violence, poison, privation or neglect; he must give the name of the ordinary medical attendant or the names of any other doctors who attended the deceased during his last illness. Finally he must state that, in his opinion, no further examination of the body is necessary.

Until 1952, form A had to be supported by a statutory declaration; now counter-signature by a 'responsible person', to whom the applicant is known, is all that is required. 'Responsible persons' are defined in the 1952 regulations, and include Magistrates, Civil Servants, and members of the professions.

FORM B – CERTIFICATE OF ATTENDING MEDICAL PRACTITIONER

Forms B, C and F are always printed together as a four-page document. Form B occupies the first two pages. It has a standard layout, with 18 questions, which must be answered by the doctor in attendance during the last illness. It requires careful study; all questions *must* be answered, and the doctor *must* see the body after death. The doctor must be fully registered. A pre-registration house officer (PRHO) may not complete the form.

Details of the cause of death are given in the same order as on the death certificate. Care should be taken that the two statements agree. In addition, the mode and time of death must be stated, not merely the date. The names of those who nursed the deceased are required and so is the nature of any operation performed in the preceding 12 months, with the name of the surgeon who performed it.

Like form A, form B requires the signatory to state his belief that there is no suspicion of violence, poison, privation or neglect. He must confirm that no further examination of the body is desirable. Finally the declaration that all the answers are true is completed and the document signed. The doctor must give his registered qualifications, and his address and telephone number.

A fee is payable by the relatives, or those arranging the funeral, for medical certificates B and C. The British Medical Association recommends a national minimum fee, currently £62.50, which is reviewed from time to time, but there is no obligation upon an individual medical practitioner to observe these recommendations; an increasing number of doctors complete the forms at a reduced or no fee. It may well be that the fee element will be removed in any new legislation, and that completion of forms B and C (or whatever replaces them) will become a statutory duty, like the completion of the MCCD.

FORM C – CONFIRMATORY MEDICAL CERTIFICATE

This forms the third page of the four-page document. It is completed by a doctor who has been fully registered for longer than five years. He must not be in partnership with, or on the same hospital 'firm' as, the doctor who has certified form B. The form requires the doctor to see the body after death, and to see the doctor who completed form B, but this latter requirement may be waived in certain circumstances, particularly in deaths occurring in hospital. A telephone conversation is usually acceptable, so long as the fact is noted in the margin of the form. The doctor must say if he has seen and questioned any other doctors, nurses, relatives or other persons concerned with the death, and whether he saw them alone. He must certify his satisfaction that the death is natural, that no further examination of the body is indicated and that referral to the Coroner is not necessary.

Since 1985, the requirement for form C to be completed may be dispensed with where:

1.   the death occurred in hospital and the deceased was an inpatient there, and

2.   a post mortem examination has been made by a doctor qualified to sign form C (i.e. one fully registered for more than five years). The doctor signing form B

must know the results of the post mortem examination before completing the certificate.

If the pathologist performing the post mortem has been fully registered for less than five years, form C must be completed in the usual way by a more senior colleague, who must see the body. Simply reading the post mortem report, or discussing the findings with the junior pathologist, is not sufficient. Many hospitals now use a modified form B, which incorporates an additional question, numbered 8a. This asks whether a post mortem has been performed, and by whom. It requires statements confirming that the doctor who performed the post mortem is:

- not a relative of the deceased

- not a relative or partner of the doctor signing form B, and

- that the results of the post mortem are known to the signatory.

If satisfactory answers can be supplied, form C need not be completed. A fee is payable by the relatives for the completion of form C. It is usually the same as that charged for form B (i.e. £62.50).

FORM F – AUTHORITY TO CREMATE (THE MEDICAL REFEREE'S FORM)

The Medical Referee, who is appointed by the Home Secretary on the recommendation of the Cremation Authority, is the final arbiter for cremation applications. He is a medical practitioner of many years' experience, and holds the office on a part-time basis, being paid a fee for each application scrutinised. He is most commonly a specialist in public health medicine, but the post can be held by a general practitioner or hospital doctor.

The Medical Referee examines forms A, B and C. If he wishes to pursue further enquiries, he may contact the doctors concerned or any other persons named in the application. He may ask to see hospital case notes, or practice records. Once he is satisfied that there is no reason for the cremation to be delayed, he issues form F. Form F, the Authority to Cremate, forms the last page of the application documents; forms B and C (see above) occupy the first three. It is a simple declaration that all the requirements of the Cremation Acts and Regulations have been complied with, that the cause of death has been definitely ascertained, and that cremation can proceed. If the Medical Referee feels that the certificates do not give sufficient information, or new facts emerge in the course of his enquiries, two courses are open to him. He can refer the case to the Coroner. Alternatively he can ask a pathologist to carry out an autopsy on his behalf (although this is nowadays an uncommon practice).

FORM D – CERTIFICATE AFTER POST MORTEM ORDERED BY THE MEDICAL REFEREE

This is completed by the pathologist carrying out the autopsy, or by the Medical Referee himself, acting upon information given to him by the pathologist. It certifies the cause of death, confirms that there is no reason for toxicological analysis or other tests, and that no Coroner's inquiry is necessary. Its satisfactory completion permits the Medical Referee to then issue form F.

FORM G – REGISTER OF CREMATIONS

This is a record, which bears the serial number of each cremation. It gives the date of cremation, the particulars of the deceased, the name of the applicant and the names of those who signed the various certificates. When cremation has been completed, the Crematorium Superintendent returns the 'tear off' Notification of Disposal to the Registrar.

FORM H – CERTIFICATE OF ANATOMICAL EXAMINATION

When a body has undergone anatomical dissection in a medical school, or similar institution, the licensed teacher of anatomy issues this form. Before 1965, anatomically dissected bodies could only be disposed of by burial (Anatomy Act 1832). The position was regularised by the Anatomy Act of 1984 (see Chapter 9) and has been re-confirmed by the Human Tissue Act (2004). The period for which a body may be retained for dissection has been also extended from two to three years.

FORM E – CORONER'S CERTIFICATE OF AUTHORITY FOR CREMATION

This form replaces pink forms B and C in cases which have been investigated by the Coroner. No fee is chargeable for its issue. It is issued by the Coroner, over his signature, after he has opened an inquest, or following post mortem without inquest (see Chapter 4). The Medical Referee must still review the case, and issue form F. After cremation has been completed, the Notification of Disposal, which forms a tear-off section of form E, is returned to the Registrar.

Cremation of body parts removed at post mortem

In 1999, there was widespread publicity surrounding the revelation that numerous organs and body parts had been retained, following autopsies at the Bristol Children's Hospital and the Royal Liverpool Children's Hospital (Alder Hey). This episode is described in more detail in Chapter 6. In the widespread Department of Health review of medical and disposal practice which followed, it was appreciated that the current cremation laws permitted the disposal only of whole bodies; other material could only be incinerated as clinical waste. New regulations were therefore introduced (Cremation (Amendment) Regulations 2000) to permit the cremation of body parts and tissues. Full returns of the numbers of 'parts' cremated are not yet available, but in 2003, 83 crematoria reported 281 disposals. It is illegal to cremate these materials unless the following forms have been completed.

- **Form AA** is completed by the applicant. It requires the full names, addresses and occupations of the applicant and the deceased. An itemised list of the organs must be given. The applicant must state by what authority he is applying (e.g. relative, executor, hospital official). The form must confirm that no relative has made objection. The date of death, and the intended place and date of disposal of the body, must be given. Finally, it must be confirmed that no further examination of the parts is necessary. As with form A, a counter-signature is required.

- **Form DD** is issued by the hospital or other institution where the parts are held. It confirms the dates of death and autopsy, the identity of the deceased, the cause of death, and a reiteration that no further examination is required. The completed forms are submitted to the Medical Referee who completes form FF. In due course, the certificate of cremation (form GG) is issued. Note that in those cases where *burial* of parts is requested, most hospitals now use the same forms, AA and DD, but without mention of cremation, and with no reference to the Medical Referee. The completed forms go to the superintendent of the cemetery or the administrator of the graveyard, who then authorises the re-opening of the grave and interment of the parts (see also Chapter 7).

Cremation of stillborn infants and fetal remains

(See also Chapter 5.)

Under the terms of the Stillbirth (Definition) Act 1992, viability is set at 24 weeks' gestation. The registration of stillbirth is covered in Chapter 5. The term 'non-viable fetus' is used to cover products of conception delivered spontaneously, or following surgical intervention, at maturity less than 24 weeks, and for which it is not possible to obtain registration documentation. There is currently no guidance from central government on the disposal of such remains. Reliance is placed upon guidelines first published by the Institute of Burial and Cremation Administration in 1985, and subsequently updated in 1992 and 2002. The IBCA document has no legal status, but is generally regarded as an authoritative document, which sets acceptable standards for the disposal of fetal remains in a seemly manner and gives guidelines for adequate records, which should be kept by the relevant authorities. Hospital records of spontaneous abortions or terminations of pregnancy are kept for, at most, 50 years; records of burials and cremations are kept in perpetuity. Terminations, under the provisions of the Abortion Act 1967, are guaranteed anonymity of disposal, and so the remains are identified in the records only by the reference number allocated by the hospital.

The midwife or doctor attending such a premature miscarriage must complete a form, certifying that the remains are of less than 24 weeks' gestation, and that there was, at no time, any sign of life (see Chapter 5). Local cremation and burial authorities supply hospitals and funeral directors with certificates and cremation application forms, prepared to the template recommended by the IBCA. Although there is as yet no legal guidance, the parent(s) should give signed consent for the disposal. As there will be no appreciable amount of ashes remaining after the cremation of such material, the parent(s) should also be required to sign a document of understanding that no remains will be available to them after completion of the process. As in all other applications for disposal by cremation, the forms must be scrutinised by the Medical Referee, and form F issued. A specific register number (and form G in the case of cremation) must also be allocated for the disposal process.

Arrangements for cremation

Arrangements for cremation are usually made by the funeral director (FBCA 2002). He obtains form A for the relatives, advises them on its completion, and delivers and collects forms B and C. He takes the documents to the Medical Referee for completion of form F, and then delivers the documents to the crematorium. He usually pays the doctors' fees for completion of forms B and C, and then recovers the money from the relatives when he submits his final account. He will advise on the facilities available at local crematoria, secure the services of the appropriate cleric, or help with the arrangements for a secular funeral.

It is now relatively easy for bereaved relatives to make their own arrangements for disposal by cremation, with appropriate secular rites of passage. Advice is readily available from the Natural Death Society, and a variety of non-religious organisations (see also Chapter 7).

For the attitudes of different faiths and ethnic minorities to cremation, consult the appropriate chapters in Part 3 of this book.

The cremated remains must be returned to the person who applied for cremation on form A, if requested. If the applicant does not wish to accept them, the authority must inter or scatter them upon land adjacent to the crematorium and dedicated to that purpose. The applicant must be given a fortnight's notice before such disposal takes place. Ashes may be scattered at a location specified by the deceased or chosen by the relatives; there is no prohibition on scattering in rivers or on shorelines, etc. In the case of disposal within a Church of England graveyard, the ashes must be 'decently interred' or 'reverently disposed' of by a minister. Likewise, although cremation is anathema in orthodox Jewry, the ashes of a 'liberal' or 'reform' Jew must be encoffined, and interred, along with a prayer shawl (tallis, for a male) and with the full burial rites, including the recitation of the mourner's Kaddish (the funeral prayer).

References

Anatomy Act (1832).

Anatomy Act (1984).

Cremation Act (1902) 2 Edward 7 c 8.

Cremation Act (1952) 15 and 16 George 6, 1 Elizabeth 2 c 31.

Cremation (Amendment) Regulations (2000) s.i. No 58.

Environmental Protection Act (1990).

Federation of British Cremation Authorities (2002) *Code of Practice*. London: FBCA.

Human Tissue Act (2004).

Institute of Burial and Cremation Administration (2002) *Guidelines*. London: IBCA.

R v Price (1884) 12 QBD 247.

R v Wrigglesworth (2005) Leeds Crown Court. *The Yorkshire Post* 22 Jan 2005.

Smale, D.A. (2002) *Davies' Law of Burial and Cremation*, 7th edn, pp. 303–312. Crayford: Shaw and Sons.

Stillbirth (Definition) Act (1992).

CHAPTER 9

ORGAN AND TISSUE DONATION AND TRANSPLANTATION

Retention and disposal of specimens, organs and tissues from living patients

These matters are beyond the scope of this book, but the current position, following the implementation of the Human Tissue Act (2004), is set out briefly here. There is no obligation to determine the wishes of the patient (except in the case of a fetus or fetal tissues; see Chapter 5). Consent to disposal is deemed to be incorporated in the written informed consent to the clinical procedure, during which the organ, tissue or fluid was removed. Blocks and slides should be returned to the patient if a request for their return was made at the time that this consent was obtained. Otherwise they form part of the clinical records and should be retained for the minimum periods of time set out below:

- Wet tissue: four weeks after final report.
- Frozen sections: ten years.
- Paraffin wax blocks (for microscope slides): 30 years.
- Blood films: seven days.
- Bone marrow and cytology slides: up to 20 years.
- Histology slides: ten years.

If a patient does demand the return of human material, it should be returned to them only if the hospital authority is satisfied that the proposed method of disposal or keeping is safe and lawful. The patient must be informed, in writing, of any hazards associated with the material. The material is disposed of by incineration in sealed bags and any identifiable specimens must be sealed in opaque bags, to conceal any details of name etc. A record is kept of the date and place of disposal of all these materials. The Human Tissue Authority (HTA) issues guidelines which are regularly updated.

History

The legal and moral aspects of organ donation have been constantly debated for over 50 years. Kidney transplantation was developed in the late 1950s. The Human Tissue Act (1961) was passed in an attempt to legalise what was, until then, a procedure which had no sound legal basis, whilst providing protection for potential donors, who were portrayed by some media outlets as helpless victims at the mercy of a predatory medical profession. The donation of bodies to medical schools for anatomical dissection had been controlled since 1832 (Anatomy Act 1832), but autopsies and the retention and use of organ and tissues were subject to no legal controls.

The assumption that there was 'no property in a dead body', which was merely 'a gift of flesh for the worms', dated back to the 17th century. This view was upheld in *Williams v Williams* (1882), in which it was held that, as there is no property in a dead body, any direction made by the deceased during life was not binding upon his executors. Consent to autopsy was regarded as a professional courtesy, not a necessity. This legal interpretation had been reinforced in the 20th century by the decision in *Doodeward v Spence* (1908). Because the body was of itself worthless, the court held that any human material became the property of the person who gave it added value by preserving it. This opinion, that processing conferred ownership, was most recently confirmed when the ownership of a retained and preserved brain was tested in *Dobson and another v North Tyneside Health Authority* (1996). The brain had been fixed in formalin; it therefore became the hospital's property. The situation remained unsatisfactory until the passage of the Human Tissue Act (2004). Repeated allegations, of premature harvesting from donors who were potentially capable of survival, led to the preparation of criteria for brainstem death by the Medical Royal Colleges. This was insufficient to totally allay public concern. The use of volunteer live donors also continued, culminating in the 'kidneys for sale' scandal of 1989 (see below). Firm guidance to the medical profession, on the ethical issues surrounding the use of living donors, was issued by the General Medical Council and this was followed by legislation forbidding the sale of human organs, in an amendment to the Human Organ Transplantation Act (1989). In consequence, although the altruistic donation of organs by living relatives receives approval, the practice of 'buying' health, usually at the expense of a Third World donor, has now ceased.

At the same time, many have felt that the criteria for obtaining consent from relatives of potential donors are unnecessarily strict, causing such delays and distress to them and to the medical attendants that many potential donors are lost. There have therefore been many attempts to obtain an 'opting-out' system, under which the lack of any objection during life would imply consent to donation after death. So far, every Private Member's Bill on the subject has fallen through lack of parliamentary time. Many people now carry organ donor cards, but these have no real legal validity; consent from relatives is still required, and the potential donor must enrol on the NHS Organ Donation Register, which is maintained by NHS UK Transplant (Tel: 0845 60 60 400).

The Human Tissue Act (2004)

OVER-ARCHING REGULATION OF EVERY ASPECT OF ORGAN AND TISSUE RETENTION IN PATHOLOGY, TREATMENT AND RESEARCH

This chapter attempts to set out the current legal position, and the practical steps to be taken, where the donation of organs or tissues is being considered. Every aspect of tissue and organ donation, and transplantation, will be regulated from April 2006 by the Human Tissue Act (2004). This Act establishes the Human Tissue Authority, which began operating in April 2005. The authority subsumes the functions of the Unrelated Live Transplantation Regulation Authority (ULTRA) and the government body which regulated the keeping of records of donors and recipients, NHS Blood and Transplant (see below).

HUMAN TISSUE ACT (2004)

The Human Tissue Act (2004) was introduced in response to the public outcry which followed revelations that numerous organs and tissues removed at autopsies, both consent and coronial, had been retained at the Bristol Royal Infirmary (Department of Health 2001) and the Royal Liverpool Children's Hospital (Redfearn 2003). The government responded, through the Department of Health, by requiring other hospitals to catalogue and declare their collections of retained material and to return individual items, wherever possible, to the next of kin. Throughout the 1990s, Elaine Isaacs, a Manchester widow, had been active in lobbying for tighter controls upon all materials removed at Coroner's autopsy. This followed her discovery that her husband's brain had not been returned to the body following a Coroner's autopsy (a procedure of itself anathema to an Orthodox Jew), but had been given to the local medical school's department of anatomy for undergraduate teaching purposes. The working parties' reports on all three of these incidents were published during 2002 and 2003 (HM Inspector of Anatomy 2003).

These led to a re-examination of the existing law, as set out in the Human Tissue Act (1961). It was realised that introduction of new legislation would provide an opportunity to clarify and enforce standards for the regulation of anatomical dissections and the preparation of teaching specimens, and for the harvesting and use of organs and tissues for transplantation. The Act, which became law in April 2006, establishes schedules of purpose for which tissues and organs may be retained, and replaces the Anatomy Act (1984), the Anatomy Regulations (1988) and the Human Organ Transplantation Act (HOTA) (1989). Most importantly, it sets out the definition for informed and valid consent, the criteria for obtaining it, and nominates those from whom it may be obtained. It sets standards for the performance of autopsies and anatomical dissections, regulates the disposal of unused and redundant tissue, and creates criminal offences to punish those who fail to obtain consent, or who exceed the limits thereof.

Additionally it creates the offence of 'DNA theft' (using material from banked tissues for research purposes with neither consent nor attribution), establishes a single authority to control the manifold uses of tissues and organs, and lays down statutory codes of practice for every aspect of treatment, research and teaching.

HOW DOES THE NEW ACT WORK?

The Act establishes the overriding principle of informed consent to the retention of material removed from both the living and the dead. Consent to their removal remains regulated by existing common and criminal law. The Act establishes schedules, setting out the various circumstances in which requests for tissue retention may be made, and specifies the purposes for which they may be used.

The first schedule deals with material removed from both the living and dead. Written and witnessed consent, given in life, is required for the retention of material after death for anatomical examination or for public display, for example in a teaching collection. The written consent from the next of kin or specified relative must be obtained for hospital autopsy to establish cause of death, the efficacy of treatment, or for teaching and for research purposes. This includes trials of new prosthetic devices and for the practising of surgical or endoscopic techniques. Nothing in the Act removes the Coroner's overriding power to order an autopsy without any consent, but clearly defines the limits upon the time of retention of any organs or tissues which are removed during such a procedure. It re-emphasises the requirement of Rule 9 of the Coroners Rules (1984) that only material which may have a bearing upon the cause of death may be removed in the first place; to remove anything else will become a criminal offence. The Act permits retention of material for the obtaining of genetic information clinically relevant to another person, living or dead, but the new offence of 'DNA theft' prevents the use of any material, including hair and nails, for 'speculative' research.

Schedule 2 of the Act permits retention, with appropriate consent, of material from a deceased person for the purposes of quality assurance, clinical audit, teaching and research activities. Exceptions to the requirement for consent are:

1. Existing holdings of tissue or organs at the time of implementation of the Act, but methods and conditions of their storage are subject to mandatory codes of practice.

2. Residual tissue left over after diagnostic tests, for example the paraffin wax fixed blocks used for the preparation of microscopic sections, may be used for research if suitably anonymised.

3. In cases where a patient, alive or dead, may have suffered from a genetic disease thought to be now present in the relative, and when the treatment of which might be modified by accurate diagnosis, tests may be carried out on the material, provided the prior approval of the Human Tissue Authority (HTA) is obtained. If a living person is incapable of giving consent to the use of retained tissue, for example in cases of dementia, or if the patient cannot be traced, the HTA may waive consent (Mental Capacity Bill 2005, which received Royal

Assent in April 2005, but is not expected to become law until 2007 at the earliest) (see p.178). (See also Department of Health 2004.)

4.   Consent is not required for the storage or use of material from imported bodies, or from those known to have been dead for over a hundred years before the implementation of the Act.

The Human Tissue Authority (HTA)

The Human Tissue Authority was established in April 2005, under the chairmanship of Baroness Helene Hayman. It has wide-ranging powers to lay down codes of practice and standard operating procedures, to license and inspect mortuaries and laboratories, and to ensure that appropriate standards of hospital and coronial autopsies are maintained. It will control every aspect of the retention and storage of human organs and tissues, and takes control of the licensing and inspection powers of Her Majesty's Inspector of Anatomy, as set out in the Anatomy Act (1984). It will also regulate organ donation and transplantation, maintaining records of the harvesting of organs and tissues for therapeutic use and of their ultimate fate, including the disposal of unused material. It will regulate public displays, for example medical school museums and teaching collections, and will supervise the return of anthropological material, such as skeletal remains, to aboriginal groups worldwide from nine specified museums. All the powers of control and registration of transplantation, including maintenance of the register of those volunteering to be donors, which were previously held by the Unrelated Live Transplant and Regulatory Authority (ULTRA), will pass to the HTA in 2006, as will those of NHS Blood and Transplant (the body which until recently regulated registration and donation).

UK Transplant is now the department with which intending donors should register, either by telephone (0845 60 60 400) or on-line at www.uktransplant.org.uk

Who can give consent?

The Act clearly states that, in every circumstance except in the rare situations described above, consent must be written and witnessed. Consent to anatomical dissections and museum display ('leaving my body to science') may only be given by the patient during life. A relative or executor may not donate a body for this purpose. Witnessed and written consent to a hospital autopsy must be given by a relative or other person specified in the Act. The Act sets out schedules of appropriate relationships (including step and half siblings) in order of priority. If none of these persons are available, nominated representative or, as a last resort, a friend of long standing may give consent. Civil partnerships, including same-sex relationships, as defined by the Civil Partnership Act 2004, are recognised for the first time.

Consent to the retention of specified organs and tissues must be fully informed; the purpose for their retention and the intentions for their ultimate disposal within a specified time must be clearly set out. Severe penalties will be imposed upon those who retain materials without consent, or use them for purposes other than those for which express consent was given; these sanctions include imprisonment for up to three years, with or without the option of a fine. The Act reaffirms the existing offences relating to anatomical dissection, as laid down in the Act of 1984. It also extends the current ban upon the payment to live donors, which was introduced in the Human Organ Transplant Act (HOTA) (1989), making it an offence to canvass or procure donors for financial reward. Health care providers have been reminded by the Department of Health that the removal of an organ or tissue from a live donor, purely for transplantation purposes, when no benefit to the patient (donor) is intended, constitutes an assault under the Offences Against the Person Act (1861). However, it is made clear that the altruistic donation of an organ, bone marrow, or stem cells, by a relative or a tissue-matched volunteer, will remain legal. A further loophole has been closed; the HOTA (1989) forbade only the sale of *organs*. The sale of tissues is now illegal also.

Implementation of the Human Tissue Act (2004)

At the time of writing, it is expected that the Act will be fully implemented in April 2006. However, prosecution for failure to obtain consent, or for the exceeding of consent, will not commence until June 2006. It is anticipated that all the promised codes of practice will have been formally published by that date, and the process of return of anthropological museum specimens will have begun.

Most of the codes of practice, which the Act will require, have already been put into operation. All NHS hospitals and medical school departments of anatomy fully comply with them. However, one piece of the new legislation has already given rise to concern amongst Coroners and to the Council of the Royal College of Pathologists. The Coroners (Amendment) Rules (2005) require that any material retained under the existing provisions of Rule 9 of the Coroners Rules (1984), which might have a bearing on the cause of death, must be returned to the relatives or disposed of, with their consent, as soon as the Coroner's interest in the case is concluded. In the past, there have been cases where a diagnosis of death from natural causes was made, but subsequent suspicious deaths in the same family led to a re-examination of the retained material from the earlier case. This re-examination sometimes led to convictions for homicide. Many Coroners and pathologists fear that relatives, whose actions might have been responsible for a death, will be the first to demand the return of material that might incriminate them in the future. The Coroners' Society and the Royal College have submitted representations to the government setting out these concerns, but at the time of writing no modification of this ruling has taken place.

Organ donation: practical considerations

Major internal organs, such as kidneys, heart, liver and lungs, deteriorate rapidly at body temperature, if they are not being continually perfused with oxygenated blood.

They must, therefore, be removed whilst the heart is still beating, and an adequate circulation is being maintained. They must then be flushed through with saline solution, rapidly chilled, maintained at near freezing temperatures (but not frozen) and transplanted as soon as possible. Other organs, notably corneas, heart valves, bone and, in some cases, skin, remain viable for a number of hours after the circulation has ceased, but also require saline irrigation and chilling as soon as possible.

Potential major organ donors are usually patients who have suffered a severe head injury or a stroke, but whose circulation and respiratory system can be satisfactorily maintained until the organs can be removed. Such donors should be under the age of 60 years, free of any transmissible disease, such as hepatitis B or HIV infection, and be in generally good health with no history of dementia, or of alcohol or drug abuse. Previous multiple blood transfusions preclude blood donation, but not necessarily donation of organs or tissues, because pre-transplantation screening for infections, including CJD (new variant Creutzfeldt–Jakob disease), is now available.

Brainstem death and selection of donors

There is no UK statutory definition of 'death'. The medical criteria for the definition of brainstem death were laid down in 1979 by a joint working party of the Royal Colleges (Conference of Medical Royal Colleges 1979) and standard protocols for its diagnosis are followed in every hospital. The brainstem, which connects the main part of the brain to the spinal cord, is the site of the centres which control heart beat, respiration and other vital body functions. These centres are damaged irreversibly when the brain swells, as a consequence of injury or disease, and the brainstem is compressed against the base of the skull. Life cannot then be maintained without artificial support.

The potential donor is examined by two independent consultants, not directly involved in the patient's management. They must satisfy themselves that there is no potentially reversible cause (e.g. drugs) for the patient's condition, that all the most basic reflexes, e.g. cough, gag, corneal and vestibular, have been lost, and that no spontaneous breathing occurs when the ventilator is disconnected. These tests must be carried out at least twice over a period of several hours. Electroencephalography (EEG testing) is of doubtful value, as many cases have been reported where a heavily sedated patient showed no signs of electrical activity, but electrical activity returned as the drugs were metabolised. It is no longer included in the criteria used in the UK. After the first set of tests have proved positive for brainstem death, it is appropriate to begin making plans for organ or tissue donation as soon as possible. Tests of liver, kidney and lung function are performed, and the necessary consent is sought from the next-of-kin (Pallis and Hartley 1996).

If the impending death is 'natural' and the attending doctor will be able to issue a death certificate, there will be no need to refer the case to the Coroner, and the procedure is fairly straightforward.

The next-of-kin should be approached sympathetically and given time to adjust to the situation. Many are helped to a decision by the knowledge that someone else is to be helped. Their written consent should be fully informed, and only obtained after detailed discussions and explanations of the procedure have taken place. If multiple organ 'harvesting' is being considered, the hospital administrators should be advised. They can then keep the media at bay and protect the family's privacy. Under no circumstances should the name of the donor or the recipient be made public by the hospital; if the relatives wish to do so, that is their affair.

Donation when the Coroner is involved

In cases of 'unnatural' death, where the Coroner is involved, the situation is more complex. Such cases may include victims of road traffic accidents or assaults, where charges of murder or manslaughter may follow. The Coroner's position is clear. He requires an autopsy to establish the cause of death. He, and the criminal courts, also require assurances as to the normality of the organs which have been removed, lest the defence put forward the hypothesis that the death may have been contributed to, or even caused by, some pre-existing illness. In the years which immediately followed the introduction of renal transplantation, several homicide defences were attempted on the grounds that it was switching off life support or the removal of the kidneys which caused the death, rather than the initial assault. This was eventually tested by the courts and rejected.

The case should be discussed with the Coroner and his pathologist beforehand. Ideally, the pathologist who is to carry out the autopsy should consult with the clinician in charge of the case, see the patient on the ward, and be present at the removal of the organs. If this is not possible, the surgeon performing the operation must prepare a statement declaring that there were no abnormalities or pre-existing diseases which might have contributed to the patient's condition. Likewise, a victim of a head injury assault may show no external injuries to the trunk, but internal bruising or bleeding may be found around the abdominal organs when the harvesting operation is commenced. In such a case, the harvesting will be almost certainly be abandoned; these other injuries may be highly relevant to the prosecuting authorities in the preparation of their case. The involvement of the Coroner does not remove the need to seek the next-of-kin's consent to donation. The Coroner can only authorise removal by the pathologist of those parts 'which may be relevant to the cause of death' (see above, and Chapter 4). The removal of organs for donation (or for research) is not covered by coronial legislation; it is subject, as in natural deaths, to the Human Tissue Act (2004). Similarly, removal of tissues such as corneas, heart valves, bone, skin or other tissue from bodies undergoing coronial autopsy still requires the consent of the next-of-kin. This is usually fairly easy to obtain in 'hospital' deaths. Consent for removal of such tissue in deaths occurring in the community is more difficult to obtain, particularly when they were sudden and unexpected, but many Coroners'

Officers are extremely helpful in arranging meetings between the relatives and the appropriate health care staff.

Live donors and commercial issues

The use of volunteer living kidney donors has been discouraged for many years but, in April 1989, the British press reported that Turkish citizens were being recruited, flown to London, and were there selling their kidneys for transplantation to unrelated recipients. Three doctors subsequently appeared before the General Medical Council and were found guilty of 'serious professional misconduct' (Dyer 1990). The publicity which these cases attracted resulted in the passing of the Human Organ Transplant Act (1989) (HOTA). Although the Act's principal purpose was to control the removal of kidneys from live donors, the allied Human Organ Transplants (Supply of Information) Regulations, which came into force on 1 April 1989, applied equally to cadaver material. Any doctor who removed any relevant organ or tissue from a dead or living person, for purposes of transplantation, had to supply information to the Unrelated Human Live Transplant Regulating Authority (ULTRA), administered by the South West Regional Health Authority (SWRHA), as to where and when the organ or tissue was removed. The functions of HOTA are now filled by the Human Tissue Authority (since April 2005) through NHS UK Transplant.

The transplant coordinator

All NHS regions have a nominated transplant coordinator, who should be consulted whenever donation is being contemplated. The coordinator will not only provide all the advice needed and protocols to be followed. He or she will initiate the matching process, which extends throughout the majority of European countries, and will arrange for the appropriate transplant team's attendance to remove and transport the organs. Most regions now issue a handbook, which sets out the criteria to be followed and provides the name(s) of the appropriate coordinators and transplant units. Finally, various self-help groups, especially for kidney donors, will provide counsel and support for the relatives during the period of decision-making, and in the days following donation. The national umbrella organisation, BODY, maintains a regularly updated website, a telephone help-line, and publishes a range of helpful leaflets, which provide guidance upon every aspect of organ donation (BODY-UK website accessed 2005) (see Appendix A).

'Leaving my body to science': donation to an anatomy department

The Anatomy Act (1984) and the regulations (1988) have been superseded by the Human Tissue Act (2004), which now regulates the inspection and regulatory functions of HM Inspector of Anatomy. Anatomical dissection for teaching purposes no longer occupies a large part of the early years of undergraduate medical training, but all medical schools in the UK require some donated bodies, though fewer than formerly. A body donated for dissection is embalmed upon reception. The Act requires that every piece of tissue, no matter how small, be retained and replaced with the body at the time of its release. If a whole organ is retained for museum display or prosection, it must be anonymised, and specific consent obtained from the next-of-kin. The body must be given a simple funeral, by either burial or cremation, within three years of its reception, with funeral rites appropriate to the religion of the deceased. The medical school pays for this. Many medical schools now hold a multi-denominational bi-annual service of thanksgiving, to which the relatives are invited. Donated bodies must be whole and not autopsied, and must be free of significant disease or deformity. They must not have lost organs by donation (except corneas) or previous major surgery. Those wishing to consider donation should contact the nearest medical school. The staff member who holds the office of Licensed Teacher of Anatomy will send the appropriate forms and answer any questions. Until April 2006, donation may also be arranged centrally through the Office of HM Inspector of Anatomy, which has both a 24 hour telephone line and a website (HM Inspector of Anatomy 2005). After April 2006, the Chief Executive of the Human Tissue Authority will coordinate the procedure. (See HM Inspector of Anatomy in Appendix A.) If donation is arranged, one should ensure that one's relatives are aware of the intended donation. They should also know the whereabouts of the forms, and should be in a position to contact the receiving medical school as soon as possible after death.

References

Anatomy Act (1832) 2 & 3 William IV ss.2 et seq.

Anatomy Act (1984) c 14 ss.2–5.

Anatomy Regulations (1988) S.I. 1988 No.44. London: HMSO

BODY-UK: national transplant support group; http://body.orpheusweb.co.uk (accessed 12 March 2006).

Civil Partnership Act (2004) c 33 all sections.

Conference of Medical Colleges and their Faculties in the United Kingdom (1979) 'Diagnosis of brainstem death.' British Medical Journal 1, 332.

Coroners (Amendment) Rules (2005) s.i. 420.

Coroners Rules (1984) s.i. 552 rule 9.

Department of Health (2001) The Inquiry into the Management and Care of Children Receiving Complex Cardiac Surgery at the Bristol Royal Infirmary 1984–1995. Cm 5207. London: The Stationery Office.

Department of Health (2004) Medicines for Human Use (Clinical Trials) Regulations 2004. SI 2004/1031.

Dobson and another v North Tyneside Health Authority (1996) 4 All ER 474.

Doodeward v Spence (1908) 6 CLR 406.

Dyer, C. (1990) 'GMC's decision on "kidneys for sale".' British Medical Journal 300, 961–962.

HM Inspector of Anatomy (2003) The Isaacs Report. The Investigation of Events that Followed the Death of Mark Isaacs. London: Department of Health.

HM Inspector of Anatomy (2005) *Donating Your Body for Anatomical Dissection.* www.dh.gov
.uk/PolicyAndGuidance/HealthAndSocialCareTopics/HMAnatomy/HMAnatomyGeneral
Information/HMAnatomyGeneralArticle/fs/en?CONTENT_ID=4118498&chk=piqbQU (accessed 12 March 2006).

Human Organ Transplantation Act (1989) c 31 ss.2–3.

Human Tissue Act (1961).

Human Tissue Act (2004) c 30 all sections.

Offences Against the Person Act (1861) c 100 ss.18 *et seq.*

Pallis, C. and Hartley, D.H. (1996) *ABC of Brain Stem Death*, 2nd edn. London: BMJ Publishing Group.

Redfearn, M. (2003) *The Royal Liverpool Children's Hospital Inquiry Report.* London: The Stationery
Office.

Williams v Williams (1882) 20 ChD 659.

CHAPTER 10

THE LAW AND PRACTICE OF EXHUMATION

History

Exhumation is the disinterment of a body from an earth burial or its removal from a vault. A dead body belongs to no-one, and the 'body snatchers', who supplied anatomy schools prior to the Anatomy Act (1832), relied upon this view for protection from prosecution (Richardson 1989). In 1867, the situation was clearly set out in *Foster v Dodd* by Byles J. 'A dead body belongs to no-one, and is therefore under the protection of the public...indignities offered to human remains in improperly and indecently disinterring them are the ground for an indictment.' In 1880, this principle was extended to protect remains disinterred during formal excavations (*R v Jacobson* 1880); this decision led to the Disused Burial Grounds Act of 1884, and subsequent amending legislation, most recently in 1981. Because of the activities of souvenir hunters on land and at sea, the Military Remains Act (1986) extends legal prohibition of unauthorised digging and diving on the sites of crashed aircraft and sunken wrecks, forbidding the taking of remains from them.

Exhumation is only permissible for one of five reasons:

1. To re-inter the body elsewhere in accordance with the wishes of the deceased or his relatives.

2. To clear a redundant burial ground for redevelopment.

3. On the order of the Home Office or a Coroner so that death might be further investigated.

4. Rarely, for the recovery of papers or property from the coffin or to confirm the identity of the deceased (Smale 2004).

5. A new circumstance arose in 2005, consequent upon new techniques in DNA identification. Researchers in the USA applied to Church of England authorities for permission to take a sample of bone from a grave in a Sussex church. The skeleton lying there was known to be that of the sister of one of the founders of the settlement of Jamestown. A skeleton, thought to be his, was recovered in 2004, and it was hoped to confirm the relationship, and thus the identity, by DNA matching. At the time of writing, the results of the tests have not been published.

Exhumation is less common than formerly in the UK. It occurs more often on the European continent and in those countries where the investigation of the circumstances surrounding a sudden death is, on the whole, more perfunctory than in England and Wales. In Germany and France, the examining magistrate, or his equivalent, usually takes the view that if a death is not suspicious, the body may be released summarily for disposal. If subsequent allegations are made, exhumation becomes necessary. Under the coronial system (see Chapter 4) more detailed initial inquiries are made. If the recommendations of the Home Office Fundamental Review or the Shipman Inquiry are implemented, even more stringent checks will be made before disposal can take place. More effective investigation of deaths in the community, the decline in allegations of homicidal poisoning, the popularity of cremation, and the slowing in the pace of new building on sites where unrecorded burial grounds were often unexpectedly discovered have all contributed to the decline in the practice.

Lawful authority for exhumation may be granted only by a Coroner, the Home Secretary or, under ecclesiastical law, by a 'faculty' granted by an ordinary of the Church of England (e.g. the Bishop of the Diocese). Without such authority, disinterment is contrary to common law and to the Burial Act, 1857. If the body lies in consecrated ground, it is also an ecclesiastical offence. The removal of bodies (and memorial stones) from disused burial grounds, under the provisions of the Disused Burial Grounds (Amendment) Act (1981) or the Town and Country Planning Act (1990), does not require the involvement of the Coroner or the Home Secretary. Such bodies must be appropriately re-interred or cremated. It should be noted that the regulations for the cremation of exhumed bodies are complex, depending upon the circumstances of the exhumation and the length of time for which the body has been interred. Advice should be sought from the local crematorium superintendent in each specific case. Due records of the disinterment and of the subsequent disposal must be added to the original register of burials, using permanent red ink.

Exhumation under the authority of the Secretary of State (Home Office)

These are rare. They are usually carried out for the same reasons as those outlined above, for example to re-inter elsewhere, or to recover property. Such authority is required when the body is buried in unconsecrated ground, for example a Local Authority graveyard. An application is made in prescribed form by a close relative. This requires the answers to fourteen questions. These include the relationship of the applicant to the deceased, the subject's name and age, the date and cause of death, and the place of interment. The application must confirm the lack of objection by other relatives. Finally, the reasons for the exhumation must be stated, as must the intended proposals for the re-interment or other disposal of the body (Smale 2004).

Exhumation by order of the Coroner

The ancient common law right of the Coroner to order exhumation is not extinguished by the Burial Act (1857); furthermore, his right to so order overrules ecclesiastical law. He does not require the Secretary of State's authority but, in practice, the Home Office is almost always consulted. If the Coroner has already completed an inquest, his right to make such an order is extinguished; Home Office authority is required. The Coroner has the power to order an exhumation for the purpose of his holding an inquest and/or for the purpose of any criminal proceedings which might be instituted, or are being contemplated, in respect of the death of that person, or some other person, in circumstances which may be related (Coroners Act 1988, s.23).

The Coroner must satisfy himself that there are reasonable grounds for exhumation. He will consult with the police and the Home Office upon this, and the exhumation must take place 'within a reasonable time of burial'. In this matter he is allowed wide discretion. Modern techniques which can detect certain poisons (for example, arsenic or thallium) have been available for many years, so time alone is no longer any bar to exhumation if death by poisoning is suspected. More recently, it has become possible to demonstrate the presence of opiates, such as morphine and many of its derivatives, in human remains which have been buried for a considerable period, whether embalmed or not (Worm, Steentoft and Christensen 1983). These techniques were successfully employed in the examination of patients of Dr Harold Shipman in 2000 (Pounder 2003), although, at present, the demonstration of these drugs has not been possible in bodies buried for more than four years.

The most common reason for the Coroner to order an exhumation nowadays is because an allegation of homicide has been made. However, allegations of mismanagement in hospital, for example overdoses of prescription drugs in patients detained in mental hospitals, has provided the grounds for further investigation in certain cases.

There is no provision for re-interment in the Coroner's 'Warrant to Exhume'. In practice, if the disposal had originally been by the authority of the Registrar, the Coroner would simply issue his burial order. If the body had already been the subject of a Coroner's burial order, this is amended to include the words, 'remains which have been exhumed by me'. (There is no longer a requirement for the Coroner to view the exhumed body, and so the form of words 'which has been exhumed and viewed by me' is no longer used.)

The practice of exhumation

The police usually handle the arrangements for exhumation. A suitable time, traditionally early morning, convenient to all parties, is arranged. An official of the cemetery or churchyard attends and formally identifies the grave from the registers available to him; if possible, the funeral director who had charge of the original interment identifies the coffin when it has been exposed. The pathologist and forensic scientist, with a police exhibits officer in attendance, supervise the digging, the collection of samples, and the raising of the coffin. Video and photographic records of the proceedings are taken. The police will have already provided appropriate screens, and will have arranged transport to a suitably equipped mortuary, where the examination can be made as soon as is possible. Exhumation always attracts the interest of the media. The police will ensure that no intrusion by photographers or reporters takes place, and that appropriate press briefings are given at intervals throughout the enquiry.

Samples of soil from above, below and to either side of the coffin are collected. Any fluid is drained off from the coffin and is also collected. If standing water is present in the grave, a sample of this is also collected. All of these are appropriately labelled and recorded. On arrival at the mortuary the coffin lid is removed and the identity of the body is formally confirmed by a relative or other appropriate person, provided putrefaction is not so far advanced as to render viewing deeply distressing and unreliable. Samples of the shroud, the coffin lining and of the coffin itself are collected, depending upon the circumstances. Many recently interred bodies have been embalmed or 'sanitised', which enhances preservation (see Chapter 7).

A meticulous autopsy is then performed. With care, even minor injuries such as injection marks can often be found. A detailed internal examination is made. Samples of tissue are taken for microscopy and for analysis; radiological and dental examinations may also be required. It is now possible to identify even badly decomposed and long buried bodies, using special techniques for the extraction of mitochondrial DNA from bones. Several members of the Russian Royal Family, murdered in 1919, were identified in this way in the 1990s. The bone marrow of members of the crew of a trawler, lost with all hands in 1974, still had demonstrable DNA when their remains were recovered in 2001 (Steel 2004). Such analyses are rendered difficult for interpretation by the presence of 'background' DNA from fungi and bacteria, and so require examination by highly skilled and experienced personnel.

When the initial examination has been completed, the body should be deep frozen until all the enquiries and tests have been brought to a satisfactory conclusion. Only then should the body be released, encoffined (in a new one if necessary), and disposed of, in accordance with the relatives' wishes. The Coroner will rarely permit cremation of a body which has been exhumed. He will be mindful of the serious allegations which have led to the exhumation, and to the fact that the defence, or other interested parties, may require even further examinations. Furthermore, the legality of such a procedure is uncertain, as there is provision in the existing legislation only for re-burial.

The procedure to be followed for Scotland differs only in minor detail. If crime is suspected, an order for the exhumation of the remains is issued by the Sheriff on the petition of the Procurator Fiscal (see Chapter 4). Private exhumations, for example for re-interment elsewhere, are authorised by the Sheriff or Court of Session upon the application of a near relative. This application must fulfil similar criteria to those embodied in the Home Office application described above. In matters of alleged crime, public concern, or where the body is that of a foreign national which is to be repatriated, the concurrence of the Lord Advocate must also be obtained.

Health and safety aspects of exhumation

It is our opinion that exhumation and work in graveyards generally poses little risk. In 1970, more than 60 bodies, which had been inhumed in a vault in Huddersfield, Yorkshire, since the early 19th century, were exhumed. Microbiological cultures produced no growth of any pathogenic organisms; only normal soil bacteria and fungi were present. In particular, neither anthrax nor tubercle bacilli were found. The risks of infection by persistent viruses, such as smallpox, are also very small. All the virological studies undertaken during the Huddersfield study were negative (Green 2006).

The risks attendant upon the exhumation of bodies recently buried are no greater than those of gardening. Tetanus bacilli may be present in the soil of a graveyard, as in any domestic vegetable garden, so workers should receive regular tetanus prophylaxis. Cuts and grazes should be promptly cleaned and properly dressed. Antibiotic cover and the wearing of masks are *not* required. Suitable coveralls, stout footwear and gloves are all that are needed.

References

Anatomy Act (1832).

Burial Act (1857) 20 and 21 Victoria c 81.

Coroners Act (1988) s.23.

Disused Burial Grounds Act (1884) 47 and 48 Victoria ch 72.

Disused Burial Grounds (Amendment) Act (1981) ss.1, 2 *et seq.*

Foster v Dodd (1867) LR3. QB67 p.77.

Green, M.A. (2006) '19th Century Pathology; the examination of 83 vault interred bodies.' *Forensic Science Medicine and Pathology 2*, 1, 19–24.

Military Remains Act (1986).

Pounder, D.J. (2003) 'The case of Dr Shipman.' *American Journal of Forensic Medicine and Pathology 24*, 3, 219–226.

R v Jacobson (1880) 14 CoxCC 522.

Richardson, R. (1989) *Death, Dissection and the Destitute.* London: Pelican Books.

Smale, D.A. (2004) *Davies' Law of Burial, Cremation and Exhumation*, 7th edn. London: Shaw and Sons.

Steel, J. (2004) *Report of the Reopened Formal Investigation into the Loss of the FV Gaul.* London: The Stationery Office.

Town and Country Planning Act (1990).

Worm, K., Steentoft, A., and Christensen, H. (1983) 'Experiences in interpretation with exhumed material illustrated by a single case of morphine intoxication.' *Journal of the Forensic Science Society 23*, 3, 209–212.

CHAPTER 11

DEATHS IN MAJOR DISASTERS

What constitutes a major disaster?

There is no easy definition of a major disaster. Perhaps any incident which overwhelms the emergency services available in the health district involved is a reasonable one. For many years, Health Districts, Local Authorities, police and emergency services have conducted mass disaster exercises. All too often, the planning for the living was realistic, but that for the dead was either 'notional' or non-existent (Edwards, Donaldson and Wade 2003).

Recent events have evoked a new international awareness of the problems (Cabinet Office 2005; National Audit Office 2002). On 11 September 2001, the twin towers of the World Trade Center in New York were destroyed by a terrorist attack, in which commercial aircraft were flown into their upper storeys. More than 4000 lives were lost in the initial fire and the subsequent collapse of the skyscrapers. Others jumped to their deaths, rather than await the inevitable. Many of the bodies were severely mutilated by burning or crush injury; many others were vaporised in the intense heat and never recovered. Identification was further compromised by putrefaction over the days and weeks which followed. The event led to worldwide reviews of disaster planning, and these efforts to provide internationally coordinated responses were tested to the full on 24 December 2004, when a tsunami, a massive tidal wave consequent upon an earthquake, devastated the coastal districts of Sri Lanka, Indonesia, Thailand, and other countries of the Pacific Rim. It is believed that nearly 300,000 perished, but many bodies were never recovered, and of those that were, very large numbers were not identified before mass interments took place.

This incident in particular highlighted many of the problems which beset planners. No matter how generous and timely the provision of personnel and material aid, if the local transport infrastructure has been destroyed, their deployment and distribution are brought to a halt. Those local facilities which survive, and which were not designed to cope with such large-scale tragedy in the first place, are overwhelmed. In Phuket, Thailand, for example, forensic investigation teams from no less than 19 countries arrived, within days of the disaster, to find that only one useable mortuary facility remained.

Planning for large-scale disasters

Planning for such large-scale disasters is beyond the scope of this book, but the general principles of planning and management remain the same. The UK experience has been on a much smaller scale. The Zeebrugge ferry sinking in 1989 (Marine Accident Investigation Board 1990) and the air crashes at Lockerbie (Busuttil 1988) and Kegworth in 1989 (Air Accident Investigation Board 1990) gave new urgency to planning for mass fatalities. The Hillsborough, Sheffield, football stadium disaster (Home Office 1989) was a timely reminder that mass transportation is not the only scenario which has to be considered. These incidents gave impetus to a new and more coordinated approach. Many counties and metropolitan authorities have now set aside designated temporary mortuary facilities, established first response teams, and conduct regular exercises for dealing with the dead, as well as the living.

Even a hotel fire or a coach crash can seriously disrupt the services provided by a smaller Local Authority. In 1995, a 20-seater passenger aircraft crashed in North Yorkshire, a large but sparsely populated county, with proportionately small emergency services. They were stretched to their limits. The lessons learned were incorporated into a training video, which is still of great value (North Yorkshire Police Authority 1996). The incidents referred to above also led to the formation of groups of bereaved relatives, whose statements have stressed the importance of sensitive and speedy identification and disposal procedures, with prolonged counselling thereafter. Their advice has been incorporated into the preparation of recent Disaster Manuals (National Audit Office 2002). In July 2005, four suicide bombers simultaneously attacked crowded trains on the London Underground and a bus in central London (Chen 2005; Easton 2005). Over 50 people were killed. Many of the bodies were disrupted by the force of the explosions, affected by fire and, as the days went by, by putrefaction. Although the numbers killed and injured were relatively small, the difficult environments in which the attacks took place tested the emergency services to the full. Body recovery was complete within five days. Nearly all the victims, and the four bombers, were identified within two weeks. Identification required DNA matching, in some cases, and was inevitably slow. Although these delays added to the distress of relatives, it was better that identification of all the bodies should be complete and accurate before any were released for disposal.

The medico-legal investigation of mass fatalities has to reconcile two conflicting areas of concern. On the one hand, the authorities seek to glean as much information as possible about the circumstances of the incident. It is important to treat every such incident as a major crime scene, and to ascertain not only who was there, but by what right, in what position in relation to the central event, and what natural diseases, drugs or extraneous factors, such as fumes, fire or explosion, may have caused or contributed to the deaths. The relatives, on the other hand, want – and need – early confirmation of the identity, and the release, of each body so that appropriate funeral rites may be observed and their grieving processes may commence. It is now generally accepted that those families who have to wait longest have the most protracted and severe problems of adjustment and acceptance of their loss.

The aim of this chapter is to reconcile these widely divergent objectives, and to offer planning suggestions for medical and nursing staff, managers, police and emergency services. It draws heavily upon experience gained from the disasters at Kegworth, Hillsborough and in North Yorkshire, and upon the most recent Royal College of Pathologists' monograph (2002) on the subject. Only a general outline of the preparations and procedures to be followed will be given. Detailed MAJAX operational policy documents already exist in every police and Local Authority area (or should do) for the emergency organisations concerned, including hospitals, and are regularly reviewed and updated.

The first priority at any major incident is the rescue of the living. The dead can wait. At the outset, plans should have been made for the recovery of the dead by other services, so that valuable ambulance space is not wasted. The bodies should be removed to a temporary mortuary at a previously selected location, some considerable distance from the admitting hospitals, so that their approach roads and car parks are not obstructed. Ideally, a cadre of suitably experienced doctors (forensic medical examiners (FMEs) or members of a volunteer casualty organisation such as BASICS) should be available to certify death at the scene, so that planned and phased removal is facilitated. It is now increasingly accepted that appropriately trained paramedic staff can also fulfil this function.

Those concerned should ask, 'Must the dead be removed now; should the dead be removed now?' In an aviation accident or explosion, for example, hasty removal of bodies, limbs or even fragments of human tissue, without adequate recording of their positions, may seriously compromise subsequent investigation. Misguided placing of nearby personal belongings with a body may delay and confuse identification. For these reasons, and many others, it may be prudent simply to guard the scene and wait for daylight – and for the mobilisation of adequate numbers of skilled helpers.

The role of the pathologist

In every district, an experienced forensic pathologist should have been nominated as a controller. His name and contact details should be known to the Coroner, police and emergency services. He should be immediately available at all times, and should provide nominated deputies.

He should have planned ahead. In consultation with the Coroner, police and emergency services, he should ensure that bearers, extra mortuary staff, odontologists, radiographers and other personnel have been identified and rehearsed in their respective roles. In any fatal aviation accident, staff from the Institute of Aviation Pathology (RAF Henlow, Beds SG16 6DN) will conduct the major part of the medical enquiry. The 24/24 telephone number is 01462 851515. The local pathologist's initial duty is to preserve evidence until these skilled reinforcements arrive.

In any disaster, the pathologist must complete the following tasks on behalf of the Coroner or Procurator Fiscal:

1.   Assist in the identification of every victim.

2.   Establish the nature of the injuries and cause of death of every victim, and identify any relevant pre-existing medical condition.

3.   Collect and retain any sample which may be relevant to the investigation (Coroners Rules 1984, Rule 9; see Chapter 4).

4.   Complete all these examinations with minimum delay, so that bodies may be released early, but only after full investigation. Great caution must be exercised here. In the Lockerbie disaster several bodies had to be recalled after their release to the funeral directors, which caused much unnecessary distress and embarrassment.

Facilities required

'REAL ESTATE'

The concerned authorities and health care professionals should, in consultation with the supervising pathologist, have identified in advance an appropriate building to be used as a mortuary. This must be on a single site, otherwise relatives may have to visit more than one, delays in identification may occur, and trace evidence may be lost. It should be dedicated solely to the incident; the use of an existing mortuary merely impedes the investigation of routine deaths in the community, spreading the distress even more widely.

The facility should be large, with an adequate running water supply and other essential services. It should be private and secure, yet easy of access. There should be adjacent office space, and a rest area for the staff, a viewing area with privacy for the relatives, adequate secure property storage and a large parking area, so that temporary mobile refrigeration can be provided. There must also be a large, well-ventilated embalming and preparation area. Victims of an air, or other transportation, accident may come from all over the world. The bodies must be embalmed and encoffined to the high standards demanded in accordance with international air transport regulations, before their repatriation can take place. Warehouses, gymnasia, redundant chapels, and commercial garages have all been successfully used. RAF stations are ideal. An aircraft hangar makes an excellent mortuary; office accommodation and a communications network are already in place, and armed services personnel are highly skilled at persuading intruders from the media to keep an appropriate distance. Local wholesale meat factors can provide refrigerated trucks. The Army (Regular and TA Reserve) can provide vehicles, portable generators, and manpower. They also may provide military ambulances, thus releasing the civilian ambulance service to attend to the living. In our experience, they welcome such requests, which provide valuable training for their troops.

FLOW PLANS

Every aspect of the operation, from the scene to the final release of the bodies to their relatives, should have been planned in advance. The composition of the search and recovery teams should have been agreed and their equipment decided upon. This should include marker pegs, waterproof labels and document cases, body and exhibit bags, and stationery. It is usually the simple items of hardware which run short.

Protocols should have been agreed for the layout of the reception area, for removal of clothing and external examination, for odontological and radiological examination, and for the autopsy proper. Every item of clothing and property must be carefully logged and securely stored. Never forget that every incident is a crime scene until the investigation is complete. Furthermore, distressed relatives are often quick to make allegations of theft. After autopsy, arrangements for disposal of the body may be handled by mortuary staff and individual funeral directors, but only after the Coroner's appropriate authority for release has been obtained, and an appropriate release register has been signed.

In many major transportation incidents, contract funeral directors, employed by the carriers or the embassies of the nationals involved, may assume responsibility for repatriation. Identification is the most urgent need, and must be established beyond doubt before any release of a body and connected property is permitted. An adequately staffed and equipped casualty identification bureau, whose staff collates every piece of information, is central to the investigation. It is here that photographs, dental records and other information, for example records of a previous surgical operation, are sorted and the information passed to the mortuary teams.

PERSONNEL AND PUBLIC RELATIONS

It has often been said that 'one volunteer is worth ten pressed men'. This is certainly true of mass fatalities. Multiple deaths, even in the relatively small numbers seen in a coach accident, are deeply distressing to anyone, no matter how wide his experience. The effects upon young and inexperienced police officers, servicemen or health care professionals can be severe. Signs of distress may be immediately obvious. One of the advantages of having a forensic pathologist, or other doctor, on-site coordinating the recovery operation is that he or she is (or should be) able to recognise these early warning signs and tactfully arrange for the person concerned to be redeployed to other duties. Many of the younger and inexperienced workers cannot cope with the sights experienced by the search team, or with the duties of bearers at the scene and in the mortuary. A nominal roll of experienced Coroners' Officers (or retired Coroners' Officers), ambulance and other emergency workers should be maintained against need. Provided appropriate medical supervision has been provided through every phase of the operation, the incidence of long-term problems, such as flashbacks or post-traumatic stress disorder (PTSD), should be very low.

Each search and recovery team should comprise a pathologist, a scribe (with knowledge of medical terminology), a police photographer, an exhibits officer, and two bearers. Each mortuary reception team should also include a pathologist, a police officer, a photographer and sufficient bearers to give frequent rest breaks.

Other professionals should have been 'hand-picked' in advance. Most radiographers, for example, have never seen a dead body, let alone a mutilated and/or burnt one.

The manning of the Casualty Identification Bureau also requires careful thought. Its staff should be skilled in communication, both face to face and by telephone. They should be meticulous in their recording and processing of information; they should have the medical and dental knowledge necessary to collect and collate the technical data as it becomes available; and they should, these days, be computer literate.

The ongoing care of the relatives requires special skills. In Australia, some large coronial departments employ social workers who are specially trained in grief and bereavement counselling; perhaps Local Authorities in the UK should give thought to this, for these workers also play a valuable role in the management of routine sudden death. Formal training in bereavement skills is now available for Coroners' Officers. The University of Teesside offers a diploma course. Such training may become mandatory in the near future (see Chapter 4 for recommendations on reform of the Coroners' Service).

Tea, coffee, comfortable surroundings and, above all, simple warmth and humanity are priceless assets, and the abilities of voluntary organisations, such as the St John Ambulance Service, the WRVS and local religious groups, in catering to the needs of both workers and visiting relatives should not be underestimated. Plans should be made to deal with the media. An appointed spokesperson should be their only channel of communication. They will frequently attempt to obtain information from all the persons involved in the mortuary operation. All staff should be warned against this. Under no circumstances should any media filming or photography be permitted in or around the mortuary, the identification bureau or the viewing area and its approaches.

This book is not the place for a detailed equipment list. The Royal College of Pathologists monograph (2002) and existing local plans should be consulted.

Finally, the importance of planning and practice cannot be over-emphasised. Every MAJAX exercise should practise the evacuation, reception, throughput and disposal of the dead; appropriate mortuary facilities should be identified and regularly reviewed; stockpiles of equipment and stationery should be regularly checked. Most importantly, the personnel lists should be regularly reviewed and updated, and all those involved, particularly volunteers, should be given regular opportunities to meet and get to know each other. Previous acquaintance forms the basis of the team-building, mutual support, trust, and self-knowledge, without which the most carefully laid plan will founder when tested by the 'real thing'.

References

Air Accident Investigation Board (1990) *No 4/90 Boeing 737-400 GOMBE near Kegworth, Leicestershire.* London: The Stationery Office.

Busuttil, A. (1988) 'Lockerbie and Dunblane: disasters and dilemmas.' *Medico Legal Journal 4,* 126–140.

Cabinet Office (2005) *UK Resilience; The Cabinet Office Civil Contingencies Secretariat.* Available at http://ukresilience.info/home.htm (accessed 19 July 2005).

Chen, A.W.Y. (2005) 'The London Bombings: a hospital doctor's experience.' *British Medical Journal 331,* 166.

Easton, G. (2005) 'Are there any doctors here?' *British Medical Journal 331,* 167.

Edwards, A., Donaldson, O. and Wade, E. (2003) 'Medical staff must be aware of major incident planning.' *British Medical Journal 326,* 2063.

Home Office (1989) *The Hillsborough Stadium Disaster 15th April 1989: Inquiry by the Rt Hon Mr Justice Taylor. Final Report.* London: HMSO.

Marine Accident Investigation Board (1990) *MV Herald of Free Enterprise: Report of Court No 8074.* London: The Stationery Office.

National Audit Office (2002) *Facing the Challenge: NHS Emergency Planning in England.* London: NAO.

North Yorkshire Police Authority (1996) *A Small Major Disaster: The Dunkeswick Air Crash 1996.* Northallerton: North Yorkshire Police Television Department.

Royal College of Pathologists (2002) *Major Disasters: The Pathologist's Role,* 2nd edn. London: RCPath.

PART 2

Considerations for the Living, Care of the Dying, and Death with Dignity

CHAPTER 12

PALLIATIVE CARE

To palliate, from the Latin *pallium*, a cloak, means to lessen the severity of pain or disease, without producing a cure.

The terminally ill patient is one whose death is certain and not too far distant. Until recently, in Britain, there would probably have been a fairly abrupt change, from therapeutic to palliative care, when death appeared to be imminent and continued active treatment deemed futile. Nowadays, relevant palliative care services should ideally be available, to those who need them, from the time of diagnosis of the life-limiting illness, up to, during and immediately after death. They should be offered in conjunction with therapies intended to prolong life, such as chemotherapy, radiotherapy or surgical procedures.

The philosophy of the palliative care approach is to neither hasten nor postpone death, but to enable dying people to live in physical comfort, with personal dignity, until death. It encompasses the holistic concept of physical, social, psychological and spiritual care for the patient and for those closest to him. Dying is a normal and ultimately inevitable process, and the patient is offered a support system to help them live as active a life as possible until death. The needs of patients and those closest to them are assessed and served by a variety of health and social care professionals in an ongoing and coordinated way.

Over the last 20 years or so, palliative care in the UK has developed into a speciality in its own right. It embraces symptom control and the social, psychological and spiritual aspects of care over an extended period of time and not just the last few days or weeks of the 'terminal' period. Initially, most palliative care was directed to cancer patients, but there is now a clear recognition that people with many other chronic illnesses may need access to similar services at the end of their lives. At the time of writing there are over 300 specialist trained palliative care consultants in the National Health Service, as well as university funded medical posts and training posts in hospices. Nurses skilled and trained in palliative care are increasingly recognised as an extremely valuable resource. There are over 2500 trained Macmillan nurses, most working in the NHS, all of whom have at least five years' general nursing experience plus two years' experience working in cancer care or palliative care. Much palliative care work is carried out by general practitioners, with varying levels of expertise and interest. All these individuals will consider themselves part of the local palliative care team.

Palliative care may be delivered in many different ways. Hospices rightly receive much publicity for the quality care they offer to the dying, but most people do not die in hospices. They die on ordinary wards in ordinary hospitals. About 30 per cent of people can expect to die at home, but most can expect to be cared for at home for the major part of the final illness. The caring will probably be done by the female members of the immediate family, mothers, daughters and sisters who regard this as a final obligation of kinship, and whose task may be eased by the appropriate provision of domiciliary services of all kinds. Often the main carers are themselves elderly and in need of support to sustain the burden of care.

In Britain, awareness of the importance of end-of-life care has grown since the late 1960s when the first hospice opened in London. St Christopher's Hospice, founded by the late Dame Cicely Saunders, offered treatment to patients with severe malignant disease, both as inpatients and as domiciliary clients. The hospice became a centre of research and teaching, particularly in the areas of symptom control and the psychosocial aspects of dying.

Other hospices followed throughout the country, and by 2003 there were 152 adult hospice inpatient units, run by voluntary organisations, and 64 NHS palliative care units for adult inpatients, together providing over 3000 beds. In addition, there were 196 beds for children in 27 units, and three units offering 64 beds for the exclusive use of those dying from HIV/AIDS. There has also been a proliferation of home and community provision, with 332 home care services, 247 day care units, 335 hospital based units and 93 hospice at home services (Hospice Information 2003). Hospices are expensive places to run and rely heavily on the local community for fund-raising, largely because of the failure of the NHS in the past to develop or adequately support this kind of service. They are labour intensive with a far higher staff-to-patient ratio than most NHS hospitals could hope to provide, although there are some NHS hospices in existence which do provide a comparable level of staffing.

Department of Health guidance

National guidance for the development of palliative care services was limited in the past. In recent years there has been much greater recognition of the need for better and more equitable services, and significant guidance has now been issued to health care commissioners and providers, together with the promise of better funding for improvements in the service. Below is a brief summary of governmental advice and instruction from 1972, when matters around death received little recognition, to 2004, when palliative care services were firmly on the national agenda.

In 1972 the DHSS memorandum (HM(72)41) *Patients Dying in Hospital* (see note below) simply gave guidance about the disposal of the bodies and effects of patients who died in NHS hospitals, where relatives were unavailable or unwilling to take that responsibility. It drew attention to the need to provide relatives with information and assistance.

It was not until 1984 that hospitals were encouraged to take a detailed look at their terminal care procedures. *Patients Dying in Hospital* (DA(84)17) was issued as a supplement to the previous memorandum, and suggested that hospitals should review their guidance to staff who may be involved when patients die, so that matters may be handled sensitively. Health Authorities were asked to draw up comprehensive written instructions on the action to be taken when a patient dies in hospital, and to ensure that these were regularly updated. The instructions were to include advice on contacting the next of kin or close friends, keeping them informed of clinical progress and the possibility of death, and enabling them to be present at the death if they so wished. The notification of death, arrangements for the transplantation of organs, removal of cardiac pacemakers, all the detail of arrangements surrounding post mortem, referral to the Coroner and death and cremation certification were included. The relatives were to be accorded privacy to view the body, and there should be regard for religious and cultural practices. The circular highlights the need for training, especially in bereavement counselling and dealing with stillbirth or infant death. It suggested that consideration be given to an existing member of staff being designated as 'bereavement officer'.

By 1987 there was already a great deal of experience of high quality terminal care and an increasing expectation that it should be more generally available. Health Circular HC(87)4, *Terminal Care*, issued in February of that year, asked Health Authorities to examine their current provision of services for the terminally ill, from whatever cause, and to plan to rectify any deficiencies, where possible in collaboration with the voluntary sector. The stated objectives of the service were: to provide special skills to terminally ill patients, their family or close friends, whether in hospital, at home or in a hospice; to control pain and other symptoms; to maintain independence; to alleviate isolation, anxiety and fear; to allow death with comfort and dignity; and to provide support for the bereaved before and after the event.

In 1989 the Royal College of Physicians gave recognition to the speciality of palliative care, and higher specialist training began for doctors in this field.

EL(90)P/10, *Funding of Hospices and Similar Organisations*, was issued in March 1990. This circular announced additional monies to enable Health Authorities to contribute to the voluntary hospice movement, eligible organisations being those who provide specialised palliative care. This money was intended to be supplementary to any funding already being donated by Health Authorities to palliative care services, and Authorities were asked to consider whether they were able to make additional contributions out of their own resources.

By 1995 there was concern over the inequalities in cancer treatment around the UK. The *Report of the Expert Advisory Group on Cancers to the Chief Medical Officers of England and Wales* (Department of Health 1995) expressed the view that some palliative care services may be required from the time of diagnosis. These should be integrated with all cancer treatment services, to provide the best quality of life for the patient and family. The report set out a framework for commissioning cancer services. This document had enormous influence on subsequent developments in palliative care.

HSG(97)43, *Patients Who Die in Hospital*, provided supplementary guidance to HSG(92)8. It set out the minimum standards for funeral, burial and cremation arrangements where NHS Trusts take responsibility for these. The NHS becomes responsible if no relatives can be traced, or if those that are contacted are unable to bear the cost, but do not qualify for Social Fund funeral payments.

Trusts are required to make a reasonable attempt to trace family. Where relatives are unwilling to pay, but the NHS has reason to believe that they could do so, the Local Authority, in which the body lies, should be asked to arrange for burial or cremation under section 46(1) of the Public Health (Control of Disease) Act 1984 (see p.197).

Trusts must take into account the views of the deceased and of any relatives, including religious preferences. If there is no known preference, cremation should be chosen. The funeral should be conducted by an appropriate minister of religion. The place of funeral service and burial should be appropriate to the faith of the deceased. The guidance also recognises that staff caring for dying patients may become very involved with the patient and family, and states that relevant staff should be given the opportunity to attend the funeral.

HSC 1998/115, *Palliative Care*, makes the important statement that 'the principles and practice of palliative care need to be integrated into the whole of NHS practice'. The benefits of significant advances in pain and symptom control should be available to all patients with life-threatening illness, wherever they are, irrespective of diagnosis. Three sets of guidelines were attached to this circular: for managing cancer pain (National Council for Hospices and Palliative Care Services 1998), for managing the last days of life in adults (NCHPCS 1997), and for palliative care in the hospital setting (NCHPCS 1996). Commissioners of health care were encouraged to work with other organisations to develop a palliative care strategy, based on the assessment of health needs and appropriate for their population.

In 2000, *The NHS Cancer Plan* (NHS Executive 2000a) recognised that the voluntary sector made a major contribution to palliative services. The plan aimed to end inequalities, and pledged an increase in funding over the subsequent three years. The NHS contribution would equal that of the voluntary sector, but all services were to work to national standards. Also in 2000, *Improving the Quality of Cancer Services* (NHS Executive 2000b) set standards for multi-disciplinary cancer services, both in hospitals and in the community.

In April 2001, a letter entitled *Education and support for district and community nurses in the general principles and practice of palliative care* requested proposals for flexible educational initiatives which demonstrated partnership between providers of palliative care education, such as palliative care teams; recipients of that education, i.e. community nursing staff; and education consortia. The aim here was to provide cancer networks with additional resources to enable patients to stay at home longer and to die there if that was their choice and if circumstances would permit.

By 2004, the National Institute for Clinical Excellence (NICE) had considered end-of-life care and published *Improving Supportive and Palliative Care for Adults with Cancer*. Apart from endorsing all the long-held principles of palliative care, it calls for more emphasis on quality issues. In NICE's view there is a need for better information and communication. Patients should receive important news from specially trained senior staff. They should also have access to a key-worker, where appropriate, to guide them through the network of services available. Cancer patients should have access to relevant services from the time of diagnosis, and those with advanced cancer should be able to access medical and nursing services 24 hours a day, seven days a week. GPs and nurses, who care for people at home, should have access to specialist advice at all times.

In July 2004, the House of Commons Health Committee reported on the state of palliative care in England and found it wanting, recommending that the NICE guidance should be fully implemented and that similar steps should be taken to ensure the good care of those who are dying from conditions other than cancer. It concludes that 'the right to "a good death" should be fundamental' and that services must operate in a far more equitable way, be delivered more strategically and bridge the gap between health and social care.

About this time, Macmillan Cancer Relief produced the *Gold Standards Framework* (Macmillan Cancer Relief 2004), to improve the organisation and quality of palliative care for patients who are at home for the last year of life. It sets standards to encourage and enable GP practices to improve such care for their patients. The standards cover communication, coordination, symptom control, continuity out-of-hours, continued learning, support of carers and care in the dying phase.

Also in 2004 the Department of Health announced a £12 million investment over three years to improve care for people coming to the end of their lives. *Building on the Best: End of Life Care Initiative* (Department of Health 2004) outlined steps to be taken to assess local needs, the mechanisms for allocating funding, and the development of a support team to coordinate and support the initiative. The aim was to 'extend the boundaries of palliative care provision by making opportunities, currently available only to cancer patients, accessible to all patients, regardless of diagnosis'. The Gold Standards Framework was to be extended to more GP practices, and the Liverpool Care Pathway for the Dying (Marie Curie 2000) used to assist staff provide hospice-type care to hospital and community settings.

Further details about many current relevant issues can be found on the website of the National Council for Palliative Care: www.ncpc.org.uk

The delivery of palliative care

Palliative care is no longer merely hospice care. There is no doubt that hospices are widely associated with high quality care in the ideal setting. But care at the end of life may be delivered in many ways, in various locations and by many different people. For many individuals, the preferred place of death would be within their own home, surrounded by their own family and friends. Available evidence suggests that over 50 per cent of patients would wish to die at home, but only about 20 per cent actually do so. In 2001, in England and Wales, 22 per cent of male deaths and 16 per cent of female deaths occurred at home. In the same year, 4 per cent of male deaths and 11 per cent of female deaths occurred in communal establishments, e.g. nursing homes (excluding hospices and hospitals). This reflects the longer life expectancy of women, as they are more likely to be widowed and to be living in residential or nursing homes at the time of death (National Statistics 2003). Home is not always the preferred place for the families and carers involved.

Services may be offered in the home throughout the illness, or patients may attend hospital or hospice for varying periods, for pain control, or for palliative procedures which improve the quality of the remaining life. They may receive care at home, in hospital or hospice for a period of respite for the carers. Final admission to hospital or hospice may be necessary because the amount of care needed is greater than circumstances will allow in the home.

Hospices may offer beds for children or adults, for long-term, day care or respite use. Hospice staff are usually deeply involved in teaching caring skills to families, carers and other health care staff, so that patients may be at home for as much of the final illness as possible. They offer bereavement support for families, often for quite a long period after the death. Private nursing homes may have specifically allocated terminal care beds for those patients requiring the extra skills, time and equipment necessary at this time.

Specialist health care staff may include nurses trained in palliative care working in the community, in daytime, night-time or as 'twilight' nurses. Marie Curie and Macmillan nurses may be part-funded by their respective charities to offer specialist care for terminally ill cancer patients. The importance of good pain and symptom control cannot be overstressed, and specialist pain clinics may be run by the hospital or the hospice. Social Service Departments provide the social and domestic support to enable a sick patient to remain comfortably in their own home. General practitioners often take a great interest in the coordination of palliative care for their patients and are increasingly involved.

Like many hospices, hospitals may have a palliative care team, offering advice and treatment in the wards and in the community. The team may include such members as consultant physician (even a specialist palliative physician), anaesthetist, Macmillan nurse, psychiatrist, psychologist, pharmacist, dietician and other relevant trained staff, and including extremely important social worker support. Hospices and hospitals increasingly seek the appointment of junior medical staff for palliative care duties as part of their specialist training. Since 1989 there have been higher specialist training opportunities for palliative care doctors in the NHS. There may be a hospice unit within the hospital, possibly with a day hospital facility. A liaison support service may be organised, whereby the liaison nurse is able to offer support to individuals and families from the time of diagnosis. This allows patients and carers the opportunities to discuss problems and fears in an unhurried manner in their own homes. Other care staff may take on a key-worker role.

Group meetings for the range of people involved in palliative care can raise relevant issues such as training, information for general practitioners, and communication between patients, relatives and staff. The palliative care team may call upon voluntary organisations for befriending or counselling or practical help. Team members may run counselling support groups for the staff involved in this work, who may find the stress of coping with dying patients and their relatives is formidable.

Caring for the dying requires much emotional currency to be spent. Some staff will prefer to work with patients who know that they are dying, and this in itself may make working in a hospice a positive experience. In a hospital ward there may be tension and anxiety concerning the patient's knowledge of his condition, and a death may be seen as a failure by the staff involved. Hospitals, public and private, may offer a similar quality of care to that in the hospice, but are unlikely to have equivalent resources and staff totally committed for this purpose. Despite recent increases in NHS funding, there is likely to be a continued requirement for the general public to dip into its pockets to sustain the hospice movement into the future.

The mix and method of the delivery of palliative care may vary widely between districts. There is no good or bad system, and issues of cost and quality must be included. Areas where deficiencies may be apparent are likely to include: lack of staff time for counselling and support for the bereaved, inadequate pain and symptom control, lack of training opportunities for all types of staff to become involved with the dying and their families, lack of awareness of ethnic minority issues, and general inexperience of the issues surrounding death. There may be an unsuitable placement for the patient because no other choice is available.

Recent national guidance and increased funding must help to improve services. The 'Gold Standards Framework' (see above), already in use in many GP practices, aims to improve the palliative care provided by the primary care team. The 'Liverpool Care Pathway for the Dying' aims to enable the best of hospice care to be transferred to other health care settings.

Symptom control

This chapter can only give a brief general overview of the principles of clinical palliative care. For detailed information a clinical text must be consulted.

The most important aspect of symptom control is anticipation and thus the prevention of symptoms.

PAIN RELIEF

Pain may be a distressing symptom, particularly for those with terminal cancers. Some 70 per cent of such patients will suffer pain, but probably 95 per cent of these can benefit considerably from skilled pain control measures, which can significantly improve the quality of life. Whilst there is now a much more scientific approach to pain relief in general (Nurmikko, Nash and Wiles 1998), the principles for palliative care remain the same. Dosage of analgesics and adjuvant therapies must be titrated against the individual's condition and symptoms, and be sufficient to prevent pain when given at regular intervals round the clock. The pain threshold will be affected by many factors and the intensity of pain may be diminished if attention is paid to such things as discomfort, insomnia, fear, sadness, depression, boredom and loneliness.

Explanation of the cause of the pain can help to allay anxiety and improve morale. It may be possible to modify the pathological processes which are causing the pain by appropriate radiotherapy, chemotherapy or hormone treatment, as long as there is no danger thereby of worsening the patient's condition. The pain pathway may be interrupted by nerve block or surgery, or comfort improved by appropriate splintage, support or seating.

The skilled pain control professional will enquire about the sites of the pain, which may be multiple, its nature and severity, its duration or periodicity, and the factors which make it better or worse. If analgesia is required then the main principles of treatment should be the following:

- to treat regularly by the clock with sufficient dosage to prevent pain from surfacing (never to wait until pain is experienced)

- dosage should be by mouth when possible

- the regime should be simple and regularly reviewed

- any potential side effects should be anticipated and minimised

- insomnia should be treated.

For mild pain, paracetamol or aspirin may suffice. Moderate pain requires a more potent preparation, such as co-proxamol (now withdrawn from the British National Formulary because of its association with self-harm) or dihydrocodeine. Severe pain calls for morphine and its derivatives. For particular kinds of pain, adjuvant therapy with various co-analgesics may be administered according to the needs of the individual. For example, in addition to the appropriate analgesic, non-steroidal anti-inflammatory agents may ease bone pain. That of raised intracranial pressure or nerve compression may respond to dexamethasone, and that of the smooth muscle of the gut to hyoscine. Transdermal fentanyl patches may be a suitable alternative for patients with cancer pain who have difficulty in swallowing.

Many of the opioid analgesics in current clinical use may produce a degree of suppression of the immune system. There is an increasing number of patients being treated today who are already immunocompromised, and may present acutely for management of their pain. These include people undergoing surgery, itself a cause of immune suppression, and those with cancer or undergoing chemotherapy for cancer. For these patients there is now a choice of opioids which do not have this suppressive effect. These drugs are structurally distinct (they have a carbonyl substitution at C6, a single bond between C7–C8 and, preferably, an hydroxyl group at C14) and include buprenorphine, hydromorphone, oxycodone, oxymorphone and tramadol (Budd and Shipton 2004). A few stoical patients may be unable to admit to the degree of pain experienced and be reluctant to take appropriate drugs. This may result in unnecessary suffering. Such patients may need to be persuaded that the recommended treatment is socially acceptable as well as medically effective. A few patients will be unable to take oral medication, because of severe nausea, vomiting, dysphagia or extreme debility, and will require a constant subcutaneous infusion of diamorphine. Battery operated syringe drivers are available for this purpose, and may often be borrowed from hospital or hospice for use in the home. There is no indication for the use of pethidine, dipipanone, dextromoramide or opioid mixtures such as 'Brompton Cocktail'. These are less effective analgesics, are shorter acting or are liable to cause more side effects than morphine. Worries about addiction to morphine in this situation appear unfounded, and are less important than good pain control.

OTHER SYMPTOMS

Other symptoms may require anticipatory control or treatment as required. Morphine is likely to produce troublesome constipation and laxatives should be given prophylactically. Nausea and vomiting may result from drug therapy, uraemia or other biochemical imbalance, intestinal obstruction or raised intracranial pressure. Several drugs are available to combat these most unpleasant and debilitating symptoms.

Breathlessness, cough, hiccoughs, anorexia, anxiety and depression, confusion and fits may all be helped to some extent by appropriate therapy. Some 25 per cent of patients in palliative care may be depressed (Ellershaw and Ward 2003). Urinary incontinence may require catheterisation for the most severely affected patients. Insomnia may call for a hypnotic. Oral hygiene is important and can contribute significantly to the wellbeing of the patient.

Diagnosing dying

It may be hard to tell when a patient is reaching his last days or hours, even for experienced practitioners for whom diagnosing dying is an important clinical skill. Patients with advanced cancer usually show a gradual deterioration, becoming bedbound, semi-comatose and unable to take food or drugs by mouth, except for small sips of fluid. Sometimes acute events, such as massive bleeding, precipitate death. Patients with heart failure may be made acutely worse by such events as infections or anaemia, which may be reversible. If their condition is worsening for no identifiable reason and does not improve within two or three days of appropriate changes in treatment, then they may be in the dying phase. Predicting the time of probable death may be even more difficult for other life-limiting diseases.

When the members of the palliative care team are in agreement that death is near, the patient, if appropriate, and family should be told and care must then be refocused. Unnecessary or futile investigations and treatment should cease. All measures to keep the patient comfortable and pain and symptom free should continue. Drugs should be administered by syringe driver rather than by mouth. The decision 'not to resuscitate' should be made clear after discussion with relatives. The entire breadth of palliative care services should be utilised as required.

Care of the dying child

Many feel that the right place for a dying child is at home with the family. That may be neither possible nor practicable, nor may it be the wish of parent or child. Children's hospices are able to provide a homely environment, the staff and the time to care for some terminally ill children and to offer support to the child and the family during this distressing period. This support may be offered in the hospice and in the home.

Caring for the dying child means caring for the family and for whatever problems, financial, social or marital, which they bring with them. The strain of caring for a dying child can wreak havoc with family life and often a great deal of support is needed.

Amongst children receiving hospice care, probably only about 15 per cent have cancer; others suffer from such diseases as muscular dystrophy and rare metabolic, genetic or congenital abnormalities. Parents may be unable to explain to the child what is going to happen to them. For parents, bereavement starts at diagnosis and the grieving process precedes death, imposing an enormous domestic toll. Staff must enable parents to remain in control of decision-making and not rush them into giving answers. They should encourage parents to involve the other siblings in the whole process of dying and death, and not exclude them, as frequently happens. Other children, however young, also need to feel loved and important and can help in many ways. Older children should be able to participate in decision making, even helping to plan the funeral arrangements.

Children are protective of their parents, and often do not ask them questions which they know the parents will find difficult to answer. They will ask people they trust for honest answers to questions, and an enquiry as to why they asked that question will often reveal the true doubts and worries of the child and the degree of knowledge which the child already has.

As with adults, anticipation is the key to good pain and symptom control, which is important for both the child and the parents. In the terminally ill child, the hearing may be the last sense to dull and parents should be warned to be careful of what they say over a dying child. After death they should be able to stay with the body, in privacy and comfort, for as long as they feel it necessary. Staff tend to become very deeply involved with the children in their care and are easily hurt themselves. They will need support and counselling to endure the harrowing nature of their work.

Quality in palliative care

What, then, are the important quality issues in the delivery of palliative care? Below are some of the quality indicators by which it may be assessed. A death, whether sudden or expected, may bring with it an intensity of reaction and grief for which staff are quite unprepared. Confidence in handling such situations obviously comes with experience, but all staff need training in this area to make them aware of the policies and procedures, encourage sensitivity to ethnic and religious issues and familiarity with the processes of death certification, registration and reporting to the Coroner. Staff must be able to offer sympathy and time, to listen to and support the relatives and guide them through the complexities of the legal process. Staff involved in dealing with death may need access to counselling facilities for themselves, and must be allowed to grieve.

The statements of policies and procedures should be clear, and should cover the medical, social, legal and administrative aspects of dealing with death. They should be available on every ward. For example, staff should be aware of any decisions regarding the possible resuscitation of a patient, and know how and where to record these decisions. They should know how to respond if a patient requests to be sent home to die, and how to request domiciliary service provision for such a patient.

For patients who spend their last days in hospital, there should be unrestricted visiting all round the clock, including children, and families should be encouraged to help deliver some of the necessary care. Visitors should have access to amenities, such as refreshments, toilets and telephones, and in some cases even a bed. Spiritual counsel should be available for all religions, and interpreting facilities as required. Patients who are being readmitted to die should ideally be nursed on a familiar ward.

For the dying patient there are many practical arrangements to be considered before death which are not discussed in this book. Advice may be sought about such things as wills, other financial matters and funeral arrangements. Detailed information may be obtained from many sources, including the Citizens' Advice Bureau, the Consumers' Association and the Department of Social Security (see Appendices A and C).

Relatives may wish to be present at death, and arrangements should be available to call them, and let them stay as long as they wish. Staff should have skill in breaking bad news and be able to spend time with the bereaved, if there is no other family support at hand. Religious rites must be accommodated.

Following a death there should be sensitive handling of the body, and any property, with due regard for ethnic and religious considerations, and arrangements for dignified removal from the ward to the mortuary. The bereaved may require counselling and ongoing support, which should be available for all ethnic and religious groups. They should be able to spend time, in privacy, with the deceased and be able to speak to a doctor who is able to answer their questions. Requests for post mortem or organ donation must be made sensitively. Relatives need clear guidance on what to do next, particularly about death certification and funeral arrangements. If community support is likely to be necessary, staff should be aware of how this may be organised. There should be a system for informing the general practitioner, not just of the death but also of the bereaved, who may need aftercare.

For the bereaved who were not present at the death, there should be arrangements for someone who knew the patient to accompany them to the mortuary, and reasonable access to the mortuary all round the clock (although this may be difficult in areas where mortuaries are closed out of hours). The viewing room should be pleasant and dignified, and someone should be available to answer any questions the relatives may wish to ask.

Many hospitals now have a bereavement officer, whose job it is to ensure the smooth arrangements following a death. Some issue a 'with sympathy' card to the relatives, which contains written instructions of immediate necessary procedures and points of contact. Some hospitals run small working groups on various aspects of dying or death, such as cot death, sudden death or pain relief, and are able to introduce improvements in good practice. They may run liaison groups with general practitioners and produce information packs for their use. They may ensure that all medical and nursing staff have access to some terminal care training, or at least gain an awareness of its importance.

References

Budd, K. and Shipton, E.A. (2004) 'Acute pain, the immune system and opioimmunosuppression.' *Acute Pain 6*, 123–135.

Department of Health Letter to Strategic Health Authorities (2004) *Building on the Best: End of Life Care Initiative.* London: Department of Health.

Department of Health and Welsh Office (1995) *Report of the Expert Advisory Group on Cancers to the Chief Medical Officers of England and Wales.* London and Cardiff: Department of Health and Welsh Office.

Ellershaw, J. and Ward, C. (2003) 'Care of the dying patient: the last hours or days of life.' *British Medical Journal 326*, 30–34.

Hospice Information (2003) *Hospice and Palliative Care Facts and Figures 2003.* London: HI.

House of Commons Select Committee on Health (2004) *Palliative Care. Fourth Report of Sessions 2003–04. Vol 1.* Printed by the Stationery Office, 14 July 2004. Available on: www.parliament.uk /parliamentary_committees/health_committee.cfm

Macmillan Cancer Relief (2004) *Gold Standards Framework.* London: Macmillan Cancer Relief. Also available on: www.macmillan.org.uk/healthprofessionals/disppage.asp?id=2062

Marie Curie (2000) *The Liverpool Care Pathway for the Dying.* London: Marie Curie Cancer Care. Available on www.lcp-mariecurie.org.uk.

National Institute for Clinical Excellence (NICE) (2004) *Improving Supportive and Palliative Care for Adults with Cancer.* London: NICE.

National Statistics (2003) *Deaths in England and Wales in 2001.* www.statistics.gov.uk.

NCHPCS (1996) *Palliative Care in the Hospital Setting.* London: National Council for Hospices and Palliative Care Services.

NCHPCS (1997) *Changing Gear – Guidelines for Managing the Last Days of Life in Adults.* London: National Council for Hospices and Palliative Care Services.

NCHPCS (1998) *Guidelines for Managing Cancer Pain in Adults.* London: National Council for Hospices and Palliative Care Services.

NHS Executive (2000a) *The NHS Cancer Plan: A Plan for Investment, a Plan for Reform.* Leeds: NHS Executive.

NHS Executive (2000b) *Improving the Quality of Cancer Services.* Leeds: NHS Executive.

Nurmikko, T.J., Nash, T.P. and Wiles, J.R. (1998) 'Recent advances – control of chronic pain.' *British Medical Journal 317,* 1438–1441.

Public Health (Control of Disease) Act (1984) Part III.

Note:

Old Department of Health letters and documents (HM, DA, HC, EL, HSG, HSC etc.) can be accessed on the Department's website at www.dh.gov.uk/PublicationsAndStatistics/LettersAndCirculars/Advanced Letters/fs/en

CHAPTER 13

MEDICO-LEGAL ISSUES AT THE END OF LIFE

With the wide variety of medical and paramedical provision, much guidance from the Department of Health and the Royal Colleges and an ever-increasing likelihood of litigation, there are, of course, numerous potential medico-legal pitfalls for health care staff. Laws cover almost everything that affects patient care. Most of these apply to the care of any patient, not simply to those with palliative care needs.

Some issues have particular relevance to people at the end of their lives, and a few are briefly outlined in this chapter. Only factual and legal aspects are considered here; the many detailed ethical arguments, for or against, are not included.

Confidentiality

The Hippocratic oath, which can be traced back to the 5th century BCE, contains the sentence: 'Whatever in connection with my professional practice, or not in connection with it, I see or hear, in the life of men, which ought not to be spoken of abroad, I will not divulge, as reckoning that all such should be kept secret.'

There is a moral duty on doctors and other health care professionals to keep confidential all that they learn in the course of a professional relationship (Finch 1994). However, this is not an absolute obligation and some disclosure may be permitted in certain circumstances. British courts have recognised the doctor's duty to respect a patient's confidence and, if a breach of that confidence were to cause recognisable damage, an action for damages could reasonably be brought to court. For Health Authorities, Trusts, hospitals, nursing homes and similar establishments, all employees are under a similar obligation of confidentiality.

However, there is also an obligation to give evidence in a court of law, if required to do so. The court does have some discretion and usually requests otherwise confidential information only when this is required in the interests of justice. In court, the doctor is not entitled to refuse to answer when directed by a judge. The court may compel disclosure by a medical practitioner of matters concerning his patient, if those matters are essential to the case.

Disclosure must be made under compulsion of law but, apart from this, there should be no disclosure (except if the patient should request it) unless the life or health of some other person or persons is put at risk by silence. This could occur, for example, in some circumstances involving infectious disease, when communication to the appropriate person or persons is necessary to allow steps to be taken to mini-mise the danger. There are regulations which, for reasons of public health, oblige doctors to notify certain infectious diseases (see p.197). Special precautions must be observed to retain absolute confidentiality for those with sexually transmitted dis-eases (including HIV/AIDS) for whom confidential information may only be trans-ferred to others for the medical purposes of treatment or prevention.

Personal information must not be disclosed to a third party, such as a solicitor or police officer, without the permission of the individual concerned, except in specific conditions when the disclosure is seen to be in the public interest.

Confidentiality may be of great importance to patients receiving palliative care, particularly those patients with HIV/AIDS.

Confidentiality does not stop at death.

Consent

The health care practitioner has a duty not to undertake any procedure without the consent of the patient. Sometimes the patient is unable to give consent. This may be for legal reasons, because the patient is under 16 and legally a 'minor', or for factual reasons, when the patient is mentally or physically unable to give consent. This may happen if there is severe mental disability or disturbance of consciousness, such as coma. For a minor, it may be necessary to seek the agreement or approval of some other person instead.

A minor aged 16 years can give consent to surgical, medical and dental treatment to the same extent as a person of full age (18) (Family Law Reform Act 1969).

A minor aged under 16 is subject to 'parental responsibility' within the meaning of the Children Act 1989. Any interference with the child's body by medical or surgi-cal treatment, without parental consent or other lawful justification, may give grounds for action for trespass to the person of the child. However, Section 8(3) of the Family Law Reform Act 1969 may reasonably be interpreted as allowing a child under 16 to consent to proposed treatment, as long as he or she understands the na-ture and likely effects of that treatment. The more serious or complex the proposed procedure, the greater the degree of understanding that is required of the child.

A PATIENT INCAPABLE OF CONSENT

Some patients are unable to give consent (see above). An adult who cannot give con-sent because of lack of understanding or severe incapacitation, such as coma or the vegetative state (see below), is legally said to be 'incompetent' or to 'lack capacity'. Relatives cannot give consent on behalf of an incompetent adult (but see Mental Ca-pacity Act 2005, below). As long as the patient is alive, the legal justification for pro-viding treatment is the principle of necessity. Treatment is necessary only if it is in the best interests of the patient. That is if, and only if, it is carried out in order to save their life or to ensure improvement, or prevent deterioration, in their physical or mental health. Treatment given must always be in the best interest of the patient.

In 1995, and again in 2004, the British Medical Association (BMA) and the Law Society jointly produced guidance for doctors and lawyers on the assessment of mental capacity (BMA/Law Society 2004). This reminded doctors that, although close relatives are usually consulted about what a mentally incapacitated patient would have wanted, getting a relative to sign a consent form is unnecessary and has no legal effect. It also pointed out that advance directives (or living wills – see below), which had been written and witnessed when the patient was capable of consent, were already legally effective and would nowadays be taken as valid consent, or refusal, if it covered the specific situation for that patient (see also Mental Capacity Act 2005, below).

For competent patients, the important legal question is whether consent is informed, full and free, and not whether the right form has been signed. A procedure carried out without consent will normally amount to actionable trespass on that person.

There is a duty to explain fully the risks inherent in treatment, as well as the potential benefits, before consent is given. Things were different in 1954, when Lord Denning, then Master of the Rolls, implied (*Hatcher v Black* 1954) that deliberate misinformation given to reassure a patient before treatment was a legitimate course of action for a medical practitioner. This is no longer acceptable. In a landmark decision in 1957, Lord Scarman (*Bolam v Friern Hospital Management Committee*) said, 'I think that English Law must recognise a duty of a doctor to warn his patient of risks inherent in the treatment which he is proposing, and especially so if the treatment is surgery.' The other Law Lords in this case agreed that a doctor is required to act in accordance with practice accepted as proper, by a responsible body of medical opinion, at the time. 'The decision as to what risk should be disclosed to a particular patient, so that he can make a rational choice whether or not to undergo the particular treatment recommended by the doctor, is primarily a matter of clinical judgement. The disclosure of a particular risk of possible adverse consequences may be so obviously necessary for the patient to make an informed choice, that no reasonably careful doctor would fail to disclose that risk.'

The necessity for full disclosure of the risks of treatment was reinforced in 1981 in the case of *Chatterton v Gerson*, when it was stated that 'the real risks inherent in careful treatment ought to be revealed, in all normal circumstances, to the patient'. There is no doubt that this approach causes much anxiety in many patients, but nowadays health care staff must take this obligation seriously.

The persistent or permanent vegetative state

A conscious patient has both wakefulness and awareness (Royal College of Physicians 2003). Some patients, after serious brain injury, appear to show signs of wakefulness, but show no evidence of awareness, either of self or of environment, for a prolonged period of time. This is known as the vegetative state. If it continues for more than four weeks, it may be termed 'persistent'. After it has been present for at least one year following head injury, or six months from other causes, it is termed a 'permanent vegetative state' (PVS), implying that recovery is most unlikely and that further treatment is futile.

It may be a stage in recovery, or it may last for a varying period until death. There are largely different brain pathways for wakefulness and awareness, allowing them to be dissociated by severe traumatic, ischaemic or hypoxic brain injury.

Patients in PVS do not interact with others in any way. They do not respond to sights, sounds, touch or pain. They make no voluntary or purposeful movement. They continue to breathe spontaneously and they retain their gag, cough, sucking and swallowing reflexes.

The functions of the hypothalamus and the brainstem are usually good enough to maintain breathing and the circulation, without the use of life support machinery. The cycle of waking and sleeping is preserved. Patients are incontinent of urine and faeces, but they may retain their cranial nerve, spinal and primitive reflexes. They may make inconsistent, non-purposeful movements, such as facial grimacing and chewing, and they may make sounds. They may move the head or eyes at times, apparently in response to peripheral sounds or movements, but there is no consistent evidence of awareness of self or environment at any time. The diagnosis of the vegetative state is not tenable if there is any degree of voluntary movement, evidence of sight or of response to threatening gestures.

PVS usually develops after a period of coma. It may be caused by acute cerebral injuries (traumatic or non-traumatic), degenerative and metabolic disorders, and developmental malformations. It may also mimic other minimally conscious states and must be distinguished from them. These include: some states of life-long severe disability; the 'locked-in syndrome', where the patient has no voluntary control of movement but has awareness and wakefulness; coma; and brainstem death. These conditions are not considered here.

There are two dimensions of recovery: recovery of awareness and that of motor function. The outlook is poor for most. Mortality is about 82 per cent at three years and 95 per cent at five years. The outcome varies according to the cause and its duration. It may also vary with the standard of care offered. Many of those who 'recover' are left with severe disability.

THE TONY BLAND CASE

The case which sparked off the current debates about appropriate end-of-life decisions in the UK was that of Tony Bland. The Medical Law Monitor (1994) described this as 'the most challenging and ethically controversial judgement of the decade'. In 1989 Tony Bland, an 18-year-old football fan, was severely crushed in a major crowd disaster at a football stadium at Hillsborough in Sheffield. He remained in a permanent vegetative state. In 1992, with the permission of his parents, Airedale Trust, the hospital treating him, applied to the High Court (Family Division) for permission to withdraw artificial feeding and allow him to die. This was Britain's first right-to-die case. At this time it was estimated that there were about 1000–1500 patients in a similar condition in Britain, with no hope of recovery. The High Court decided that the hospital could stop feeding Tony 'in his best interests'. Three Appeal Court judges then upheld that decision. They rejected arguments that withdrawing the feeding tube would amount to murder. 'Patients unable to choose for themselves whether to continue treatment should not be deprived of the right to have a rational decision taken on their behalf in their best interests. I cannot believe that a patient in the situation of Mr Bland should be subjected to therapeutically useless treatment, contrary to good medical practice and medical ethics, which would not be inflicted on those able to choose.'

The judges distinguished this case from a recent 'mercy killing'. Tony Bland would have died without the tube and was being kept artificially alive with it. They thought it would show greater respect to allow him to die and be mourned by his family than to keep him grotesquely alive. They laid down guidelines for future cases and said that doctors should always seek court sanction before withdrawing feeding 'for the protection of the patient, the protection of doctors, the reassurance of patients' families and the reassurance of the public'. The Official Solicitor, representing Tony Bland, then took the case to the House of Lords because of the life and death issues involved. In February 1993, the House of Lords ruled that doctors caring for Tony would not be acting unlawfully if they stopped artificially feeding him. A committee of peers was set up to examine the area of medical ethics and the criminal law, including the issue of euthanasia. Lord Keith said, 'A doctor was under no duty to continue to treat a patient, when a large body of informed and responsible medical opinion was to the effect that no benefit would be conferred by continuing. It did no violence to the principle of the sanctity of life to hold that it was lawful to cease giving medical treatment to a patient who had been in a persistent vegetative state for three years, considering that treatment involved manipulation of the patient's body without his consent and conferred no benefit on him.'

The judgement brought Britain into line with other countries sharing similar legal, ethical and medical principles: the United States, Canada and New Zealand.

In May 1993, the House of Lords Select Committee on Medical Ethics took evidence from the Department of Health and the Home Office. The Government at this time saw no need to change the homicide laws, it rejected euthanasia, and while it saw no objection to doctors being guided by 'living wills', it was against any legislation for them.

The following year, in January 1994, a patient who had been in PVS for over two years, after an overdose of drugs, was allowed to die after the Court of Appeal sanctioned a decision by doctors not to replace his gastrostomy tube. The judges said it was not in the patient's best interests for the tube to be replaced.

In February of that year, the House of Lords Select Committee on Medical Ethics ruled that it is a crime for a doctor to kill a patient intentionally, even when the patient requests it. There was concern that there could be no way of ensuring that all

such acts were truly voluntary. People who were elderly, lonely, sick or otherwise vul-
nerable might feel under pressure, real or imagined, to request an early death.

The committee ruled that if pain and distress could not be controlled satisfactorily, doctors should give relief by increasing doses of analgesics and sedatives, even if
this shortens life. Competent patients have every right to refuse to consent to treatment, and patients who are incompetent to give or withhold consent to treatment
have to be protected from the aggressive overtreatment to which competent patients
would object.

If doctors and relatives disagree, there should be local judicial forums set up to
adjudicate. The committee suggested that the health professions should develop a
definition of PVS and a code of practice for managing it. They also called for better
training in palliative care, pain relief and medical ethics.

By April, guidelines had been set for the end-of-life management of PVS. These
stated that the patient must have been insentient for at least 12 months before an application could be made to the Family Division of the High Court for permission to
withdraw treatment. The application could be made by the next of kin, the hospital
or the Health Authority. The views of the family and of the patient, if known, were
important to any decisions made, and there were to be at least two neurological reports, including one commissioned by the Official Solicitor from an independent expert. Doctors had to consult Health Authority solicitors if there were issues of
consent, and lawyers in the Official Solicitor's Office were willing to discuss cases
informally before proceedings were started.

In May 1994, the Government issued a White Paper, stating their overriding
concern to protect the interests of patients. British law would not be changed to permit euthanasia, mercy killing or assisted suicide. Actions that have as their intention
another person's death would continue to be unlawful. Decisions that limit treatment
should be made jointly by all concerned in the care of an incompetent patient. The
Government agreed to begin discussions with health professionals on a code of practice for the management of PVS and the use of advance directives.

In August 1995 the Supreme Court in Dublin (Ireland) ruled that a 45-year-old
woman in a 'near permanent vegetative state' should be allowed to die. She had suffered brain damage in an operation 23 years before. The Chief Justice said that the
true cause of her death would be the injuries she sustained in 1972 and not the withdrawal of nourishment.

Later that year the first ever application to a Scottish Court sought to end the life
of a woman patient. Aged 51, she had been in PVS since an overdose of prescribed
medicines more than three years before. It was made clear to doctors in Scotland that
they would now have to follow the same procedure as in England, taking all similar
cases to court. The Lord Advocate would give no undertaking that charges of murder
or culpable homicide would not be brought against them. Later it was ruled that a
single judge in the Court of Session could sanction the withdrawal of feeding but, as
a civil court, it could not grant immunity from prosecution to the health care staff involved. However, in May 1996, the Lord Advocate, Lord Mackay of Drumadoon,

said that doctors who allowed patients to die with court approval would not be prosecuted.

In July 1996, a research article and an accompanying editorial (Andrews *et al.* 1996) appeared in the *British Medical Journal*, highlighting a number of cases of the misdiagnosis of the vegetative state in a rehabilitation unit. In this series of patients, some 17 out of 40 of those who were referred to this unit with a diagnosis of the vegetative state were misdiagnosed. They apparently had sufficient means of communication to consistently use eye movements to point, or were able to use a touch sensitive buzzer. Most of these misdiagnosed patients were blind or visually impaired and all remained severely physically disabled. The study concluded that the diagnosis of PVS needs considerable skill to diagnose, requiring multidisciplinary assessment over a long period of time, and that the diagnosis cannot be made from a one-off bedside examination, even by an experienced clinician. Those who retain a degree of awareness must be recognised, if their quality of life is to be maximised and inappropriate withdrawal of tube feeding prevented.

In 1996, the Royal College of Physicians produced new guidelines for the diagnosis of PVS. They preferred the term permanent (rather than persistent) vegetative state, and the diagnosis should only be made when the condition had been stable for more than one year after head injury, or more than six months after brain damage from other causes. The diagnosis must be made independently by two doctors, both with experience in the assessment of disturbances of consciousness. They must ask staff and carers about the patient's reactions and responses. The diagnosis is based on clinical criteria: no awareness of self or environment; no evidence of language comprehension or expression; no response to visual, auditory or tactile stimuli.

Guidance on the diagnosis and management of the vegetative state (RCP 2003) was again issued in 2003. Building on previous guidance, it requires additional safeguards. Before the diagnosis is confirmed, the cause should be established as far as possible and the effects of drugs, metabolic disturbances and treatable structural causes should be excluded. Medical, nursing and therapy staff must agree with family and friends that there are no signs of awareness. As before, it requires the same timescale and the views of two independent doctors, experienced in the assessment of disorders of consciousness. In addition, in case of doubt, there should be an assessment by an expert clinical neuropsychologist.

Once the definitive diagnosis of PVS has been made, recovery cannot be expected and continuation of treatment is futile. The clinical team, in consultation with relatives, must review the situation and consider the implications, including the possibility of withholding or withdrawing nutrition and hydration. Withdrawal of treatment from an incompetent adult means that feeding or hydration, which is artificially keeping a patient alive, is withdrawn and death is allowed to occur (refraining from an act). These cases must be referred to the courts before further action is taken. Decisions to withdraw life-sustaining medication, such as insulin for diabetic patients, must also be referred to the courts, as the legal position is uncertain. Decisions not to treat, as with antibiotics, other drugs or life-saving procedures such as cardiopulmonary resuscitation, can be made by the caring team, in discussion with the family, and do not need to be referred for legal opinion.

Once the courts have given permission for the withdrawal of nutrition and hydration, it is recommended that sedatives should be administered, to reduce the possibility of suffering, however remote that may be. Good palliative care should be offered until death.

Advance directives or living wills

In recent years there has been much public discussion about end-of-life matters. There is a large body of public opinion that believes people should have much more choice and control over their treatment at the end-of-life, and their mode and time of death. There are those who wish to refuse futile treatment, and those who wish to stay alive as long as possible, however unpleasant their physical circumstances. Many people have a fear of losing their capacity to control what happens to them at the end of their lives. They worry about severe stroke or dementia or many other disabling conditions. Many think they would not wish to be kept alive, with life support, when the outlook was clinically hopeless and their quality of life would be, to them, unbearable. Without the patient making a living will, the family have no legal right to influence the health care for the individual in the future. If patients are competent, they may themselves consent to, or refuse, treatment as they think fit. If patients are not mentally competent, then treatment may only be given if it is in their best interests. Other people cannot consent to treatment on behalf of an adult except in very specialised circumstances.

An advance directive, otherwise known as a 'living will', is a declaration of the treatment wished or expressly refused in the future, should the person be unable to consent to, or refuse, treatment at the time. It may take various forms, such as a witnessed oral statement, a signed printed card or even the note of a discussion written in the patient's case notes. Usually it is a written document. It is written when the patient is of sound mind and the document appropriately witnessed. In 1995 the Law Commission recommended that living wills in the UK should be given official support of statute, but this did not happen. Although there is no actual legislation about living wills yet in force in the UK, there is case law, which has given them legal validity for some years in England and Wales. The Mental Capacity Act 2005, which will give legal validity to advance directives, should come into force in 2007 (see below). In England and Wales, refusals of treatment are legally binding for doctors but requests for specific treatment to be administered are not.

In Scotland, living wills are not legally binding for doctors. They are useful for enabling doctors to be aware of what the patient would have wanted, but doctors are not required to act in accordance with the advance statement if they feel it would be against good medical practice or not in the patient's best interests. The Adults with Incapacity (Scotland) Act 2000 formalises the right of health care proxies. A person may grant either a 'continuing' or a 'welfare' power of attorney to another person, authorising them to act in matters concerning financial affairs or the welfare of the individual, should he or she become incapable of making his or her own decisions. The Act ensures that the proxy must be consulted about treatment decisions, unless this is unreasonable or impracticable. The grant of the proxy must be registered with the Office of the Public Guardian, where it is open to inspection and could be challenged.

In England and Wales, the views of the health care proxy are not yet legally binding, but will be after the Mental Capacity Act 2005 comes into force in 2007 (see below).

Living wills made by persons under the age of 18 years are not legally binding and may be overruled by a parent or a court. People writing these directives must understand the nature and consequences of them, and not be under mental distress at the time. Doctors must be satisfied that the writing of the living will was not influenced by illness, medication, false information or undue pressure from other people. Doctors must comply with the patient's requests, even if they themselves disagree. Living wills can be altered, by competent patients, as often as necessary. If the patient should become incompetent, the carefully worded, witnessed and signed directive will override any conflicting decisions by the medical team. Only in exceptional circumstances are doctors and nurses able to override a living will. There must be evidence to show that the writer did not fully understand the implications of the will when it was drafted, or that the situation is quite different from the one envisaged in the document. Emergency treatment would not be delayed until a living will came to light, unless there was sure knowledge of its existence and content.

Living wills are recognised as legal documents by the British Medical Association (Voluntary Euthanasia Society 2004), the Royal College of Nursing, the General Medical Council, the Nursing and Midwifery Council, the Law Society and Age Concern. They are given legal validity in the Mental Capacity Act 2005, which is proposed to come into force in 2007 (see below).

The living will can only reflect the wishes of the person at the time it was written, and needs to be regularly reviewed. People may change their minds as treatment improves or their circumstances change.

Living wills may only be used to refuse treatments or procedures, not to request specific ones. They can be used to state what quality of life and kind of treatment would be deemed acceptable if the person were to be so ill as to be unable to make their own decisions at the time. They cannot be used to request euthanasia or help in committing suicide, both of which remain illegal in the UK. Nor can they be used to refuse basic nursing care, such as washing, bathing and toileting, nor to refuse the giving of food and drink by mouth. They cannot refuse care which specifically aids personal comfort, such as painkillers, nor demand care or treatment which would be considered inappropriate by the health care team.

The living will needs to specify a clearly identifiable point in care which will trigger the wishes of the now incompetent patient. This could be, for example, the onset of incompetence or possibly some subsequent happening after the onset of incompetence, such as pneumonia or other severe infection. The health care team and family, or proxy, must agree that the trigger event has occurred, and will then be bound by the conditions of the will.

It has been suggested that a living will could also express the wish to stay alive, with life prolonging measures, for as long as possible. Various organisations, working for a change in the laws surrounding assisted death, have developed so-called 'pro-choice living wills' (Irwin 2004), which, they claim, can enable doctors to have full and frank discussions about end-of-life medical care with their patients.

Elderly or chronically sick people often confer the Power of Attorney to another. This gives the other person the authority to act on their behalf in financial and legal matters, but, in England and Wales, does not confer the right of the other person to make decisions about future health care for the individual concerned. Within a living will, it is possible to nominate a 'health care proxy', who has permission to make health and treatment decisions on behalf of the individual, should he or she become legally incompetent.

The Voluntary Euthanasia Society, VES, produces a suitable document for a living will. Visit their website on www.livingwill.org.uk

Resuscitation

To resuscitate means to restore to consciousness, to revive (from the Latin *resuscitare*, from *re* and *suscitare*, to raise (from *sub-*, up from below, and *citare*, to rouse)) (*Collins English Dictionary* 1986).

In health care terms, it means the restoration of respiration and circulation after an acute event has caused the heart to stop. The purpose is to maintain adequate ventilation and circulation until means can be obtained to reverse the underlying cause. The three elements of basic life support, after initial assessment of the situation, are airway, breathing and circulation, commonly remembered as ABC. Details of how to perform resuscitation are not given here. Interested readers are urged to consult the guidelines produced by the Resuscitation Council (UK) (RCUK 2000).

Attempts at resuscitation are not new. There are accounts of different methods of resuscitation in ancient texts, and even in the Bible, where terms such as 'mouth to mouth' and 'breathing into' are used (Ardagh 2004). The prophet Elisha revived an apparently dead child. He 'lay upon the child and put his mouth upon his mouth...and the flesh of the child waxed warm' (Bible, Kings 2, iv 34). Many different methods were used during the early ages to revive the apparently dead. The application of hot ashes or hot water to warm the body; whipping or pain to stimulate a response; the use of bellows to blow air into the chest.

The seeds for modern cardiopulmonary resuscitation (CPR) were probably sown some 500 years ago (DeBard 1980). Artificial respiration began with the Belgian anatomist, Andreas Vesalius, working on live animals in the 16th century. Tossach reported successful mouth-to-mouth ventilation in 1744. The Paris Academy of Sciences officially recommended mouth-to-mouth resuscitation for the victims of drowning in 1740. In 1767, the Dutch Society for the Recovery of Drowned Persons was formed, in response to increased numbers of drownings. It recommended warmth for the victim; draining the water from the head and chest by placing the head lower than the feet, applying manual pressure to the abdomen and inducing vomiting by tickling the back of the throat with a feather; stimulation with strong odours or rectal fumigation with tobacco smoke: restoring breathing by means of a bellows; and bloodletting. The Royal Humane Society was set up in England in 1774, with similar motives. Another method in use at this time was rolling the victim to and fro while stretched out over a barrel, in order to fill and empty the lungs. Over the next 40 or so years various methods came into favour, such as placing the victim over a trotting horse, rolling him from side to side or pulling at his tongue.

External chest compression is variously ascribed to John Howard in the 18th century, to Boehm in 1878 and to Dr Friedrich Mass in 1891. Open chest cardiac massage was increasingly used right up to 1960. Defibrillation may have begun in 1775, but was not proved successful, when used internally, until 1899. Dr George Crile, who had described an experimental method of resuscitation, using chest compression plus artificial respiration and parenteral adrenaline in animals, reported the first successful use of external chest compressions in human resuscitation in 1903. The following year he performed the first American case of closed-chest cardiac massage.

In 1954, James Elam proved that expired air could maintain adequate oxygenation, and two years later he and Peter Safar used mouth-to-mouth resuscitation with significant success. They presented their findings formally in 1958, by which time the United States military had adopted mouth-to-mouth resuscitation to revive unresponsive victims. Also in 1954, Zoll published his accounts of cardiac defibrillation. In 1956, electrical defibrillation, which had been shown to be successful when applied directly to the heart in 1947, was successfully applied externally through the closed chest wall. In 1960, Kouwenhoven, Jude and Knickerbocker rediscovered the value of external cardiac compression whilst working on ventricular fibrillation of the heart in animal models. Their paper described the effective use of closed chest compressions in resuscitation. This was the beginning of the modern use of CPR techniques, which were rapidly developed by the American Heart Association (AHA 2005). They began a programme to disseminate CPR to physicians and the general public, although training was not standardised until several years later. The open chest method of cardiac massage was no longer used after 1960, when closed chest massage was shown to be equally effective. This coincided with the increased use of mouth-to-mouth ventilation. It was the simultaneous use of artificial ventilation, chest compressions and cardiac defibrillation which allowed the successes of modern CPR. Resuscitation using modern CPR techniques has only been possible in the last 40 years.

CPR has now evolved into widespread general use, with international committees, councils and associations. These produce concensus guidelines, for professional and lay people, for people managing a cardiac arrest on their own outside hospital, and for professionals working as a team with modern technical equipment (ERC 1998 a and b). Following the guidelines may produce difficult decisions and potential medico-legal pitfalls.

Cardiac arrest can strike people of all ages and all fitness levels, usually without warning. In the industrialised world, the commonest cause of adult sudden cardiac death is ischaemic heart disease (BMA, RCUK and RCN 2002). Other precipitating causes include trauma, overdose of drugs, hypothermia, immersion, anaphylactic shock, pregnancy and low blood volume. If bystanders are able to act quickly and begin CPR, and trained responders are able to administer defibrillation within minutes, some of these lives might be saved.

CPR does not have 100 per cent success, even in expert hands. The outcome depends on the cause of the original cardiac arrest, the age and level of previous fitness of the patient and the level of support available at the time. For people who are already seriously terminally ill and near the end of life, there may be little or no benefit in restarting the heart if it stops. For others who were previously well, as in drowning or after a heart attack, CPR may be a life saver. Estimates of success vary widely. Some four out of ten adult patients will have their heartbeat and breathing restored by CPR, but only half this number will survive to leave hospital. For the others, CPR fails.

For otherwise healthy, full-term babies who fail to breathe spontaneously at birth, almost all resuscitations are successful, if instituted by a trained practitioner at delivery. These cases are not considered here.

Normal breathing introduces oxygenated air into the lungs, where oxygen is transferred into the bloodstream and thence to the heart and the general circulation, including the brain. At the same time, waste carbon dioxide is breathed out. If breathing stops, oxygen cannot reach the heart muscle and, most importantly, cannot reach the brain. Serious brain damage can result if the brain is starved of oxygen for as little as three to four minutes in normal temperatures, a bit longer in cases of hypothermia and even less if the patient is already short of oxygen. Artificial respiration aims to fill and empty the lungs in a regular cycle, using either exhaled air from the resuscitator, or air or oxygen if available. To do this, the mouth and airway must be cleared quickly of debris, such as vomit, the patient laid on a firm surface, and the head held slightly extended, with the jaw held forward to prevent the tongue falling back and obstructing the tracheal entrance. If no made airway is available, the operator kneels at the patient's head, closes the nostrils with the free hand, places his lips on those of the patient and breathes his own exhaled air into the mouth of the other. If the airway is clear, the patient's chest will be seen to rise and fall as the air enters and leaves. In hospital, where technical equipment is available, the airway may be kept open by the use of an artificial airway in the mouth or through the nostril, or preferably by an endotracheal tube, attached to a source of oxygen or air.

Because the heart has stopped, there is no pump action available to circulate this newly oxygenated blood from the lungs. Regular compression of the chest will help to circulate the blood. Artificial ventilation and chest compression together are known as 'basic life support'. Both the artificial breathing and the chest compression must continue together, the recommended ratio of the former to the latter being 2 to 15. Guidelines recommend a rate of 100 chest compressions a minute, a hard task indeed for an unaided person to do. Even in expert hands, chest compressions will only achieve about 30 per cent of the usual blood flow to the brain.

Various heart rhythms may be associated with cardiac arrest. Most commonly in adults, the heart stops beating regularly but the heart muscle fibres continue to contract irregularly in an uncoordinated manner, in so-called ventricular fibrillation. The only interventions that have been shown unequivocally to improve long-term survival from this condition are basic life support and defibrillation. Defibrillation, carried out by the application of electric shock over the heart, may restore normal rhythm to the heart, but the chances of successful defibrillation decline by 7 to 10 per cent for each minute that the condition persists. To be successful, the defibrillating shock must be delivered as soon as practicable. Defibrillators vary in the type of shock they deliver, and details of their use is outside the scope of this book. Many are automated and can deliver a current based shock appropriate to the patient in question. Only a small proportion of the electrical energy gets through the heart muscle, and it is important that the defibrillator is correctly placed for maximum effect. Up to three shocks are administered, if necessary, preferably within the space of one minute. Modern automated defribrillators, intended for the use of the general public, may be able to reinforce CPR training with voice and visual prompts, taking the user through the recommended steps of CPR.

Mouth-to-mouth ventilation can be a less than pleasant experience for the rescuer. It can be made pleasanter by the use of a Brooke, or similar, emergency airway, which enables the resuscitator to breathe down one end, separated by a flange from the lips of the patient. The other end of the device forms an airway which is inserted into the patient's mouth, over the tongue. This simple device can assist the effort required to maintain adequate ventilation.

For advanced life support, carried out by trained health professionals, certain drugs may be used in addition. Epinephrine (adrenaline) is a powerful cardiac stimulant and improves the efficacy of CPR. It causes blood vessels to constrict, raising the perfusion pressure of the blood in the heart muscle and the brain. It may be administered intravenously or, diluted, via the trachea, from where continued ventilatory breaths will disperse it into the bronchial tree. Other drugs may be of value in specific circumstances.

RISKS TO THE RESCUER

The need for resuscitation may obscure other safety concerns. Rescuers should be careful not to place themselves, or others, at more risk than the victim. Before starting a resuscitation attempt, rescuers must quickly assess any risks, such as traffic, toxic fumes, dangerous masonry or the need to switch off the car ignition after a road accident, to minimise the risk of fire.

Poisoning in the victim seldom poses a threat to the rescuer, but exceptions are incidents involving hydrogen cyanide and hydrogen sulphide gas poisoning, when the resuscitator must take care not to inspire the toxic exhaled air from the victim. In these cases, if assisted ventilation is required, it should be given only using a mask and non-return valve system. Other cases of poisoning may involve corrosive chemicals, which may contaminate the victim's clothing and skin. Rescuers in these cases require appropriate protective clothing.

The possibility of infection being transmitted during mouth-to-mouth ventilation has been a cause of concern, especially with regard to hepatitis and HIV/AIDS. Worldwide, there have been occasional reports of transmission of cutaneous tuberculosis, shigellosis (bacillary dysentery), herpes simplex virus (cold sores), meningococcal meningitis and salmonella infection. These are rare incidents. To date there have been no recorded cases of the transmission of either hepatitis B or HIV by this method. Blood is the single most important source of infection for these viruses and, as the infective status of the victim is generally unknown, care must be taken to avoid contact with any body fluid containing visible blood, as well as semen, vaginal secretions, cerebrospinal, pleural, peritoneal, pericardial and amniotic fluids. In particular, these fluids should not be allowed to come in contact with broken skin or mucous membranes of the rescuer.

It became common practice in hospitals to attempt resuscitation during the 1960s. It was quickly realised that this was not always desirable. The procedure is difficult and frequently futile. Some patients were less than delighted to have been revived, many experienced days of intensive care before dying, and many survivors were left with severe disabilities, frequently worse than their original condition. It became customary, where a patient was considered to be terminally ill and near to natural death, for medical and nursing staff to agree 'do not resuscitate' (DNR) and for a note to that effect to be put in the patient's notes.

'DO NOT RESUSCITATE'

Decisions about 'do not resuscitate' and 'no treatment' were challenged in the High Court for the first time in February 1966. The patient, known as 'R', was 23, had a malformation of the brain, was severely handicapped and had severe epilepsy. The hospital had agreed with his parents to apply a policy not to resuscitate, but social workers had disagreed and contacted the Disability Law Service.

When the case came to court, England's Senior Family Judge, Sir Stephen Brown, ruled that the 'do not resuscitate' policy was not unlawful and that R need not be resuscitated in an acute crisis, such as a heart attack or severe chest infection, as long as the parents were consulted and agreed at the time.

After several further cases of complaint by relatives, where DNR decisions had been made without reference to them, guidance was issued in 2002 (BMA, RCUK, RCN 2002). Jointly produced by the BMA, the Resuscitation Council (UK) and the Royal College of Nursing, this recommended that decisions about resuscitation should be based on consultation between health professionals, the patient and those closest to him, taking note of his informed opinions and reflecting his best interests. An advanced directive, if available, would be honoured. If the patient's wishes about resuscitation are unknown, or cannot be ascertained, health professionals should make every effort to revive him. The views of children and young people must also be taken into consideration, although, for incompetent children, parents will decide on their behalf. Resuscitation follows the same principles as any other treatment for an incompetent adult. It must be used appropriately to maximise benefit and minimise potential harm. Resuscitation decisions must be based on the circumstances of the individual patient. They must be regularly reviewed as the situation changes. For some people, attempted resuscitation may be considered inappropriate. It may be refused. All establishments where decisions about life support may arise, such as hospitals, surgeries, nursing homes and ambulance services, are expected to have policies to guide decision making in such an event and to make these policies available to patients and their families.

THE LEGAL STATUS OF THOSE WHO ATTEMPT RESUSCITATION

In these litigious days, there is concern that persons who attempt to resuscitate may find themselves sued if any harm is suffered by the victim as a result of the act. There are no statutory obligations relating to the field of resuscitation but, theoretically, there is potential liability which could arise in common law. In the UK there have been several cases where a claim has been made against a rescuer, but by 2000 there had been no cases of successful prosecution against anyone who came to the aid of a casualty in an emergency situation. Claims might be made on the grounds of assault on the casualty (the law of trespass) or of a breach of duty of care (the law of negligence). An individual who witnesses a situation 'in the street' where resuscitation might be required has no obligation to assist as long as he did not cause that situation. This holds for both professional and lay witnesses. However, if that individual chooses to help the victim, he then assumes a duty of care towards him.

A person who attempts resuscitation, whether under positive duty of care or assumed duty of care, will only be legally liable if the casualty is left in a worse position than he would have been in, had no attempt to resuscitate been made. As the person would otherwise die, it would be difficult to leave him any worse off, unless the resuscitation was being given inappropriately and, for example, the casualty sustained fractured ribs or other injury. It is possible that the relatives of a victim, who has been revived but left in a seriously brain-injured state, would consider that death would have been a better outcome for that individual. In the UK, this type of argument, known as a claim for 'wrongful life', is unlikely to succeed. The standard of care to be expected from a health professional, a non-professional first-aider or a member of the general public would differ in legal terms. For the trained professional, acting competently within current guidelines, it is unlikely that a successful claim could be brought. For lay people, liability will only arise if the standard of care given is below that expected of any reasonably careful person in the rescuer's position.

A person who attempts resuscitation will only be liable for damages if, by negligent intervention, he causes an injury which would not otherwise have occurred, or makes an existing injury worse. He may be held culpable if the standard of care given was below that which would be expected of him in the given circumstances, whether he is a health professional, a volunteer first-aider or a member of the general public.

Many countries, including a number of states in the USA, have enacted 'Good Samaritan' legislation. This gives various levels of immunity from legal liability to people who provide first aid, but no such legislation currently exists in the UK.

Elective ventilation of potential organ donors

The Exeter protocol for elective ventilation of potential organ donors was published in 1991. Patients dying from rapidly progressive intracranial haemorrhage were transferred from medical wards to intensive care units for a brief period of ventilation before confirmation of brainstem death and harvesting of organs for transplantation. This approach led to Exeter having a rate of kidney retrieval and transplant higher than anywhere else in the UK.

But in 1994, doubt was cast on the legality of this practice on the grounds that relatives cannot consent to treatment of an incompetent adult, when that treatment is not in that person's best interest. The protocol was declared illegal in 1994.

The spirit of the protocol is defined in the *Code of Practice – Cadaveric Organs for Transplantation* (Department of Health 1983). This has not been withdrawn.

The legal difficulty is that the donor is incompetent and has probably not made an advance declaration. Relatives cannot give consent on behalf of an incompetent adult. As long as the patient is alive, the legal justification for providing treatment is the principle of necessity. Treatment is necessary only if it is in the best interests of the patient. That is if, and only if, it is carried out in order to save their life or to ensure improvement or prevent deterioration in their physical or mental health. Unless the treatment can be shown to be in the patient's best interest, it is not lawful. Elective ventilation may be desirable from the point of view of the potential recipient, but it is evidently not in the best interests of the donor, for whom it is a futile act. An advance directive (e.g. a well-worded donor card) would be taken as informed consent.

Euthanasia

Euthanasia is the name given to the situation where someone other than the patient intentionally ends the life of a patient at the patient's request. This is an 'act' in legal terms. 'Acts' are voluntary. They cannot apply to minors or to incompetent patients, and the intention is to bring about death.

There have been many well-publicised cases where people with severely disabling or terminal conditions have requested to be able to end their lives with dignity at a time and in a manner of their choosing. There have also been many cases when a loving spouse has brought about the death of a seriously ill partner, often called 'mercy killings' by the press.

Two doctors have subsequently been charged with murder, after helping terminally ill patients to die (*R v Arthur* 1981; *R v Cox* 1992). Arthur was acquitted but Cox was convicted.

Despite much public debate and sympathy for legalisation of euthanasia, it remains illegal in Britain. However, there is much ongoing debate about the Assisted Dying for the Terminally Ill Bill 2004, which was introduced in the House of Lords on 8 January 2004. Interested readers should visit the website of the National Council for Palliative Care (www.ncpc.org.uk), or similar active sites, for up-to-date developments on this issue.

Suicide

The situation in which an individual brings about his or her own death is known as suicide. A variety of means may be used to achieve this, but it is a lone and unaided act.

Probably from the 13th century, suicide was treated as a crime under English common law. It was held to be an offence against nature and God, and was punished in various ways. Property was confiscated and burial was refused in consecrated ground. Sometimes the culprit would receive a stake through the heart. In Scotland, attempting suicide was a crime under common law until the 18th century, but by the 20th century had disappeared as a crime. Neither committing suicide, nor attempting it, are punishable in Scots law. Suicide ceased to be a crime in England and Wales in 1961 (Suicide Act 1961). Ireland repealed its law in 1993.

ASSISTED SUICIDE

Assisted suicide is one in which a person brings about their own death with the help or advice of another person. This is an 'act' in legal terms. 'Acts' are voluntary. They cannot apply to minors or to incompetent patients, and the intention is to bring about death.

Many people might instinctively feel that suicide and assisted suicide are such individual acts of freedom and free will that there are no legal prohibitions. This is incorrect and has brought many people into trouble with the law. Laws on assisting suicide vary considerably round the world (Humphrey 2003).

It remains a crime in England and Wales to aid, abet, counsel or procure the suicide of another person. There is a maximum penalty of 14 years' imprisonment. In Scotland the legal position is less clear (Gavaghan 2005) and not set out in statute, but assisting, or attempting to assist, a suicide does constitute a criminal offence. The nature of the charge may vary. Whether prosecution is deemed to be in the public interest depends entirely on the opinion of Scotland's chief prosecutor, the Lord Advocate. In theory, the assistant could be charged with murder or, more likely, culpable homicide, and the sentence is decided by the judge.

In Britain, no case against the assistant may be brought without the permission of the Director of Public Prosecutions. There have been eight Bills or Amendments introduced into Parliament between 1936 and 2003, all trying to modify the law to allow careful, hastened death. None have succeeded and assisting a suicide remains a crime. There are laws which can ban a publication if it encourages suicide or assisted suicide.

The treatment of pain

The treatment of pain by increasing doses of drugs is justified even if it shortens life. The shortening of life is not the prime objective of the treatment (see also p.165).

Terminal sedation

Terminal sedation is recommended in the latest guidance on management of the incompetent patient in a permanent vegetative state when, after permission has been given by the court, nutrition and hydration are being withdrawn. This is to minimise any remote chance of suffering being caused by the procedure.

For other patients, terminal sedation means that the suffering patient is sedated to unconsciousness. This is intended to relieve suffering, not to cause death. All life-sustaining treatment is withheld and the patient dies of dehydration, starvation or some intercurrent complication, such as pneumonia. The only outcome is death, and this may take days or even weeks.

Terminal sedation is now enshrined in English common law, following a case which came to the High Court in London in 1997. The patient suffered from motor neurone disease, a progressive and severely disabling condition. She sought the assurance that, when she could no longer swallow, her general practitioner would be able to administer enough diamorphine to her to keep her unconscious. She had prepared a living will in which she stressed that she had no wish to be tube fed. The court agreed that this was acceptable medical practice.

Terminal sedation is often appropriate for patients near death, from cancer or other diseases, and is part of the armamentarium of good palliative care.

Human Rights Act (1998)

The Universal Declaration of Human Rights was first adopted and proclaimed by the General Assembly of the United Nations in December 1948. The rights defined in that declaration were, in essence, similar to those defined in the later Human Rights Act 1998, which incorporates the European Convention on Human Rights into UK law.

The Human Rights Act 1998 is now in force, bringing with it a whole minefield of issues, which could potentially affect health care staff in many situations.

- Article 2, 'Right to Life', states that everyone's life shall be protected by law.

- Article 3, 'Prohibition of Torture', prohibits torture or treating people in an inhuman or degrading manner.

- Article 5, 'Right to Liberty and Security', states that, with a few exceptions such as in the lawful detention of common criminals and persons of unsound mind or those detained for the prevention of the spread of infectious disease, everyone has a right to liberty and to security of person.

- Article 6, 'Right to a Fair Trial', covers the right to a fair, and public, trial, within a reasonable time and by an independent and impartial tribunal established by law.

- Article 8, 'Right to Respect for Private and Family Life', states that everyone has the right to respect for his family life, his home and his correspondence.

- Article 14, 'Prohibition of Discrimination', prohibits discrimination on the grounds of sex, race, colour, language, religion, political opinion, nationality, property, birth or other status.

The General Medical Council recommends careful documentation in all situations where the Act may be invoked at a later date (GMC 2000/1).

Mental Capacity Act (2005)

The Mental Capacity Bill had its first reading in the House of Commons on 17 June 2004. It received Royal Assent on 7 April 2005 and the proposed date for it to come into force (as the Mental Capacity Act 2005) is 2007. Part of it (the Independent Mental Capacity Advocate service), has had wide consultation and a pilot service has been commissioned by the Department of Health for a period of one year from January to December 2006 (POhWER 2006).

The Act (Mental Capacity Act 2005), which applies only to England and Wales, clarifies a number of legal uncertainties and reforms and updates the current law under which decisions have to be made on behalf of other adults (over 16 years) who are unable to make those decisions for themselves. The Act applies to those who have lost mental capacity at some point in their life, be it temporary or permanent, whether as a result of disease, trauma or congenital defect, and covers a broad spectrum of decisions, including personal welfare, financial matters, health issues and research. The Act will replace Part 7 of the Mental Health Act 1983 and the whole of the Enduring Powers of Attorney Act 1985.

The Act makes new provision for persons who lack capacity. It will establish a new Court of Protection (in place of the present Supreme Court of Protection) and a new office of Public Guardian (who will take over from the current Public Guardianship Office) and introduce a new type of power of attorney, to be called a Lasting

Power of Attorney (LPA, which will replace the present Enduring Powers of Attorney for new cases). Adults of sound mind will be able to choose someone to make personal decisions on their behalf (the Attorney), should they lose capacity at a later date. Those decisions will cover finance and welfare, including health.

The key health provisions in the new Act are given briefly below.

- There are five key principles which state that a person should be assumed to have capacity, unless proved otherwise. For the purposes of the Act, 'a person lacks capacity in relation to a matter if at the material time he is unable to make a decision for himself in relation to the matter because of an impairment of, or a disturbance in the functioning of, the mind or brain'.

- A 'best interests' checklist takes into account the wishes, feelings, beliefs and values of the individual, including any advance directive written before he or she lost capacity, and the views of family and friends.

- There will be protection from liability, subject to certain rules and limitations, for carers and professionals to lawfully care for a person who cannot consent.

- There will be the ability to choose a Lasting Power of Attorney while able to do so, to act for them if they should lose capacity at a later date.

- There will be court-appointed deputies to make decisions on matters about which the individual lacks capacity.

- The creation of Independent Mental Capacity Advocates (IMCAs) to support people without capacity, when there is no one to speak for them in matters relating to serious medical treatment or long-term residential care.

- There will be safeguards to control research involving people who lack capacity.

- An advance directive (living will), made whilst the person has capacity, comes into the legal framework.

- It will be a criminal offence to ill treat or neglect a person who lacks capacity.

- The new Court of Protection will have jurisdiction in relation to the Mental Capacity Act. There will be special procedures and judges.

- The new Public Guardian will be the registering authority for LPAs and deputies.

With regard to health decisions, the powers of the LPA or deputy include 'giving or refusing consent to the carrying out or continuation of a treatment by a person providing health care for P' (P is used as an abbreviation for the person without capacity in the Act) (Section 17d) and 'giving a direction that a person responsible for P's health care allow a different person to take over that responsibility' (Section 17e).

Section 4 (5) importantly states: 'Where the determination relates to life-sustaining treatment he must not, in considering whether the treatment is in the best interests of the person concerned, be motivated by a desire to bring about his death.'

Advance decisions, made by a person over 18 years when he has capacity, must be respected. They may be changed whilst he still has capacity and this does not need to be in writing. They must be valid and applicable to the treatment in question. The validity of the directive may be challenged on many counts, including change of circumstance that P may not have foreseen. It may only be applicable to life sustaining treatment under certain conditions. The existence of an LPA does not prevent the advance decision from being regarded as valid and applicable. The court may need to make a declaration as to whether the directive is valid and applicable to the proposed treatment.

Section 37 of the Act mentions the provision of 'serious medical treatment' by an NHS body, meaning treatment which involves providing, withholding or withdrawing treatment of a kind prescribed by regulations made by the appropriate authority.

If P's treatment is regulated by Part 4 of the Mental Health Act, the NHS body treating him must instruct an independent mental capacity advocate (IMCA) to represent him. Emergency treatment is allowed as an exception.

References

Adults with Incapacity (Scotland) Act (2000).

American Heart Association (2005) *Highlights of the History of Cardiopulmonary Resuscitation.* Website of the American Heart Association: www.americanheart.org. Dated 17 February 2005 (accessed July 2005).

Andrews, K., Murphy, L., Munday, R., Littlewood, C. (1996) 'Misdiagnosis of the vegetative state: retrospective study in rehabilitation unit.' *British Medical Journal 313,* 13.

Ardagh, M. (2004) 'A brief history of resuscitation.' *New Zealand Medical Journal 117,* 1193.

Bolam v Friern Hospital Management Committee (1957) 1 WLR 582.

British Medical Association and the Law Society (2004) *Assessment of Mental Capacity: Guidance for Doctors and Lawyers,* 2nd edn. London: BMA.

British Medical Association, the Resuscitation Council (UK) and the Royal College of Nursing (2002) *Joint Statement: Decisions Relating to Cardiopulmonary Resuscitation.* London: BMA, RSUK and RCN.

Chatterton v Gerson (1981) AllER 257.

Children Act (1989).

Collins English Dictionary, 2nd edn. (1986) Glasgow: William Collins.

DeBard, M.L. (1980) 'The history of cardiopulmonary resuscitation.' *Annals of Emergency Medicine 9,* 5, 273–275.

Department of Health (1983) *Cadaveric Organs for Transplantation: A Code of Practice Including the Diagnosis of Brain Death.* London: HMSO.

European Resuscitation Council Advanced Life Support Working Group (1998a) 'The 1998 European Resuscitation Council guidelines for adult advanced life support.' *British Medical Journal 316,* 1863–1868.

European Resuscitation Council Basic Life Support Working Group (1998b) 'The 1998 European Resuscitation Council guidelines for adult single rescuer basic life support.' *British Medical Journal 316*, 1870–1876.

Family Law Reform Act (1969) s.8 (3).

Finch, J. (1994) *Speller's Law Relating to Hospitals*, 7th edn. Cambridge: Chapman and Hall.

Gavaghan, C. (2005) *Assisting Suicide in Scotland – Where does the Law Stand Now?* www.euthanasia .cc/97-3as.html (Scottish suicide laws) (site accessed 9 February 2005).

General Medical Council (2000/1) 'Human Rights Act, what are the implications?' *General Medical Council UK Casebook.*

Hatcher v Black (1954) *The Times* 2 July QBD.

House of Lords (2004) *Assisted Dying for the Terminally Ill Bill (HL)* as introduced in the House of Lords on 8 January 2004. Available on www.publications.parliament.uk/pa/ld200304/ldbills/017 /2004017.htm

Human Rights Act (1998). London: The Stationery Office. The text of the Human Rights Act can be found at www.gov.pe.ca/law/statutes/pdf/h-12.pdf

Humphrey, D. (2003) *Assisted Suicide Laws Around the World*. www.assistedsuicide.org (updated 18 September 2003, accessed August 2005).

Irwin, M. (2004) 'Prochoice living wills.' *Bulletin of Medical Ethics*, 21–24.

Kouwenhoven, W.B., Jude, J.R. and Knickerbocker, G.G. (1960) 'Close chest cardiac massage.' *Journal of the American Medical Association 173*, 1064–1067.

Medical Law Monitor (1994) 1, January, 5.

Mental Capacity Act (2005). London: The Stationery Office. [The text of the Mental Capacity Act.]

POhWER, The Advocacy Agency (2006) Website: www.pohwer.net/how_we_can_help/independent_2.html (accessed 31 March 2006).

R v Arthur (1981) *The Times* 6 October, 1 and 12.

R v Cox (1992) 12 BMLR 38.

Resuscitation Council UK (2000) *Resuscitation Guidelines: Basic Life Support. And Advanced Life Support.* London: RCUK.

Royal College of Physicians (2003) *The Vegetative State. Guidance on Diagnosis and Management.* London: RCP.

Suicide Act (1961) Chapter 60.

Voluntary Euthanasia Society (2004) 'Living Wills.' www.livingwill.org.uk (accessed July 2005).

CHAPTER 14

LAST OFFICES

Last Offices – the laying out of a body – epitomises our respect for the dead. Maintaining modesty and privacy, the body is cleaned and tidied, straightened, protected, made safe for others to handle and pleasant for others to see.

The ritual and traditional aspects of laying out vary considerably between ethnic and religious groups. In some there is a requirement for specific individuals to carry out the proceedings, if this is at all practicable. It is essential to consult members of the family, if available, before Last Offices are performed. Their wishes should be respected and their presence welcomed. If no member of the family is present, and no other advocate for the deceased available, then the information on the following pages may be helpful.

In Britain the majority ethnic group consists of white Caucasians who are associated with one of the many churches of the Christian faith. Later chapters will help to clarify some of the differences between their beliefs and rituals associated with death, but all would accept the standard hospital procedure for the laying out of the dead.

This chapter covers the routine laying out of a body after an expected, natural, hospital death, prior to the removal to the hospital mortuary to await collection by the funeral director. It also explains when the routine procedure is not appropriate.

Over the last few years, there have been rumours that some hospitals have dispensed with Last Offices (Faugier *et al.* 1992), claiming that it wastes resources because the funeral director will repeat the procedures, and also that junior nurses may be distressed by the procedure. In other hospitals, the procedures may be of a more limited nature than described here. Many hospitals now have detailed Last Offices policies, which may be very similar to this chapter but with local variation.

Hospital nurses used to regard Last Offices as the final special service to the patient. Often the deceased was known, cared for and loved by them during the last days of life, and the ritual is a fitting conclusion to this special relationship. Today, with many temporary agency nurses, shorter hospital stays and much less continuity of care, Last Offices may not have the same meaning to the practitioner on the ward.

When not to perform Last Offices

Appropriate advice should always be sought before performing Last Offices if the death has been reported to the Coroner, for example when the doctor is unable to fill out the death certificate, the death has occurred within 24 hours after surgery, anaesthetic or any invasive procedure, or if someone thinks the death is 'suspicious' or potentially litigious. The Coroner should also be informed if the deceased was not seen by a doctor within 14 days of death (see Chapter 4).

In particular, do not remove any tubes or cannulae, or pack any orifices, until the doctor in charge of the case has been consulted. If in doubt seek advice from the nearest University Department of Pathology or Forensic Medicine, local coronial pathologist, or Coroner's Officer (see Appendix B).

Routine Last Offices are not appropriate for Jewish (see p.257), Muslim (p.274), Hindu (p.281) or Sikh bodies (p.287), unless requested by the family. In all the above, a 'limited laying out' may be appropriate (see p.189).

If the deceased is a potential corneal donor, the eyes must be closed and protected from the time of death, whether or not Last Offices are carried out (see p.189).

Donors of other organs (heart, kidneys, liver) may be kept on a life support system following their serious accidents until brain death is confirmed, heralding the optimum time for surgery, after which they will be taken directly to the mortuary. Some may be the subject of coronial inquiry and need to undergo autopsy following the removal of the organs. Indeed, some Coroners expect the pathologist to be present during the transplant removal procedure (see p.128).

Last Offices should be performed in the usual manner on those whose entire body is being donated for medical teaching or research.

When to perform Last Offices

Once death has been confirmed by a doctor (preferably one who attended the deceased during the last illness) and it has been ascertained that 'routine' laying-out is appropriate, the senior nurse may delegate a member of staff to perform Last Offices. The senior nurse will contact absent relatives, and, in due course, the portering staff must be alerted to the impending removal of the body from the ward to the mortuary.

Last Offices should be carried out for all groups, after appropriate consultation with relatives if necessary, as soon as practicable and certainly within two to three hours of death. Ideally it should be completed before stiffening ('rigor mortis') commences, which greatly increases the difficulty of handling a body. If the body temperature was high at the time of death, rigor may set in as early as two hours after death, so the laying out should not be delayed unnecessarily.

When death occurs, the bed should be screened or moved to a side ward to minimise distress for family and other patients. The body is laid flat, with one thin pillow supporting the head. Dentures are inserted, the jaw is supported, and the eyes are closed. The bed and immediate area should be tidied, and the body covered by a sheet. Some hospitals leave the body for up to an hour, as a mark of respect, allowing relatives time with the deceased. Preparation may then be made for Last Offices to be performed.

Equipment for Last Offices

The trolley should contain:

- Gowns or disposable plastic aprons for staff.
- Disposable gloves.
- Bowl of warm water, soap, the deceased's own toilet articles or disposable face cloth and disposable towels.
- Razor (disposable), comb, scissors.
- Mouth cleaning materials.
- Waterproof tape, Micropore tape.
- Cotton bandage, cotton wool, appropriate dressing packs.
- Incontinence pad.
- Petroleum jelly.
- Shroud of appropriate size.
- Identification bracelets, tags or labels.
- Plastic bags for waste and soiled instruments.
- Sharps bin if appropriate.
- Documents for hospital administration, e.g. notification of death forms.
- Nursing policy documents as relevant.
- Bags for the deceased's personal possessions and valuables.
- Record books for property and valuables.
- Clean sheets.
- Appropriate body bag.
- Laundry skip.

In hospitals, some of the above may be supplied in packs, either from the Central Sterile Supply Department of the hospital or from a commercial supplier.

Procedure

Any blankets or coverlets should be removed, the body being covered by a sheet and with one small pillow under the head. The body should be laid flat, face upwards, and the limbs straightened. A body with flexed limbs is difficult to fit easily onto a trolley or shell for removal from the ward, and for arranging on the bier for viewing purposes. A flexed body may not fit inside a standard coffin, causing additional distress (and expense) to bereaved relatives. Rigor passes off in due course, and the body may still be able to fit comfortably into the coffin in time for the funeral, unless this is scheduled to take place very rapidly, as may be the case for Jews, Muslims and, less commonly, other people of Asian origin.

If the body cannot be straightened, do not force it, but extend the limbs as much as possible. Major spinal deformity, such as severe kyphoscoliosis, will be corrected later, at autopsy or by the funeral director.

The clothing should be removed, and the body inspected for bruises or other signs of injury. Any unexpected findings should be noted in the nursing record, and the relevant doctor should be informed immediately before proceeding further.

The eyes should be closed and may occasionally require a little sticky tape to keep them closed. Micropore tape is ideal for this and can easily be removed after rigor is complete, leaving no mark. Alternatively, a damp cotton wool pad may be used to keep the eyelids in place.

After death the mouth tends to gape open and needs to be supported until rigor is complete. First the mouth should be cleaned. It is often extremely dirty, dry and unpleasant at death. Dentures should be cleaned and replaced, or inserted if they had been left out during the last illness. Natural teeth should be cleaned as thoroughly as possible. The mouth should be closed and maintained by the judicious use of a length of cotton bandage over the head, a small pillow or wad of material or cotton wool firmly placed under the chin, or a 7.5 cm (3 in) length of 2–3 cm (1 in) diameter plastic tubing similarly used as a temporary chin prop until the body has stiffened. Whatever is used, it should leave no mark and may be removed by others after rigor is complete.

We do not recommend 'binding up' the jaw. If the bandage is applied too tightly, it may leave pressure marks on the cheeks, which are difficult to remove.

Care of orifices

The bladder can usually be emptied by applying firm pressure over the lower abdomen. The practice of tying a bandage tightly round the penis may still persist, but we suggest that most families would find that unacceptable if they knew about it. Any serious leakage, from vagina or bowel, can be stopped by packing the orifice with cotton wool. Some hospital policies forbid the packing of orifices on the grounds that it may cause damage to the body, but done with care it has been safely used for many years. Minor leakage can be safely contained by the use of an incontinence pad for both sexes. Leaking of body fluids represents a potential infectious hazard to others who have to handle the body. This applies to all body fluids.

Any intravenous needles or cannulae need to be removed (and disposed of with care), and the wounds made by them must be securely covered with waterproof tape. Any drainage tubes need removal, and the holes sealing likewise. Surgical scars not yet healed require a leakproof cover. Any stoma (colostomy, ileostomy) needs to be rendered leakproof. Fistulae (as in regional ileitis for example) need similar treatment. Stitches and clips should be left intact.

General toilet

For hygienic and aesthetic reasons the body is washed all over. The front of the body is washed first, including the face, not forgetting nostrils and ears. The back is then cleaned, and any bedsores covered with waterproof dressings. A large incontinence pad should be placed under the buttocks. If the bottom sheet is soiled, it should be replaced with a clean one at this point. Male patients should be shaved unless they chose to wear a beard during life. After the wet shave, some hospitals recommend the use of E45 cream to the face, to prevent the development of brown streaks on the skin (Ashford and St Peter's Hospitals NHS Trust 2005). Hair should be clean and combed; nails should be cleaned and trimmed if necessary.

Apply a little petroleum jelly to the lips and perioral area. This not only prevents drying out, but also protects against the potentially corrosive effects of stomach contents.

Jewellery and religious emblems

Both men and women often wear wedding rings and other jewellery. Earrings and neck chains are common for both sexes and often have religious significance, for example the cross for Christians, the Star of David for Jews, and the symbolic dagger for Sikhs. Hindus may have a sacred thread tied round neck or wrist. For Hindus and Sikhs, it is important that these emblems be left undisturbed but, for most bodies, it is appropriate to remove them unless relatives request that they should be left in place.

Jewellery should be removed by a nurse only in the presence of a witness. A note of the valuables removed should be entered in the valuables record book, and the items sealed in an envelope to be held in safekeeping as appropriate until collected by the family. Any jewellery left on the body should be listed on the card, which accompanies the body to the mortuary.

Rings left on the body should be secured with adhesive tape, such as Micropore, if at all loose. Avoid the use of the names of precious metals or gems when describing the jewellery in the property book or the mortuary card. You may be wrong, and run the risk of later accusations if the 'gold' bracelet turns out to be brass, and the 'diamond' ring to be mere crystal. Use the terms 'yellow metal' and 'white metal' instead of gold and silver.

Labelling the body

The body must be clearly identified in some indelible fashion. Many hospitals use a strong plastic irremovable bracelet, which contains the patient's admission details on a pre-printed label, which is put onto the wrist at admission and remains there during the hospital stay. Hence, the body is likely to already have such a label on one wrist but, if not, one should be applied. A second similar label should be affixed to one ankle.

For a death in a nursing home such bracelets may not be available, but any strongly tied, clearly written label will do just as well. Mortuary staff and funeral directors frequently use a waterproof felt-tip type of marker and write the name and mortuary reference number clearly on the side of the lower leg and the soles of the feet, thus making identification simple from the refrigerator shelves in the mortuary, where bodies are often stored with the feet towards the door.

Further identification of the body is contained on the 'notification of death' cards, which should also accompany the body from ward to mortuary. One may be attached to the shroud, and one to the covering sheet.

Shrouding the body

Occasionally a request is made for the deceased to be dressed in personal clothing, but usually a white garment, traditionally called a shroud, is used, for aesthetic reasons for the viewing of the body.

Modern shrouds are usually made of waterproofed paper or plastic, but cotton shrouds may still be occasionally used. They are supplied in various sizes, with ties at neck and wrists. If the head has been injured or operated upon, a cap of tubular gauze may be used to cover any wounds (which have been sealed with waterproof dressings). A 'notification of death' card should be pinned, taped or stapled to the shroud. Often the feet are tied together with cotton bandage, for ease of handling, but this is not absolutely necessary.

The body is then wrapped in a sheet, for protection and for aesthetic reasons. The sheet on which the body lies is first folded down over the head and up over the feet, and then firmly wrapped round the body. This also holds the limbs securely in position. The sheet should be taped or pinned, and a 'notification of death' card pinned securely to the front of the sheet. Hospitals often have special mortuary sheets for this purpose, which are larger and stronger than ordinary bed sheets.

In recent years, there has been increasing use of black plastic body bags, instead of sheets, for transportation of the body. If the body is infected, or there is a suspicion of infection with a category 3 or 4 infection hazard, white zipped body bags should be used (see p.205) and appropriately labelled.

Additional information required

The card which accompanies the body to the mortuary should contain any relevant information which mortuary and funeral direction staff may need to know. The presence of an implanted pacemaker must be noted, as these devices are liable to explode at high temperature and must be removed (by a doctor) if the body is to be cremated.

The card should also clearly indicate if the body is potentially infectious (see p.198), or if the case has been reported to the Coroner.

The body is now ready to be moved to the mortuary, and should be removed rapidly and discreetly. A variety of specialised biers are available, some of which are designed to resemble a theatre trolley.

Clearing up and checking property

Finally, the equipment used must be cleared away, all linen sent to the laundry, and the bed area thoroughly cleaned. The plastic covered mattress and pillow case are washed with soap and water, and dried.

Soiled linen (that which has been used but is not foul or infected) and infected linen should be treated according to the hospital policy for infection control. All washable fabrics are easily disinfected by hot water. Foul linen is usually placed in a colour coded plastic bag, which has a special tape at the closure. At the laundry the bag is placed directly into the appropriate washing machine without being further handled by the laundry staff. The cold water of the sluicing cycle dissolves the tape and allows water to enter the bag. The hot water then melts either the soluble stitching of the bag, or the alginate bag itself, and allows the linen to be washed at a hot enough temperature for a long enough time for disinfection to be carried out.

If the patient died from certain infections, the bedding and bed are treated as for 'terminal disinfection' according to hospital policy (see p.204).

The property of the deceased must be checked in the presence of a witness, and a list carefully entered in the property record book. The toothbrush, face flannel, and any food items are all discarded. Other property should be placed in a bag, which is labelled, secured and locked away. Valuables should also be carefully recorded in the 'valuables' book, and placed in a bag which is secured, labelled and then locked away acccording to hospital policy. Any nursing and administrative documentation should then be completed.

Helping the bereaved

Nursing, medical and administrative staff can greatly assist the relatives and friends by offering, as well as sympathy and understanding, information which is timely and relevant. The death certificate, and cremation forms, should be ready for collection within a reasonable time, even at a weekend. Many large hospitals will have a Coroner's Liaison Officer, or Bereavement Counsellor, who will explain the requirements and procedures to confused families. If such a person is available, then staff should ensure that the family have access to the help which can be offered. The Hospital Chaplains of all persuasions will be pleased to offer counselling, comfort and help.

In some hospitals, a type of condolence card or booklet is given to relatives. This contains useful information regarding necessary procedures and useful contacts for information, advice and practical help.

If other agencies or individuals have been concerned in the care of the patient, such as Social Workers, District Nurses or specialist palliative care teams, then the ward should also inform them of the death.

'Limited laying out'

If death occurs within 24 hours of admission, or of an operation, anaesthetic or invasive procedure, or if the cause of death is unknown or there are any suspicious circumstances, the death must be reported to the Coroner (see p.59). It must also be reported if death occurred in police custody or prison or if caused by accident or industrial disease, such as pneumoconiosis or asbestosis.

In such situations, leave all tubes, drains and packs in position. Spigot any catheters and cannulae and leave dressings untouched. A post mortem examination will usually be ordered to ascertain the cause of death, but this may take several hours to arrange.

For all ethnic groups the body should be straightened before rigor mortis commences, the eyes closed and the chin supported as described. Ward staff should carry out only limited 'cleaning up'. Orifices should not be packed, but an incontinence pad should be used. The preparation of the body for disposal will be carried out, by others, after the post mortem is complete.

Procedure following an alleged assault

If a patient dies as a result of an alleged assault, the preservation of trace evidence is imperative. Hairs, fibres, dust and flakes of paint on the patient or the clothing may all serve to establish that contact has occurred between the deceased and his assailant. In such cases clothing should be left undisturbed, if it is still on the body. Any items of clothing which have been removed should be placed in a separate plastic bag, sealed and labelled. Plastic bags should be placed over the head, hands and feet, and tied or taped in place. Any pretransfusion blood samples should be retained in case subsequent grouping or analysis is necessary. Ideally the body should be placed in a plastic sheet or body bag for transport to the mortuary. *Never* pack the mouth, vagina or anus in such cases. This will reduce the chances of recovery of semen, lubricants or other signs of interference.

Corneal transplant donors

If the patient is a potential corneal transplant donor, then the eyes must be safeguarded from the moment of death by keeping the eyelids securely closed at all times, but not weighted. The corneas may be removed up to 12 hours after death, and it is most important that the body is handled carefully and is refrigerated as soon as possible.

The ease of collection of donated corneal tissue will vary according to the area where the donor is located. If collection has not been pre-arranged, contact should be made with the nearest ophthalmic department, or with the local transplant coordinator. The address of Moorfields Eye Hospital Eye Bank is given in Appendix A.

The procedures to be followed if death was due to certain infectious diseases are explained in Part 2, Chapter 16.

References

Ashford and St Peter's Hospitals NHS Trust (2005) *Last Offices Nursing Procedure.* (Reviewed February 2005.)

Faugier, J., Andrews, J., Rundel, S., Speck, P., Booth, B., Pitkeathley, J. (1992) 'Care after death.' *Nursing Times 88*, 6, 20.

CHAPTER 15

BEREAVEMENT

Bereaved, or bereft, from the Old English 'bereafean', means robbed, dispossessed, left desolate.

For those deeply affected by a death, the start of the grieving process is immediate, particularly so if the death is unexpected or is that of a baby or young child. Health care staff may have had little experience in breaking bad news and may be quite unprepared for the intensity of grief reaction which follows. Junior staff may be horrified at the apparent lack of sensitivity shown by their seniors. Doctors may have received little or no training in this field, and learn largely from empathetic nursing staff.

Breaking bad news is never easy, and relatives need time to understand and accept the situation. They may need physical nearness and sympathetic contact with health care staff. If possible, a third person should be present when the doctor is answering their questions, to later verify what was said and reinforce the explanations.

Grief

Grief is an intensely personal reaction, but common elements are experienced in varying degrees by all bereaved relatives and are normal components of the process. Feelings of fear, helplessness, sadness and longing, guilt, shame and anger may overwhelm the bereaved. There may be a deep sense of disappointment. Physical and mental symptoms are common and may include tiredness and lethargy, the inability to think clearly, insomnia and bad dreams. Dizziness and palpitations, nausea and diarrhoea, headaches, menstrual disorders and loss of sexual appetite are frequent, and alcohol intake may be significantly increased.

The timescale of the grief reaction varies considerably, and may be helped or hindered significantly by the amount of support available for the bereaved, to help them explore their loss and continue with their lives. Usually the immediate family, close friends and clergy will supply all the necessary support, and outside 'professional' help is not required. The expectation must be that, after bereavement, people will ultimately return to a normal, healthy level of functioning.

The pattern of grief

For the first week or two the bereaved may feel themselves to be in a state of shock, with psychological numbness, feelings of depersonalisation, indecision and, for some, inappropriate behaviour and denial of the situation. They may experience auditory hallucinations of the voice of the deceased. A period of anguished yearning and acute emotional pain may ensue, with idealisation of the dead person and restless searching to fill the void. There is anxiety, insecurity, anger, guilt and loneliness. This period may extend over several weeks or months, and merge into a longer depressive period, which may bring with it the exacerbation of any pre-existing personality problems. The loss of a spouse brings the loss of marital status and associated loss of social status, companionship and sexual fulfilment. Apathy may persist for many months.

Full acceptance of the loss may take over a year, and healing of the life may take much longer. In many circumstances, particularly in the elderly, depression may continue to be a problem, an expression of abnormal, or complicated, grief.

Complicated grief

Sometimes the intensity of the grief reaction is magnified, particularly if the death was sudden or violent, or occurred in horrifying circumstances. Particular problems arise when the start of grieving is delayed, for example when there is a delay in recovering and formally identifying the body. A complicated grieving process may be anticipated if the death was that of a baby or child, or if the death was part of a major accident or disaster in which many people have been killed or injured. Grief may likewise be complicated if there are no immediate close family or friends to offer extended support. In such cases, the timely offer of professional help can be of great benefit to those with particular difficulties, such as those who continue to have physical symptoms or deep mental anguish, nightmares or insomnia, those without close supportive networks to listen and share the experiences, those with difficulties in relationships, and those who are becoming accident prone or who cannot cope with their work.

If sufficient support can be offered to those at risk of a complicated grief reaction, the need for difficult and extended bereavement counselling may be averted.

THE DEATH OF A BABY

Families whose children have died of the sudden infant death syndrome (SIDS; see p.86) may need particular help. By definition, the death was unexpected and parents are totally unprepared for the event. They are overwhelmed by their feelings of loss, guilt and anger, feelings so intense that the young parents may believe they are losing their minds. The death of a baby bereaves not just the parents, but the grandparents and siblings too. It can cause continuing marital stress. Every sudden death of a baby is the subject of detailed police and coronial inquiries (see Chapters 4 and 5). These often cause the parents to feel that they are under suspicion, which adds to their distress.

Parents need time for explanations and questions with a face-to-face interview with a well-informed doctor. They may need social and domestic support until they can continue their normal lives, and they may need ongoing support and counselling. They will seek answers to such questions as: why did our baby die; did he suffer; did he suffocate; what more could we have done; are other children likely to die in our family; and was it anyone's fault? The Foundation for the Study of Infant Deaths, together with the Department of Health, has produced a helpful booklet (2002), which answers these and other questions simply and clearly, but booklets are not a substitute for the concerned doctor discussing that special baby with those particular parents.

Many staff need advice on how to handle a dead baby, and how to present the child to the parents in the most sympathetic way, for example by the use of a Moses basket or crib instead of a bare trolley. Parents may need to spend time with their dead child, and keepsakes are of great importance. Many hospitals will take photographs of the child for the parents to keep, if requested, or encourage the parents to snip a lock of hair or retain the name bracelet (Tom-Johnson 1990). The name may be placed in a Book of Remembrance in the hospital chapel.

Much help can be offered by other parents who have been through a similar experience. Compassionate Friends is one organisation which offers such help (see Appendix A), with the offer of a sympathetic ear as the first gesture of friendship. SANDS (The Stillbirth and Neonatal Death Society) likewise offers support to parents and other family members whose baby has died around the time of birth (see Appendix A). The sharing of experiences and intense feelings between the newly bereaved and the befriender can bring consolation and social contact.

MAJOR DISASTERS

In recent years, there have been many well-publicised major disasters, at home and abroad, including fires, accidents at sports grounds, aircraft crashes, terrorist atrocities and natural disasters. In any sudden violent death the bereaved may be expected to experience a severe grief reaction, but for many bereaved by these major disasters the situation was rather different. They may have actually witnessed the disaster, or its aftermath, on their television screens, not just at the time of the accident but replayed on numerous occasions thereafter, even years later on the anniversary of the event. It has been evident for some time that grief is more likely to be complicated in such situations, and anticipatory counselling has been accepted and welcomed as good practice.

COVERT RELATIONSHIPS

Another area where complicated grief may be anticipated is the death which may not be openly discussed. Secrecy may hinder the normal grief process for the bereaved, and is likely to be a particular problem for same-sex partners. In Britain today there is still felt to be some discrimination against homosexual people in the spheres of employment, housing and social activity. Consequently, many gay men and women keep their relationships so secret that the death of one is not automatically connected to the grief reaction of the other in the minds of their relatives and colleagues. Many doctors, nurses and other staff are still not aware that same-sex partners feel bereavement every bit as keenly as a spouse. Organisations such as the Lesbian and Gay Bereavement Project offer ongoing support (see Appendix A).

What is counselling?

A key element in coping with death and bereavement is finding an appropriate person with whom to share the grief. Given time, the intensity of the grief reaction will lessen. Bereavement counselling may be regarded as a willingness and readiness to listen to all the thoughts and feelings of the bereaved, often over a long period of time, until they feel ready to let go of the offered support.

Bereavement counselling is increasingly being recognised as important in the prevention, or alleviation, of the many psychological problems which may follow a death, particularly in high-risk groups. Personal counselling may be required for up to a third of elderly bereaved, particularly if there is no existing support network, if another crisis occurs at the same time, if the death was particularly traumatic or if the marital relationship was especially dependent. Counselling may also be required by professional staff who are experiencing the pain of personal loss.

The principles of bereavement counselling

Effective counselling enables the bereaved person to explore their loss and come to terms with their own life, ready to face the future. The counsellor will guide the bereaved through several well-defined areas. Starting with admission by the bereaved that the loss has occurred, by letting him talk about the circumstances of the death, he is then encouraged to identify and ventilate feelings associated with it, such as anger, guilt or anxiety. The future potential problems of life without the deceased may require practical solutions. The counsellor should encourage the bereaved to fight against emotional withdrawal and to nurture old and new friendships, without feeling the guilt of breaking faith with the memory of the loved one. Time must be allowed for grief to run its course. During this period the counsellor must ensure that the bereaved person understands that his reaction and feelings are quite normal and expected, and that there is no evidence that he is losing his sanity (Jones 1989).

Continued support is essential and may be needed for many months after a death. Any psychopathology which is evident to the counsellor should be referred on for specialist grief therapy or psychotherapy as relevant.

Grief work is difficult, time consuming and exhausting for practitioner and client, bringing inevitable pain to both sides. The dead cannot be brought back, and the bereaved can never be really grateful for the work of the counsellor and the total acceptance of the death.

The Watch Tower Bible and Tract Society has produced a very readable booklet entitled *When Someone You Love Dies,* and advice to the bereaved within it is applicable to people of all denominations. It suggests the bereaved person should accept proffered help from friends, take care of their health, postpone any major decisions until thought becomes clearer, realise that grief takes time and that others may feel awkward in the situation, beware of turning to alcohol or drugs to cope, keep to a regular routine and be willing to let intense grief lessen and be replaced by treasured memories (Watch Tower Bible and Tract Society 1994).

Support organisations

Many organisations are deeply aware of the bereavement problems of special at-risk groups. Detailed information about some of them is given in Appendix A of this book. Staff involved in bereavement counselling may themselves require outside or inside support and help for this work. Staff counselling sessions and time should be made available to all who feel the need.

References

Foundation for the Study of Infant Deaths and Department of Health (2002) *Reduce the Risk of Cot Death.* Available on the FSID website: www.sids.org.uk/fsid/

Jones, A. (1989) 'Bereavement counselling: applying ten principles.' *Geriatric Medicine* 55–58.

Tom-Johnson, C. (1990) 'Talking through grief.' *Nursing Times 86,* 1, 44–46.

Watch Tower Bible and Tract Society (1994) *When Someone You Love Dies.* WTBTS.

CHAPTER 16

THE CONTROL OF INFECTION IN LIFE AND IN DEATH

The routes of infection

Infection, in life, may be transmitted by various routes. A sound knowledge of the routes of transmission will enable sensible and appropriate infection control measures to be instituted.

Infecting organisms may, for example, be airborne in dust or respiratory droplets from coughs and sneezes. They are commonly transmitted by direct contact with unwashed hands. Fomites are those intermediate objects such as toys, bedding, books or handles which are capable of transmitting infection because blood or body fluids have been spilt upon them or, more commonly, because bowel organisms from unwashed hands have been deposited there. Food may carry infection because of inadequate cleaning or cooking, or because of contact with unwashed hands, utensils or with contaminated raw food, after cooking is complete. In some countries drinking water may be a source of disease.

Blood and body fluids infected with certain viruses, such as those which cause HIV disease/AIDS or hepatitis B, C and others, can transmit these diseases if introduced into the circulation of a healthy subject. This may happen with, for example, the shared needles of drug abuse, unprotected sexual intercourse with an infected person, or the accidental needlestick or inoculation injury in the health care professional. The increased understanding of these two diseases in recent years has brought with it an awareness of the risk of both to health care staff and others who have to deal with blood in their professional lives and has prompted careful reviews of infection control guidelines.

In hospital, special measures are instituted to reduce the risk: of transferring infective organisms from person to person, from patient to patient, from staff to patient and from patient to staff. Different levels of isolation are appropriate for different infections in life, and if death occurs during the course of the infection staff should continue to observe the same infection control precautions during the preparation of the body as were observed during the illness itself.

The law and infectious disease

NOTIFIABLE INFECTIOUS DISEASES

Some infectious diseases are notifiable by law (see Table 16.1) so that appropriate measures may be instituted to control the spread. The doctor who suspects or diagnoses the illness must notify the patient to the 'Proper Officer' of the Local Authority (as set out in HSC 73 (35)). The Proper Officer may also be known as the Medical Officer of Environmental Health (MOEH) for the Local Authority, and may also hold the title of Consultant for Communicable Disease Control (CCDC) or Consultant in Public Health Medicine (CPHM) for the Health Protection Agency (HPA). The HPA, set up in April 2003, has taken over the work of the old Public Health Laboratory Service and that which used to be carried out by CCDCs and CPHMs in the old Health Authorities. 'Proper Officers' now are mainly employed by this new agency, but make their services available to Local Authorities. Proper Officers no longer need to be medically qualified, and a few non-medical Proper Officers are already in post.

The notification of infectious disease should be made to the Proper Officer of the district where the patient is normally resident, but in practice Proper Officers will notify their counterparts in other districts if the situation calls for infection control procedures to be carried out to prevent the spread of the infection to others.

There are some slight differences in the lists of diseases notifiable in England and Wales, in Scotland and in Northern Ireland. The diseases are notifiable under the Public Health (Control of Disease) Act 1984, as set out in the Public Health (Infectious Disease) Regulations 1988. Since 1989, the Department of Health has been reviewing the law on infectious disease control (Department of Health 1989), but there had been no change in the laws of notification by early 2006.

Other infections may kill or cause severe disease, but are not statutorily notifiable (for example: Legionnaires's disease, psittacosis), and others have a voluntary reporting system for surveillance purposes (HIV infection and AIDS).

CURRENT LAW RELATING TO DEATH DURING THE COURSE OF INFECTIOUS DISEASE

Death may occur because of the infection, or because of some intercurrent event, such as a heart attack, an accident or an assault. When the death of a person suffering from a notifiable disease occurs in hospital, and the Proper Officer believes it to be desirable to prevent the spread of infection, the Public Health Act 1936 (ss. 163, 164) prohibits the removal of the body from the hospital except for the purpose of being taken directly to a mortuary, or to be directly buried or cremated. Under the Act, the person in charge of the premises where such a body lies must take steps to prevent other people from having unnecessary contact with it. The Act also prohibits wakes (a watch or vigil over the dead body on the night before burial) over such bodies.

Table 16.1 Currently notifiable infectious diseases

Public Health (Control of Disease) Act 1984

Cholera

Plague

Relapsing fever

Typhus

Smallpox (laboratory, eradicated)

Public Health (Infectious Diseases) Regulations 1988

Acute encephalitis	Mumps
Acute poliomyelitis	Ophthalmia neonatorum
Anthrax	Paratyphoid fever
Diphtheria	Rabies
Dysentery (amoebic, bacillary)	Rubella
Food poisoning	Scarlet fever
Leprosy	Tetanus
Leptospirosis	Tuberculosis
Malaria	Typhoid fever
Measles	Viral haemorrhagic fever
Meningitis	Viral hepatitis
Meningococcal septicaemia (without meningitis)	Whooping cough
	Yellow fever

Notification is not only a statutory duty, it is a valuable tool in the prevention and control of disease

Local Authorities have a duty to dispose of bodies if no arrangements for their disposal have been made by others. A Justice of the Peace may order the removal and burial of a corpse by the Local Authority if he is satisfied, on a certificate from the Proper Officer, that it is a potential health hazard to the residents of the building, or of neighbouring buildings.

Regulation 14 of the Cremation, England, Regulations, 1930, gives power to the medical referee of a crematorium to order cremation contrary to the usual provisions if the body had died from plague, cholera or yellow fever, whether on board ship, in hospital or in a temporary place of reception provided under the Public Health Acts, even if this is contrary to the wishes of the relatives. Such powers are available generally during epidemics 'or other sufficient reason' on approval by the Secretary of State.

Remember that not all infectious diseases are notifiable, and that death may also be due to non-notifiable infection. A body may be a source of infection to those who handle it for some time after the death.

Classification of infective organisms

Because of the range of infectivity and severity of disease caused by different infectious agents, the Advisory Committee on Dangerous Pathogens (ACDP) has in the past classified them into four groups according to the level of hazard they present to laboratory and mortuary workers (ACDP 1983, 1995, 1998). Similar classifications are used in other countries.

- *Group 1* organisms are most unlikely to cause human disease.

- *Group 2* organisms may cause human disease and may pose a hazard for laboratory workers, but the infection is unlikely to spread into the community. Laboratory exposure rarely produces infection, and effective prophylaxis or treatment is usually available. This group includes the agents which cause tetanus, botulism, Legionnaire's disease, listeriosis, mumps, measles and many others.

- *Group 3* contains organisms which may cause severe human disease and also are a potentially serious hazard to laboratory workers. There may be a risk of spread in the community but there is usually effective prophylaxis or treatment available. This group includes the agents causing anthrax, tuberculosis, rickettsial diseases, typhoid, paratyphoid, rabies and yellow fever. The human immunodeficiency viruses (HIV) and hepatitis B virus are also in this group.

- *Group 4* contains organisms which cause severe human disease and are a potentially serious hazard to laboratory workers. There may be a risk of spread in the community, and there is usually no effective prophylaxis or treatment. This group includes the viruses which cause Lassa fever and other viral haemorrhagic fevers, smallpox (now eradicated) and some encephalitis viruses. Special laboratory accommodation is required for any work relating to these agents.

The above categorisation of pathogens superseded that detailed in the *Code of Practice for the Prevention of Infection in Clinical Laboratories and Post Mortem Rooms* (originally known as the 'Howie Code') (UK Health Departments 1984) which has itself undergone review. It has recently been reissued as two separate publications, one for laboratory practice and one for mortuary practice, in 2003 (HSE/HSAC 2003, HSE 2003, HSC/HSAC 1989a (mortuary and post mortem room) and HSC/HSAC 1989b (for laboratory practice)).

Place of treatment for infectious disease

Some of the above diseases are potentially very serious, both from the point of view of the individual patient and from the potential for the infection to spread to others. Diseases such as anthrax, cholera, diphtheria, poliomyelitis, typhoid, paratyphoid and the viral haemorrhagic fevers would need to be admitted to hospitals with facilities and expertise in the treatment of infectious cases. The treatment of Group 4 infections must be confined to special high-security infectious disease units, of which there are only two in England. These are Newcastle General Infirmary and Coppett's Wood Hospital near London.

Most other diseases can be treated in general hospitals, or at home, with standard infection control precautions (such as single room, careful handling of stools, isolation nursing and restriction of at-risk visitors).

Standard infection control precautions

HAND WASHING

In all situations, hand washing is probably the most important measure in preventing the spread of infection. A liquid soap preparation is preferable to a soap bar for routine hand washing at ward level, and should be used where visible soiling is apparent. This requires disposable paper hand towels. A hot-air hand dryer is no longer advised. A soggy terry towel is a likely source of cross infection (Garner and Favero 1985) and is to be condemned for use in health care facilities. Hands can be re-contaminated by incorrect drying (Blackmore 1987). These days, in hospitals, in a bid to reduce cross infection with antibiotic-resistant organisms, a hand-rub gel containing alcohol and glycerine should be available for use by all who come into contact with patients. This does not require the use of water or towels. It has been shown to be effective against bacteria, but less so against viruses. Alcohol is not a cleansing agent and is not recommended when hands are physically dirty, but is good for use when a higher level of hand hygiene is required (Lawrence and May 2003). At home, soap and clean separate towels for patient and carer are advised.

COVER CUTS AND ABRASIONS

Any cuts or abrasions on the hands should be covered with waterproof dressings, fingernails should be kept short and clean, and jewellery on the hands kept to a minimum (wedding ring only) when in potentially infective situations.

AVOID PERSONAL CONTAMINATION

Avoid contamination of skin, mucous membrane (of eyes, mouth and nose) or clothing with blood or body fluids. Body fluids include cerebrospinal, peritoneal, pericardial, synovial and amniotic fluids, urine, faeces, vaginal secretions, any other fluid containing visible blood, saliva associated with dentistry, and also unfixed tissues or organs.

PREVENT PUNCTURE WOUNDS

Prevent puncture wounds, cuts or abrasions in the presence of blood. If one is sustained, follow the first aid procedure: bleed it, wash it, report it. In some cases, prophylactic treatment will be necessary, for example where HIV is involved. Consult local policies for appropriate treatment.

SHARPS

Avoid the use of sharps (needles, blades, glass items) if at all possible. Whether at hospital or at home, all sharps must be disposed of safely into an approved type of puncture-proof sharps bin immediately after use (British Standard BS 7320 1990). Needles must not be resheathed. About 40 per cent of self-inoculation accidents occur whilst resheathing needles, and this must not be done unless there is a safe method available to do it. The sharps bin should be sent for incineration as soon as it is two-thirds full. The bin should always be labelled with the source of its contents and the date of its removal.

SPILLAGES OF BLOOD AND BODY FLUIDS

Spillages of blood or body fluids must be cleared up promptly, and surfaces disinfected in the appropriate manner. Put on protective gloves and apron: cover spillage with disposable towels to absorb any wetness, and disinfect the contaminated area, including the towels, with freshly prepared sodium hypochlorite solution. (If no blood visible use 0.1 per cent solution which is equivalent to a 1:100 dilution of household bleach, e.g. Domestos, or 1000 parts per million of chlorine. If blood is visible use 1.0 per cent solution, which is equivalent to a 1:10 dilution of Domestos or a neat solution of Milton.) Leave in contact for at least ten minutes, preferably 30 minutes; mop up with disposable towels or cloths; dispose of cloths and towels into colour coded incinerator bags. Colour coding may change with European directives in the future. Dry granules are also available instead of liquid hypochlorite solutions, but may give off chlorine fumes if used incorrectly, particularly if poured onto urine. Seek advice about the disinfection of non-disposable items.

Hypochlorite must not be used on carpeted areas. To clean a blood spill on a domestic carpet, wear disposable plastic apron and disposable latex gloves, soak up as much spillage as possible using paper towels, then use water, detergent and a disposable cloth to clean the area. Discard the apron, gloves, paper and cloth into a yellow clinical waste bag. If using the domestic waste collection service, double wrap the bag before putting it into the bin. Hands must be thoroughly washed after completion of the task (Lawrence and May 2003).

CONTAMINATED WASTE

Contaminated waste must be disposed of safely. In hospital, items for disposal (swabs, dressings, gloves etc.) should be placed in a colour coded plastic bag (yellow is recommended by the Health and Safety Executive), which is then sealed and sent for incineration in accordance with hospital infection control procedures. At home a similar system should be used, the colour coded 'clinical waste' bags being collected by a special service run by the Local Authority Cleansing Department or by a private refuse concern, which takes the waste for incineration or for special safe disposal. If only a very small quantity of clinical waste is produced at home, this should be sealed in a polythene bag, which is then sealed inside a second bag, and the double-bagged waste may then be deposited in the household rubbish bin for routine collection. At the time of writing, changes are being made to recommendations for the disposal of clinical/hazardous waste.

LAUNDRY
In hospital, items of laundry from infected patients should be placed in a water-soluble bag inside the room, then placed in the appropriate colour coded bag outside the room, preparatory to being sent to the laundry. At home, soiled linen should be washed in the hottest cycle of the domestic washing machine (which may damage some fabrics). If there is no washing machine, then arrangements must be made for appropriate laundering, possibly through the Local Authority services.

ROOM CLEANING
Hospital policy will dictate the frequency and quality of room cleaning for infected patients. Protective clothing (gloves and aprons) must be worn by cleaning staff. Disposable cloths should be used, and incinerated after use. Special buckets, and mops which can be autoclaved, may be used for floors, which should be mopped at least daily.

DECONTAMINATION OF EQUIPMENT
Equipment must be decontaminated according to hospital policy.

PROTECTIVE CLOTHING
An understanding of the route of transmission of the particular infection will dictate the appropriate protective clothing for carers or visitors.

Protective clothing for staff in most infective situations will consist of a disposable plastic apron and gloves. They should be placed in the yellow bag for incineration after use. Visitors may need to be similarly protected, and must be encouraged to wash their hands. They should not eat or drink while visiting an infected patient.

If a gown is considered necessary it may be of a waterproofed disposable variety, or a plastic pinafore may be worn under a cotton gown. Occasionally the possibility of splashing (surgery, pathology) makes it desirable that the eyes, nose and mouth are protected with a visor and a facemask. Sometimes special footwear (boots or oversocks) is needed.

Antibiotic-resistant organisms
In recent years there has been an increasing incidence of methicillin resistant *Staphylococcus aureus* (MRSA) infection amongst hospital patients. *Staphylococcus aureus* is the greatest single cause of infections acquired in hospital and accounts for about a

third of them. It has been blamed, by the media, largely on the poor quality of hand washing of hospital staff and ward cleaning in general. In fact, there are several additional reasons why antibiotic-resistant organisms, not merely MRSA, are more prevalent. Everyone carries vast numbers of bacteria, most of them either not harmful or positively beneficial. *Staphylococcus aureus* is common, and carried by some 33 per cent of the population in their nostrils and on their skin. For most healthy people, it causes no problems unless it breaks through the skin. It has always been a common cause of skin and wound infections, abscesses and septicaemia in susceptible patients.

For a variety of reasons, some 40 per cent of *Staphylococcus aureus* strains have now become resistant to methicillin and other antibiotics. This does not mean that such infections are incurable, but they require higher dosages and longer treatment times than non-resistant infections. With the changing practices in modern hospitals, beds are more frequently occupied, often for shorter periods, by patients from a wider range of wards, from other hospitals and other districts. Visiting hours are longer, more visitors come more often and stay longer than in the past. They may visit several wards. There are an increasing number of people with more serious illnesses being treated by more 'high tech' methods, and there are more patients with weakened immunity from a variety of causes, such as patients with cancer and the aftermaths of treatment, after transplant surgery or those with HIV infection. Indwelling tubes and devices are more frequently used and are a common route for infection. Over 60 per cent of blood infections are introduced by intravenous feeding lines and the commonest sites for health care associated infections in 2002 were the urinary tract (23%), the lung (22%), wound infections (9%) and blood infections (6%) (Emmerson *et al.* 1996). The number of death certificates mentioning *Staphylococcus aureus* infection, in England and Wales, has increased year on year from 1993 (just over 400) to 2003 (about 1400). All of this increase has been due to increased infections with MRSA. Most of these deaths were in older people (Health Protection Agency 2004).

MRSA is a worldwide problem. For many years it was regarded as a purely hospital pathogen, but in recent years variations have been found also in the community outside hospitals (Morrison 2005). Other organisms currently causing concern in British hospitals include *Clostridium difficile* and glycopeptide-resistant enterococci as well as surgical wound infections in general.

Poor compliance with hand washing may result from poor training, lack of washbasins or other poor facilities, such as toilets without soap or towels. Walls and floors may not be adequately cleaned, instruments not properly cleaned and sterilised. The inappropriate use of antibiotics, both in medicine and farming, around the world has added to the problem. The main route of transmission of MRSA is thought to be via dirty hands.

There has been a huge amount of central guidance on infection control in hospitals issued over the last few years (ACDP 2003; CMO 2003), as the incidence of hospital-acquired infection has risen. By 2002 it was estimated that the prevalence of health care associated infection was about 9 per cent in England, slightly higher than that of many other European countries (HPA 2004). At this time, the proportion of *Staphylococcus aureus* blood isolates which were resistant to methicillin varied widely between countries. In Denmark, the lowest, the proportion was a mere 1 per cent. In the UK, the highest, 44 per cent of such isolates were MRSA (CMO 2003).

Most countries are promoting similar strategies to reduce hospital-acquired infection. These include better surveillance systems, clarification of standards for infection control, cleaner hospitals and better hygiene practices, strict policies for antibiotic prescribing, better isolation facilities for infected patients, and the involvement of staff and management, at all levels, in action to control the infection rates. Some countries screen for the organism prior to surgery and screen and treat infected, or colonised, health care staff before they are allowed contact with patients. Further research and development must be a priority. New guidelines are currently under consultation (July 2005) and may be available by the time this book is published.

Ward practice for infectious disease deaths

LAST OFFICES

For most infective situations, Last Offices should be carried out routinely (see p.182), but any infection control procedures observed during the illness must be adhered to during the process. The washed and shrouded body should be placed in a cadaver bag (a thick plastic bag with a long zip up the front), and all the documentation which accompanies the body (identification bracelets, death notice on shroud and sheet, case notes and mortuary card) should be labelled with a 'Danger of Infection' sticker, as should the body bag itself, to alert porters, mortuary staff, pathologists and funeral directors that special care may be needed. The request forms must give enough clinical information for the pathologist and mortuary staff to take appropriate precautions, and should make it clear from whom additional information can be obtained. The hazard warnings must be prominent, but the clinical information need be available only to relevant staff. Results of serological testing for the human immunodeficiency virus (HIV) or hepatitis B must be made available to mortuary staff and funeral directors.

TERMINAL CLEANING

After a death or the discharge of a patient, where there has been danger of infection, a special cleaning routine may be appropriate. Staff should wear disposable apron and gloves, and place any used disposable items from the deceased in a yellow plastic bag for incineration. Any cubicle curtains should be placed in a water-soluble bag, then in a designated colour coded bag with a 'danger of infection' yellow diamond. Waterproof mattress and pillow covers should be cleaned with freshly prepared sodium hypochlorite solution (0.1% or 1000 ppm available chlorine), which should be left in contact with the surfaces for ten minutes, then washed with hot soapy water and dried. Beds, cots and other furniture should be similarly treated, as should floors.

Mop heads so used should be autoclaved or incinerated, and the mop handles wiped with the hypochlorite solution, and washed. Walls and ceilings need cleaning only if splashing has occurred, and may be requested by the Control of Infection Team or appropriate medical officer. Gloves and apron must be discarded into the yellow bag and hands washed before staff leave the cubicle. Staff must refer to local policies and the NHS Healthcare Cleaning Manual (Department of Health/NHS Estates 2004).

Mortuary practice for infectious disease deaths

Any body which is unidentified, particularly if no medical history is available, should be treated as if it were infected.

Local rules must ensure that the mortuary staff are forewarned of the arrival of an infectious body, so that any necessary preparations may be made. Funeral directors also need to be aware of any risk.

Infected bodies will be enclosed in a leakproof body bag. In high-risk cases, the bag should be opened only sufficiently to allow for identification, and the body should not be removed from the bag. Relatives should be warned of potential risk. They may be allowed to see the face but must be discouraged from touching the body or kissing it. In some mortuaries, highly infectious bodies may only be viewed through a window. Those who are concerned about the possibility of exposure to infection themselves may be referred to the physician who cared for the patient in the last illness.

Post mortem examinations

In some cases of known infectious disease, post mortems are forbidden unless absolutely essential (UK Health Departments 1984). If carried out, special care is required.

Risks to health during post mortem examination are largely those due to infection transmitted via airborne spray and splashing, or via accidental inoculation through a cut or puncture wound, and both are minimised by good technique.

Guidance on all aspects of mortuary practice was previously given in 'Safe Working and the Prevention of Infection in the Mortuary and Post Mortem Room', and has now been amplified in new guidance (HSE 2003; HSE/HSAC 1989a; HSE/HSAC 2003).

If death occurs from a Group 4 pathogen, special arrangements and precautions are necessary for handling the body. All staff must wear full protective clothing and footwear, including aprons, caps, masks, gloves, gowns and rubber overboots. The body is placed in a plastic bag. Wadding, soaked in embalming fluid (a compound of formaldehyde, methanol, ethanol and other solvents), is packed round the body inside the bag which is then sealed and sponged with White Fluid 1:40 (BS 2462: 1961 Group WD, a phenolic disinfectant). The coffin seams are soaked in a phenolic disinfectant, and the body placed inside. The lid is screwed down and the outside of the coffin treated with disinfectant. The disposable clothing is placed in impermeable plastic bags, sealed and incinerated. Non-disposable clothing must be autoclaved.

The body is taken for cremation. The usual cremation certificates are unnecessary because the Consultant for Communicable Disease Control (the Medical Officer for Environmental Health), now at the Health Protection Agency, is empowered to certify the cause of death and to authorise cremation in such a case, but form F (the Medical Referee's certificate) is still required (see p.116).

Post mortems must never be made on cases of Group 4 disease, except under conditions approved by the Dangerous Pathogens Advisory Group.

Special situations

HEPATITIS B
A vaccine is now available which gives a high degree of protection against hepatitis B. As yet, no vaccine is available for hepatitis C. All health care staff likely to be handling blood or body fluids from infected, or unknown, persons should ensure that they are protected by immunisation. Nurses, pathologists and mortuary staff in particular should review their level of immunity at regular intervals. Whatever their vaccine status, staff must take great care when dealing with blood or body fluids, whether from the living or from the dead. Most cases of infection will be unrecognised; therefore all body fluids must be regarded as potentially infective and consistently good practices adopted. The virus may remain potentially infective for humans for months or years in stored serum, even after freezing (Robinson 1979).

Post mortem examinations should not be carried out unless absolutely necessary. If it is necessary, full protective clothing must be worn by mortuary staff, including full face protection. Detailed instructions for disinfection following the autopsy are given in the 'Code of Practice for the Prevention of Infection in Clinical Laboratories and Post Mortem Rooms' (UK Health Departments 1984).

HIV INFECTION
At present there is still no immunisation against HIV infection, the virus which causes AIDS, although world-wide there is much research being carried out for this purpose. Everyone is potentially susceptible to the infection if contamination from infected blood or body fluids gains access to their own circulation, through a needlestick injury, an accident in the post mortem room, or a splash onto the mucous membranes of the eyes or mouth or onto unprotected broken skin. A body may remain infectious for some time after death. Experimentally, infectious virus can be recovered from an aqueous environment for at least a week at room temperature (Resnick et al. 1986), although the virus is said to be far less robust than that of hepatitis B and easily killed outside the body. (There is no risk of transmission of the disease in life through shared household articles such as cups, cutlery or toilet seats.)

In hospital, all necessary care and procedures must be available to known HIV infected patients, but investigations and procedures which are not essential for the patient's wellbeing should not be carried out, as the handling of specimens does pose a potential risk for all who are involved in the chain, from the houseman or phlebotomist who takes the specimen, the porter who transports it and the pathologist who tests it, to the laboratory staff who ensure its safe ultimate disposal.

Many patients with clinical AIDS also have infection with the cytomegalovirus (CMV), which is capable of causing infection in unborn children. Because of this risk, any pregnant staff should minimise their contact with known AIDS patients. Some AIDS patients are also infected with tuberculosis (TB), which may be highly infectious before treatment is established. The risks are further increased because an increasing number of strains of TB are now multi-drug resistant.

Protective clothing needs to be worn if there is any likelihood of contact with blood or body fluids. If splashing is likely (operating theatre, mortuary) then eye protection should be worn. Direct mouth to mouth resuscitation of known HIV infected patients should be avoided if possible (although there is no record of infection being transmitted this way) and a Brooke, or similar, airway used if cardiopulmonary resuscitation is instituted.

Razors, toothbrushes and other implements likely to be contaminated with blood, however minutely, should never be shared between patients.

Post mortem is unlikely to be required if AIDS is given as the cause of death. Many cases of HIV infection will be unrecognised. Pathologists and mortuary staff, like surgeons, must assume that all bodies are potentially infected and practise their art accordingly.

HIV INFECTION AND COMMUNITY CARE

The majority of AIDS patients will be cared for in a domestic environment for most of the duration of their illness, but the principles of infection control remain the same (see Standard infection control precautions, p.200). Carers should wear protective clothing appropriate to the task. Normal household cleaning with detergents and hand-hot water is adequate for most situations, including bathrooms and toilets. Contamination of surfaces by blood and body fluids should be treated with a one-in-ten solution of ordinary household bleach. Where this would spoil carpets or other fabrics, detergent and hand-hot water will suffice. Disposable cloths should be used, and disposed of with other infected items in a yellow colour coded plastic bag which is sent for incineration by the Local Authority cleansing department or by a private refuse disposal concern.

HIV DEATHS IN THE COMMUNITY

It is the responsibility of the general practitioner to inform the funeral director of the danger of infection. The funeral director will provide a cadaver bag and a leakproof shell or coffin for the removal of the body from the house.

MENINGITIS AND SEPTICAEMIA

There are many causes of meningitis. The only ones which are likely to pose a threat to those handling the body are *Mycobacterium tuberculosis* (see below) and *Neisseria meningitides*, the cause of the highly infectious meningococcal meningitis. Septicaemia likewise may result from a variety of infections, most of which do not cause problems after death. Risk to the handler may be caused by bodies with meningococcal septicaemia or with group A streptococci, and infection control guidance must be followed.

RABIES

Rabies is a notifiable disease under the Public Health (Infectious Disease) Regulations 1988. It is caused by a bite from an animal infected with the rabies virus, usually a dog or cat. At present it is not endemic in Britain, but cases do occur which are attributed to animal bites overseas. The virus is transmitted in the saliva of the rabid animal. The incubation period may be prolonged (it may be over a year), giving the sufferer time to return home before seeking treatment or becoming ill. Treatment will be given in a specialised infectious diseases hospital.

Person-to-person infection is extremely unlikely, but theoretically there may be a small risk to carers from intimate contact, particularly with the saliva of the patient. Nurses assigned to care for such a patient should be offered rabies immunisation and wear protective clothing. Staff who have cuts or abrasions on their hands, or who are pregnant (because of possible risk to the infant of administering the vaccine), must not be allowed to handle the patient. Direct mouth-to-mouth resuscitation should not be used.

Post mortems should not be undertaken unless in exceptional circumstances, and preferably the pathologist should receive immunisation prior to the autopsy. Special facilities would be needed to sterilise equipment after the autopsy, as 3 per cent formalin is not thought to be adequate to kill the rabies virus.

The risk of infection from the corpse would be slight, but protective clothing should be worn by anyone handling it. Embalming should be prohibited, and cremation encouraged. Any ritual washing should utilise 0.1 per cent cetrimide solution or other quaternary ammonium compound solution.

VIRAL HAEMORRHAGIC FEVERS

Four diseases, not endemic in Britain, form this group of serious imported infections. They are Lassa fever, Marburg disease, Ebola fever and Congo/Crimea haemorrhagic fevers. They have an incubation period of about 21 days so that people becoming infected while abroad may not become ill until after their return to Britain. These serious, highly infectious fevers would be treated in special high-security infectious disease hospitals. Malaria needs to be excluded as a cause of the fever in people returning from exotic places.

Post mortems should be avoided on the grounds of unwarranted risk, but essential limited sampling may be necessary to establish a diagnosis. Full protective clothing should be worn, including high performance respiratory protection (breathing apparatus). Disposal for a body infected with such a Group 4 pathogen is described on p.205.

CREUTZFELDT – JAKOB DISEASE

This rare form of dementia, caused by a filterable, self-replicating agent known as a prion, has been reported from some 50 countries. Human cases constitute the only known reservoir of infection and the mode of transmission is usually unknown. Several cases had a history of brain or eye surgery within two years of onset, some had a history of treatment with pituitary hormones derived from human cadaver donors, and at least one case has been attributed to a corneal transplant. A special variant of this infection, which tends to affect younger people, vCJD, has been attributed to infection with bovine spongiform encephalitis (BSE), a disease of cattle which was epidemic in the UK during the 1980s and early 1990s. People became infected through eating meat from an infected cow, but infectivity by this route is thought to be very low. Infection is also theoretically possible via infected transfused whole blood in humans, as has been shown in sheep, but there is as yet no evidence that this has occurred. Whole blood is no longer used for transfusion in the UK. The white cells, thought to be the likely site of possible infectivity, are extracted before use (Wilson, Code and Ricketts 2000). The death rate from vCJD in the UK shows evidence of levelling off, with 18 deaths being reported in 2003, down from 28 deaths in 2000 (Andrews 2004).

Great care must be taken to avoid using tissues from infected patients in transplants. Corneas should not be taken from demented patients, from those who die in psychiatric hospitals, or from those who die from obscure undiagnosed neurological disease. Material from such patients should not be used for the preparation of thromboplastin, growth hormone or other biological extracts used as reagents or treatment (Advisory Group for CJD 1981). Surgical instruments contaminated from such patients must be autoclaved twice before further use, or disposable ones used where possible. Normal infection control measures are appropriate after death, with the body placed in a leakproof bag for transportation to the mortuary.

The bodies of patients who have died from CJD must not be used for teaching anatomy or pathology. If a post mortem is essential, it should be carried out only by fully trained staff, according to the detailed guidance given in *The Code of Practice for the Prevention of Infection in Clinical Laboratories and Post Mortem Rooms*, 2nd edn (2002). The post mortem may be carried out in any mortuary, care being taken not to contaminate the environment. The body should remain in the opened bag, with absorbent wadding placed inside, alongside the body, to absorb body fluids. For the examination of the brain, the entire head should be enclosed within a large plastic bag while the skull is being opened. Disposable protective clothing must be worn, including a face visor, which completely encloses the operator's head, to protect eyes and mouth from contamination.

For an intact body, normal procedures are appropriate for funeral directors. Embalming should be discouraged, but relatives may have superficial contact with the washed body. Either burial or cremation is suitable. Any retained tissues may be potentially infected, and should only be returned to the family via the funeral director, for appropriate disposal.

ENTERIC INFECTIONS
If death is known or suspected to be due to *Salmonella* infection, or other enteric infections such as bacillary dysentery, special care must be taken in washing down and opening the gut, returning the viscera to the body and sewing up and washing the body. The mortuary surfaces and pathologists' clothing must all be carefully disinfected with phenolic disinfectant.

TUBERCULOSIS
If the death was known or suspected of being due to respiratory tuberculosis, special precautions are taken to minimise the risk of infection. Ten per cent formalin solution is introduced into the lungs after collecting specimens for bacteriology and before commencing the post mortem. Care must be taken not to cause any aerosol spray, handling should be kept to a minimum and all instruments used must be autoclaved at the end of the session. Disposable gowns should be worn.

ANTHRAX
Post mortems should be avoided if death is known to be due to anthrax. If an autopsy is performed, care must be taken not to cause splashing of body fluids onto clothing or surfaces. The mortuary surfaces need careful treatment for at least half an hour with a freshly prepared disinfectant solution, which is then washed down with running water. Clothing must be autoclaved before laundering. Anthrax spores may survive for many years in soil. The body should be cremated.

BRUCELLOSIS AND LEPTOSPIROSIS
These infections may be transmitted through the conjunctiva as well as by other routes. If post mortems are performed, then visor protection must be worn.

SARS
Severe acute respiratory syndrome (SARS) was the name given to a sudden epidemic of severe respiratory disease, which began in Beijing in February 2003 and spread rapidly round 16 areas of China and to other countries, including Singapore, Hong Kong, India and Canada. The cough and breathing difficulties were often preceded by symptoms of fever, chills, malaise, myalgia, rigors, abdominal pain and headache. The causative organism was identified as a coronavirus, apparently unlike any other virus of the same family, either human or animal. Transmission is mainly by the spread of infected droplets from the respiratory system of the infected person to another. There were almost 4000 cases identified, with deaths in 26 countries by the end of April 2003. The sequences of the genomes of two of the SARS strains were known by May 2003, indicating that the virus was genuinely new in humans. By mid May, almost 8000 people had been affected and 643 had died in 29 countries,

and the UK had its first possible cases reported. In China, over 16,000 people were put in quarantine. Strict isolation of victims and the follow up of contacts, for the signs of early infection, remained the main strategy for stopping the epidemic. The SARS virus may be viable in the environment for several days, so precautionary measures, including rigorous disinfection and hygiene procedures, should provide the highest standard of protection. Cases were treated with broad-spectrum antibiotics and supportive care, as well as antiviral agents and immunomodulatory therapy. Assisted ventilation in a non-invasive or invasive form would be instituted in SARS patients complicated by respiratory failure (Camps and Hoffman 2005). No specific guidance was issued to mortuary staff in the UK during the SARS epidemic.

MRSA

The usual mortuary infection control procedures should be adequate for MRSA (see Standard infection control precautions, p.200).

Stillbirth

Some stillbirths are likely to be associated with infection. The most likely are rubella, syphilis, toxoplasma, cytomegalovirus, parvovirus B19 and listeria monocytogenes. There is little additional risk to the father from handling the body, as he has most probably been exposed to the infection from the mother, or may indeed be the source of it. Basic cleaning and wrapping of the body should reduce any small residual risk (Healing, Hoffman and Young 1995).

Infection and bereaved contacts

It is possible that the bereaved relatives and friends may be at risk of incubating the infection and require prophylactic treatment for themselves, as in contacts of meningococcal meningitis or septicaemia and some other serious diseases. The Medical Officer for Environmental Health/Consultant in Communicable Disease Control at the Health Protection Agency (HPA) is responsible for contact tracing and the institution of appropriate control measures.

Sources of local advice

For further advice on any aspect of infection control, contact:

- The Consultant for Communicable Disease Control at your nearest branch of the Health Protection Agency.
- The Director of Public Health at any Primary Care Trust.

- For NHS staff, each National Health Service hospital, Community and Mental Health Trust has an Infection Control Team.

- Consultant microbiologists in hospitals, university departments, and the Health Protection Agency will usually be happy to help. In particular, the HPA may be able to give advice about the more dangerous and lesser known infections.

References

Advisory Committee on Dangerous Pathogens (1983) *Categorisation of Pathogens According to Hazard and Categories of Containment.* London: Department of Health.

Advisory Committee on Dangerous Pathogens (1995) *Categorization of Biological Agents According to Hazard and Categories of Containment.* London: HSE Books.

Advisory Committee on Dangerous Pathogens (1998) *Supplement to Categorization of Biological Agents According to Hazards and Categories of Containment.* London: HSE Books.

Advisory Committee on Dangerous Pathogens (2003) *Infection at Work: Controlling the Risks. A Guide for Employers and the Self Employed on Identifying, Assessing and Controlling the Risks of Infection in the Workplace.* London: Department of Health.

Advisory group on the management of patients with spongiform encephalopathy (Creutzfeldt–Jakob Disease (CJD)) (1981) *Report to the Chief Medical Officers of the Department of Health and Social Security, the Scottish Home and Health Department and the Welsh Office.* London: HMSO.

Andrews, N. (2004) 'vCJD incidence in the UK shows evidence of having peaked or reached a plateau.' *Eurosurveillance Weekly 8*, 6, 2–3. London: Health Protection Agency Communicable Disease Surveillance Centre.

Blackmore, M.A. (1987) 'Hand drying methods.' *Nursing Times Journal of Infection Control 83*, 37, 71–74. In: *Hand Decontamination Guidelines* (2002). London: Infection Control Nurses Association.

Camps, B.S. and Hoffman, C. (eds) (2005) 'SARS Reference.' Website: www.sarsreference.com/sarsref/prevent.htm (accessed July 2005).

Chief Medical Officer (2003) *Winning Ways. Working Together to Reduce Healthcare Associated Infections in England.* London: Department of Health.

Department of Health (1989) *Review of Law on Infectious Disease Control – Consultation Document.* London: Department of Health.

Department of Health/NHS Estates (2004) *34335 The NHS Healthcare Cleaning Manual, Section 2 'Infection Control'.* London: Department of Health/NHS Estates. Also available on www.dh.gov.uk/

Emmerson, A.M., Enstone, J.E., Griffin, M., Kelsey, M.C., Smyth, E.T.M. (1996) 'The second national prevalence survey of infection in hospitals – overview of results.' *Journal of Hospital Infection 32*, 175–190.

Garner, J.S. and Favero, M.S. (1985) 'CDC guidelines for handwashing and hospital environmental control.' US Department of Health and Human Services, Public Health Service, Atlanta, USA. In: *Hand Decontamination Guidelines* (2002). London: Infection Control Nurses Association.

Healing, T.D., Hoffman, P.N. and Young, S.E.J. (1995) 'The infection hazards of human cadavers.' *CDR Review Communicable Disease Report 5*, 5, RR61–73.

Health Protection Agency (2004) *Staphylococcus aureus bacteraemia Laboratory Reports and Methicillin Susceptibility (Voluntary Reporting Scheme): England and Wales, 1990–2003.* National Statistics website: www.statistics.gov.uk/ (accessed 24 February 2005).

Health and Safety Commission and Health Services Advisory Committee (1989a) *Safe Working and the Prevention of Infection in the Mortuary and Post Mortem Room.* Draft document for consultation. Bristol: Health Services Advisory Committee.

Health and Safety Commission and Health Services Advisory Committee (1989b) *Safe Working and the Prevention of Infection in Clinical Laboratories and Similar Facilities.* Draft document for consultation. Bristol: Health Services Advisory Committee.

Health and Safety Executive (2003) *Safe Working and the Prevention of Infection in Clinical Laboratories and Similar Facilities.* London: HSE/HSAC.

Health and Safety Executive and Health Services Advisory Committee (2003) *Safe Working and the Prevention of Infection in the Mortuary and Post-Mortem Room.* London: HSE/HSAC.

Lawrence, J. and May, D. (2003) *Infection Control in the Community.* London: Churchill Livingstone.

Morrison, D. (2005) 'MRSA – from hospital superbug to community threat.' *Bulletin of the Royal College of Pathologists 129*, 14–16.

Resnick, L., Veren, K., Salahuddin, S.Z., Tondreau, S., Markham, P.D. (1986) 'Stability and inactivity of HTLV III/LAV under clinical and laboratory environments.' *Journal of the American Medical Association 255*, 14, 1887–1891.

Robinson, W.S. (1979) 'Hepatitis B virus.' In: *Principles and Practice of Infectious Diseases*, Vol 2. New York: John Wiley.

Royal College of Nursing Safety Representatives Conference Co-ordinating Committee (1987) *Introduction to Hepatitis B and Nursing Guidelines for Infection Control.* London: Royal College of Nursing.

UK Health Departments (1984) *Code of Practice for the Prevention of Infection in Clinical Laboratories and Post Mortem Rooms (The Howie Code).* London: HMSO.

UK Health Departments (1999) *AIDS/HIV Infected Health Care Workers: Guidance on the Management of Infected Health Care Workers and Patient Notification.* NHS MEL(1999)29, Scottish Executive, UK Health Departments.

Wilson, K., Code, C. and Ricketts, M.N. (2000) 'Risk of acquiring Creutzfeldt–Jakob disease from blood transfusions: systematic review of case–control studies.' *British Medical Journal 321*, 17–19.

PART 3

Religious, Ethnic and Cultural Aspects of Dying and Death

CHAPTER 17

CHRISTIANITY AND THE SACRAMENTS

This handbook is not intended as a manual of comparative theology. Death, which touches every one of us several times during our own lives, is associated with beliefs, rituals and traditions, which vary widely between different ethnic groups. Within each of those groups there is the whole spectrum of observance, from the ultra-orthodox to the non-believing, non-practising atheist or agnostic. However, the death of a non-believer may have great impact on religious members of the family, and non-observance of religious laws may be a cause of anguish, shame and family disagreement.

Many Health Authorities have written policy documents to ensure that all patients have the right to have their way of life – and death – respected, acknowledging that many people have traditions, beliefs, food, customs and manners which are different from the majority.

These chapters touch only on issues surrounding death, and how beliefs and customs may differ. Health care staff who are sensitive to these issues can contribute greatly to the welfare of all their patients. We hope that our readers are of many cultural backgrounds, so we have included the ethnic majority groups of Britain, as being of special interest to others.

Christianity

Christianity is the religion which acknowledges the divinity of Jesus Christ, with the belief that God became man on earth in the person of Jesus Christ. There are many Christian churches and sects. In 2002, it was estimated that Christianity had over 2038 million adherents. It is the largest world religion, with almost 33 per cent of the world's population claiming to be an adherent of one or another of the various churches (Encyclopaedia Britannica 2004). Central to its teaching is the belief of God as a Trinity, with one God who reveals Himself as a Father, a Son, and a Holy Spirit. God created the world, and redeems mankind through the work of his divine son, Jesus Christ, who was crucified, rose from the dead and ascended to heaven. The symbol of the cross is often worn by followers of the faith. Some may wear the fish symbol, which is derived from the Greek 'ichthos' – an acronym for Jesus Christ, Son of God, Saviour.

Sacraments are outward and visible signs, believed by Christians to have been ordained by Jesus Christ to symbolise and convey spiritual gifts. An example is the use of bread and wine in the Communion service (Eucharist), which symbolises the presence and power of Christ. Christian tradition came to recognise seven Sacraments, of which the most important are Baptism and Eucharist. The others are confirmation, penance, extreme unction (anointing of the sick), matrimony and priestly ordination. The importance given to the different Sacraments varies between the different churches.

Baptism is the sprinkling with, or immersion in, water as a sign that the person is cleansed from sin and may be admitted as a member of the church. It is known as the essential Sacrament, and all the mainstream Christian churches recognise the validity of each other's Baptism.

Eucharist is the principal Sacrament and is the central act of Christian worship in most Christian traditions. It is also called Holy Communion, Lord's Supper, or Mass. (Notable exceptions to this would include the Society of Friends (Quakers) and the Salvation Army.) Communion bread and wine is taken in memory of the body and blood of Jesus Christ, who blessed both at his final meal (the Last Supper) with the words 'this is my body' and 'this is my blood' and commanded that both should be taken in remembrance of Him. For some, it is the source and summit of the life of the church. Many Christians draw great comfort and strength from participation in the regular service of Communion, and find that it invigorates them and refreshes their faith. For a person who is too sick to attend a place of worship for Communion, the hospital Chaplain, or, increasingly, an authorised lay person, may offer Communion at the bedside, by saying brief prayers and giving the Sacrament of bread and wine, which has been blessed and consecrated at a previous service.

In Britain the 'established church' is called the Church of England or the Anglican Church. Its adherents are called Anglicans.

Reference

Encyclopaedia Britannica CD (2004) *Worldwide Adherents of All Religions by Six Continental Areas, Mid 2002*. Rugeley: Focus Multimedia.

CHAPTER 18

THE ANGLICAN CHURCH

(The Church in Wales, the Church in Ireland, the Episcopalian Church in Scotland)

Anglicans are initiated into the faith at Baptism. Their approach to death is influenced by the Christian conviction that all will share in Christ's resurrection and eternal life.

Baptism

Baptism is the official entry into the Christian fellowship of faith, and in infancy and childhood is usually associated with the giving of a name to the child – the 'Christening'. Traditionally it was regarded as important that a child should have a name before it died, and it may yet be a source of great distress if the baby has not been named. Anglicans, however, no longer adhere to the old-fashioned view that an unbaptised child may be taken by the devil rather than by God, and the religious importance of naming before death has diminished accordingly. These days, some churches will offer a special naming ceremony for a child, separating this from the declaration of religious commitment of the traditional Baptism.

The Baptism is so called because of St John the Baptist who, before the birth of Christ, used immersion in water as an act of repentance and preparation for the arrival of the 'Coming One', and who later baptised Christ himself. During the ceremony, a priest makes the holy sign of the cross, with water, on the baby's (or adult's) forehead. This is regarded as the outward sign of God's love and marks the entry of a person into the family of Christ, acknowledging them as a son or daughter of God. It also marks the beginning of a process of being 'born again' and the development of spiritual awareness. It can have deep significance for individuals and their families.

There is no age limit for Baptism, and it may be offered in many circumstances where life is in danger, for example to premature babies, before surgical operations and in serious illness. Similarly there is no age limit for the Baptism of a healthy individual. Baptism of a young child is carried out with promises made on the child's behalf, and many believers have a similar ceremony again when they are old enough to understand and commit themselves to the principles of the faith, usually from 11 or 12 years onwards. This is known as 'Confirmation'.

If a child receives an emergency Baptism in hospital, and subsequently recovers, the second part of the service can be offered by the child's own church at a later date.

Should a child die unbaptised, the priest is able to give a naming and blessing ceremony immediately after death if the parents wish it. This is particularly appropriate following a stillbirth. A certificate to commemorate the Baptism may be provided by the priest.

In an emergency any confirmed Anglican believer may baptise. In extremis any Christian may do so, regardless of denomination.

Anointing

For adults, if death is imminent, the anointing ceremony may be requested. This may be done more than once. Anointing is regarded as a preparation for something special, for some life-affecting event, rather than specifically a preparation for death. It may be equally performed before a major operation, childbirth, or if the patient is returning home again after surgery or a long illness. Olive oil, sanctified by a Bishop, is used to make the sign of the cross on the forehead, chest and wrist of the patient, and prayers are offered.

The dying patient will usually regard it as important that family and close friends have unrestricted access to the bedside. The relatives may wish to share a Communion or anointing ceremony, if necessary at the bedside, with the sick family member.

It is now many years since Christian prayers were said every morning, by nursing staff, on wards in British hospitals. Older patients may remember this and lament its passing. Most large hospitals have a hospital chapel where services are held, and where mobile patients can seek personal refuge, but such places are unlikely to be visited by the dying patient. Such chapels have an interfaith function nowadays. Visits from the hospital Chaplain may therefore be appreciated, and requests may be made for prayer, Communion, anointing, or simply counselling and comfort. The church would wish each dying Anglican patient to know that he or she is deeply loved. Comfort is offered to the atheist, the agnostic and to those who feel themselves to be in a state of sin, as well as to committed believers.

At death a prayer of commendation may be said for the benefit of the family. The prayer may be said at the point of death or over the body of the patient after death, in the ward or mortuary chapel. It gives thanks to God for the life passed, and commends the soul to God's keeping.

Last Offices are 'routine' (see p.182). Christian bodies are frequently laid in the coffin with the hands crossed over the chest or placed in an attitude of prayer.

Post mortem examinations

There is no church teaching with regard to the disfigurement of a body. It is only the soul which transcends to the next world. Post mortems may be disliked at a personal level, but are not forbidden on religious grounds.

Donation of the body for research and teaching

This would also be quite acceptable from the religious point of view. On a practical level, the church would offer a memorial service instead of a funeral at the time, and a funeral service when the body is finally interred a year or so later. This, of course, means extra grieving for the family, and the church will help greatly in the grieving process by emphasising the importance of the 'gift' to medical research.

Blood transfusion

There is no ethical problem with the giving or receiving of blood.

Organ transplantation

There is no religious objection to donation or reception of organs such as kidney, heart or liver. The church remains concerned about such ethical issues as the use of fetal tissue transplants for the treatment of Parkinson's disease, but the church will follow the laws of the land.

Abortion

Most Anglican ministers would agree with the terms of the Abortion Act 1967 and the more recent (1990) amendments to the Human Fertilisation and Embryology Bill (see p.78) and would be happy to provide counselling if requested. As with any other group of people, there will be a wide variety of views held by different clergy, and some may feel that the current law is misguided.

Stillbirths

Stillbirths (babies born dead after 26 weeks' gestation) are regarded as natural births, and frequently the family wishes to have a funeral for the baby. A special children's service is provided in the Alternative Services Book. Even for a younger stillbirth, or fetal remains, many parents wish to have a naming ceremony and burial. The burial service for a child is appropriate for this situation.

Suicide

There is no longer any stigma associated with suicide, and the body of a suicide would be treated in exactly the same way as any other, including burial in consecrated ground. The clergy would respond to the needs of the relatives.

Euthanasia

It is not an appropriate course of action to deliberately end life or to assist the person to end their life.

Funerals

Burial and cremation are both equally acceptable. There is no specific teaching as to tissue retention and its ultimate disposal. The clergy will always strive to help individuals and families overcome such problems and will offer prayers as requested. They will always cooperate with the law of the land. If a second funeral is requested for a retained body part, a prayer of commendation may be offered, rather than the full funeral service, and comfort offered to the family.

CHAPTER 19

THE ROMAN CATHOLIC CHURCH

The Roman Catholic Church is the name given to the religious organisation of those Christians who acknowledge the supreme jurisdiction of the Bishop of Rome (the Pope). The Pope is recognised as the lawful successor to St Peter the Apostle, who was appointed by Christ to be the head of His church. About one-third of the world population is estimated to be Christian and, worldwide, Roman Catholics constitute by far the most numerous body of Christians, about 57 per cent of the total. Probably almost a fifth of the human race belongs to the Roman Catholic Church (Encyclopaedia Britannica 2004). There may be five million Catholics in Britain (Stanford 2005).

There are many similarities in the practices of Anglicans and Catholics, and indeed of the many other branches of Christianity.

The Catholic Church understands life here and now as the first chapter of eternal existence. From the moment of conception, through birth until natural death, which is itself a birth into that eternal existence, a person prepares for eternal life (the fullness of life). God freely invites followers into His life, Heaven. The rejection of this, by deliberate and free choice, leads to Hell.

The Sacraments

On the whole, the Sacraments are of greater importance to Catholics than to other Christian groups. They are of great significance to believers, assisting them in the journey through this world and helping them to make that ultimate choice for God and eternal life.

Baptism is the essential Sacrament for all mainstream Christian groups, and of great significance to Catholics. Worldwide, adult baptism is common, alongside infant baptism, but infant baptism is the usual practice in Britain. There is no upper age limit. It is regarded as extremely important that a child is baptised before, or at, death. This is so important that anyone, even a non-believer, may baptise in an emergency. A little water is poured on the forehead of the child, with the words '(Name of child) I baptise you in the name of the Father, the Son and the Holy Spirit'. (The Chaplain should always be informed of the baptism, so that it can be registered.)

Holy Communion is the sharing of the body and blood of Christ in the form of bread and wine, remembering his death and resurrection and giving thanks for his love. Children usually take their first Communion at the age of seven or eight, when parents, teachers and clergy feel that they have the use of reason. They will attend confession for the first time, before this first Communion, but do not require to be 'confirmed' at this time. (Pope Pius X, in about 1910, wanted children to be able to share in Communion and said that those over 'the age of reason' could do so, even before Confirmation.) They may attend 'confession' after this, but are not deemed capable of committing mortal sin until they are old enough to take full responsibility for their moral decisions.

The Sacrament of the Sick symbolises Christ's present healing and loving, to help a person to be well again. It can be adapted to different degrees of illness, and can be repeated in changing circumstances. When a person is dying, they can receive the Sacrament of the Sick as 'extreme unction' or last anointing. The dying person is anointed with holy oil on the forehead and hands, and the ceremony becomes one of absolving the patient from sin, of healing and of reconciliation. (There are three kinds of holy oil. The Bishops of the Diocese meet together each year on Maundy Thursday, for the Chrism Mass. Here the oils are blessed for their different purposes. One is for Confirmation and Ordination, one for Baptism, and the third for the Sacrament for the Sick.) This Sacrament is primarily for healing, not simply for extreme unction. Older patients may still not be aware of this, and be afraid to request the sacrament for healing, as they may consider this to be their last anointing.

If the patient is well enough, Holy Communion may be taken also. For a Catholic patient in hospital, it is extremely important to have access to a priest and to receive Holy Communion. Many large hospitals will have a full-time Catholic priest. Catholic Chaplains regard it as their duty to visit all Catholic patients, probably more so than for other Christian groups. They will ensure that one of their number is on-call, round the clock, for the emergency administration of the Sacraments.

Health care staff should never hesitate to call a Roman Catholic Chaplain at any time of the night or day in appropriate situations.

Diet

Catholic patients in hospital would not request any special diet. Friday is a day of abstinence and self-denial for Catholics in health, and, by tradition, this became a meat-free day. This is no longer considered necessary, but many British hospitals and other institutions have long been accustomed to serving fish on Fridays to minimise any offence to Catholic clients, both patients and staff. Observance of any dietary 'rules' would, in any event, not be expected of sick patients, either in hospital or at home.

The dying Roman Catholic

At the point of death, and up to three hours after apparent death, the anointing of the sick (extreme unction) may be carried out, for the sake of the family and friends.

Last Offices

Last Offices are 'routine' (see p.182). There is no religious objection to non-Catholics handling the body.

Post mortems

As with Anglicans, there is no religious objection to post mortems. The body is to be treated with reverence, as befits the dignity of a human person, one who shares the life of God. A 'whole' body is not essential for the fullness of life. Donation of the body for research or teaching is likewise not prohibited.

Blood transfusion

There is no religious objection to the giving or to the receiving of blood.

Organ donation

There is no religious objection to donation or to reception of organs. The Church does have ethical concerns about a donor being kept artificially alive for the purpose of transplantation of an organ. Respect for the dignity of the dead body is of primary importance.

Abortion

Catholic teaching is utterly opposed to abortion in all circumstances.

Miscarriage or stillbirth

The Church teaching is that the infant should be baptised. The clergy would do this if the parents requested it, and a funeral service may be offered.

Euthanasia

Euthanasia would never be condoned.

Suicide

The Church does not believe that a person has the right to commit suicide, but does not judge the deceased after the event, rather to 'let God judge'. No reference would be made to the mode of death at the funeral service, and burial may take place in consecrated ground.

Funerals

Traditionally, Catholics in Britain were buried rather than cremated, but there is no religious prohibition upon cremation, which is increasingly the choice. It was customary in some Catholic communities, particularly amongst Irish Catholics, to display the body after death or at the funeral, but this too is a declining tradition. If the body is to be displayed, it should preferably be embalmed (see p.102).

If retained pathological specimens or body parts are released to the family after death, they would be disposed of according to the wishes of the family.

A service (Mass) will be held in church, with a homily for the family and prayers for the individual. Holy water is used to remind the congregation of baptism and of the Easter mystery of Jesus' death and resurrection. It is sprinkled on the coffin as a sign of the hope of sharing in the glory of the resurrection. The coffin may then be covered with a pall (a cloth), a reminder of the white garment given at baptism, and other Christian symbols, such as the Bible or a cross, which symbolise key aspects of the faith. The Paschal candle stands beside the coffin as a symbol of the light Christ brings to the world. Incense is burned, symbolising the prayers of the church rising to heaven.

A child who had not yet made confession and received Communion would have the 'Mass of Angels', rather than a requiem mass. A child who had already received Communion would have a requiem mass, whatever the age. Funeral rites may also be celebrated for a child who dies before baptism. In this case the pall and holy waters, both reminders of baptism, are omitted from the ceremony.

References

Encyclopaedia Britannica CD (2004) *Worldwide Adherents of all Religions by Six Continental Areas, Mid 2002*. Rugeley: Focus Multimedia.

Stanford, P. (2005) *The Catholic Church*. At www.bbc.co.uk/religion (accessed 11 July 2005).

CHAPTER 20

FREE CHURCHES AND OTHER CHURCHES

There are many variants of Christianity which do not conform to Anglican or Catholic tradition of hierarchical church organisation and are not tied to the State or to Rome. They are known as 'non-conformist' or 'free' churches. As with some other religious groups, membership of some of these shows a significant reduction in the UK over the last ten years or so, whilst apparently increasing in numbers worldwide. Figures given here are taken from Whitaker's Almanacks (1989, 2005).

The Methodist Church, founded by the Wesley brothers in 1739, has spread to some 90 countries and includes several different Methodist groups. In 2004 it was estimated that there were about 341,000 Methodists in Britain (a drop from over 450,000 in 1987).

The Baptist Churches have over 40 million members worldwide, over 143,000 of whom live in Britain. (This too shows a reduction in Britain from about 170,000 in 1988.)

The Salvation Army, by 2004, had about 45,000 members in the UK, some 1400 officers engaged in evangelistic and social work and about 800 centres of worship. (In 1987 it had 924 centres, and 1800 active officers.)

The Society of Friends (Quakers) has no separate ministry. In Great Britain there are about 500 places of worship, and about 16,000 members.

The Seventh Day Adventists have over 240 churches and companies and over 22,200 members in the British Isles (an increase from 16,500 in 1989).

There are many others, including the General Assembly of Unitarian and Free Christian Churches, the Free Church of England, and the United Reformed Church.

The Eastern Orthodox Churches (Greek Orthodox, Russian Orthodox and Serbian Orthodox) are part of the most ancient mainstream Christian churches worldwide, but congregations in most parts of Britain are small. They are not properly considered 'Free Churches' because of their links to other States, but are mentioned here for convenience.

The list is almost endless. The Lutheran Church is one of the largest Protestant denominations, particularly in Northern Europe and the USA. It has over 70 million members worldwide. There are about 100,000 in Great Britain, in a hundred congregations. (This shows a significant increase in Britain, from about 27,000 in 1989.) Lutheran services in Britain are often held in other languages to serve immigrant communities.

Finally, the Church of Scotland is the established church in Scotland, and the Presbyterian Churches of Wales and Ireland represent a large body of Christianity in those countries.

All the above will call themselves 'Christians' and, on the whole, their attitudes and practices with regard to death are similar to those of Anglicans. There are no special requirements for Free Church adherents in hospital. The usual ward practice is unlikely to cause offence, and there are no special dietary requirements.

When facing crisis or illness in hospital Free Church believers will, on the whole, be happy to be visited by a minister from any Free Church, not necessarily their own. They are likely to place less emphasis on sacramental ceremonies, and to want the minister to join them in informal prayer, rather than administer the sacraments of Holy Communion or Extreme Unction, and they will value his presence. Baptism of a sick infant is not necessarily seen as essential, but for some families these details assume particular importance. Methodists of Afro-Caribbean origin may have some different beliefs and customs from those of native British origin (see p.246), and are likely to regard baptism as of greater significance than do their white neighbours.

Last Offices

For all the Christian groups 'routine' Last Offices are appropriate (see p.182).

Post mortems

There is no objection to post mortem examination on religious grounds.

Blood transfusion and organ transplantation

There is no religious objection to the giving or receiving of blood. There is no religious objection to the donation or reception of organs.

Donation of the body

There is no religious prohibition to the donation of the body for research or teaching purposes.

Funerals

Burial and cremation are equally acceptable.

References

Whitaker's Almanack (shorter edition) (1989) *The Churches*. London: J. Whitaker.

Whitaker's Almanack (2005) *The Churches*. London: A & C Black.

CHAPTER 21

JEHOVAH'S WITNESSES

'Jehovah' is an English translation of the Hebrew name for God, as written in the Scriptures. 'Witness' is taken from the passage in Isaiah 43:10 (and similar passages): 'My witnesses, says the Lord, are you, my servants, you whom I have chosen to know me and put your faith in me and understand that I am He' (New English Bible). Jehovah's Witnesses believe that God has had His Witnesses since the time of Abel, but the modern organisation is a Christian religion, which began in the USA in the 19th century and has since spread all over the world. It is estimated that there are some 6.4 million Witnesses worldwide, and over a million in America. There are about 125,500 Witnesses in Britain, in almost 1500 congregations (Watch Tower and Bible Tract Society 2004).

Jehovah's Witnesses are deeply religious people, who believe that the entire Bible is inspired by God. It is, for them, of great importance to try and live their lives by God's commands and requests, as written in the Old and the New Testaments. They believe that Jesus was created by God, and that he is subordinate to Him (Colossians 1:15; Corinthians 11:3), unlike the belief in the Trinity of most other Christian groups. They believe that the rule of the Kingdom of God under Christ will soon be established over the earth, at which time God will resurrect many former inhabitants to live in peace, with freedom from sickness and disease, on paradise earth. At this time, the complete number of those called to rule with Christ in heaven will be in place (Revelation 14:1–3).

Witnesses differ in practice and belief in many respects from other Christian groups. In particular, health care staff may have many misconceptions about them because of their well-known religious objection to the giving or receiving of blood, but there are many other points to note when caring for Witnesses as patients.

Jehovah's Witnesses and the question of blood

Some people may have mistakenly concluded that Jehovah's Witnesses disagree with the modern practice of medicine, or that they wish to become martyrs to their cause. Both ideas are incorrect. When ill or injured, Jehovah's Witnesses will willingly seek medical help in all respects except in the question of blood (WTBTS 1977; Governing Body of Jehovah's Witnesses undated). Health care staff must appreciate that this is a religious objection and is fundamental to the faith.

It is founded upon Biblical teachings. In a number of places the Bible forbids the consuming of blood ('only flesh with its soul – its blood – you must not eat', Genesis 9:3–4). Christians are commanded to 'abstain from…blood' in several verses of Acts (15:20, 28, 29; 21:25). Jehovah's Witnesses interpret these passages to mean that blood must be neither consumed by mouth nor taken intravenously, whether as whole blood, packed red cells, plasma, white cells or platelets. However, there are many issues of modern medicine which are not covered by the Bible, and individual Witnesses will decide according to the dictates of their personal conscience whether to accept such derivatives as albumin, immune globulins or coagulation factors (haemophiliac preparations).

Passages such as [you must] 'pour out and cover it [the blood] with dust' (Leviticus 17:13–14) indicate to Witnesses how Jehovah God requires blood to be handled, namely with respect and appreciation for the fact that it represents life. They believe that it should not be stored or used again after it has left the circulation, for example as in autologous transfusion of predeposited blood. However, a Witness may accept the use of dialysis or heart–lung equipment as long as no other source of blood is used, and where the extra-corporeal circulation is uninterrupted and continuous with the body circulation (WTBTS 1989). There is no religious objection to these. Neither is there any religious objection to blood samples being taken for pathological examinations, as long as the blood is disposed of appropriately after the tests.

Increasingly, there are reports of major surgery, including heart bypass surgery and organ transplantation, being successfully carried out without the use of transfused blood (Varela et al. 2003).

Bloodless medicine and surgery

Worldwide, there are many specialist clinicians who are skilled in the use of medical alternatives to donor blood. There is an extensive body of literature on the subject, available from the Jehovah's Witnesses Hospital Information Service in London. A recent study in a trauma centre (Varela et al. 2003) showed that Jehovah's Witnesses were no more likely to die from their trauma than were other patients. Major surgery of all kinds has been performed successfully without donor blood (Dixon and Smalley 1981).

There have been many deaths worldwide in recent years due to the transfusion of blood which was infected, in particular with the viruses which cause HIV and hepatitis B. Safe, bloodless surgery is therefore of potential benefit to all patients, not only to Jehovah's Witnesses.

FLUIDS

Alternative treatments include intravenous fluids, which help to maintain blood volume and prevent hypovolemic shock. These include such things as Ringer's lactate solution, dextran, hydroxyethyl starch and others. Some newer fluids are able to transport oxygen, but none as yet can do this as well as the haemoglobin in real blood. (Witnesses will not accept the re-use of their own previously collected and stored blood.)

DRUGS
Genetically engineered proteins, such as erythropoietin, stimulate the production of new red blood cells. Other substances stimulate production of other blood components, such as interleukin-11 for platelets. Some preparations can help to minimise blood loss during surgical procedures (aprotinin, antifibrinolytics).

BIOLOGICAL HAEMOSTATICS
The direct application of haemostatic pads, woven from collagen and cellulose, can control bleeding. Glues and sealants made with fibrin can be used to close puncture wounds, or can be spread over wide areas of bleeding tissue.

BLOOD SALVAGE
Machines are now available which are able to recover blood after surgery or trauma. The blood is cleansed and returned to the patient via closed circuit tubing. The use of such machinery is a matter of personal choice for patients who are Jehovah's Witnesses.

SURGICAL TECHNIQUES AND TOOLS
Properly planned surgery should avoid most complications. There must be very prompt action to control any bleeding. Devices are available which can cut and seal blood vessels at the same time. Minimally invasive (keyhole) surgery will cause less bleeding than conventional surgery. Over 180 hospitals round the world now specialise in bloodless medicine and surgery.

There are over 1400 Hospital Liaison Committees worldwide which are equipped to provide health care staff with relevant and up-to-date information from a large database of research and literature on 'bloodless' medicine, including their national office in London (see below). By invitation, they will make presentations to hospital medical staff or support patients through their treatment.

Religious ceremonies (the Sacraments)

BAPTISM
Witnesses commit themselves to the faith and to God at baptism. For this they must be of an age of understanding.

There is no requirement to baptise the infant of a Witness couple, even in the case of extreme illness. Should a child die, the child is protected by the dedicated state of the parents (1 Corinthians 7:14). Baptised parents will not give their consent to transfusion for their children, since they see their duty to raise their children 'in the nurture and advice of the Lord' (Ephesians 6:4).

Many Witnesses are adult converts, and baptism follows study by the individual and personal examination by elders in the local congregation as to whether the person is qualified. Thus, until a person is baptised, no sanctions can be taken against a person who accepts a blood transfusion, as he is not a Jehovah's Witness until he is baptised. However, many students preparing for baptism have refused transfusions.

BREAD AND WINE (THE MEMORIAL)
The emblems of the bread and wine, representing the body and blood of Christ, are taken only on the anniversary of Christ's death and only by those Witnesses who know they are of the heavenly calling.

Witnesses believe that only those whom God has called and anointed with His spirit will rule with Christ in the Kingdom of God. The rest will be subjects of that Kingdom, living on a paradise earth during the 1000-year reign of Christ, when the earth will be restored to the state God first intended, before sin and death entered the human condition (Revelation 20:4–6; 21:1–4).

While there are well over six million preaching Witnesses in the world, less than 9000 partook of the bread and wine at the 2004 annual 'Memorial' of the death of Christ (Religious Tolerance 2005).

If a Witness professes to be of the heavenly calling, the local elders will ensure that, subject to the physical state of the individual, they are given the opportunity to partake of the emblems, should they be in hospital at the date of the Memorial.

Jehovah's Witnesses in hospital

In a hospital setting, Witnesses would not expect to receive care which was in any way different from that given to others. The dietary prohibition against blood (and against eating animals which have been strangled) is not problematic in Britain. It is considered that the slaughter methods used in Britain are adequate to pour away the unwanted blood. The extra bleeding processes which are used in the production of kosher meat are not required. Each Witness has the responsibility to determine and make reasonable enquiry as to whether blood or blood products are included in any food offered. The only foodstuffs which would offend would be the 'Black Pudding' type of sausage, which is made from the blood of the pig, or game which has been shot and not properly bled.

Witnesses will seek treatment for illness like anyone else, but will be mindful of the possible question of blood. Most will carry an advance directive in the form of a small personal card, which directs that no blood should be given and which releases doctors and hospitals from responsibility in this regard. The card is signed, dated and witnessed by two other Jehovah's Witnesses (one is usually a member of the family, the other a congregation elder or the family solicitor) who are authorised to uphold the bearer's decision in the event of his or her loss of consciousness.

Most hospitals will have a standard form for refusal of blood, which a Witness will gladly sign for himself, or the parents will sign on behalf of their child. Doctors and hospitals will thus be released from responsibility for any untoward results caused by refusal, despite their competent care. There will be no objection to blood samples being taken for diagnostic or treatment purposes, and no objection to most types of medical care.

In Britain, a 'competent' adult (over 18 years and of sound mind) is perfectly free to refuse to consent to any aspects of treatment. In an emergency, however, doctors must act as they deem necessary to save life (the so-called 'principle of necessity'; see p.161). An advance directive of blood refusal, signed by the Witness and others, would be respected.

In the case of a child, doctors must act as they deem necessary for the welfare of the child, but must be able to defend their actions. In this case, a second opinion is always desirable. Occasionally, if the wishes of the parents conflict with what the medical team considers is in the best interest of the child, legal advice may be necessary and a court order obtained by the hospital for the treatment of the child.

The dying Witness will wish to be visited by family and friends, and also by the elders of the congregation. Elders are not clergy, since all Jehovah's Witnesses are ministers in the sense that the apostles of Jesus' day were, but they do provide spiritual services for the members of the congregation and they must be accorded the same respect, privilege and access which is shown by health care staff to the ministers of other faiths.

At death

There are no ceremonial rites at death. The usual Last Offices are appropriate (see p.182).

Post mortem examination and body donation

The dead body has no special religious significance and there is no religious objection to post mortem. The use of the body for teaching or research is viewed as a matter for the family to decide, unless the deceased made their wishes known before death.

Organ transplantation

Obviously there are no direct references to organ transplantation in the Bible, and in general there are no religious principles against them. Many aspects of this difficult area would be a matter of personal decision by the individual Witness.

There is no absolute prohibition against the receiving of body components, and each Witness must decide individually if he or she can accept. Some transplants, for example corneas, do not require the use of blood. These days, many other transplant procedures may be undertaken without the use of blood.

Donation of organs would be left to the personal choice of the individual.

Abortion

Witnesses believe that life is sacred. They believe that scripture indicates that life begins at conception. Deliberately induced abortion, simply to avoid the birth of an unwanted child, is unacceptable.

In cases such as tubal pregnancy where there is no possibility that the embryo can develop and a child be born, intervention is viewed as a matter for the mother to decide.

If, at childbirth, there must be a choice between the life of the child or the life of the mother, the mother is responsible for such a dire decision.

There is no biblical guidance on the burial of a fetus, and the decision is personal to the parents.

Euthanasia

It is forbidden to hasten death in any way, but Witnesses would not strive unnecessarily to prolong life or to prolong the dying process.

Suicide

The person's body is dedicated to God. As life is sacred, suicide is thus against the law of God. If the balance of the person's mind was disturbed, then Witnesses believe that such situations are left in God's hands and the prospects for resurrection would not necessarily be precluded.

Funerals

Burial and cremation are equally acceptable. The dead body is not regarded as significant once the 'breath of life' has left it.

The funeral ceremony would take place at the Kingdom Hall (church), which is the meeting place of the local congregation, or at the crematorium. There is no formal written funeral service. Each is put together to suit the individual Witness. It will usually begin and end with prayer, with a short address by an elder, and may include music and songs of praise if the family wish it.

Evangelising

Jehovah's Witnesses commit themselves, as a personal responsibility, to spread the word of their faith, and 'Pioneers', many of whom are young, will volunteer to spend 1000 hours per year in preaching from house to house (Acts 5:42; 20:20) and conducting Bible studies in people's homes. They also distribute literature (the well known *Watchtower* is now printed in 150 languages, and over 26 million copies are distributed worldwide for each edition). Both men and women may become 'preachers' but only men are appointed as 'Elders' and 'Ministerial Servants' (1 Timothy

3:1–13). All Witnesses receive continuous training at their Ministry School (local evening class at the Kingdom Hall), but Elders and Ministerial Servants are provided with extra courses, as are Pioneers and those wishing to enrol for foreign missionary service.

Further queries may be directed to:

Hospital Information Service
Watch Tower Bible and Tract Society
IBSA House
The Ridgeway
London NW7 1RN
Tel: 020 8906 2211 (24 hour)
Fax: 020 8349 4545
Email: his@wtbts.org.uk

References

Dixon, J.L. and Smalley, M.G. (1981) 'Jehovah's Witnesses. The surgical/ethical challenge.' *Journal of the American Medical Association 246*, 21, 2471–2472.

Governing Body of Jehovah's Witnesses (undated) *Blood Transfusion – Why Not for Jehovah's Witnesses?* New York: WTBTS.

Religious Tolerance (2005) 'Jehovah's Witnesses.' www.religioustolerance.org/witness2.htm (accessed May 2005).

Varela, J., Varela, J.E., Gomez-Marin, O., Fleming, L.E., Cohn, S. (2003) 'The risk of death for Jehovah's Witnesses after major trauma.' *Journal of Trauma 54*, 967–972.

Watch Tower Bible and Tract Society (1977) *Jehovah's Witnesses and the Question of Blood*. New York: WTBTS.

Watch Tower Bible and Tract Society (1989) 'Do Jehovah's Witnesses allow the use of autologous blood (autotransfusion) such as by having their own blood stored and later put back into them?' (Answer to reader's letter.) *The Watch Tower*, 1 March, p.30.

Watch Tower Bible and Tract Society (2004) 'Statistics 2004 and Report of Jehovah's Witnesses Worldwide.' www.watchtower.org (accessed May 2005).

CHAPTER 22

THE MORMON CHURCH

The Church of Jesus Christ of Latter-Day Saints is also known as the Mormon Church. This branch of Christianity arose in America in the early 19th century, and now has over 12 million members worldwide and is growing fast, with an estimated 250,000 converts per year. It is the fourth largest church in the USA.

The first mission to the UK took place in 1837 and by 1852 there were some 57,000 converts. These increased to over 80,000 by 1880, but most of these then emigrated to the USA. There are now about 180,000 Mormons in Britain (an increase of some 28,000 over the number in 1990), with 500 congregations, living in all parts of the country (Personal communication from the Leeds Mission, England).

The Book of Mormon is central to the beliefs of the church and is regarded as scripture, in addition to the Old and New Testaments of the Bible. The Book, 'Another Testament of Jesus Christ', was written in America. It is an account of the revelations of many prophets whose words, written on gold plates, were quoted and abridged by a prophet historian named Mormon. The record gives an account of two great civilisations. One originated from Jerusalem in 600 BCE and later divided into the Nephites and the Lamanites. The other, earlier civilisation is that of the Jaredites. After thousands of years all were destroyed except the Lamanites, whom Mormons believe to be the ancestors of the American Indians.

Mormon's son, Moroni, having himself added to the plates, then hid them in the Hill Cumorah (near Palmyra, New York, USA) where they remained for some fourteen centuries. On 21 September 1823, the glorified resurrected being of Moroni appeared to the Prophet Joseph Smith and instructed him about the plates, and in due course the plates were delivered to him and he translated them into the English language by the gift and power of God.

There is a prophet today at the head of the church, which is organised after that of Christ, with 12 apostles as part of the structure. Unlike Anglicanism and Roman Catholicism, the Mormon Church views the Holy Trinity (Father, Son and Holy Ghost) as three separate members of the Godhead.

There is a belief in pre-existence, a spirit world prior to mortal birth. The spiritual being from that world has all memory erased, and the new infant is born on this earth with no recollection of previous existence. After death the spirit leaves the physical body and goes to some spiritual place, and eventually at some time and in some place the body and spirit will reunite and be resurrected. Life on this earth is seen as a probationary period to determine the status in the next. The purpose of mortal life is to prove oneself, to eventually return to live in the presence of Jesus Christ and God the Father.

Those who are worthy may undergo an endowment ceremony at the Temple. 'Worthiness' includes a sound knowledge of the commandments of the faith, with reference to chastity, tithing and living the world of wisdom. Smoking and alcohol are forbidden. The individual declares himself 'worthy' to accept the responsibility of priesthood, and may then attain the different levels: Aaronic priesthood, for boys from the age of 12 to young adult; Melchizedek priesthood thereafter, with several levels of increasing responsibility. Only boys and men can attain priesthood.

The importance of family unity is emphasised by the 'sealing' ceremony at the Temple, at which man and wife are 'sealed' together for eternity. Children, including those who have died in infancy or childhood, may be sealed with their parents. Antecedents, already dead but not members of the church, may be baptised into the church and sealed with their families. This work for the dead is carried out in the Temple so that they may have the privilege of being with their families after the resurrection.

Death is regarded only as a temporary sadness because of the knowledge that the family will eventually be reunited. Mormons believe implicitly that there is a plan of salvation, and that it encompasses the past life, the reasons for this life and the progress in the next.

The Sacraments

The Sacraments have differences from those of other Christian groups.

BAPTISM

Baptism provides entry into the Gospel. It is very important to the faith and is carried out with immersion. Children, however, are not required to be baptised before the age of eight years, which is regarded as the 'age of accountability'. Before that they are deemed incapable of sin. A young child who is seriously ill would therefore not require emergency baptism ('Little children need no repentance, neither baptism', Book of Mormon, Moro 8:11). Baptism is followed by confirmation as a member of the church, as one who has received the gift of the Holy Ghost. This gift provides comfort and guidance throughout life. For older members of the church there is no form of rite or ceremony associated with dying or death.

THE SACRAMENT OF BREAD AND WATER

This is equivalent to the Eucharist of other Christians, but uses bread and water instead of bread and wine as Mormons abstain from alcohol. The Sacrament is performed each Sunday, and all worthy members may participate. In hospital the ceremony may be requested, but would not be viewed as essential. The Sacrament may be taken into hospital or into the home of a sick member.

SACRAMENT FOR THE SICK
There is no ritual at dying or death, but members of the Melchizedek Priesthood may give 'priesthood blessings' and minister to the sick in hospital or at home.

The Mormon patient in hospital

Mormons try to take care of their bodies and eat healthy diets, take proper rest and proper exercise. They are not usually vegetarians, but eat meat sparingly and avoid eating blood products (such as Black Pudding). They are concerned about the stimulant effects of caffeine and alcohol, and drink neither tea nor coffee. Some will avoid all hot beverages. In hospital, acceptable alternatives are milk, water or fruit juices. Alcohol and smoking are forbidden.

Those who have been through a special Temple ceremony wear a sacred undergarment. This may be a one-piece or two-piece garment and may be made of different fabrics. It is an intensely private item. It is removable for hygiene purposes and is washable, but would be worn by those eligible to wear it at all times, in health and sickness and ultimately in death. The garment may be removed, for example when going to the operating theatre, but must at all times be kept from public display and treated with great respect.

The dying Mormon

There is no ritual for the dying. Spiritual contact is important, and any active member of the church will know his own Bishop and how to contact him. 'Home Teachers' are charged to look after various needs, and will offer home support when needed and make visits to the hospital.

At death

There is no special requirement for health care staff to observe. 'Routine' Last Offices are appropriate (see p.182) but the sacred garment, if worn, must be replaced on the body after the toilet is complete.

Post mortem examinations

There is no religious objection to these, and the family of the deceased may choose freely whether to allow the examination.

Blood transfusion

There is no religious objection to blood transfusion; indeed the church positively encourages its employees to participate in blood donation, and makes its meetinghouses available for this purpose.

Organ transplantation

Members are counselled that whether an individual chooses to donate his own organs, or authorises the transplants of organs from a deceased family member, is a decision for that individual and family to make. There is no religious objection to donation or reception, and the decision to receive an organ should be made with competent medical counsel and confirmation through prayer.

Donation of the body

There is no church policy on donation of the body for teaching and research, and it would be for the family concerned to make the decision.

Abortion

The Mormon Church has consistently opposed elective abortion, and would urge all to preserve the sanctity of life.

Euthanasia

Deliberately assisting the death of a person suffering from incurable disease violates the commandment of God. In instances of severe illness or accident, members exercise faith in the Lord and also seek competent medical assistance. If death is inevitable it should be regarded as a blessing and a purposeful part of eternal existence. One should not feel obliged to extend mortal life by unreasonable means.

Suicide

To take life is to offend God. Mormons would accept that one who takes his or her own life may not be responsible for their actions. Only God can judge such a matter.

Funerals

Burial is preferred. Cremation is not encouraged because of important symbolic references to burial in the doctrines of the church, but it is the responsibility of the family to decide. The Bishop will call on the family to offer comfort and solace and to provide assistance with the funeral service and other practical matters, as requested by the family.

The body may be viewed prior to the funeral, followed by family prayer before the service. The service may be held in a church meetinghouse and will follow the general pattern of the Sunday service, simple and dignified, with an invocation and benediction, reverential prelude and postlude music, special musical pieces and brief sermons centred on the gospel of Jesus Christ. The Bishop who conducts the service should be invited to make brief remarks.

At the cemetery, a simple prayer to dedicate the grave site is offered by a bearer of the Melchizedek Priesthood, who is chosen in consultation with the family.

There would be no second funeral given for the disposal of body parts which had been retained after death. The church teaches that it is the spirit, the soul, which defines a person. There is no requirement for the body to be complete for resurrection.

For the death of an infant, there may only be a graveside service. An older child would have the same funeral as an adult.

The church does permit the use of its meetinghouses for funeral services for those who are not members of the Church of Jesus Christ of Latter-Day Saints. Such services may be held as prescribed by the church of the deceased and conducted by a clergyman of that church, provided that the service is dignified and appropriate. Members of the Mormon Church who participate in the provision of any part of a funeral service must accept no fee, whether the funeral service is on behalf of a member of the church or of a non-member.

The president of the Relief Society, the women's organisation of the church, will assist the bereaved family in many practical ways, including providing assistance in dressing the body of a deceased female for burial. The Society will care for young children, prepare meals and safeguard the home during the funeral service.

Further information may be obtained from your local Church of Jesus Christ of Latter-Day Saints, or by writing to:

The Church of Jesus Christ of Latter-Day Saints
Public Communications/Special Affairs Department
50 East North Temple Street
Salt Lake City
Utah 84150, USA

CHAPTER 23

CHRISTIAN SCIENCE

The Church of Christ, Scientist, was founded in America in 1879 by Mary Baker Eddy (1821–1910). She herself suffered much physical ill health and became preoccupied with the question of God's responsibility for human suffering. She experimented with various alternative healing methods, while maintaining her lifelong interest in the Bible, especially in the promise of Jesus that his followers would 'heal the sick' (Matthew 10:8). She eventually experienced personal healing, recovering from the life-threatening effects of an accident. This episode, in 1866, marked the point of her discovery of Christian Science. In 1875 she published *Science and Health*, later revised as *Science and Health with Key to the Scriptures*. The Bible and this work formed the textbooks of the new faith and were looked on as the 'dual and impersonal pastor' of the Church (Miscellaneous Writings 1883–1896). The faith grew rapidly in America and elsewhere. There are now about 1700 congregations in some 80 countries, including 143 congregations in the UK (Personal communication from the Christian Science Committees on Publication for the UK and N. Ireland). *Science and Health* is currently published in 17 languages, in Braille and on the Internet (www.spirituality.com). There are numerous Christian Science publications, including the well-known international daily paper, the *Christian Science Monitor*, also available on-line (www.csmonitor.com).

Christian Science is a prayer-based system of healing. It has been practised around the world as a healing theology for over a century, by members of the Church of Christ, Scientist, as well as by individuals of other faith traditions, and by those with no formal faith tradition.

The Church aims to 'commemorate the word and works of our Master [Jesus Christ], which should reinstate primitive Christianity and its lost element of healing' (*Church Manual*, p.17). It sees itself as an institution, which proves its usefulness by 'elevating the race' and 'rousing the dormant understanding from material beliefs to the apprehension of spiritual ideas and the demonstration of divine Science' (*Science and Health*, p.583), in order to change thought for the better and heal sickness.

Like other churches, this one is primarily concerned with spiritual regeneration and redemption from sin, but among health care staff it is probably best known for its reliance on prayer alone for the healing of sickness and disease. Those who practise Christian Science believe such healing is an integral part of a Christian lifestyle and the natural result of drawing closer to God in one's thought and life.

There is now over a century of experience of Christian Science healing through prayer alone, and written accounts of healings continue to appear in the many Christian Science publications as a testament to the faith. Accounts of healings are also broadcast, and are shared spontaneously at Wednesday evening meetings to '[scale] the pinnacle of praise and [illustrate] the demonstration of Christ, "who healeth all thy diseases" (Psalm 103:3)' (*Church Manual*).

In the practice of Christian Science, respect for individual choice in questions of health care, or any other aspect of daily life, is paramount. Many Christian Scientists rely on their own prayer for the healing of adverse health conditions. Some may also ask for help from a Christian Science practitioner, a professional spiritual healer, who employs the Christian Science method of healing. (There is a worldwide directory of practitioners in each issue of *The Christian Science Journal*, a monthly magazine.) However, individuals are always free to choose conventional medical treatment or other complementary and alternative therapies. Christian Scientists respect health care professionals.

However, those choosing to apply Christian Science to their own need for healing believe that treatment must be purely spiritual, seeking regeneration and a deeper understanding of man's relationship with God. For most illnesses, therefore, Christian Scientists will not normally be patients in hospitals, but will either pray for themselves or seek prayer from an experienced Christian Science practitioner. If there is a need for practical care while they are doing this, they can seek nursing care at home from a visiting Christian Science nurse or gain admission to a Christian Science House (registered as a 'Care home not providing medicines or medical treatment' under the Care Standards Act 2000). However, those who practise Christian Science may be in hospital following accidents, through personal choice, or because of family or legal pressures. They also follow legal requirements regarding pregnancy and childbirth, as well as for the care of children. Christian Scientists are known to work cooperatively with public health officials and comply with public health regulations, wherever there is no specific space in law to allow for a different course of action.

The Christian Scientist in hospital

A Christian Scientist in hospital voluntarily would have few special requirements. He or she would probably accept conventional medical treatment, but might ask that drugs and therapy be kept to a minimum, where possible. There are no dietary prohibitions and no fasting requirement, although most Christian Scientists do not smoke or drink alcohol. There are no special garments. Individuals relying on Christian Science may ask to be retested, or to have a pending procedure re-evaluated, after having had time to pray for healing. Privacy would be appreciated, but the act of prayer is silent and unlikely to cause difficulties. Access to the Bible and the denominational textbook *Science and Health with Key to the Scriptures*, and to other Christian Science literature, would be regarded as important.

If a Christian Scientist were not in a hospital through choice – because of an accident, for example – and chose to decline conventional medical treatment, this would *not* mean that such a decision was made on dogmatic grounds, nor on the basis of a fear of going to hell or from any sense of fearing to displease God. It would, instead, mean that a positive choice had been made, by a competent adult, to rely on prayer for healing, individually or with the help of a Christian Science practitioner. This choice would generally be based on the individual's own experience of the effectiveness of such healing, or it might even be made on the basis of several generations of a family who have experienced successful healing.

Such an individual would cooperate with authorities to take appropriate actions, such as quarantine, if considered necessary to protect the health of others.

Health care staff can greatly assist their Christian Science patients by ensuring they have access to the Bible and *Science and Health* and are given time and a quiet space to pray during the various stages of diagnosis and treatment. Contact with other Christian Scientists is important, including a Christian Science practitioner. Readings of passages from the above books (or other Christian Science literature) may be appreciated.

Where possible, the best way to ascertain what would be most helpful in any circumstance is to ask the individual patient.

The Sacraments

The Sacraments of Baptism and Communion are deeply important to Christian Scientists, but are regarded as profound inner experiences essential to Christian regeneration, rather than as outward ceremonies. Baptism is understood as the purification and spiritualisation of thought and life, while Communion is regarded as communing with God through prayer. The symbols of water, bread and wine are therefore not used by Christian Scientists, and there would generally be no ceremony of any kind for a sick patient, whether adult or child.

The dying Christian Scientist

There are no specified last rites. The approach to this situation remains an individual or family decision. In a case of incapacity, it should be explored whether or not a Christian Scientist has written an advance directive (see p.167) or nominated a lasting power of attorney to make health care decisions for him or her (under the Mental Capacity Act 2005) (see p.178). In the case of Christian Scientists, such an advance directive is most likely to have been prepared without consultation with a medical practitioner.

At death

Questions relating to care of the body should be answered by the individual and the family.

'Routine' Last Offices are appropriate (see p.182). It is preferred that the body of a female should be handled by female staff.

Post mortem examinations

The governing By-Laws of the Church of Christ, Scientist make provision for post mortem examinations: 'Sudden Decease. Sect. 2. If a member of The Mother Church shall decease suddenly, without previous injury or illness, and the cause thereof be unknown, an autopsy shall be made by qualified experts' (Manual of The Mother Church, p.50). Consent for non-coronial post mortems is a matter for the family to decide.

Blood transfusion

Individual Christian Scientists make their own decisions about the donation and reception of blood.

Christian Scientists are law-abiding citizens, and parents comply with the requirement of the law in the UK that a doctor should be called to attend a child in time of illness (Children and Young Persons Act 1933). If, in accord with this requirement, the child of Christian Scientist parents was under medical care, the parents would consider blood transfusion as most other parents would, if the doctors concerned felt that this was essential.

Organ transplantation

Individuals make their own decisions about organ or tissue donation and reception.

Donation of the body

Individuals make their own decisions about donation of the body for teaching and research.

Abortion

The teachings of Christian Science emphasise the importance of a spiritual approach to life, and support the effort of individuals to live in accord with the moral values of the Bible, but individuals make their own decisions about abortion.

Suicide

Christian Science does not condemn anyone who commits suicide, but it does not view suicide as a solution to life's problems. Instead, Christian Science opens up a path by which one can draw closer to God and come to understand that life is spiritual and of limitless promise. Through this prayer-based approach, many individuals, including those tempted to commit suicide, have found answers to problems of every description and have gone on to lead lives of progress, fulfilment and great happiness.

Euthanasia

Christian Scientists endeavour to live in accord with Jesus' Sermon on the Mount, and the Ten Commandments. Killing one's fellow beings is expressly forbidden in these. Death is regarded not as a friend, but as 'the last enemy that shall be destroyed' (1 Corinthians 15:26), and the experience of many Christian Scientists over the last century has shown that even apparently hopeless terminal conditions have been healed. They would not regard any case as being beyond the healing power of God.

Funerals

Both burial and cremation are acceptable, and the decision is for the family to make. There is no requirement for a speedy funeral.

There is no special requirement for the disposal of separate body parts, which would be a decision for the family. As a practical matter, however, it is unlikely in the extreme that a Christian Scientist would request a funeral for separate body parts.

Further information may be obtained from the local Christian Science Reading Room, or by contacting:

The District Manager
Christian Science Committees on Publication for the United Kingdom and the Republic of Ireland
Claridge House
29 Barnes High Street
London SW13 9LW
Tel: 020 8282 1645
Email: LondonCS@csps.com
Website: www.christianscience.com

CHAPTER 24

THE AFRICAN-CARIBBEAN COMMUNITY

The main religion of the Caribbean islands is Christianity, but with wide variations in ritual practice. Different island communities have different religious backgrounds; most belong to Anglican, Methodist or Pentecostal churches. When they come to Britain they bring with them their traditional religious customs. A high proportion of them are church attenders, particularly amongst the older generations. In the British West Indies the church is still very much a social and community centre, as well as a religious one.

African-Caribbean Christians are likely to be much more demonstrative in the practice of religion than are their English counterparts. For them, Baptism is more important, and a naming ceremony for a child is a major occasion. In the Pentecostal Churches there is no 'Confirmation'. Instead, adult baptism, with total immersion, marks the voluntary acceptance of the faith and is symbolic of being 'born again'. There are strict rules to follow for those undergoing baptism. For example, smoking and alcohol are forbidden.

It is very important that a child should have a name before it dies and the Christening ceremony has great religious significance.

African-Caribbeans deal with death in their community in their own special way. On the whole, at such times, religious differences melt into the background and cultural and island identity takes over.

The family structure may be complex, but the family influence is strong. Every member, no matter how distantly related, is acknowledged to have a contribution to make to the family, and is regarded as important. Frequently mothers and fathers do not marry each other and may not even live together. Grandparents are very important in the family structure and they often play a major part in bringing up their grandchildren. The extended family tends to maintain good relations with one another, and comes together at the death of one of its members.

Many, probably the vast majority, of the younger African-Caribbean population in Britain were born here, and the Caribbean influence may be less strong for them than for their parents and grandparents.

African-Caribbean patients in hospital

Sick patients in hospital would probably wish to be treated no differently from other patients, and are unlikely to make any special requests. If they are in for a long stay, they may find English hospital cooking very plain and unappetising.

For those who are church attenders, prayer is very important. They will feel a need for privacy so that visitors may pray together and sing hymns with the patient. Few hospital wards have appropriate facilities for this, but it could be anticipated and a side-ward made available for a dying patient. Families would much appreciate the freedom to be rather more demonstrative than the average white family would be. They do feel emotionally restricted and inhibited in our hospitals.

African-Caribbean families used to feel that hospital doctors, particularly consultants, were too remote. These days, families are less inhibited and more ready to ask questions in a hospital situation.

It is important that the dying person is visited, not only by close family but also by church and community leaders. The extended family will wish to make frequent and prolonged visits, and close family will wish to be present at death. African-Caribbean patients may, therefore, require facilities for more than the average number of visitors, and ward staff could do much to accommodate this, if at all possible.

It may be important that the church is advised of the patient's admission to hospital, that the clergy visit, and that prayers are said together. Sacraments are not seen as so necessary as prayer, and only a few will ask to take Holy Communion.

At death

For those in hospital there are no special Last Offices. 'Routine' Last Offices are appropriate (see p.182).

There is no religious objection to staff of other persuasions handling the body, but there is often a hidden hope that it will be done by a black sister or someone who understands such things as the care of the hair, and who will show the proper respect to the body.

If death occurs at home, the laying-out may be done by neighbours, friends or family, in the first instance. The family will wish to wash and dress the body, either at home or at the funeral parlour.

Post mortem

Older members of the community are likely to have a firm belief in the sanctity of the body and will be offended by the idea of a post mortem. Whilst agreement must be given for a post mortem ordered by the Coroner, older people are unlikely to give consent for any other reason, and would need careful explanation of why the examination is required.

Blood transfusion

There is no religious objection to donation or acceptance.

Organ transplantation

There is unlikely to be any objection to the receiving of a transplanted organ. However, as older people are likely to believe that a whole body is necessary for the next life, they are unlikely to consent for the removal of an organ. Younger members may have different views.

Donation of the body

Again, older members of the family would probably not agree to the disfigurement of the body.

Abortion

African-Caribbean families have a great love and acceptance of children in all circumstances. Families, particularly grandparents, are traditionally very supportive. Most African-Caribbean families would be personally against abortion.

For an early miscarriage, hospital disposal would be acceptable. If the fetus is recognisable as a child (probably about 20 weeks), then it would be accorded the full funeral rites.

Suicide

Life is considered sacred and suicide is unforgiveable. The victim would receive the usual funeral rites, with no mention of suicide, but it would remain a stigma to the family.

Euthanasia

Euthanasia is unacceptable.

Funerals

Some African-Caribbeans are cremated and, in some communities, a proportion are returned to their homeland for burial, but the great majority are buried in Britain.

The funeral is an elaborate and important occasion for all who loved the deceased during life, and the whole community will wish to attend. The funeral may be delayed for several days, allowing time for the extended family to gather together. Traditionally, the body was kept at home until the funeral and may have been viewed on many occasions during this period. Today, most bodies will be kept at the funeral parlour until the time of the funeral, but the body will always be taken back to the house of the deceased for the start of the funeral. The funeral procession will always commence at the house. The body may be viewed in church prior to the funeral service, particularly for the Pentecostal community. For these reasons the body should, ideally, be embalmed.

Because of the importance attached to funerals, it is important that African-Caribbean families and friends are allowed time off work to attend, and not just for very close relatives. If there is a member of the clergy in the family, then he (or occasionally she) will be expected to conduct the funeral service, alongside the minister of the church.

The funeral service may be long, with flowers, carefully chosen hymns and tributes from many people about many aspects of the life of the deceased. There may be a steel band or a choir providing the music, gospel singing, and a variation of the service to suit the individual.

At the graveside the family will fill up the grave themselves, only leaving when it is filled completely. The singing may continue throughout, and the congregation then return to the church hall for an ongoing gathering. The family home then becomes 'open' for people to call, and for prayer, and would remain so for a week or more.

There is a strong belief that an entire body is a requirement for resurrection. Any retained tissues or organs, which were made available to the family after the funeral, would be regarded with rage, horror and shame. The parts would certainly be accorded a second ceremony and burial in the same plot as the body, but this ceremony would be attended by close family only. The matter would not be disclosed to anyone outside the immediate family. If the family were aware that a body part would be made available some time after death, then the funeral would be postponed until the part was released.

CHAPTER 25

RASTAFARIANISM

Rastafarians are followers of a growing movement which began in the West Indies, largely in Jamaica and Dominica, in the 1930s. The movement is linked to the roots of resistance to slavery (Campbell 1985) among the descendants of the black African slave families, and the identification with Africa is central to the doctrine of Rastafari. Much inspiration came from the 'Back to Africa' movement led by Marcus Garvey (1887–1940) which raised black consciousness and self-respect. Garvey promoted the 'Universal Negro Improvement Association' in the 1920s, the main goal of which was to unite black people with their homeland, Africa. His mission was to restore the lost dignity of black people, after generations of slavery.

The accession of Ras (Prince) Tafari as the Emperor of Ethiopia (Haile Selassie I) in 1930 was seen as fulfilment of a belief that a ruler would emerge in Africa and lead all black people to freedom. Believers claim that there is direct lineage from the biblical King David to Ras Tafari (hence the name Rastafarian), and the Emperor Haile Selassie I became the only king descended from that throne through to the present era. He has the titles also of King of Kings and the Lion of Judah. Rastafarians consider that the Ethiopian Emperor is a divine being and the Messiah of the human race. They believe that they are the true Jews who will eventually be redeemed by repatriation to Africa, which is their true home and heaven on earth (Encyclopaedia Britannica 1989).

Until the mid-1960s Rastafarianism was little more than a local Jamaican religious movement. Various groups have influenced the modern Rastafarian movement which has, in many ways, rejected both Jamaican–European culture and the Christian revivalist religion predominant in Jamaica. The Black Power movement, started in 1968 by Walter Rodney, was significant. In the 1970s, Bob Marley, a popular reggae musician, came to symbolise Rastafarian values and beliefs and greatly increased the profile and the following of the faith.

The result is a distinct entity. Rastafarians do not consider themselves as ordinary Christians. For them, Christ's spirit has been reborn in Ras Tafari, the true Messiah. Rastafarians mainly reject the Christian version of the Bible. Some parts of the Old and New Testaments are still regarded as scriptures, but the true foundation of Rastafari is the Holy Piby, the 'Black Man's Bible', compiled by Robert Athlyi Rogers of Anguilla between 1913 and 1917 and brought to Jamaica in 1925 by the Rev. Charles Goodridge and his colleague Grace Jenkins Garrison. Followers believed that this Bible was the closest to the first Bible. It was written in Ampharic (once the official language of Ethiopia and believed to be the original language of mankind). Goodridge and Garrison taught that the original (white) church scholars had mistranslated the early Bible to make God and His prophets Caucasian instead of black. This apparent misinterpretation of black history is known as 'Babylon', which has come to represent the white power structure in the world. Rastafarians also give special significance to the Kebra Negast, the Ethiopian Holy Book.

Despite increasing secularisation, the Rastafarian movement retains great moral authority as a result of its stance on racial identity and prejudice. There is no clearly defined leader or formal organisational structure, people meeting in groups or remaining as individuals, with a few exceptions. The 'House of Nyabinghi' is run by an Assembly of Elders, unappointed and unelected, making the faith less structured than most other world religions. Most worship occurs during rituals, which are of two basic types. 'Reasonings' are informal gatherings for discussion, at which the holy weed, ganja (marijuana), is smoked in a ritual manner. The 'nyabinghi', or dance ritual, marks special occasions during the year, such as the coronation of Emperor Selassie (2 November) or the Emperor's birthday (6 January). Contrary to popular belief, not all Rastas smoke marijuana recreationally, although it is widely used for religious reasons, to aid meditation and for medicinal purposes.

Rastafarian culture has a puritan ethic, which assists personal dignity. It may reject Western medical treatment. For some, legal marriage is regarded as unnecessary, and the extended family may be complex. Many young Rastafarians are converts to the faith. Many young people have adopted the traditional Rastafarian hairstyles, the dreadlocks, without necessarily being followers of the faith. Believers may wear the colours of the faith: red symbolises the blood that has been shed by Rastafarian martyrs throughout their history; yellow symbolises the riches of the homeland; green represents the beauty of Ethiopia, their 'promised land'.

Worldwide, there may be 1 million adherents (Littman 2000). The 2001 census showed some 4672 practising Rastafarians in the UK. Most members are male.

The Rastafarian patient in hospital

Some Rastafarians may have an antipathy to Western-style medicine and be reluctant to take treatment, which they fear will contaminate the body. They may prefer to try 'alternative' therapies, such as herbalism, homeopathy or acupuncture. Those who choose to use the general practitioner as the first source of advice are likely to accept conventional medical treatment, if they feel it will be beneficial.

Both men and women are readily identified by their distinctive hairstyle. The 'dreadlocks' or 'locks' are a symbol of the faith and a sign of black pride. The orthodox may not permit their hair to be cut, but it is up to the individual to decide whether or not to cut the locks. Sometimes men may choose to cover their heads with a soft hat.

Rastafarian women prefer to dress modestly at all times, and will wish to do so in hospital. There is a taboo on the wearing of second-hand clothing, and the orthodox patient may thus be reluctant to wear a hospital gown previously worn by many others. A disposable paper gown for theatre use may be an acceptable alternative.

It is important to visit the sick in hospital or at home. Visits are often made in groups, and the visitors often feel restricted and unwelcome in the hospital situation.

Diet

True Rastas eat only food which is uncontaminated by chemicals and is completely natural. This is becoming known as 'I-tal' food in Jamaica. The food is minimally cooked and served without salt, preservatives or other condiments. They prefer to drink herbal products, such as tea, rather than milk, coffee or soft drinks.

All forms of pig meat are forbidden, as are foods cooked in pig fat. Many believe it is unnecessary to eat meat and devout Rastas follow a vegetarian diet. Some fish are regarded as unwholesome and belonging to 'the scum of the sea'. For this reason herring and sardines, among others, are not acceptable. At home many Rastafarians would prefer to eat fresh, organically grown produce rather than canned food.

The dying patient

Rastafarianism is a personal religion. Its adherents have a deep love of God and believe that wherever people are God is present, and that the Temple itself is within each individual. There are no church buildings as such, no set services and no official clergy. All members of the faith share in the religious aspects, and the family may pray by the bedside of a dying member. Other than this there are no last rites. There is a firm belief in the resurrection of the soul after death, but not of the flesh.

At death

Routine Last Offices are appropriate (see p.182). Any funeral director may prepare the body for disposal.

Post mortem and donation of the body

Despite the lack of belief in physical resurrection, the idea of a post mortem examination would be extremely distasteful to most Rastafarians. Few would agree to autopsy except where it is ordered by the Coroner. It is unlikely that families would agree to donate a body for teaching or research.

Blood transfusion

The fear of contamination of the body may influence the attitude to transfusion. Some may need to be assured that there is no risk of disease being transmitted by the blood, and objections may be raised both to donation and reception of blood for this reason. However, both donation to and reception from other family members might be considered.

Organ transplantation

As with blood transfusion, the fear of contamination of the body may cause extreme reluctance to participate in organ transplants. There is also a deeply held feeling that to do so is to interfere with God's plan for mankind.

Abortion

Abortion and contraception are both totally forbidden.

Suicide and euthanasia

Both are forbidden. Anyone who takes a life, including their own, is condemned for-ever.

Funerals

Burial is preferred but cremation is not forbidden. The funeral is not the elaborate af-fair seen in other African-Caribbean groups and the dead body is accorded little cer-emony. Only the intimate family and friends will attend. There is no special mourning ritual, but family and friends are very supportive of the bereaved.

There is no belief in the afterlife, neither heaven nor hell. Sometimes a body may be flown back to the country of origin for disposal (see p.62).

References

Campbell, H. (1985) *Rasta and Resistance*. London: Hansib Publishing.

Encyclopaedia Britannica, 15th edn. (1989) 5, p.620; 9, p.949.

Littman, K. (2000) *New Religious Movements: Rastafarianism*. http://religiousmovements.lib.virginia .edu/nrms/rast.html (accessed July 2005).

CHAPTER 26

THE JEWISH FAITH

Judaism, the religion of the Jewish people, preceded Christianity. 'Jew' is the name given, since the 6th century BCE, to the members of the Tribe of Judah, themselves descendants of the Patriarch Abraham from about the year 2000 BCE. Jacob, a grandson of Abraham, was given the name of 'Israel' by God, in recognition of his deeds (Genesis 35, 9–12), and his descendants are also known as the 'Children of Israel'.

Jews believe there is only one God, who created the universe. The first five books of the Old Testament (known as the Torah) contain laws and rules for daily life, which are regarded by orthodox Jews as commands from God. Amongst the main precepts of Judaism are: to worship one God, to obey the Ten Commandments, and to practise charity and tolerance towards other people. The family is of great importance in Jewish life.

Jews do not believe that Christ was the son of God or the Messiah, but believe that the Messiah, who will redeem mankind, is yet to come.

It has been estimated that there are about 14.5 million Jews worldwide (Encyclopaedia Britannica 2004). Their spiritual centre is Jerusalem, in Israel.

Jews in Britain

There are about 300,000 Jews in Britain (Personal communication from community leaders), over half of whom live in Greater London. Between them they encompass a wide spectrum of religious observance, from the ultra-orthodox communities who follow scrupulously the code of laws of the Torah, to the less strict 'liberal' congregations, and the 'reform' synagogues where much of the service is conducted in English, instead of the traditional Hebrew. Religion and culture are inextricably entwined, and the extent to which different families observe different tenets of Judaism will vary considerably.

Religious principles of medical treatment

Human life is precious, and its preservation takes precedence over every other consideration.

Almost all forms of required medical treatment are permitted, even encouraged, in Jewish law. All treatment is permitted, and required, if it is necessary in order to save life. This even extends to the giving of non-kosher food, or breaking the laws of the sanctity of the Sabbath, in a potentially life-threatening situation. Medication which must be 'taken with food' may be taken even on the holiest fast day, Yom Kippur, if it is essential to save life. The orthodox will draw a clear distinction between 'saving life' and general therapeutic treatment. They may seek advice from Rabbinic authorities in difficult situations.

The only exceptions to permitted medical treatments are those which involve the death of another person, as in organ transplantation or abortion (see below).

In practice, then, the medical and nursing staff may assume that any required treatment is not prohibited in Jewish law. Exceptions are those situations which involve issues of abortion, fertility treatment or contraception, organ transplantation, or treatment which of itself carries a significant risk to the life of the patient. In all these situations the orthodox patient may wish to consult a Rabbi, and may wish the doctor to be present at that discussion.

The Jewish patient in hospital

Most Jews hospitalised in Britain would appreciate some dietary considerations (see below). Apart from this, the less orthodox are not likely to expect to be treated in any way differently from other patients. However, orthodox patients will wish to observe religious customs even in hospital.

Male patients may choose to wear their traditional head covering, usually a small skullcap, and wish for privacy and time for the three sessions of daily prayer. Morning prayers, usually said before breakfast, may take half an hour, and require the wearing of a prayer shawl and of phylacteries (tiny leather boxes containing passages from the Bible, which are bound round the head and hand). Afternoon and evening prayers take only five or ten minutes.

Orthodox women will dress modestly at all times, and in hospital will prefer to keep body and limbs covered. They may not wish others to look upon their hair, and may ordinarily wear a wig. In hospital they may choose to keep their head covered with a scarf. They may be reluctant to expose themselves to others, as in a teaching situation. Despite this modesty, Jewish women are unlikely to request to be seen by a female doctor.

Both sexes may wish to observe the Sabbath, which commences just before sunset on Friday afternoon and ends on Saturday evening just after nightfall. Hence it starts and finishes at different times through the year. The Sabbath commemorates God's creation of the world, and is a day of rest. Religious Jews do no 'creative' work on the Sabbath, and this includes travel by vehicle, use of the telephone, the switching on and off of electrical appliances, carrying goods outside the house and the use of money, among others.

Orthodox patients, and their visitors, will therefore not wish to travel, switch on bedside lights or television sets, make phone calls or write during that time. They may even be reluctant to press their nurse-call bell. They will appreciate hospital staff taking the trouble to do these things for them, and anticipating their needs. Similar rules apply to the major Jewish festivals.

The rules of the Sabbath may, indeed must, be ignored if life is in danger.

Dietary laws

Orthodox Jews follow a religious diet, and for them the dietary laws are strict and only 'kosher' food will be acceptable. However, if the patient is seriously ill and no kosher food is available, then non-kosher food would be permitted if it would help to save life.

Meat is only kosher if it comes from an animal which both chews the cud and has a cloven hoof, or from domesticated poultry, and which has been slaughtered and handled according to ritual. Acceptable meat includes beef and veal, mutton and lamb, chicken, turkey, duck and goose. Such meats will only be accepted as 'kosher', however, if they bear the seal of a recognised Rabbinic authority, confirming that they have been slaughtered and prepared in accordance with the rules of Jewish law.

The meat of the pig, rabbit and birds of prey is forbidden, as are products containing their fats, milk or eggs. Most Jews would be offended to be offered pig meat in any form. However, they are only regarded as non-acceptable in dietary terms. Medical products made using pigs, such as porcine insulin, would be acceptable for treatment purposes. A pig's heart would be acceptable for transplant purposes if the technique becomes acceptable and safe (Jewish Chronicle 1998).

Fish must have both fins and scales to be kosher. All shellfish are forbidden.

Milk and meat are not eaten at the same meal, and milk products are not eaten for at least three hours after a meat meal.

Many hospitals will have access to a 'Kosher Kitchen', which will supply a daily kosher meal to patients who request it. If a kosher meal is not available, many Jewish patients will prefer a vegetarian diet.

The dying patient

Jewish law forbids any active intervention to hasten death, and a dying patient may not be moved. Orthodox families will wish to consult a Rabbi in any such circumstances, for example, when it is considered appropriate to switch off a respirator, which is keeping alive a person with confirmed brain death.

There is no special ceremony of Last Rites, and it is not required that a Rabbi is present in the event of an impending death. However, the dying Jew may wish to hear or recite the special prayer (The Shema), which is a declaration of belief in God, and special psalms, particularly Psalm 23 (The Lord is my Shepherd). Some may wish to make a deathbed confession. For many, visits from the Rabbi will be welcomed.

A dying Jew should not be left alone. It is a great 'Mitzvah' (commandment, good deed) to be present at 'Yetziat Neshamah' – the departure of the soul.

Death is presumed when breathing stops. Traditionally the body is left untouched for about ten minutes, after which a feather is laid across the lips and nose to detect any signs of breath.

Jews believe in life after death. Orthodox Jews retain a belief in physical resurrection, and therefore require the body to be buried intact. The Reform and Liberal end of the Jewish spectrum of belief considers the survival of the soul after death to be independent of the condition of the body. Hence there are different approaches to some aspects of death, such as organ donation and cremation.

At death

The disposal of the Jewish dead is undertaken by burial societies in the community. A detailed ritual will be observed, characterised by reverence for the dead, simplicity, equality between rich and poor, and speed of the funeral process. Considerable importance is attached to the ritual cleansing and clothing of the body, and it is only undertaken by Jews who are specially qualified and of the same sex as the deceased. The burial societies will attend any Jew who dies within their area, even if he or she was not a member of a synagogue.

Therefore, the body should be handled as little as possible, by others, after death. In normal circumstances, burial should ideally take place within 24 hours, or as soon as is practicable, and will be delayed only for the Sabbath and major festivals.

IN NORMAL CIRCUMSTANCES

For a hospital death, where there is no requirement to notify the Coroner, the eyes should be closed after death. If practicable this is carried out by one of the children of the deceased. The jaw should be supported (see 'limited laying out'; p.189), the limbs straightened, including the fingers, and the arms placed by the sides. The body should be labelled, then be covered with a white sheet and otherwise left untouched, but not left unattended.

If the family are present, they will contact the burial society, synagogue or Jewish undertaker, any of whom will initiate the process of disposal. If no family are available, the local synagogue or undertaker should be contacted for advice and help.

IN ABNORMAL CIRCUMSTANCES

If the death must be notified to the Coroner (see p.183) any undue delay in funeral arrangements will cause distress to the relatives, as will the necessity for a post mortem examination (see below). The family should make contact with their preferred undertaker, who will be able to keep in contact with the Coroner's Officer during the Coroner's investigation into the cause of death. A post mortem is not always required, but, if one is ordered by the Coroner, the family do not have any choice in the matter. Even if a post mortem is ordered, the funeral need not be unduly delayed.

To notify the Coroner, someone in authority should contact the local police station and speak to the Duty Inspector. He will have a list of the Coroners' Officers who are on-call for each geographical area, and will arrange for the appropriate Officer to communicate with the doctor.

The doctor should inform the Coroner's Officer that the body is Jewish, and that the family wishes the funeral to take place within 24 hours of death for religious reasons. He should ask if it is possible to arrange for any post mortem to be carried out later that day, or early next morning. If the Coroner will agree to receive the pathologist's findings over the telephone (or by 'fax') after the post mortem, he will then be able to furnish his death certificate (form B; see p.65) without too much delay in a straightforward case.

If the body needs to be moved for the post mortem, for example after death at home or in a nursing home, the family may use their chosen funeral director or the Coroner's Officer will arrange the transport.

Ritual preparation of the body will commence after the autopsy.

Post mortem examinations

Man was created in God's image, therefore mutilation of the body is regarded with abhorrence.

Post mortem examinations are not permitted in Jewish law, except where civil law requires it. They are deeply disliked, even among the less orthodox, and every effort will be made to avoid them unless absolutely essential. Any part of the body removed during the examination must be returned to the body for burial.

Sometimes, if the Coroner feels it is appropriate, an MRI (magnetic resonance imaging) scan of the body may be carried out instead of a post mortem. This has been used on several occasions in orthodox Jewish communities in Britain, the cost being borne by the relevant community (see p.65).

Blood transfusion

The preservation of life is an important guiding principle in Judaism. There is no religious prohibition to the giving or receiving of blood.

Organ transplantation

Jewish law does have specific guidelines regarding certain medico-ethical matters when the life of a second individual is involved. If a patient is, or might be, in a potentially life-threatening situation, any treatment deemed necessary by medical staff should be carried out without delay. There is no objection, in principle, to receiving a transplant, always provided that no organ is removed until the death of the donor is definitely established (the exception being a living kidney donation). Since there may be differing views as to the criteria for death, Rabbinical advice should be sought in all such cases for orthodox patients.

Organ donation, however, may be regarded differently by different groups of Jews. Orthodox Jews, with a belief in the sanctity of the body, have been unwilling donors in the past. But there has been a softening of attitude in recent years, and an increasing sympathy for transplant procedures. This has been influenced by the situation in Israel, where transplants are a reality and necessity and donation is encouraged. These days, even some orthodox Rabbis carry transplant donor cards. Those of Reform persuasion may find no religious objection to organ donation.

Donation of the body

Again there will be mixed views on body donation for research, but the more orthodox would not consider such a proposal, and would be deeply offended by it.

Abortion and miscarriage

Where a potentially life-threatening situation arises at any stage during a pregnancy, or during, or after, delivery of the child, all necessary treatment must be given to save the life of the woman. If the only way to save her life is by aborting the fetus, then this is permitted, even obligatory. However, once the head (or the majority of the limbs) is born, the fetus is regarded as an independent human being whose life may not be sacrificed, even to save that of the mother. Any question of abortion in a non-life threatening situation must be referred to a Rabbinical authority. For the orthodox community, abortion on demand is prohibited.

After a miscarriage, the fetus should be buried. Traditionally, there was no requirement for the usual funeral service if a child died under the age of 30 days. However, a burial would take place. The preparations for burial include a circumcision for a boy, and the giving of a Hebrew name both to a boy and a girl. However, in recent years there has been increasing demand for some form of ceremony at this time and a funeral service may be offered.

Suicide and euthanasia

In Judaism, life is sacred. Nothing may be done to hasten death, in sickness or in health. Jews believe that they do not have autonomy over their bodies. The body has been 'loaned' by the Almighty and therefore it is essential to safeguard the body and safeguard life.

In past history, if a person committed suicide they were shunned. Their body was buried in a separate part of the cemetery and accorded no mourning rites. However, towards the end of the 19th century, a classic halachic (Jewish Law) authority, Rabbi Y.M. Epstein, said that if a person was not of sound mind when they committed suicide, then they should not be penalised so harshly. It being unlikely that a person would do such an act unless they were under duress, except where it can be proven that they were of sound mind at the time of suicide, they were assumed not to have been of sound mind.

In recent times there has been a more sympathetic attitude in general. Suicide is not condoned, but would receive the usual burial and mourning rites as for other Jews.

The same principles apply to euthanasia and, strictly speaking, no action may be taken to shorten life. But this is a complex area nowadays. Matters of serious nature and complexity, such as the withdrawal of treatment or sustenance, should always be discussed with a competent rabbi.

Disposal of body parts

In orthodox belief, an amputated limb, removed before death, should be buried. The request for this must be made known in advance of surgery so that the part will not be sent for incineration, as is customary hospital practice. If the patient is a member of a synagogue, he or she already has a reserved plot in a Jewish cemetery and the part would be interred there. The part would be wrapped in a sheet and possibly placed in a container before burial. The grave would be dug deeper than is usual, the part laid in the bottom and then, in some instances, concreted over. This ensures that it will not be damaged when the coffin is eventually laid to rest. As the owner of the part is still living, there is no ceremony at this time. Occasionally, the amputated part may be frozen and stored, and eventually buried at the same time as the rest of the body.

Body parts that come to light after death, such as pathological specimens, would be reburied with the body. The parts would be placed in a small casket, which would be laid on top of the coffin. Again, if the family is aware that some parts had been retained by the Coroner or pathologist, the grave would be dug deeper to accommodate the later burial of these tissues. If the family wish, some form of ceremony would be offered.

Preparation of the body for disposal

To assist in the preparation of the dead for burial is one of the greatest 'Mitzvot' (commandments, good deeds) of Judaism. The ritual is carried out by the Chevrah Kadisha (the Holy Society), who receive special training for the task. Ideally, all are volunteers from the community, and a minimum of three persons of the same sex as the deceased are necessary to carry out the procedures. It is not the practice for family members to take part.

Preparation may be done at the home, but is most often carried out at the Jewish, or other, mortuary. It may begin half an hour after the death is confirmed. The body is undressed and covered with a sheet. The Chevrah Kadisha then address the body and ask to be forgiven for any unavoidable indignity. If at a Jewish mortuary, the body is placed on a marble slab, feet towards the door. Candles are lit and placed on the window ledge. If the preparation takes place in the home, a protective waterproof sheet is spread on the floor. The Tahara (Purification) Board, a shaped metal tray rather like a very shallow bath with a hole for drainage, is placed on two trestles or chairs and the body is placed upon it, feet towards the door. A large receptacle such as a baby bath is placed underneath the drainage hole. Candles are lit near the head. The windows of the room are opened.

The eyes are closed, the limbs straightened and the jaw supported, if necessary, with a cotton binding. The body is kept covered with a sheet through the entire process and, except for the purposes of identification, no other person may look upon it. Prayers are said throughout. Nowadays, the members of the Chevrah usually wear disposable gloves. The actual process of ritual washing and cleansing takes place on the Tahara Board and follows a prescribed pattern, with prayer, and the body is kept covered all the time. A member of the Chevrah will hold the sheet above the body whilst the others carry out the duties.

The finger and toe nails are cleaned and the hair is combed. Anything which comes away from the body, such as hair, is placed in a linen bag, which becomes a pillow for the head in the coffin. The body is carefully dried with a clean white sheet. Limbs and fingers are straightened.

The body is then clothed in special shrouds. These must be appropriate for one who is shortly to stand in judgement before God, and should be simple, hand made, perfectly clean and white. They are usually made of cotton. For men, the headdress is first put on and covers the entire head and neck. Trousers with closed feet are drawn up to the belly and secured with a bow; no knots are allowed. Tapes are also tied under the knees. The first upper garment is like a loose shirt, large enough to cover the entire body, with sleeves and tied at the neck. Over this goes a second shirt-like garment, and then a sash is wound round the body and fastened with a bow. The ends of the tapes are sometimes fashioned to resemble the Hebrew letter 'Shin', the first letter of the declaration of faith. A prayer shawl and, finally, a linen sheet complete the attire for the coffin.

For women the prayer shawl is omitted. A face cloth, of calico, is used to cover the face and the headdress is smaller and more like a pixie-hood in style.

The linen bag is placed in the coffin, and into this is placed any clippings or scrapings from the nails, hairs from the hairbrush, and any dressings with blood upon them, which were on the body at the time of death. The bag will also contain some padding material, such as polystyrene bits or soft foam pieces, and is used as a pillow to keep the head secure in the coffin. A handful of soil from the Holy Land of Israel may be sprinkled over the eyes, heart and hand of the body, with the words 'unto your people shall you be gathered'. The Chevrah Kadisha then ask forgiveness of the deceased, and the lid is closed. It is exceptional for the lid to be re-opened prior to interment.

During the process of Tahara, blood which flowed before death can be cleansed away, but that which flowed at, or after, the moment of death must be left and buried with the body. Theoretically, if death was due to accident or violence and the body and clothing were bloodied, no Tahara would be permitted, and the body and clothing would simply be wrapped in a sheet and placed in the coffin. In practice, in Britain, such cases would be subject to coronial inquiry and a post mortem would almost certainly be performed. The customary mortuary practice would be to leave the body clean and tidy. The bloody clothing, however, would be buried with the body, apart from any which needed to be retained for forensic examination.

Funerals

It is considered a humiliation to the dead to leave them unburied, and early funeral is obligatory to the practising Jew. The body returns to the earth, but the soul returns to God who gave it. Orthodox Jews believe in the resurrection of the body. The righteous will be resurrected at God's will, but the wicked will remain in the dust.

Orthodox Jews are always buried, but cremation is now preferred by some Jews of more liberal persuasion. The ashes may then be scattered, or placed in a wooden container and buried in the (non-orthodox) Jewish cemetery, according to personal request.

After mentioning the name of a dead person it is traditional to add 'Alav Hashalom' – 'may peace be upon him'. When speaking to one who is in mourning, the accepted greeting is to wish the person 'long life'.

Mourning

There are detailed requirements for the mourning period, the rending of garments, and the anniversaries of the death. The immediate mourning period, the Shiva (sitting), lasts seven days. Anyone who knew the deceased during life is welcome to the house to offer condolences and to attend prayers.

For advice

Queries relating to fertility treatment, abortion, contraception, organ donation, intervention in a dying patient, autopsy or any other topics affecting orthodox Jewish patients may be addressed to:

London Beth Din
735 High Road
London N12 0US
Tel: 020 8343 6270
Fax: 020 8343 6257

References

Encyclopaedia Britannica CD (2004) *Worldwide Adherents of All Religions by Six Continental Areas, Mid 2002.* Rugeley: Focus Multimedia.

Jewish Chronicle (1998) 'No objection to pig transplants.' *Jewish Chronicle*, 5 August, 40.

CHAPTER 27

BUDDHISM

Buddhism is the tradition of thought and practice associated with the Buddha (The Enlightened One) who lived in northern India during the 6th/5th centuries BCE. He is revered, not as a god, but as the founder of a spiritual way of life.

Over the centuries Buddhism has spread widely and there are over 364 million Buddhists worldwide (Encyclopaedia Britannica 2004) and many regional variations. Many adherents are found in India, Sri Lanka, Central Asia, China, Japan, South-East Asia and Tibet.

The main teachings (known as the Four Noble Truths) are held to be universal and sum up the true nature of life. The Four Noble Truths are as follows:

- all existence involves suffering (*dukkha*)

- the cause of that suffering is craving (*tanha*)

- the suffering can be brought to an end by extinguishing that craving (*nirvana*)

- the way to do this is by following the Noble Eightfold Path (*marga*) of the Buddha. This involves developing: Right Understanding, Right Thought, Right Speech, Right Action, Right Livelihood, Right Effort and Right Mindfulness and Right Concentration in daily life.

For the lay follower, this Buddhist way of life involves the cultivation of morality, meditation and wisdom, together with the keeping of special festivals, pilgrimages to sacred Buddhist places and the acceptance of social responsibility.

Buddhists accept the doctrine of karma and rebirth, which teaches that actions in this life will influence the quality of the next life, and this leads to the acceptance of ongoing personal responsibility. It is important that a Buddhist behaves morally at all times. All killing is considered unskilful and against Buddhist teachings. Because there is no concept of a Creator God in Buddhism, there is no 'worship' in the Judaeo-Christian sense. There is, however, the act of *Puja*, a ritual that is an act of respect or reverence for the Buddha and his teachings.

Buddhists in Britain

In 1986 there were estimated to be at least 20,000 Buddhists in Britain (Personal communication). According to the 2001 government census there are now at least

152,000 with 500 groups and centres and around 20 temples and monasteries (details can be found at www.statistics.gov.uk).

Until the 1960s, virtually all were native converts, apart from small numbers among the Chinese communities. In recent years refugees from Tibet and Vietnam have joined them.

Three main traditions of Buddhism predominate in Britain now. They are Theravada (from established schools in Sri Lanka, Burma and Thailand); Vajrayana (from Tibetan traditions that migrated from their homeland after the Chinese occupation in 1959); and Zen (from China, Japan and Indo-China). All three traditions have established centres in the UK and they are likely to have a monk (either of native or overseas origin) as a spiritual director.

The Buddhist patient in hospital

The Buddhist patient may, therefore, come from one of many ethnic backgrounds. He/she may have customs and preferences associated with the country of origin rather than with religious differences. He/she may not be able to speak, write or understand very much English. He/she may also find hospital food plain and unappetising. Since the killing of animals is considered incompatible with following the Buddha's teachings, most (but not necessarily all) Buddhists prefer a vegetarian diet.

The dying Buddhist patient

For Buddhists who are dying, the state of mind at the moment of death is of paramount importance, as this will influence the circumstances of a future rebirth. A Buddhist facing death would wish for a mind that is tranquil and at peace. Where possible, therefore, Buddhists should have the opportunity to have a period of peace and quiet for meditation and spiritual reflection. Many would also appreciate receiving spiritual support from fellow Buddhists as death approaches. A small Buddhist shrine placed where it can be seen and the opportunity to chant some appropriate Buddhist scriptures would also be welcomed.

Most Buddhist patients would be happy to give a contact name for spiritual/religious support when entering hospital, and a hospital chaplain might also be able to assist in creating the arrangements for peace and privacy. For dying Buddhists who have no particular affiliation to a local Buddhist centre or group, a nationwide Buddhist befriending network for those who are dying or bereaved (known as 'The Ananda Network') might be able to offer support (see below).

At death

No specific ritual is required for a lay Buddhist at the moment of death, or after death. Routine laying out is appropriate (see p.182). A monk of the appropriate school of Buddhism should be informed of the death as soon as possible.

However, if the patient is a Buddhist monk or nun, certain considerations would be welcomed. When a Buddhist monastic dies the body is often left untouched for a specified time, depending upon which Buddhist tradition he/she follows. This can range from a few hours to (in some Tibetan schools) 49 days. Buddhists living in Britain recognise that this is impractical for hospitals, so the best advice is to contact the Buddhist centre/organisation he/she attends as soon as possible for advice.

Post mortem

There is no religious objection to post mortem.

Blood transfusion and organ transplant

Helping others is fundamental to Buddhists. Giving and receiving blood or organs, before or after death, are viewed as acts of compassion and so there are no specific religious objections.

Donation of the body

There is no religious objection to this.

Abortion and euthanasia

The Buddha did not lay down absolute rules. These issues are for individual Buddhists to consider in the light of their daily practice.

Suicide

Attitudes vary on the question of suicide. Some would argue that it is detrimental to the spiritual life and contrary to the Buddha's teachings. Others say that there are no hard and fast rules. There is an account, in Buddhist scriptures, of an enlightened monk called Channa, who took his own life because he had an incurable illness, which caused him great pain and suffering. Some Buddhists who feel that suicide is wrong would argue that his actions were justified because he was an enlightened being, but his action cannot be seen as condoning suicide. Modern Buddhists may point out that there is free will to make moral decisions.

Funerals

Buddhist funerals are usually based on the diverse cultural funeral practices of the different Buddhist countries, rather than on specific religious instructions. The time between death and disposal is usually between three and seven days. Cremation is usual, with subsequent interment of the ashes. For Western Buddhists, funeral services are usually a mixture of Buddhist readings and rituals from whatever tradition they follow. The stone marking the grave should bear the Buddhist symbol of the eight-spoked wheel of the law.

If, for any reason, a Buddhist funeral cannot be carried out, any funeral service may be used with modification. All reference to Christian doctrine or God should be omitted, as should any Christian prayer. A memorial address is given, and passages read from a Buddhist book, if available.

Any retained tissues or organs which become available after the funeral would not be problematic. The physical body is seen as essentially impermanent and is simply a vehicle through which spiritual awareness develops. What happens to the body after death would not be of great concern to Buddhists.

Buddhist Hospice Trust

The Buddhist Hospice Trust, a small UK-based charity, was launched in 1986 to offer information and support to those who are seriously ill, dying or bereaved, from a Buddhist perspective. It has set up a nationwide befriending service called 'The Ananda Network' which is available, free of charge, to both Buddhists and non-Buddhists alike. It also publishes a twice-yearly journal called *raft*, which is available through subscription. The Buddhist Hospice Trust website is at: www.buddhisthospice.org.uk

For further information contact:

Dennis Sibley
The Buddhist Hospice Trust
I Laurel House, Trafalgar Road
Newport, Isle of Wight PO30 1QN
Tel: 01983 526945
Email: dsibley@buddhisthospice.org.uk

Reference

Encyclopaedia Britannica CD (2004) *Worldwide Adherents of All Religions by Six Continental Areas, Mid 2002.* Rugeley: Focus Multimedia.

CHAPTER 28

THE BAHÁ'I FAITH

The Bahá'i faith, the youngest of the world's independent, monotheistic religions, arose in Iran (Persia) during the middle of the 19th century from the teachings of the founder, Bahá'u'lláh.

The religion has been carried to virtually every part of the world. According to the Encyclopaedia Britannica 2004, there are some seven and a half million adherents worldwide, living in 232 countries, but figures from the National Spiritual Assembly of the Bahá'is of the UK estimate about five million. They come from some 2000 ethnic groups. The faith has spread to Europe, Australasia, Oceania, the Americas and Africa, while still remaining strong in its country of origin. The census of 2001 revealed almost 5000 Bahá'is resident in the UK, but figures from the website of the National Spiritual Assembly of the UK give the figure as 6000 in 2005.

The faith began in a Muslim country, but is not a sect of Islam or of any other faith. It is a quite distinct and separate religion, which has attracted believers from virtually every cultural, racial, social and ethnic background by its universalist and humanitarian principles.

Bahá'is believe that humanity is a single race with a common destiny. The faith recognises the essential unity of God and the Prophets of all faiths. It has belief in one God, whose will has been revealed to mankind by a series of messengers, divinely inspired prophets, including Zoroaster, Abraham, Moses, Buddha, Krishna, Christ, Muhammad, the Báb and Bahá'u'lláh. These founded the separate great religions, but had the common purpose, regarded as a single divine purpose, to bring God's message to mankind. Bahá'u'lláh explicitly states that there will be further messages from God in the future.

To Bahá'is, all races are equal. The faith condemns superstition and prejudice, and teaches that the fundamental purpose of religion is to promote concord and harmony. Religion must go hand in hand with science in order to promote an ordered, progressive and peaceful society. There is emphasis on education, equal opportunities with rights and privileges for both sexes, monogamy and the attainment of world peace. Religious conflict is seen as a serious threat to world peace.

There is no formal public ritual or priesthood. Each local community elects a local assembly, which coordinates activities, enrols members, assists, counsels and conducts marriages and funerals. There are annual elections to the National Spiritual

Assembly. Every five years, the members of the National Assemblies elect the su-preme international governing body, the Universal House of Justice.

Bahá'is strive to live a life of virtue, to prepare for the life after death.

The Bahá'i patient in hospital

Bahá'is believe in the healing power of modern medicine for both physical and men-tal ills, while recognising the role of the spirit, of prayer and of turning to God.

Bahá'is have a number of requirements for their daily spiritual life. These are simple personal responsibilities and do not require the intervention of another Bahá'i. They include reading a passage from the Bahá'i scriptures each night and morning, daily obligatory prayer, for which a quiet room or prayer room is appreci-ated (but not essential), an annual period of fasting (although those who are ill are ex-empt from this requirement), and observance of nine holy days during the year.

Bahá'i patients may come from diverse backgrounds and have needs which are unrelated to religion. For example, they may not have English as their first language.

The dying patient

If an illness is incurable, Bahá'is can accept palliative treatment if they wish, details of which can be discussed with the appropriate medical professionals as well as with the spiritual care-givers. Whenever possible it is up to the patient to decide, in coopera-tion with his or her doctors, what course of action to take. If the patient is unable to take decisions on his or her own behalf, the family should consult with the medical professionals.

A Bahá'i who is near death does not require the intervention of a spiritual care giver or chaplain, but clearly they will want to have their loved ones around them at that time. If there is time to prepare for death, it is very much up to the individual and those close to him or her to choose how to approach this.

At death

Bahá'is recognise death as a transition to a further stage of life akin to the transition made when a baby is born.

Following a death, care staff should follow normal hospital procedures. 'Rou-tine' laying out of a body is appropriate (see p.182). Some families may wish to per-form this service for their deceased relative.

Post mortem, transfusion, transplant and research

There is no religious objection to blood transfusion, post mortem or organ transplan-tation, or to the donation of a body for research or teaching purposes. However, whatever remains of the body after research must be buried and the Prayer for the Dead recited. Cremation is forbidden.

Suicide

The act of suicide is condemned in the Bahá'i teachings, but Bahá'is do not take a condemnatory attitude towards someone who commits suicide. People who suffer hardship and distress deserve compassion. Questions of forgiveness and judgement are left for God to decide.

Euthanasia

It is not for one person actively to end the life of another, so euthanasia is not permitted, although it is recognised that steps to ease suffering may, as a side effect, shorten life and this is accepted. There may come a time in the life of the patient when it becomes appropriate to withhold treatment, other than the palliation of suffering. The family will wish to discuss this with the relevant medical professionals.

Funerals

Bahá'i teachings require that the body is treated with great respect, and that it is to be allowed to decompose naturally, with no means used to hasten or prevent this process. Therefore embalming and cremation are not usually permitted.

The body is carefully washed and may be wrapped in cloth of silk, linen or cotton. Reflecting the diversity of the Bahá'i community, some relatives may wish to perform these tasks themselves, and some may have brought material in preparation for this, but there is no religious requirement for them to do so and the funeral director may be asked to perform these services. If it is not feasible to wrap the body, or if it is not done, it is not considered damaging to the spiritual wellbeing of the dead.

If the deceased is 15 years or older, Bahá'is may wish to place a 'burial ring' on a forefinger of the body. This simple ring bears the inscription (in Arabic) 'I came forth from God and return unto Him, detached from all save Him, holding fast to His Name, the Merciful, the Compassionate'.

There is no religious requirement for the body to be packed, though this may be done for aesthetic reasons. There is no restriction on the gender of the individual performing these services, regardless of the gender of the dead person.

When circumstances do not permit speedy interment, the body may be embalmed, provided that the process used has the effect only of retarding the natural decomposition for a short period only. The body should not be subjected to an embalming process, which has the effect of preserving it, without decomposition, for a lengthy period.

These requirements apply equally to stillbirths and neonates. Bahá'is believe the human soul comes into being at, and develops from, the time of conception. An unviable fetus, no matter how young, is still regarded as a person. Therefore it should be buried if possible. As there is nothing in Bahá'i scripture specifically referring to the manner of burial of embryos, how this is arranged is left to the discretion of the parents.

The funeral service should be carried out in a respectful and dignified manner as befits what is regarded as a solemn and important occasion.

While there is no concept of ritual purity or defilement relating to the treatment of the body of a deceased, there are a few simple and specific requirements relating to Bahá'i burial and the Bahá'i funeral service.

These are that:

- the body is not cremated
- it is interred as close as reasonably possible to the place of death and at most within an hour's travelling time from that place
- the body is not embalmed, the natural process of decomposition being allowed to take place
- it is buried in a coffin of as durable a material as possible
- at some time before interment a special prayer for the dead, the only specific requirement of a Bahá'i funeral service, is recited for Bahá'i deceased aged 15 or over.

These requirements apart, there is no definite system of practices or rigid rituals, and the observation of simplicity and flexibility is encouraged. There is no requirement to hold a funeral within a set time of death, although this should not be unnecessarily delayed.

The prayers and observations will be arranged either by the family or by the local Bahá'i community. If neither is available, advice and help may be sought from the National Bahá'i Centre (see below).

Bahá'is believe that, throughout eternity, the soul continues its progression toward God. Prayers are said for those who have died. Any funeral director may be used. In the absence of relatives or a local Bahá'i community, health care staff may deal with disposal in the usual manner as long as the above conditions are fulfilled.

Body tissue that becomes available after a person's funeral should also be buried and not cremated or disposed of in other ways. In this case, there is no need for a second funeral, since the Prayer for the Dead will have been recited at the time the main part of the body was buried.

The address of the National Bahá'i Centre is:

27 Rutland Gate
London SW7 1PD
Tel: 020 7584 2566
Fax: 020 7584 9402
Email: nsa@bahai.org.uk
Website: www.bahai.org.uk

Reference

Encyclopaedia Britannica CD (2004) *Worldwide Adherents of All Religions by Six Continental Areas, Mid 2002*. Rugeley: Focus Multimedia.

CHAPTER 29

ISLAM

The Arabic word 'Islam' means 'submission to God', and the Muslim is one who surrenders himself, or herself, unconditionally to God's will. For a true believer, desires will always accord with Islamic teachings. Muhammad (p.b.u.h.)[*], who lived from 570–632, was the channel through which God's final revelation came to man.

Islam is a complete system of faith and behaviour, and draws no distinction between the religious and the practical spheres of life. The all-embracing Law of Islam (Shari'a) covers all facets of human activity.

Islam is the religion of almost one-fifth of the world's population, about three-quarters of whom are widely scattered from the Adriatic to Malaysia. There are over 858 million Muslims in Asia, and over 329 million in Africa (Encyclopaedia Britannica 2004b). Most Muslims resident in Britain have come here from the Indian subcontinent, mainly Pakistan, Bangladesh and parts of Kashmir. Others come from places as diverse as Yemen, Iraq, Bosnia, Afghanistan, Iran, Mauritius, West Africa, Indonesia, Somalia and Central Asia. Some are of Turkish or Turkish-Cypriot origin. Students and visitors may also come from Africa or from Arab countries. Muslims are not of one race, colour or ethnic group, but come from all parts of the world. Increasing numbers of native British people are also Muslim. In the 2001 UK census, 1,591,000 people claimed to belong to the faith, some 2.7 per cent of the population.

Mecca (Makka), near Jedda (Jadda) on the Red Sea coast of Saudi Arabia, is the place where God's Messenger, Muhammad[*], was born and, at the age of 40 years, began his prophethood of Islam. Hence, Mecca is the religious centre of Islam and contains the most sacred place, the Holy Haram Mosque, which is a place of pilgrimage. (Haram means 'sanctuary'.) Muslims have five important religious duties, known as the 'Pillars of Islam'. The first is to declare that 'there is no God but one God (Allah), and Muhammad (peace and a blessing upon him) is His Messenger'. The other four are: prayer five times a day, with rituals of purification; the giving of alms; fasting; and pilgrimage to Mecca.

On the whole, practices around death are similar for all Muslims, but there may be some variation between Muslims from Arab lands and those from Asian countries.

---

[*]   'Peace and a blessing upon him' is given after every mention of the name of the Prophet and the phrase is replaced in the text of this chapter by the asterisk symbol.

Most of the customs are laid down in the Shari'a laws, derived from the words of the Prophet (the Hadith) rather than from the Qur'an.

There is no initiation ceremony into Islam. Friday is the holy day, from sunset on Thursday to sunset on Friday, but there are no religious restrictions for this day except that any work being done should stop for prayer.

The Muslim patient in hospital

For many Muslim patients, English may not be the first language. Elderly people, particularly women, may have spent much of their time in the home and never had the opportunity to acquire skills in spoken or written English. Translating and interpreting in medical situations may require special care.

Cleanliness is of great importance to Muslims. Hands, mouth, nose, face, arms and feet, in that order, are always washed before prayer.

Women are required to wash the entire body after menstruation. Both sexes would wish to use fresh running water, hence a shower rather than a bath would be preferred. Water is also needed to wash down after both urination and defecation; toilet paper alone is not considered adequate. Water therefore must be available in toilets, and if bedpans have to be used, a bowl of water must be provided also. The only contraindication for this would be if the water was, in any way, harmful for the patient.

Modesty is extremely important. Muslim women will prefer to be examined by a female doctor. If there is only a male doctor available, then he will be acceptable if another female is also present. Some may not agree to be seen at all by a male doctor, so the availability of a female doctor will be essential. In Islam, free mixing of the sexes is restricted, and Muslim women cover their heads and bodies to maintain modesty. It would be inappropriate to treat Muslim women on mixed wards, or to ask them to expose themselves in any way unnecessarily to other people. Special care is needed in X-ray or operating theatre situations, and suitable gowns should be provided.

It is a religious recommendation that an ill person should be visited, hence a Muslim patient may have many visitors.

Diet

Some meat may be eaten provided that it has been slaughtered according to Halal ritual, which drains the meat of blood. Halal lamb, beef, chicken, rabbit and goat are permitted, but pork meat, carrion and blood are forbidden, as are products made from them or cooked in pig fat. Fish, sea food and eggs may be eaten, as long as they are not prepared or served alongside non-Halal foods. Plates which may have been used for non-Halal foods must be carefully washed before use. Alcohol is forbidden.

Many Muslims will be accustomed to food which is well seasoned and spiced, and may not take kindly to British hospital diets. As with Jewish patients, some may prefer a vegetarian diet whilst in hospital.

During the month of Ramadan, Muslims fast between dawn and sunset. Although those who are sick are not expected to fast, in hospital, during Ramadan, food may need to be presented as part of the necessary medicine that is required for treatment of the patient. However, if the patient is not so ill that food is essential for recovery, for example if the patient has a broken leg, then they should be enabled to fast and to eat at the appropriate time without being made to feel that they are causing inconvenience.

The dying patient

Islam teaches that suffering and death are part of God's plan. There is belief in the day of judgement and a life beyond. At the approach of death, it is important to beg for God's forgiveness for sins committed during life. Then is the time to ask fellow humans for forgiveness, if wrong has been done to them, and settle any kinds of debts outstanding. The visiting Imam will remind the dying Muslim of this duty. Sudden death is regarded as undesirable, because this deprives the devout Muslim of the opportunity to make amends in this way.

There is no requirement for a religious leader (Imam) to be present at the death of a Muslim patient. The choice of place of death is a personal one, though it is often said that Muslims would prefer to die in their own homes. Members of the family may join the patient in prayer and recite verses from the Qur'an. The declaration of faith (the Shahada) is said gently and soothingly in order that the dying person may be prompted to utter, with their last breath, the words 'I bear witness that there is no God but Allah, and Muhammad* is His Messenger' ('Ashadu an la elaha ella Allah wa ashadu anna Muhammadan Rasulullah').

The dying patient may wish to sit or lie with the face towards Mecca, and may appreciate the bed being moved or turned to make this possible (to face the South East if in the UK).

If no relatives are available, any practising Muslim can give help and religious comfort. The local Muslim community should be contacted for help and advice.

At death

There is no religious prohibition on the touching of the body by non-Muslims. Whilst modern health care staff will usually wear disposable gloves to handle a body, this is for the protection of the staff and is not a religious requirement. Staff should, if possible, consult with members of the family before carrying out any procedure.

Funerals should take place as soon as practicable, preferably within 24 hours of death. Relatives will be distressed if there is a delay, and staff should take care to ensure that they understand why any delay is unavoidable.

IN NORMAL CIRCUMSTANCES

Where the attending doctor is able to sign a death certificate and there is no reason to notify the Coroner, the body should be prepared according to the wishes of the family. If no family members or other Muslim advocate is present, a limited laying-out is appropriate which differs in some details from that given on p.189.

Disposable gloves must be worn. The eyes should be closed and the mouth supported, traditionally by a bandage under the chin and round the head. The body should be straightened, and this is done by first flexing the elbows, shoulders, knees and hips before straightening them. This is believed to delay the onset of stiffening, making it easier to wash and shroud the body. Normally the large toes are tied together. The head is turned towards the right shoulder. This is so that the body can be buried with the face towards Mecca. Hair and nails should be left untrimmed. The body should not be washed, but simply labelled and covered totally with a plain sheet. Advice should then be sought from the local Muslim community.

IN ABNORMAL CIRCUMSTANCES

Where the death must be reported to the Coroner, it will help greatly if health care staff and others can expedite the process, so that the funeral need not be unduly delayed.

First, the family must be informed of the death, if they are not already present. The family should contact their preferred funeral director, who will be able to keep in touch with the Coroner's Officer during the inquiry. If no family are available, the local Muslim community or Mosque should be contacted for advice and help.

The Coroner's Officer must then be informed of the death. He is contacted by a phone call to the Duty Inspector at the local Police Station. The Duty Inspector has a list of Coroners' Officers who are on duty for each geographical area, and will arrange for the relevant Officer to contact the doctor in charge of the case.

Reporting to the Coroner does not necessarily involve a post mortem examination, but may do so. Even so, the funeral need not necessarily be delayed.

The doctor should inform the Coroner's Officer that this is a Muslim body, and that the family wish for a speedy disposal. He should ask the Officer if it is possible to arrange for the post mortem to be performed later that day, or early next morning, and to arrange for the findings of the pathologist (the cause of death) to be telephoned (or faxed) to the Coroner, by the pathologist, immediately after the autopsy is complete. In this way the Coroner is able to issue a death certificate as soon as practicable, often within the 24 hours.

Some Coroners may insist on an initial written provisional report, but this causes no additional delay. As with Jewish bodies, Coroners' Officers are usually extremely helpful in expediting these arrangements, and pathologists, particularly in areas with significantly large ethnic populations, will usually gladly accommodate requests for speedy autopsy for religious reasons. However, difficulties may still be encountered in some areas because of restricted opening times of public mortuaries at weekends and public holidays, and because of limited hours of work of Registrars of Births,

Marriages and Deaths at these times. It is important that the family understands any reasons for delay.

If the body needs to be moved for the post mortem, either the family may use their preferred funeral director or the Coroner's Officer will arrange the transport. Ritual preparation of the body will commence after the autopsy is complete.

A late miscarriage or a baby who is stillborn or who dies after birth should have a name. A stillbirth does not necessarily need a full funeral service, but does require burial in a cemetery, and the parents will usually wish to take the body for burial.

Post mortem examinations

Islam teaches that the body belongs to God. Strictly speaking, no part of it should be cut out, harmed or donated to another. Post mortems are therefore disliked. If a post mortem is ordered by the Coroner, then the family must understand the reason why it is necessary, and be reassured that all organs will be returned to the body for burial.

Blood transfusion

There is no religious objection to the donation or reception of blood. The preservation of life has high priority and blood donation is commendable.

Organ transplantation

At one time, Muslims were not likely to agree to organ transplants except in special circumstances, but there is much variation in practice related to the level of religious commitment. Tissue donations and transplants and other essential examinations may be allowed according to the principle that 'necessity removes restrictions'. Anything that is essential to save life may be permitted. With proper reasoning and encouragement, consent may be obtained.

In 1982, the donation of organs after death was declared 'hallal' (permissible) in Saudi Arabia by the highest religious authority, the Senior 'Ulama' Commission (Encyclopaedia Britannica 2004a). The Commission has influence throughout the Islamic world. In 1991, the National Committee for Transplantation in Iran sought clarification from senior religious leaders, who confirmed that any organ from a brain-dead person may be used for transplantation (Lancet 1992). However, Muslims from the Indian subcontinent may disagree with these pronouncements and, in some areas, public acceptance of transplantation remains low.

Donation of the body

The majority of Muslims would not agree to the donation of the body for teaching or research purposes.

Abortion

In Islamic law, termination of pregnancy is allowed only if necessary to save the life of the mother.

According to Islam, life after conception begins at 120 days. Termination prior to this is less objectionable and for the mother to decide. Termination after this time is unacceptable, except where the life of the mother is at risk.

Any product of conception over the age of 120 days would require burial.

Euthanasia and suicide

Euthanasia is strictly prohibited.

Suicide is regarded as a very grievous sin, but the body would receive the customary funeral rites. Islam teaches that a suicide victim will not enter Paradise, but that God will judge the circumstances.

Preparation of the body for the funeral

The body is usually prepared for burial by the family and, in Britain, this may take place at the mortuary, at the funeral director's, or at home. The body is washed, either by a professional washer or by any members of the same sex as the deceased. There is no ritual to be observed except that the person who performs the task must be worthy, and shall recite the phrases which acknowledge God and Muhammad* as His Messenger.

The body is carefully washed an uneven number of times (at least three) until no impurities remain. Warm water is used, to which camphor or rosewater has been added. Private parts are always kept covered with a sheet while the body is washed with a sponge. These days, gloves are worn for the procedure. A woman who has given birth may be regarded as unclean for 40 days thereafter and, in some traditions, may not pray or handle a body during this time, nor may a woman who is menstruating. However, if no other appropriate persons are available, any able person may assist.

After washing, the arms are placed across the chest, and the body is clothed in three pieces of unstitched white cloth, which must cover the entire body and head. Those who have been on a pilgrimage to Mecca (the Hajj) may have brought back a special white shroud for themselves. Silk cloth is not permitted for men.

Funerals

Muslims are always buried, never cremated, and should be buried as soon as possible, according to Islamic law. Cremation is not practised, because the soul, which leaves the body immediately after death, is believed to remain close by the body until the time of burial. The Qur'an gives clear direction for burial of the dead. Should the death occur at sea, sea burial would be acceptable.

In Britain, a simple wooden coffin is usually used. In other parts of the Muslim world, the dead are laid to rest without a coffin. The shrouded body is placed in a niche dug out of the side of the bottom of the grave. This is so that the weight of the earth will not fall upon the body. The niche is bricked up before the grave is filled. Some Local Authorities in the UK allow this practice.

In some Islamic cultures women take no part in the burial ceremony, while in others women do attend the burial at the graveside. The menfolk take the body to the mosque or the graveside for prayer and readings from the Holy Qur'an before burial. The service is conducted by a respected member of the community, as there is no priesthood. If no Muslim attendant is present at the funeral of a Muslim, then prayers are omitted, as they may not be offered by non-believers. As a mark of respect, in some cultures, the immediate family may not eat until after the funeral.

There is some variation in customs following the funeral. There are three days of mourning, during which friends and relatives offer condolences and bring food to the house for the family. Condolences should not be offered after this time, as they will reawaken the pain of the death for the family. After this, life should return to 'normality' as life must go on. The widowed wife will stay at home for a longer period. The grave may be visited and alms given to the poor.

A widow is expected to mourn for 130 days, dressing with simplicity and without jewellery. She is confined to the home unless it is absolutely necessary to leave it for that time. Subsequently she may resume her place in society, and is encouraged to remarry.

These days, in Britain, there are Muslim funeral directors who will arrange all aspects of a Muslim funeral.

Any tissues or body parts which are released to the family after the funeral should be buried, but no second funeral would be necessary.

Some families may wish to take the body back to their country of origin for burial (see Chapter 1).

Readers are reminded that the address of the IQRA Trust is given in Appendix A, p.327.

References

Encyclopaedia Britannica CD (2004a) *Islam: Death*. Rugeley: Focus Multimedia.

Encyclopaedia Britannica CD (2004b) *Worldwide Adherents of All Religions by Six Continental Areas, Mid 2002*. Rugeley: Focus Multimedia.

Lancet (News item) (1992) 'Organ transplantation.' *Lancet 340*, 300.

CHAPTER 30

HINDUISM

Hinduism is the name given to the religious beliefs, practices and cultural codes of conduct of the Hindus. In the 8th century, the Muslims invaded the Indian subcontinent from the Northwest, and gave the name 'Hindus' to the people who lived in the land beyond the Indus River, predominantly the inhabitants of India.

According to the census of 1971, about one-fifth of the population of India profess a specific religion other than Hinduism (Hinnels 1984). The rest constitute the Hindu population.

Hinduism is a culture quite as much as a religion, and its origins may date back to 1500 BCE. It is totally bound up with the social, or caste, structure of society, and is a culture based on an acceptance of differences rather than insistence of one unequivocal truth. The range of belief and practice is very great, and Hinduism varies in its nature from village to village, with major differences from region to region. Different deities, scriptures, festivals and caste structures exist in different areas.

Common to all is the belief in re-incarnation and the 'Moksha' or 'release' from the cycle of repeated birth, death and re-birth. A person's deeds in his previous life have determined his position and caste in this life (Karma – the law of cause and effect), and his behaviour in this life will likewise determine his station in the next (Dharma – the duty that dictates the conduct of one's life). Each person must try to live life such that he rises above the cycle of re-birth when the soul is released and becomes one with God, the attainment of 'Moksha'. Until then he will be reborn again and again.

Unlike Judaism and Christianity, Hinduism has no religious belief in historical personalities and does not see events on earth as manifesting the action or purpose of God. There is no historical founder of the faith. Truthfulness, non-violence, honesty, sincerity and devotion to God are considered essential to good living. There are no initiation rites and there is a great tolerance of belief. Hindus believe that there is one Supreme Being, Brahman, who is omniscient, omnipotent, limitless and all-providing, who may be worshipped in many different forms and understood in many different ways. Different aspects of the Deity are worshipped through one or several gods and godesses, the most important being Brahma, Vishnu and Shiva, but Hindus are essentially monotheistic in their belief that only one, all encompassing, Divine Essence pervades the entire universe. Most families worship at a shrine at their home, and attend the temple for communal worship. Each temple has a priest, but there is no central religious authority.

Every Hindu should pray, revere the old, and offer generous hospitality to any that seek food and shelter. In India, the influence of the caste system is powerful and different castes vary in their interpretation of the laws on diet, prayer and ritual purification. Each caste contains many sub-castes, each made up of a group of people of like social, occupational and geographical background, identifiable to each other by their surnames or sub-caste names.

People regard their own sub-caste as a large kin group or extended family. They feel at ease with them, and feel obligations to them. Most Hindu marriages will take place within the sub-caste groups. In Britain the importance of the caste structure may be lessening in some ways, but it probably still has great influence on social behaviour.

About 13 per cent of the world's population follows some variant of Hinduism (Encyclopaedia Britannica 2004). Almost all of them, over 821 million, live in Asia. Figures from the 2001 census show that there are at least 559,000 Hindus in the UK. The majority of them will come from Gujurat, in Western India, or from East Africa where they settled earlier. Some have come from Sri Lanka.

The Hindu patient in hospital

As with other Asian patients, the Hindu patient may not have English as a first language, and may need skilled help for translation and interpretation in hospital situations. Occasionally caste differences, or, more likely, differences in what is considered as acceptable social behaviour, may cause friction between doctor and patient, or between doctor and doctor or patient and patient.

Many Hindus pray at least once a day, at sunrise, and, though they may want to continue to pray in hospital, they are unlikely to request space or isolation to perform rituals associated with the prayer. They may, however, want to wash and change their clothes before prayer.

Like all Asian women, Hindu women dress modestly. They will probably prefer to be seen by a female doctor if at all possible. Staff should be considerate when dressing patients for operation or for X-ray, or in similar situations.

The use of water is required after using the lavatory. If the bedpan must be used, a bowl of water must also be supplied for washing.

Diet

Most Hindus believe in non-violence and refuse to take life. Many are vegetarian on the grounds of conscience, and will not eat off a plate which has been used for meat. They may prefer to eat off a disposable plate. Even with those who eat meat, beef will be taboo on cultural rather than religious grounds, for there is no religious constraint on the eating of beef. Some will not eat eggs or onions, but, for most, cow's milk and dairy products are acceptable.

The dying patient

The Bhagavad Gita (The Song of the Lord) and the Ramayna are parts of the Hindu scriptures. Both represent the essence of the Hindu religion and point the many ways to salvation (Nirvana). Devout Hindus will derive comfort from their readings. Some may wish to lie on the floor, symbolising closeness to Mother Earth, but also possibly expressing a desire to release a bed for someone more worthy, or with a need greater than their own, even at a time when death is approaching.

The patient or the family may wish to invite the family priest, or one from the temple, to perform holy rites. If there are no family members, and the patient wishes it, staff should seek help and advice from the local Hindu Temple. The rites may include the tying of a holy thread, as a blessing, round the neck or wrist of the dying person, and he or she may be sprinkled with holy water from the River Ganges (Ganga, the river most sacred to Hindus, is regarded as flowing from the head of Shiva and its waters as having the power to wash away sins), or be marked on the forehead with vermillion or sandal-wood paste. A sacred tulsi leaf may be placed in the mouth of the patient. These religious tokens should not be removed by health care staff.

Sometimes family members may bring clothes or money for the dying person to touch before their distribution to the needy.

Devout Hindu patients would prefer to die at home. This has religious and social significance, and death in hospital can cause additional distress. If the patient has requested to go home to die, and all reasonable treatment has been offered, then all possible steps should be taken to comply with this request.

At death

As with Jews and Muslims, Hindu funerals in India would take place as soon as practicable, ideally within 24 hours. Hindus in Britain are less likely to demand such speedy disposal. Because adult Hindus are cremated, and there may be a delay for the use of crematorium services, funerals may, in practice, take much longer than this to arrange, but health care staff can help to speed up the process.

Some Hindus may object to non-Hindus touching a dead body and, if so, disposable gloves should be worn by health care staff. Traditionally the washing and laying out is done by the family, at home or at the funeral parlour. If health care staff must handle the body, they should do so with great respect.

IN NORMAL CIRCUMSTANCES

Where the doctor is able to complete the death certificate, and there is no requirement to notify the Coroner, the body may be prepared according to the wishes of the family or the instructions from the priest.

If no family members are present, a limited laying out is appropriate. Wearing disposable gloves the nurse should close the eyes, straighten the limbs and support the chin. Jewellery, sacred threads or other religious objects should be left on the body. The body should not be washed, and the hair and nails should be left untrimmed. The body should be labelled before being wrapped in a plain white sheet, without religious emblem.

The local Hindu Temple should be contacted for advice and help.

IN ABNORMAL CIRCUMSTANCES

Where the death must be reported to the Coroner, health care staff must ensure that the family understands why this is necessary. Should the family be very concerned because of the delay to the funeral, the doctor in charge of the case can help to expedite the process by following the advice given on pp.257, 275 (Muslim or Jewish bodies).

If the family understands that the cremation will take several days to arrange anyway, then it is appropriate to follow normal hospital procedure.

If a post mortem is necessary, ritual preparation of the body will commence after the post mortem is complete. Doctors should ensure that death and cremation certificates are made available as soon after death as practicable.

Post mortem examinations

Post mortems are disliked but, if the reason for them is explained sympathetically, they may be accepted by some families. There is no religious prohibition of autopsy.

Blood transfusion

There is no religious objection to the giving or receiving of blood.

Organ transplantation

There is no religious objection to donation or reception.

Donation of the body

There is no religious objection, but families are unlikely to agree to this.

Abortion

There is considerable variation in attitude, which is cultural and tribal rather than religious. Some groups will consider termination for an unmarried woman who becomes pregnant. Care must be taken to ascertain the degree of pressure being applied either way by hierarchically superior family members. (There tends to be a more strict hierarchical family structure among Hindus from the North of India than amongst those from the South.) Genetic defects are commoner in communities with much inter-marriage, as may happen in sub-caste groups. Prenatal testing for fetal abnormality may need to be followed by advice to terminate the pregnancy, and should be embarked upon only with careful explanation. The woman or couple may agree to take on problems, which may well be beyond their actual capabilities, in the belief that these misfortunes are pre-ordained and part of their 'Karma', a result of misdeeds in the previous life and therefore inevitable.

The products of an early miscarriage or abortion may be disposed of by the hospital. Once the fetus is recognisably a baby, then it would be accorded the normal funeral rites.

Suicide

There are no 'religious' views as to suicide and no special requirements for the funeral of a suicide. There may be differing tribal views in some areas. In Hinduism, where duty is considered very important, one has choice to do what one feels is right, according to conscience. One must be able to justify one's actions to one's own conscience.

Euthanasia

There are no 'official' religious views on this. The same criteria would apply as in the paragraph above.

Funerals

All adult Hindus are cremated. The practice is based on the belief that, so long as the physical body remains whole, the soul, which departs the body at death, will remain near it. Cremation (purification by fire) allows them to separate and aids the release of the soul.

Before cremation the body is washed, usually by the women of the family, shrouded and decked with flowers. A special service, at home or at the Chapel of Rest, will precede the cremation, and religious objects may be placed beside the body in the coffin. For some cultural groups, it is traditional that the eldest son, who shaves his head as a sign of grief, is responsible for the arrangement of the funeral, and in India he would be the one to light the funeral pyre. In Britain, he would expect to be able to press the switch at the crematorium, and this can usually be arranged. Practices vary, and for some groups the eldest son will prepare the funeral for his father and the youngest son prepare that for his mother. For a child death, the father would light the pyre. Prayers and hymns are read during the ceremony and 'mantras' chanted by the priest and the congregation.

There is great regional variation in the disposal of the ashes, based on what is believed to be happening to the soul between death and re-incarnation. Various customs, 'rituals of respect', aim to prevent the soul from re-entering the body of the deceased and, subsequently, enable it to be handed over to Yama, the god of death. In some parts of India, the ashes are gathered on the third day, placed in a container and buried near the cremation site. They are disinterred on the tenth day, and may be cast into the Ganges then or on the 13th, 16th or the 31st day. This final scattering of the ashes is of great religious importance to all Hindus. If it is not possible to consign the ashes to the Ganga, then any river, ocean or body of water may be used. The ashes may also be kept until the family has the right opportunity for disposal, as on a visit to India. Usually a priest will lead the ritual for the mourners at the time of disposal of the ashes.

In Britain, the law is unclear. There is no specific general prohibition upon the disposal of ashes in rivers and lakes, but in some areas local bylaws or Water Authority regulations may forbid the practice. The ashes may be scattered in the sea. Frequently the ashes, or a portion of them, are sent to India so that they may be cast into the Ganges.

In the mourning period, friends and relatives will visit the bereaved family. Close family members, particularly the women, will not cook until the cremation has taken place, and some may not eat, although the extended family will provide food during this period. This is one reason why Hindu funerals should not be unnecessarily delayed.

White clothing is worn, as a sign of mourning, for the first ten days. The widow and the eldest son may shave their heads. Older women may wail and keen loudly, as is traditional to show grief. Widows in Hindu culture are expected to spend much time in prayer and assume the role of mediators, advisers and comforters for the community. They should always wear white and spend most of their time within the home. Traditionally widows did not remarry, although widowers were encouraged to do so.

The family may hold a special ceremony, with a priest, on the anniversary of a death and, in some cultures, the family may give alms at this time.

In the case of a retained organ or tissue specimen being made available after the funeral, this would not be seen as a problem. The soul and body are already dissociated and no second funeral would be necessary. The disposal by the hospital would be appropriate.

References

Encyclopaedia Britannica CD (2004) *Worldwide Adherents of All Religions by Six Continental Areas, Mid 2002*. Rugeley: Focus Multimedia.

Hinnels, J. (ed) (1984) *The Penguin Dictionary of Religions*. Harmondsworth: Penguin Books.

CHAPTER 31

SIKHISM

Sikhs are members of a relatively young religious faith. Sikhism arose in the 16th century, in the Punjab in Northern India, as a reformist movement of Hinduism. The word 'Sikh' (from the Sanskrit 'siksati' – 'he studies') literally means a disciple, and Sikhs follow the teachings of the founder, Guru Nanak (born in 1469), and his nine Guru successors, who tried to combine the best features of Hinduism and Islam. 'Guru' means 'teacher', but has come to represent the inner spiritual guidance, which comes from the divine presence of God. The ten Gurus are revered as saints, and the collection of their writings, the Guru Granth Sahib, is the Sikh holy book. The tenth Guru, Guru Gobind Singh (1675–1708), commanded that, after him, Sikhs should use the Guru Granth Sahib as their teacher.

Historically, Sikhs have experienced a great deal of persecution and the tenth Guru organised the sect into a people with military organisation in the defence of their faith. He also instituted the 'amrit', which is the baptism and initiation into the faith. All those baptised adopt the same family names of Singh (lion) for men and Kaur (princess) for women. They are then bound to observe special rules, such as daily attendance at the temple and special prayers. They wear the five symbols of the faith, popularly known as the Five Ks. These are:

1. Kesh – uncut hair.

2. Kangha – the wooden comb which fixes the uncut hair into a bun.

3. Kara – an iron, steel or occasionally gold bracelet worn on the right wrist.

4. Kirpan – a symbolic sword worn under the clothing in a small fabric sheath, or as a small brooch or pendant.

5. Kach – short trousers or breeches, often nowadays replaced by ordinary under-garments but with the same significance.

The hair is sanctified at initiation and must be kept covered at all times. The turban is worn even in death.

Sikhs believe in one God, and each makes their personal relationship with God in their own way. They reject idolatry and caste, and believe in the equality of all people, irrespective of their colour, creed or sex. They believe in re-incarnation, aiming to achieve unity and understanding with God after many cycles of re-birth as different forms of life. After death there is the judgement of God, and the soul then undergoes pleasure or pain in the next life according to past actions in the last. 'The soul neither dies, nor can it be destroyed' (Adi Granth 1026/1). There are no professional priests in this faith, having been abolished by Guru Gobind Singh, who felt they had become corrupt and self-important. The main religious centre for the Sikhs is Harmiandir Sahib at Amritsar (otherwise known as The Golden Temple) in the Punjab of Northern India.

In 2002 there were estimated to be almost 24 million Sikhs worldwide, most of them in Southern Asia (Encyclopaedia Britannica 2004). According to the 2001 UK census, there may be some 336,000 Sikhs living in Britain, mostly from families who originated in the Punjab or in East Africa. Other sources put the figure at 500,000 (Whitaker's Almanack 2005). If not born in Britain, their native tongue is likely to be Punjabi.

The Sikh patient in hospital

As with other patients of Asian origin, Sikhs may not have English as a first language. They may need skilled help to translate and interpret medical needs.

Sikh women dress modestly and will be unwilling to expose themselves before men. In such a situation there must always be a female present. They should be treated with consideration when being dressed for surgery or X-ray examination, and are likely to prefer to be seen by a female doctor if possible. Treatment on a mixed-sex ward would be inappropriate except in an emergency situation.

Sikh men will wish to keep their hair covered at all times. They will be embarrassed if asked to remove the turban, or the breeches, in view of others. For both sexes the Five Ks should not be disturbed, in life or death, unless it is absolutely necessary.

Running water is preferred for washing and water is regarded as essential for toileting. Water must be provided if bedpans or commodes must be used. Sikhs will want to wash their hands and rinse their mouths before meals.

Diet

Many Sikhs are vegetarian, particularly the women. Some believe that meat defiles the body, giving rise to such ills as cancer, high blood pressure and even bad temper. Few non-vegetarian Sikhs will eat beef, and some will not eat pork. All Halal meat (meat which is killed according to Muslim ritual) is forbidden, whatever the animal. Some Sikhs may not eat fish or eggs. In hospital Sikh patients may prefer a vegetarian diet, or at least require explanation of the constituents of the hospital menu with its unfamiliar names, such as stew, hotpot or shepherd's pie. Intoxicants of all kinds, including tobacco and alcohol, are forbidden.

The dying patient

There are no priests in Sikhism. The comforting words of the Guru Granth Sahib may be read by the patient, one of the family, a friend or the reader from the Gurdwara (Temple). In the absence of family, any practising Sikh may give religious comfort and, if the patient wishes it, the local Gurdwara should be approached for assistance. There are no last rites to be performed other than that the dying person should be encouraged to utter 'Waheguru, Waheguru' ('Wonderful Lord'). Death is regarded as God's will, and the family are discouraged from making extravagant displays of emotion. Sikhs are taught that those who have the spirit of God are not afraid of death.

At death

In India, Sikh funerals take place within 24 hours of death. Traditionally, Sikh families will want to wash and lay out the body themselves, but there is no religious objection to others touching the body.

IN NORMAL CIRCUMSTANCES

Where the doctor is able to sign a death certificate and there is no requirement to notify the Coroner (see p.183), if family members are available they must be consulted before health care staff perform any Last Offices. The body may then be prepared according to the wishes of the family.

If no family are available, a limited laying-out is appropriate. The Five Ks should be left intact, and the hair should be kept covered. Hair and beard, which are felt to contribute greatly to the personality of the Sikh, must not be trimmed.

The eyes should be closed, the jaw supported and the limbs straightened. The face will be displayed on several occasions prior to the funeral, and should be cleaned and straightened so that the much-valued expression of peace and tranquillity is attained.

The body should be clearly labelled on wrist and ankle, and then covered with a plain white sheet, without religious emblem.

IN ABNORMAL CIRCUMSTANCES

Where the death must be reported to the Coroner, the family must be sympathetically and clearly told why this is necessary. The Five Ks must be respected, and normal hospital procedure should be followed. The ritual proceedings will take place after the post mortem has been carried out. If the family are upset at the prospect of a delayed funeral, the process may be speeded up by following the advice given for Jewish (p.257) or Muslim (p.275) funerals. Because Sikhs are cremated, the traditional disposal within 24 hours is unlikely to happen in Britain, and there may be a wait of several days for cremation. Because of this, it is appropriate to follow usual hospital practice rather than to try and complete the investigations unnecessarily rapidly, unless the family insist.

Post mortem examinations

There are no religious objections to post mortems, but, as with other Asian groups, the funeral should ideally take place as soon as possible and families will need a clear explanation of any reason for delay.

Sikhs believe life after death is a continuous cycle of re-birth, but the physical body is not needed in this rebirth. The real essence of a person is their soul.

Blood transfusion

There are no religious objections to the donation or the reception of blood.

Organ transplantation

There are no religious objections to the donation or the reception of organs for transplant. The Sikh philosophy and teachings place great emphasis on the importance of giving and putting others before oneself and stresses the importance of performing noble deeds. There are many examples of selfless giving and sacrifice in the teachings of the ten Gurus:

> Where self exists, there is no God.
> Where God exists, there is no self.
>
> (Guru Nanak, Guru Granth Sahib)

> The dead sustain their bond with the living through virtuous deeds.
>
> (Guru Nanak, Guru Granth Sahib)

> The true servants of God are those who serve Him through helping others.
>
> (Guru Nanak, Guru Granth Sahib)

Donation of the body

There are no religious objections to donation of the body for research and teaching.

Suicide

Suicide is regarded as tragic, but not as a grievous sin.

Euthanasia

Sikhs have a great respect for life, which they see as a gift from God. Sikhism teaches that we have a duty to use life in a responsible way. If a person is suffering, there is a reason for it. Most Sikhs would be against euthanasia, as they believe that the timing of birth and death should be in God's hands.

Sikhs contemplating euthanasia for themselves or others should look at the whole picture and make appropriate distinctions between ending life and not artificially prolonging a terminal state.

Abortion

Abortion is not generally supported except possibly in the case of an unmarried woman. Prenatal testing for fetal abnormalities is likely to require a great deal of explanation, and may not be justified if there is no likelihood of any recommended termination being acceptable. There are no religious objections to family planning.

Funerals

The bodies of stillborn babies or late miscarriages will normally be given the usual funeral rites prior to burial. Burial may also be accorded to neonates who die within a few days of birth. All other Sikhs are cremated. There are no special rites for older children, who are treated as for adults.

In India, cremation would take place within 24 hours of death, but is likely to take considerably longer in many parts of Britain. Delays must be kept to a minimum, and the reasons for them clearly explained. If organ or tissue specimens had been retained, as by the Coroner, and this was known prior to the funeral, the funeral would be delayed to take account of this. It may also be delayed to allow family and friends to congregate.

Usually family members of the same sex will wash and dress the body, either at home or at the funeral parlour. Every Sikh who has been baptised is cremated wearing the five symbols of the faith. Men are wrapped in a white shroud and retain the turban. Older women wear a white shroud, and younger ones are shrouded in red.

In Britain, the coffin is usually brought to the family home before the funeral. Here the face will be displayed for the family to see for the last time. Prayers are offered, and the procession may move to the Gurdwara for further prayer before the journey to the crematorium. In India, the oldest son would light the funeral pyre and, in Britain, he may expect to press the switch at the crematorium instead, which can usually be arranged. Prayers are recited by the granthi of the local Gurdwara, or by any one of the mourners, while the corpse is consumed by the fire.

Traditionally the ashes are scattered at a Sikh holy place, usually in the Punjab where Sikhism was founded. A family member may undertake this task. Otherwise ashes may be scattered in a river or at sea.

The Gurdwara is more than a place of worship, it is the social centre of the Sikh community. The family will usually return there for ritual washing and prayers after the cremation. Some close female relatives will refuse to eat until after the cremation.

The whole family mourns for some days, and relatives and friends will come to share their grief. White is worn as a sign of mourning.

A ceremony, 'Bhog', takes place after the death, either at the Gurdwara or at home. Antim Ardas comprises a complete reading of Guru Granth Sahib. This is called a Sahaj Path and is usually completed in ten days. If the family can read, they must take part in the reading. If they cannot read, they must sit and listen to the recitation of Gurbani (The Lord's word contained in the Guru Granth Sahib). The reading provides spiritual support and consolation to the bereaved. During Ardas, the blessings of God are sought for the departed soul. Generally, family and friends gather for the Bhog ceremony on the completion of reading the holy book. Musicians sing appropriate hymns, for example Saloks of the ninth Nanak and Ramkali Sadd are recited. After the final prayer, the Hukam is taken and Karah Parsad is distributed to the congregation. (The Hukam is a random reading of the Guru Granth Sahib. When a Sikh rises in the morning and opens the Guru Granth Sahib at random, the first verses on the page are read. This is a daily command from the Guru and the reading is interpreted as how the Sikh should live that day. Karah Parsad, made from flour, ghee, sugar and water, is distributed to the congregation as a form of communion.)

It is forbidden to erect a monument in the name of the dead lest it should become an object of worship.

References

Encyclopaedia Britannica CD (2004) *Worldwide Adherents of All Religions by Six Continental Areas, Mid 2002*. Rugeley: Focus Multimedia.

Whitaker's Almanack, 137th edn. (2005) *Religion in the UK*. London: A&C Black (Publishers).

CHAPTER 32

ZOROASTRIANS (PARSEES)

Zoroastrianism is the religion of the followers of the Iranian prophet Zoroaster (Zarathushtra). Zoroastrians believe that the prophet lived about 6000 BCE, although other historians believe it was much later than this, possibly between 1700 and 1400 BCE. Between approximately 549 BCE and 642 CE it was the state religion of three successive Iranian empires, the boundaries of whose territories extended into what is now Afghanistan and Pakistan, Iraq, Israel and Turkey. It was overtaken by the expansion of Islam, and its adherents have been the victims of much persecution over the years (Hinnells 1984).

In the 10th century CE some members of the faith left Iran to seek a new place of religious freedom. They settled in northwest India, where they were known as Parsees (Persians).

The Zoroastrian holy book is the Avesta, which contains the prophet's words in 238 verses of songs (the Gathas) and other scriptures. The faith teaches of a wholly good God, the Wise Lord Ahura Mazda, who is omnipotent and omniscient and responsible for all creation. The Wise Lord is opposed, but never overcome, by the evil Angra Mainyu. As both the spiritual and material worlds are created by God, man has a religious duty to care for both of these aspects of his existence. Believers should respect nature and protect air, earth and water. The Gathas teach that all humans have free will to choose between good and evil. An essential feature of all worship is physical and moral purity and the faith has a highly developed moral code. Followers should seek to do hard work, good deeds and charitable acts. They should think Good (Humata), speak Good (Hukhta) and act Good (Huvreshta). After death, the immortal soul will be judged by God and then will dwell in paradise or hell until the end of time. It will be resurrected in the final judgement.

Zoroastrian worship is distinctively characterised by tendance of the temple fire. Fire symbolises purity, light and truth and is a visible symbol of the presence of Ahura Mazda in every human being. (Ahu meaning to be or to exist, Mazda meaning wisdom.)

Zoroastrianism was the earliest monotheistic religion. It has influenced all the monotheistic major world religions (Judaism, Christianity and Islam) in particular with regard to beliefs of a supreme divine force, heaven and hell, resurrection of the dead and the final judgement.

Children are initiated into the faith some time between the ages of seven and 15 years, and the child will wear the sacred garments – the Sudreh (shirt) and the Kusti (girdle) – for the first time on the Day of Initiation, which is called Navjot. The Kusti is worn over the Sudreh, and both garments are worn for life.

Zoroastrianism stresses that one practises good thoughts, good words and good deeds, along with cleanliness, every minute of the day and night. The Almighty is revered through the medium of fire, which is venerated only with sandalwood and incense. Pollution of air, earth and water is forbidden in this self-declared eco-friendly religion.

The largest Zoroastrian communities are in India, Iran, Pakistan, USA and Britain. There are conflicting estimates of numbers. The Encyclopaedia Britannica 2004 estimates that there are just over two and a half million Zoroastrians worldwide, with most of these living in Asia and few in Europe. According to Whitaker's Almanack 2005, however, there are now fewer than 150,000 Zoroastrians worldwide, and about 7000 in the UK, mainly living in London (Whitaker's Almanack 2005). In the 2001 census in Britain, only 3738 people claimed to belong to the faith. The Zoroastrian Trust Funds of Europe believe there are about 150,000 worldwide and 5000 in the UK.

The Zoroastrian patient in hospital

As with other patients of Asian origin, English may not be the mother tongue. Zoroastrian patients in British hospitals would wish to maintain their customary standard of cleanliness and hygiene, as required by their religion. Running water is preferred for washing, but if the patient cannot reach the tap then fresh water in a clean vessel will be acceptable. There is usually no dietary restriction, but some will not eat pork or beef.

Daily prayers are fundamental to a Zoroastrian's way of life. The sacred girdle, the 'Kusti', is worn by adherents of both sexes, and is untied and tied whilst reciting the Kusti prayers. A sick patient may need help to carry out this important daily ritual.

The dying patient

Zoroastrians would wish their loved ones to be near them at the time of death, and relatives and friends will say prayers where possible. Occasionally, a Zoroastrian Priest may be called to the bedside for prayer, but this is not a usual event. There are no last rites before death.

At death

It is important that the body is bathed before being dressed, and normal Last Offices would be appropriate (see p.182).

The body should be wrapped in white clothing, and families may provide the special 'Sudreh' to be put next to the skin beneath the shroud. They may request that the head is covered with a cap or a white scarf and that the sacred 'Kusti' should be replaced on the body.

It is very important that the funeral of a Zoroastrian body takes place as soon as possible after death. If the death must be reported to the Coroner, the reasons for any delay must be carefully explained to the family. (See p.257 for how to expedite arrangements as for Jewish bodies.)

Post mortem examinations

Post mortems are forbidden in religious law, and much disliked. They would be refused except in cases where the Coroner is involved.

Blood transfusion

Staunch and orthodox Zoroastrians would not take blood transfusion on the grounds that the purity of their blood would then be polluted, which is considered to be against the will of God. They may not wish to donate blood for the same reason.

Organ transplantation and donation of the body

According to strict religious law both would be forbidden, but there may be some individuals who would agree. For the orthodox, organ transplantation would again introduce the concept of bodily or genetic pollution, which is against the will of God. Indeed, intermarriage itself is forbidden, to preserve the genetic purity of the Zoroastrian race. It is believed that one should return to one's keeper with all that one was given at birth.

Abortion and euthanasia

Birth and death are in the hands of God, and, in strict religious terms, no life should be taken. Abortion is not allowed for any reason and euthanasia is forbidden. Views differ, however, and some individuals may make a personal choice in this regard, as well as in the matter of blood transfusion.

Suicide

Suicide is totally unacceptable. In Mumbai (Bombay), where bodies are disposed of in the Towers of Silence (see below), the corpse of a suicide would be deposited in a different tower from that which is usually used.

Funerals

Traditionally, in India, the body is washed and dressed in clean white garments, including the sacred 'Sudreh' and 'Kusti'. There must be no distinction between rich and poor at death, for at this time all are equal. Inexpensive materials are used to clothe the body, and there must be no display of ostentation at the funeral.

After death a dog is brought before the corpse. The gaze of the dog is believed to put the evil spirits to flight.

Until the funeral (in India), the body is laid on the stone floor of the house, and a priest offers continuous prayer. No one is allowed to touch the body except the bearers. A fire is lit, and kept burning for three days after the death. During the funeral service the body is placed on a stretcher, covered with a white cloth and carried by the bearers, who must be Parsee Zoroastrians, on foot to the Tower of Silence.

Zoroastrians believe that earth-burial, cremation and disposal by water contaminate the sacred elements (earth, fire and water). The Tower of Silence is usually on a hill outside the town, circular and built of stone. It has three concentric circles, one each for men, women and children. It has neither roof nor windows and only certain bearers are allowed to enter it. The body is placed on the stone slabs of the Tower floor, and left exposed to the sun and the vultures, who strip the bones clean of flesh within a couple of hours. The bones, dried by the sun, are later swept into the central well (Encyclopaedia Britannica 1989; Polson and Marshall 1975). There is a solemn observance on the morning of the fourth day when, it is believed, the departed soul reaches the next world and undergoes judgement.

Note: In recent years, the vulture population of parts of India has been severely depleted, making disposal of the Zoroastrian dead a real problem and leading to forced changes in funeral practice (see p.25).

There are no Towers of Silence in Britain, and Zoroastrians here recognise that other methods of disposal must be used.

In Britain, family members may sometimes prepare the body for the funeral, but in most cases they instruct a funeral director as to the desired method, including the dressing of the body with the Sudreh and Kusti, and the covering of the head.

Funerals should take place as soon after death as possible, if not the same day then at least on the next. In Britain burial and cremation are both accepted. The rites are the same for adults and for children, but cremation is forbidden for a young child. Burial only is permissible under the age of seven years. If the child is nearly seven years old, he/she may be cremated, along with the Sudreh and Kusti, even though he or she may not have been confirmed into the religion.

In India, when a body part is amputated, prayers would normally be said as in a funeral, and the part deposited in the Tower of Silence. There is no experience of this practice in the UK.

There is at least one Parsee cemetery, at Brookwood near London.

The family may wish for the body to be sent back to the country of origin for disposal (see p.62).

If a Zoroastrian patient has no relatives or friends to attend his last illness, health care staff should contact the address below. The association will gladly arrange for the last rites to be performed in the Zoroastrian manner.

For further information and advice, contact:

The Zoroastrian Trust Funds of Europe (Incorporated)
Zoroastrian Centre
440 Alexandra Avenue
Harrow, Middlesex HA2 9TL
Tel: 020 8866 0765
Fax: 020 8868 4572
Email: secretary@ztfe.com

References

Encyclopaedia Britannica, 15th edn (1989) *Zoroastrianism and Parsiism.* Chicago: EB.

Hinnells, J.R. (ed) (1984) 'Zoroaster/Zoroastrianism.' In *The Penguin Dictionary of Religions.* Harmondsworth: Penguin Books.

Polson, C.J. and Marshall, T.K. (1975) *The Disposal of the Dead,* 3rd edn. London: English Universities Press.

Whitaker's Almanack, 137th edn. (2005) *Religion in the UK.* London: A&C Black (Publishers).

CHAPTER 33

THE CHINESE COMMUNITY

Most Chinese residents came to Britain after 1965, with a peak in 1980 when a number of Vietnamese 'boat people' sought asylum. Chinese people now make up 0.4 per cent of the population of England.

According to the census, there were just over a quarter of a million Chinese people living in England and Wales in 2001, double the figure of the 1991 census. Over half of them (53%) claim to have no particular religious beliefs. About 20 per cent are Christian, some 15 per cent are Buddhists and barely 1 per cent claim to belong to a variety of 'other' religions, including Islam and Shintō. Almost 10 per cent did not answer the (voluntary) census question on religion. In China, some would hold to ancestral worship beliefs or Taoism.

Although there are some localities in Britain which have a 'Chinatown' and a significant Chinese population, most Chinese are widely dispersed round the country and still largely concerned with the restaurant trade.

Irrespective of religion, Chinese traditional culture is strong and there are many facets which can affect health care. Traditional beliefs and practices often show great diversity, but all have great respect for the ancestors. Graves are visited, headstones cleaned and offerings made on two special days each year.

Chinese in Britain come mainly from Hong Kong and the New Territory rural area, although a small proportion (often students) come from mainland China, Taiwan or Singapore and Vietnam. They speak mainly Cantonese, with some other dialects. Younger Chinese, born or educated in Britain, will have no language problems, but older people, because of their restricted social life (often in the catering trade), may have very little English, even after living here for many years.

Christian Chinese will probably have Western or Christian sounding names; those from traditional and Buddhist cultures will usually have Chinese sounding names. Different 'dialect groups' have different customs, and some traditional practices are disappearing.

Whatever their religion, most Chinese will have a belief in re-incarnation. After death, the deceased faces the Ten Courts of Hell (graphically depicted in the Tiger Balm Gardens in Singapore). He appears before the appropriate Court (one for thieves, one for tax-dodgers etc.) and receives the appropriate punishment. Following this, he receives a cup of magic to obliterate all previous experiences, after which he is re-incarnated via one of six pathways, including insects, animals, poor and rich people, depending on the quality of his behaviour in his former life. Because of the belief that behaviour in this life will influence the quality and status of the next, virtue becomes the most important thing for a Chinese person to attain. Likewise, filial piety is essential. These are the personal qualities which they will try and demonstrate at the time of the death of a parent, in order to influence their own afterlife.

The points made below have largely been made by Chinese health care staff in Britain and by European health care staff in Chinese communities in Singapore and Malaysia.

The Chinese patient in hospital

There are many cultural influences which may impinge on a Chinese patient's stay in hospital. They will affect older Chinese people much more than younger, more Westernised, individuals.

The traditional Chinese health belief is that of balance between two vital and opposing life forces, Yin (breath) and Yang (blood). Yin equates to feminine, interior and cold; Yang to masculine, exterior and heat. The Chinese would traditionally take various foods or herbs to balance these forces. They also recognise four vices which are detrimental to health: 'womanising', gambling, drinking and smoking narcotics (Fong 1994).

The number 4 sounds like 'death' in Chinese. It is widely regarded as an unlucky number, and to be in bed 4 or Ward 4 would be seen as an ill omen. Likewise, the 7th lunar month is felt to be unlucky for operations and other procedures because, during this month, the spirits, which are released from graves, are hungry and must be appeased with offerings. (In China, opera performances are given to amuse the spirits at this time.)

The number 8 sounds, in Chinese, like 'good luck', so that 8 and 88 are lucky numbers. Jade is worn as a good luck charm, to keep away the evil eye.

Older Chinese people are reluctant to talk about death and regard doing so as unlucky. They try and protect each other from the knowledge of the diagnosis, particularly the diagnosis of cancer. They hate to use the word 'cancer', which they fear, often regarding it as a single disease. They may also regard swollen feet as a sign of imminent death.

Younger, more Westernised, people will discuss cancer and death and try and discuss it with their elders. Chinese people may also have a fear of surgery, and this often causes a delay in seeking conventional treatment. There is a great stigma attached to mental illness in the family.

There is great faith in traditional Chinese medicines and herbs. Many Chinese patients will have already sought traditional remedies before seeking Western help and will take both kinds of treatments concurrently. Some may have even been back to Hong Kong for this purpose, prior to their admission to a British hospital. Some may go to the Temple for healing. Some will pay for a piece of yellow 'charm paper', which is then burnt, dissolved in water and given to the patient to drink.

English language may be a problem, especially for older patients. A study a few years ago showed that some 70 per cent of first-generation Chinese immigrants did not speak English (Kerrie and Kwong 1992). Some older people may also be illiterate in Chinese. Because of this, older women do not find it easy to access breast or cervical screening or other medical services, and may prefer to see a female doctor in hospital. Within the traditional culture, the male is superior, and this may prevent him going for a medical consultation. He would rather consult a male doctor than a female one. Chinese women may be reluctant to speak up for themselves. Chinese women, especially the older ones, would strongly object to being on a mixed-sex ward. They may need explanation of items of which they have no experience, such as sputum pot or dental pot.

Flowers of all colours are associated with death and are used for funerals, but are not welcomed by the patient in hospital, who may be alarmed that death is near. Men particularly would not want gifts of flowers, or want nurses to place flowers anywhere near their bed, especially white ones.

English food may be unacceptable. A choice of rice would be preferred to potatoes. Older people will be unaccustomed to potatoes, which are also associated with poverty in China: 'comfortable' people eat rice. Orthodox Buddhists may observe a meat-free (or blood-free) day twice a month, on the 1st and 15th day of each lunar month, when only vegetarian or vegan food would be acceptable. Acceptable food would depend on the illness in question, and patients will strive to eat the right foods to keep their 'balance' and to heat up or cool down their bodies as deemed appropriate. Families will often bring herbal drinks and medicines into hospital for their sick member.

The colour white is associated with death, and patients may be unwilling to wear white clothing in hospital. This applies to both sexes.

The dying Chinese patient

Families expect to care for their dying parents and to be present throughout the last illness. They frequently feel guilt as their family member is dying, their concern being their fear of not having done enough to help him or her in life. The family tends to become very demonstrative at this time and will want to be with the patient all day long, and all night too. They will want to prepare food for the patient, not special dishes, just to prove that they are doing everything possible for the good of the patient. They will ask the dying patient for his wishes regarding food and will try and fulfil any requests.

It is important that there are many visitors, but especially that the son, daughter and grandchildren are present. Of particular importance is the presence of the eldest son and the eldest grandson. If there are no boys, a nephew or a close male relative may 'deputise'. This presence at the bedside is a well-understood obligation of kinship. If the patient dies in hospital, the nearest relative, not necessarily male, will arrange the funeral.

Unless they are Christian, they are unlikely to request a priest to be present. His presence would be associated with death.

Black and white clothing is likewise associated with death. No red clothing, or anything red, should be near the patient, as this will prevent the soul from being released. The soul would 'bear a grudge' if red was worn and would vow to stay near the body.

Chinese people are very frightened of cancer, and discussion of this is taboo within the community. A woman with breast cancer may not even let her husband know of her plight. Some even believe that cancer is contagious and may not wish to visit the patient because of this. The word 'cancer' tends to avoided and referred to as 'that thing'.

Chinese people usually have great respect for health care professionals and will want to cooperate with doctors and nurses.

At death

There is nothing special to be done at the time of death. The family is unlikely to want to touch the body and generally leave the preparation to the funeral director. In Singapore, some families will place a small omelette over the mouth after death, to absorb the evil spirits coming out of the body. In Malaysia, the family may burn red candles and incense outside the hospital mortuary, to be as near to the body as possible and protect the spirit.

After death, a monk will usually say prayers and comfort the mourners. Last Offices are 'routine' (see p.182).

Blood transfusion

There will probably be no objection to the receiving of blood, as this is associated with 'serious illness' which requires Western medicine, but Chinese people may be unwilling donors.

Post mortem examinations

Post mortems are disliked. It is regarded as necessary to have a whole body for the afterlife.

Organ transplantation

The language barrier may be a cause of lack of understanding about transplantation issues, but many Chinese believe that an intact body is needed for the next world. There is unlikely to be objection to receipt of an organ, but Chinese people, especially the elderly, may be unwilling donors. They may believe that 'the other person is living inside you'. However, the reception of corneas is probably already quite common.

Abortion

Abortion is usually regarded as necessary and acceptable.

Suicide

Suicide is seen as tragic but not sinful. If death was by suicide, there may be extra ceremonial chanting, both at the wake after the funeral and at the site of the suicide.

Euthanasia

Chinese people may have quite a liberal view about end-of-life decisions. They do not wish anyone to suffer unnecessarily and are likely to accept death more readily than many.

Funerals

In China, burial would take place within a short time of death. Burial is preferred to cremation. Sometimes cremation is used for older people, and the ashes taken back to the land of origin.

The body will be embalmed and dressed in best clothes for the funeral. Each 'dialect' of the Toaist belief differs in the funeral costume for the deceased. Traditional costume, often worn by older people, may consist of several layers of shirts and trousers of various designs. Sometimes a special garment is used, particularly for older people, consisting of trousers and a long gown, usually in blue or black, and often made of silk. Sometimes women prepare their own funeral clothes.

Sometimes, families will not want their parents to wear make-up or powder after death. The face will be exposed to the family after death.

The family will do a lot of the preparation but a funeral director is always involved. A rice grain will be placed between the lips or, in a wealthier family, a pearl. This will light the path to the next world. A red parcel will be tied to the clothes. In Taoist belief, the soul does not depart from the body completely and therefore the dead body can still hear. Accordingly, conversation must be cautious, so as not to offend the dead.

The Taoists believe that the deceased only realises the reality of death on the 7th day, when he washes his hands and finds that his fingers have decomposed. Because of this belief, much ritual is included in the funeral rites. For example, the daughter must call her father every morning to wake up and wash his face, and a basin, mug, toothbrush and flannel are left near the coffin for this purpose. Food offerings are also left by the coffin, for three meals a day.

The lifestyle of the dead is believed to be quite similar to that on earth. Offerings of many kinds, made of paper, are burned for the use of the deceased in the next world. These may include paper gold bars, paper currency, a paper mansion, paper credit cards, cars, ships, television sets, even paper maids.

Buddhists and Christians may not burn offerings to the dead, but some traditional customs do transcend religious barriers.

To ward off evil spirits after a death, the family will cover lanterns and incense burners in red outside the house door, and in lift entrances and main entrances, if an apartment block. At funerals, visitors are given a red thread to wear as a protection, or a coin wrapped in red paper.

A wake follows the funeral and will last an odd number of days (1, 3, 5 or 7). The length of time depends on the age of the deceased, the wealth of the family and the distance the relatives have to travel. It is important that relatives return from far places for the funeral. In Singapore, if the bereaved family lives in an apartment block, a tent will be erected in the space below it, to hold the wake. Anyone can go and pay their respects and, as gambling, cards and games such as 'Mah Jong' fill a great deal of the time, it can become a less than solemn social occasion.

If the deceased has surviving parents, normally the death costume is not worn and a 'mourning tag' is attached to the body. If the deceased is a child under 18 years, the parents should not attend the funeral. If 'black hair dies before white hair', this is wrong within nature. The corpse must mourn for its parents, as it is not right that the child should die before they do. Older people would prefer not to attend the funeral of a child.

If a wife should die before her husband, a single flower, often a white lily, will be laid at the side of the coffin, so that people may be aware of the relationship.

Black and white clothing is associated with death and is worn to funerals. In Buddhist tradition, the close family will wear white, friends will wear black. Black is usually worn at a Christian funeral. Traditionally, the family was not allowed to laugh or wear bright clothes, jewellery or make-up, but these restrictions are disappearing.

Old people often arrange their own coffin money. There are funeral clubs in the UK, which may be a help to some. Culturally, it is very important that the deceased is buried properly. Cremation is seldom wanted by older people. They may not be aware that there is a choice.

If cremated, the monk will arrange a place in the Temple for the ashes and a memorial plaque for the deceased. This ensures that the soul has a place to go and be settled.

In a traditional Chinese funeral, there would be several monks, with chanting, musical instruments and dancing round the coffin. This all helps the soul on its way to the next world. The coffin would be open, and the immediate family kneel near it, crying to demonstrate their sorrow. There would be lots of flowers at such a funeral. There would be open house during this time. Afterwards, the family will partake of a funeral meal.

Mourning would traditionally last at least 49 days (7 × 7). Every 7 days, the monk will say prayers and everyone will attend. In the UK, mourning probably lasts only for the first seven days in this manner, but may continue privately for much longer, with close family staying largely within the home.

There is a colour code for mourning wear, so that people are aware of which relative has died. For example, close female relatives may wear a woollen decoration in their hair, the colour, often white or blue, depending on their relationship to the deceased. This will be worn for some time after the death.

At the end of the mourning period, perhaps a year after the death, there will be a family ceremony. Black mourning ribbons or badges and the hair ornaments will be ceremonially burnt.

In Hong Kong, families tend to care for their elderly members. Marriages may be arranged, and the son and daughter-in-law traditionally are obliged to care for the son's parents. If there are no sons in the daughter-in-law's family, then they will look after her parents also.

References

Fong, C.L. (1994) 'Chinese health behaviour: breaking barriers to better understanding.' *Health Trends* 26, 1, 14–15.

Kerrie, P.K. and Kwong, L. (1992) *Working with Chinese Carers. A Handbook for Professionals.* London: Health Education Authority in conjunction with the King's Fund.

CHAPTER 34

THE JAPANESE COMMUNITY

In Japan, the indigenous religion, Shintō, exists alongside various sects of Buddhism and also Christianity. There are also some ancient shamanistic practices and a number of 'new religions', which have emerged during the last century or so. Shintō is a polytheistic religion in which objects and people, often historical religious figures, may be enshrined as gods. Shintō has no known founder, no official sacred scriptures or fixed dogmas, but it has preserved its guiding beliefs throughout the ages.

'Kami' means mystical, or divine, referring to the sacred or divine power of the various gods. The word 'Shintō' means 'the way of kami' and came into use in order to distinguish indigenous Japanese beliefs from those of Buddhism, which had been introduced into Japan in the 6th century CE and became the national religion in the 8th century CE. Christianity arrived much later, being introduced into Japan, by Jesuit and Franciscan missionaries, in the mid-16th century.

No religion has dominance, and each influences the others. It is perfectly possible to belong to a Buddhist sect and yet still believe in Shintō gods. Japanese children usually do not receive formal religious education, but many homes will have a Buddhist altar, the centrepoint of various rituals to commemorate dead family members. The temple remains important in Japanese culture. Funeral rites and other religious ceremonies are conducted in these beautiful buildings. Buddhist ceremonies are favoured for unhappy occasions, such as funerals, while Shintō ones are preferred for happy events.

There are many ways of telling fortunes in Japan. A popular one is a six-day divination marked on the calendar. Each day is noted with one of six prophesies, adopted from China, with various degrees of luck or misfortune allotted to each. For example, people would not wish to conduct a funeral on a 'Tomobiki' day, which prophesises 'lucky in the morning and evening, but unlucky at noon'.

Traditionally, the Japanese have viewed the individual in the context of the society and community. A newborn baby had to undergo various family and community rituals and was not considered a 'person' until after these had been carried out, and was not given a name until that time. Similarly, the death of a person was not recognised until communal rituals were complete. Thus, the notion of a person had a communal, rather than an individual, basis. This is a cultural, rather than religious, tradition and many of these rites are still practised in modern Japan (Nudeshima 1991).

The Japanese patient in hospital

There are no prohibitions on food or drink. The patient will probably prefer simple, healthy food, not fatty and not milky. Fresh fruit and vegetables, cooked or raw, are appreciated, as these are expensive commodities in Japan. Lemon tea (made with green tea) is a popular drink and brown sugar is considered to be better than white. Elderly people prefer rice to bread, and like a mixture of white and brown rice.

Patients, particularly older people, will prefer to be called by their 'family' name. Japanese women are often very shy and modest, and older ones would probably prefer to see a female doctor.

They are likely to believe that heart disease, infections and acute illnesses require Western medicine, but that many other complaints need traditional Japanese medicines.

The dying Japanese patient

The hospice movement is growing in Japan and many dying patients would prefer care in a hospice-type of environment. Despite the wish to die at home, which has a traditional significance, most Japanese do die in hospital. The family will be criticised if they are not present at the death of their member. In Japan, dying patients are frequently transferred to their homes, so that death may take place there.

There are no special rituals or prayers for the dying patient. Water may be offered (known as 'last water'), as may boiled rice at the time of dying. This may even be offered after the dying (or newly dead) person has been transferred home.

At death

Japanese patients would prefer to die at home. If death occurs in hospital, the body will be brought home as soon as practicable after the death. Sometimes the family will prepare the body, or the funeral agency will be called to the house, where the body will lie for two or three days in the best room. The body is seldom embalmed, but kept cool with dry ice in the house. The shroud is usually white, and is sometimes covered with a white kimono. The 'death clothes' also include a handkerchief to cover the face, white socks on the feet and white gloves on the top of the hands. The wooden coffin will have a window to reveal the face. Books, flowers, dolls and other special favourite things may be placed inside the coffin.

For Japanese people dying in hospital in Britain, 'routine' Last Offices would be appropriate (see p.182).

Post mortem and body donation

Body or organ donation was long thought to be wrong, even dishonourable, when disposal of the dead was not just a family duty, but a community responsibility. Traditionally, relatives and neighbours had a social and religious duty to care for the body.

This tradition is weakening; public attitudes are changing and there is a steady increase in people willing to donate (Nudeshima 1991).

There is unlikely to be much objection to post mortem, except where there is belief in the need for an intact body for the next world.

Blood transfusion

There is unlikely to be any objection to donation or reception of blood.

Organ transplantation

By 1992, Japan was the only highly industrialised and medically developed nation which did not use organ donations from brain-dead donors. Live donors were frequently used for renal transplants and a few live donors were used for liver transplants (Takao 1992).

Until 1997, there was considerable resistance to organ transplantation in Japan, despite the fact that neither Buddhism nor Shintō object to the concept of brain death. Two traditional beliefs go against the practice: there is a link between body and soul and therefore, in donating an organ, the soul will be lost; and a body should be undefiled for its journey to the next world. The Buddhist belief, however, is that the spirit alone is re-incarnated.

Although one of the most technically advanced parts of the world, transplantation was only slowly accepted and many Japanese were flown overseas for such surgery. In 1997, the lower house of the Japanese parliament voted to officially recognise the concept of brain death, paving the way for official recognition of transplantation and the Organ Transplant Law of that year (Wise 1997).

Suicide

In Japan, there is a deeply ingrained culture which regards suicide as an honourable act. It is seen as an acceptable way to sincerely atone for failure and to express remorse, responsibility and shortcomings. One suicide manual has apparently been on Japan's bestseller list for a number of years (Giarelli 1999).

However, the suicide rate has been increasing alarmingly in recent years and is now the sixth largest cause of death (Motohashi, Kaneko and Sasaki 2005). There are now over 30,000 suicides a year (23.8 per 100,000), which is the highest rate of suicide in the developed world, according to the World Health Organization. Higher in some rural areas, it has reached 40 per cent of deaths. Better acceptability for, and access to treatment for, depression have helped to reduce this figure.

Suicide in Japan is most prevalent in those in their fifties, and men are more than twice as likely to kill themselves as women (BBC News 1999). The rise in suicides has been said to be linked to overwork and redundancies, particularly at the time of recession in 1998.

Recent concerns include the development of group suicides, often in teenagers and young people, who link up to 'matchmaker' websites or 'suicide clubs' on the internet (Cameron 2005). These websites are not illegal, although they are causing alarm, and there is, as yet, no restriction in their content.

Assisting a suicide is an illegal act.

Euthanasia

As in other parts of the world, euthanasia and decisions around the end of life have received much debate in Japan in recent years, with large sections of the public apparently approving of the choice to 'die with dignity' rather than to merely prolong life with no thought to its quality.

The Japan Society for Dying with Dignity (formerly called the Japanese Euthanasia Society) was established in 1976 and initiated a law allowing for the withdrawal of life-sustaining treatment. Living wills were already being respected, although not legally binding at this time (LifeSiteNews.com 2002). Membership rose after 1990, when the Japanese Medical Association re-affirmed the right of terminally ill patients to refuse life-prolonging treatments. By 2002, the Society claimed 100,000 members in support of a 'dignified death' for the terminally ill, most being women over the age of 65.

In 1995, a legal distinction was made between euthanasia and murder, by redefining the legal requisites for euthanasia and reducing them from six in 1962 to four in 1995. The conditions laid down were difficult to comply with. In particular, improved terminal care meant that the patient's pain and suffering were seldom 'unbearable'.

The government will allow cessation of life support as long as it fulfils certain conditions, and a manual of terminal care to guide end-of-life decisions was issued in 1989 (Ministry of Health and Welfare and the Japan Medical Association 1989). Living wills were also given approval.

There is no movement for legislation at present and no organisations claim to condone the practice of active euthanasia or physician assisted suicide. Active euthanasia is not permitted in practice and the cessation of life support still remains a controversial issue in Japan (Akabayashi 2002). No cases of active euthanasia had been performed by 2002, strongly indicating that euthanasia is not 'publicly permitted' in Japan.

Article 13 of the Japanese Constitution guarantees respect for each person as an individual, and therefore the right of the individual to self-determination. However, whether this right extends to issues such as euthanasia or the refusal of medical care remains controversial. Participation in another's suicide remains illegal.

Abortion

Although all religions encourage the sanctity of life, abortion is actually widely used as a method of choice for contraception and family planning in Japan (Qureshi 1994).

Funerals

Japanese people may not seem to be much concerned with religion in their daily lives, but many are sticklers for tradition at times of funerals. There are strict rules of protocol, which cover clothing and adornment of mourners, behaviour and gifts. To attend a funeral, men must wear dark suits and black ties, women must wear black clothes and even the handbag is expected to be black. The only acceptable jewellery is pearls. Neither red nor bright blue is used in funerals, neither for the mourners nor for the body. It is particularly important to be present at the death of a parent; failure to do so will mean a 'loss of face' within the community.

The funeral will take place as soon after death as practicable, often within 24 hours. Prior to a funeral, mourners will spend the evening together, keeping watch over their dead. Originally a practice just for the family, this custom has now evolved into a religious ceremony and callers come to express their sympathy. The funeral altar is set up and, if the family is Buddhist, a priest will chant sutras. This service of 'tsuya' is held in the early evening and is less formal than the funeral itself.

A Buddhist priest will attend the house between the death and the funeral. He will give a posthumous Buddhist name to the soul of the newly departed person. This name will be written on a wooden memorial tablet and sometimes engraved on the gravestone. Different sects have their own way of naming. A rich family may have several priests.

Mourners at the funeral follow a traditional ritual. On arrival they will bow once, then hand over their condolence money (the 'kōden') and sign the condolence book. Then, kneeling, they bow to the bereaved family and offer incense three times, in a prescribed manner, finally holding their hands together in prayer before bowing to the family once more and departing.

The 'kōden' is an obituary gift, presented by relatives and friends at the funeral to the family of the deceased. In ancient times, food was often given, but today it will be a monetary gift. The 'kōden' is placed in an envelope and tied with black and white strings, used exclusively for mournful occasions. It is considered a very important social courtesy to make this monetary offering. The names of donors – and their donations – are noted so that the courtesy may be returned in the future.

Most funerals last two days: the 'tsuya' or wake of the night before and the 'kokubetsushiki' or 'leave-taking' of the funeral day itself. Mourners will choose which of these to attend. Guests attending the 'kokubetsushiki' will first offer incense and then wait outside for the coffin. The mourning period lasts two or three days after the funeral. The family will come together on the first anniversary of the death, and visit the (Buddhist) temple. Further remembrance will take place at years

3, 7, 13, 17, 23, 27 and 33, that is all the years with '3' and '7'. If the death has occurred overseas, the body will almost always be transported back to the home for the
funeral.

Because of the shortage of land, Japanese law no longer permits burial and all
bodies are cremated in Japan. Burial may be chosen outside Japan.

After the funeral, the family will partake of a meal, the 'otoki', at a special funeral
restaurant. The 'otoki' will include meat, as the family has eaten no meat or fish during the funeral process. Everyone who attended the funeral is given a small packet of
salt. This must be sprinkled over them before they enter their house, as a sacred purification rite. It is believed to remove any traces of other-worldly influences, which
may linger about the person after attendance at a funeral.

'Hoji' is the Buddhist memorial service, held on the anniversary of the person's
death. They are usually held on the 1st, 2nd, 7th, 13th and 17th anniversaries of the
death and usually in the home. The family will attend the service and pray for the re-
pose of the dead, while the priest reads a sutra. The term also refers to services held
on the 35th or 49th day after the death. Customarily, the family will dine together
after the service, cherishing the memory of the deceased. It is usual for meals to be
strictly vegetarian during the funeral and mourning period.

The Bon Festival (originally 15 July by the lunar calendar, now 13–16 August) is
when ancestral spirits and departed souls were believed to return to their families,
and this period is a festival to welcome them home. Offerings are made and memorial services held. The family grave will be visited, prayers offered, flowers laid and
candles and incense burnt. Communal bonfires may be lit both to welcome the spirits home and to speed them back from whence they came. In seaside places, wooden
or straw lanterns may be offered afloat on the water. Music and folk dancing,
sometimes in the temple grounds, are included in the festival.

'Higan', the equinoctial weeks, twice a year, are the times when Buddhists believe they can meet their ancestors. At these times, people pay a respectful visit to
their family graves, which are tidied up, and food, flowers and incense are offered
at the graveside. This ceremony, said to have been started by Prince Shotoku
(574–622), seems to be practised by all Japanese, regardless of religion.

With the modernisation of Japan, the traditional practices may be dying out in
some areas. In 1991 it was estimated that merely 30 per cent of Japanese followed
ritual funeral practices. Funerals may not be the long and complex events they once
were, but may be brief events managed by funeral agencies. Family graves, which
were once used by several generations, are now used by the nuclear family. The view
of the individual as a communal responsibility, from birth to death, is no longer
widely held (Nudeshima 1991).

References

Akabayashi, A. (August 2002) 'Euthanasia, assisted suicide, and cessation of life support: Japan's policy, law, and an analysis of whistle blowing in two recent mercy killing cases.' *Social Science and Medicine 55*, 4, 517–527.

BBC News (1999) on www.news.bbc.co.uk/1/hi/world/asia-pacific/383823.stm (accessed September 2005).

Cameron, D. (2005) 'Five dead in Japanese net suicide pact.' *The Age.* Melbourne: The Age.

Giarelli, A. (1999) 'The suicide trend.' *World Press Review 46*, 10 (accessed via www.worldpress .org/Asia/1543.cfm, September 2005).

Japan Travel Bureau (1994) *Japanese Family and Culture.* Japan: Japan Travel Bureau.

LifeSiteNews.com on www.lifesite.net/ldn/2002/dec/02121708.html, Tuesday 17 December 2002 (accessed September 2005).

Ministry of Health and Welfare and the Japan Medical Association (1989) *Manual of Terminal Care.* Tokyo: Chuo-Hoki [in Japanese].

Motohashi, Y., Kaneko, Y. and Sasaki, H. (2005) 'Lowering suicide rates in rural Japan.' *Akita Journal of Public Health 2*, 105–106.

Nudeshima, J. (1991) 'Obstacles to brain death and organ transplantation in Japan.' *The Lancet 338*, 1063.

Qureshi, B. (1994) *Transcultural Medicine: Dealing with Patients from Different Cultures.* Lancaster: Kluwer Academic Publishers.

Takao, M. (1992) 'Brain-death and transplantation in Japan.' *The Lancet 340*, 1164.

Wise, J. (1997) 'Japan to allow organ transplants.' *British Medical Journal 314*, 1298.

CHAPTER 35

HIV/AIDS

The changing picture

HIV/AIDS still requires a short chapter of its own, not to elaborate on the varied multi-system clinical aspects of this unkind disease, nor to give advice on treatment, but because dealing with dying and death in AIDS patients may still present some health care staff with situations with which they are not comfortable, and through which their misconceptions, inexperience and prejudices become all too evident to the patients, their partners and their families.

At the time of the first edition of this book (1992), AIDS was, almost by definition, fatal (MMWR 1987). Happily, in the intervening period, significant treatment regimes have become available, although there is as yet no immunisation for prophylaxis, nor yet a cure. People with known HIV infection now may live long and otherwise healthy lives. With appropriate treatment and health education, they need pose few dangers for partners, carers and families.

Under consideration in this chapter are those who have been newly diagnosed as having some AIDS-related symptom or sign, such as the skin manifestations of Kaposi's sarcoma or an acute episode of *Pneumocystis carinii* pneumonia (PCP). A definite diagnosis of AIDS has been made, and from that point the patient may feel under sentence of, at least, life restriction or, at worst, even premature death.

Surveillance of 1995 known AIDS sufferers by the Communicable Disease Surveillance Centre (CDSC), early in the epidemic, showed that cases diagnosed before 1987 lived, on average, for a mere nine or ten months between diagnosis and death, but those diagnosed in 1987 had an average survival around 18 months, with further improvement apparent for those diagnosed in 1988 (Day Report 1990). By 1990, many adult AIDS patients lived for as much as 18 months after diagnosis, and some were known to live as long as three years.

Today people diagnosed with HIV/AIDS, in countries where treatment is available and affordable, can expect many years of apparent normality of life. (There may be some 40 million people worldwide who are living with HIV/AIDS, only 12 per cent of whom had access to treatment in 2005.) HIV positive people can expect to live longer, but are also more likely to have a long period of increasing dependency, with many acute episodes of illness along the way.

At the outbreak of the epidemic in the UK, sufferers were mainly young and most were gay (about 85 per cent of all reported AIDS cases in England and Wales up to the end of September 1989 were homosexual or bisexual, as were 55 per cent of all known HIV infected persons). Some had a history of drug abuse (about 3 per cent of reported AIDS cases and about 9 per cent of reported HIV positive persons). Some (at that time about 7 per cent of AIDS cases and 12 per cent of HIV infected persons) had been the recipients of blood products used for transfusion or for the treatment of haemophilia. Recent estimates from the Health Protection Agency (HPA 2005) show that, by 2003, some 50,000 people were living with the virus in the UK, although up to a third of this number may yet be unaware of their diagnosis. In 2003, 3572 new diagnoses were made and 500 people died, bringing the total number of deaths from AIDS in the UK to 12,760 since reporting began in 1982.

The routes of infection remain the same, but the proportions differ markedly. In 2002, 58 per cent of new infections were acquired heterosexually, many of these being acquired abroad. Only 30 per cent were acquired by men having sex with men, and only 2 per cent from injecting drug use. A small number, about 2 per cent, have been acquired by babies during delivery or breastfeeding from an HIV positive mother, and a few, less than 1 per cent, from blood or tissue transfer. There are still a proportion of infections where the route of infection is unknown, about 8 per cent in the UK.

With treatment, the number of deaths is decreasing, and the number of new cases continues to increase. It is estimated that the number of people living with known HIV has increased by about 47 per cent between the years 2000 and 2005.

The following paragraphs contain points made by people who themselves were HIV positive. Although originally made quite early on in the epidemic, these issues are still felt to be relevant today.

Although there has been much publicity about HIV and AIDS in the years since the outbreak began and, it is hoped, a softening of public attitude toward sufferers, many people so diagnosed will still be overwhelmed by the prospects of being known to carry the virus. They may wish to keep their diagnosis a close secret, not to be shared with workmates, neighbours or even families.

For most of us, in many situations, a trouble shared is a trouble halved. For AIDS patients, the blessed relief of sharing the bad news is probably still not realistic for the minority. Indeed, the cloak of secrecy surrounding the progressive illness may mean a gradual loss of contact with family and friends, repeated deception and increasing isolation.

Despite increasing social and sexual liberalisation, health care staff, and others, may have a deep-seated personal antipathy to other ways of life. They may have an unconscious distaste of drug abuse, homosexuality or promiscuity, which makes it difficult to take a non-judgemental stance. It is essential to accept that there are many ways to live a life, and that misfortune is equally worthy of care and compassion however acquired. Staff who cannot come to terms with their own prejudices should avoid situations where their attitudes may cause offence.

Counselling

Counselling for newly diagnosed AIDS patients must be optimistic and counsellors must try and be positive in their attitudes. Advice at this point must be geared to build up the confidence of the individual to live positively and enjoy the time that is left, to do the things they always wanted to do while they are well enough to enjoy them. The old advice to go away, write a will and prepare for death was exceedingly discouraging, frequently excessively pessimistic and, these days, probably applies to very few newly diagnosed people.

Treatment

Details of current clinical treatment are not given in this book. Readers must refer to current clinical texts.

AIDS sufferers know that, at present, there is no permanent cure for their disease, which may be variable and unpredictable. Although appropriate treatments may have significant long-lasting benefit, untreated patients will surely die of their condition. Doctors who are seen as 'very professional' are perceived as being totally committed to the fact that AIDS is a serious condition which needs treating in a 'sledgehammer' way. They are felt to have knowledge only of the 'medical model' of therapy, to be unwilling to discuss or provide information about alternative or complementary therapies, and to be reluctant to provide detailed information about the potentially frequent and unpleasant side effects of current therapy. In short, the patient may not be allowed truly informed choice for his own treatment plan within the conventional health care setting. These days, there is much more information available and people should have a much greater choice of treatment regime, but the medical profession and the alternative therapist are often still suspicious of one another and seldom get together to discuss a more 'rounded' approach for a particular patient.

Several self-help organisations give up-to-date information on new alternative and complementary therapies, which many HIV-positive people believe are helpful, and which may cause less unpleasantness for the patient. Many patients try a combination of orthodox and complementary medicines but, in the past, often felt they could not discuss the latter with their doctors because of their dismissive or sceptical response. These days, one hopes that doctors are better informed and more likely to listen.

The dedicated AIDS unit

From an infection-control point of view, most AIDS patients do not need to be treated in a special ward or unit. Even if they are bleeding or suffering from diarrhoea, vomiting or incontinence, they are no more risk to others in the ward than is any other patient, as long as standard infection control procedures are adhered to (see p.200).

The advantage of a special AIDS ward is, for the individual, the relief of secrecy, the freedom of unrestricted visiting and the permissible demonstration of affection, and the empathy and understanding of the dedicated staff. There are fewer of these dedicated units now in the UK than when the first edition of this book was published, as most treatment is now offered on an outpatient basis.

The dying patient

Some AIDS victims will become acutely ill away from their usual place of residence, or return to the home of family or friends when in need. Like other patients, most would wish to be in comfortable homely surroundings rather than in hospital. Appropriate domiciliary services should enable most to live and die with dignity at home. General practitioners must be willing to accept them as 'temporary residents', if necessary, and act as gatekeepers for necessary domiciliary services, a position which some doctors in the past have seemed reluctant to accept. The current NHS reforms may further discourage general practitioners from taking on these time-consuming and potentially costly patients.

Care of the dying AIDS patient is similar to care for any other dying patient, with attention as necessary to hygiene, comfort and pain relief, the control of infection and the prevention of pressure sores, and in general a holistic approach to physical and spiritual wellbeing. Careful washing of hands, the wearing of disposable gloves for handling body fluids, and the scrupulous disposal of soiled dressings and sharps are necessary for the safety of the carers and others.

Especially among drug abusers and homosexuals, there may be a carer who is not legally the next-of-kin, but whose relationship to the patient is as close as that of any husband or wife, and who will feel the devastating loss at bereavement just as keenly. This relationship must be respected, and support offered to the bereaved partner in exactly the same way as it would be offered to a widow or widower.

In many cases the surviving partner will be only too aware that he or she too is HIV positive and must, in time, follow a similar path, but without the love, care and compassion which they have been able to give to their lover. Sometimes the family of the deceased are unaware of the existence of the partner, or reluctant to acknowledge the intensity of their relationship. They may be left to grieve and suffer alone, often deprived even of the rights to property and inheritance that a marriage certificate would have ensured.

The Civil Partnership Act (2004)

The Civil Partnership Act became law in November 2004, consequent on the Human Rights Act 1998, and will come into force in the UK in December 2005. This Act will give lesbian and gay couples the right to register their commitment to each other, by formalising their permanent relationship by registration. This is not the same as marriage, although it will confer many of the same rights. It is available only to same-sex couples and the intention is for them to receive greater social acceptance and recognition. The partnership *must* be registered to have validity.

The Civil Partnership Act introduces the following rights, and responsibilities, for couples registered as partners under the Act:

1.   There will be a duty to provide reasonable maintenance for the civil partner and any children of the family, if the partnership is formally dissolved.

2.   Civil partners will be assessed in the same way as spouses for child support.

3.   Civil partners will receive equitable treatment for the purposes of life assurance.

4.   They will receive employment and pension benefits, as do married couples.

5.   They will get recognition under intestacy rules.

6.   They will have access to fatal accidents compensation.

7.   They will receive protection from domestic violence.

8.   They will receive recognition for immigration and nationality.

Civil partnerships must be registered and the register will be searchable by the public. This does not authorise an institution to discuss an individual's sexual orientation without their consent.

Further information on this Act can be obtained on many websites. Search for the Act by name.

M. died in 1989. C. is alive and very well, having lived with HIV and AIDS for over 16 years. Apart from the statistics given at the beginning, the points raised in this chapter are theirs and this chapter is dedicated to them.

References

Day Report (1990) Working Group Report to the Director of Public Health Laboratory Service. 'Acquired Immune Deficiency Syndrome in England and Wales to end 1993, projections using data to end September 1989.' *Communicable Disease Report Suppl.* London: Communicable Disease Surveillance Centre (CDSC).

HPA (2005) Figures from the Health Protection Agency: www.hpa.org.uk/infections/topics_az/hiv_and_sti/epidemiology/epidemiology.htm.

MMWR (1987) For a detailed description of the case definition, see the 1987 Revision of Case Definition for AIDS for Surveillance Purposes. *Morbidity and Mortality Weekly Report (MMWR) 36,* 1–5. Atlanta: Center for Disease Control.

ORGANISATIONS WHICH MAY BE ABLE TO OFFER HELP WITH VARIOUS ASPECTS OF DYING AND DEATH

The following information has been provided by the organisations themselves, and is reprinted here with their permission. The information is accurate as of April 2006. The entries are in alphabetical order.

As contact details tend to change over time, it is suggested that you visit the websites first for up-to-date contact details.

AB Welfare and Wildlife Trust (also known as the Alice Barker Trust)

Supports those who need to pursue their own plans, when faced with 'emotional emergencies' because someone is dying or has died. Contact this charity if you suspect that advice from any other sources may be incorrect or misleading, e.g. about burials or cremations. It challenges public officials even at the highest levels and has never been proven wrong – see Research and Quality of Advice Service via www.abtrust.info. It persuaded the library in the Houses of Parliament to destroy flawed information received from local authority solicitors and environmental health officers. Its work has been praised in Parliament, and MPs from the main parties have called for a new law, so the charity can get on with providing a new type of national public service. If that happens, it will range from protected burials in bona fide nature reserves, through to powers to end unacceptable practices in other organisations. It is currently limited to providing burials in the Harrogate area.

AB Welfare and Wildlife Trust
7 Knox Road, Harrogate HG1 3EF
Tel: 01423 530 900
Email: ab-welfare-wildlife-trust@burials.freeserve.co.uk (email not suitable for urgent help)
Website: www.abtrust.info

Age Concern Cymru works to improve the lives of older people in Wales, through consultation, research, campaigning and influencing policy. They can provide information to members of the public and there is a specialist library on issues affecting older people. Local Age Concern organisations provide a range of services, including advice, advocacy and assistance to claim welfare benefits.

Age Concern Cymru
Ty John Pathy, 13–14 Neptune Court, Vanguard Way, Cardiff CF24 5PJ
Tel: 029 2043 1555   Fax: 029 2047 1418
Email: enquiries@accymru.org.uk   Website: www.accymru.org.uk

Age Concern England

Age Concern is the UK's largest organisation working for and with older people. It is a federation of over 400 charities working together to promote the wellbeing of all older people.

Age Concern England campaigns at national level on issues that matter to older people. It publishes a wide range of books for older people, their carers and professionals. A range of factsheets dealing with issues around income, housing, long-term care, health and consumer issues are available through the helpline, which operates seven days a week. The website contains over 1000 pages that contain information about publications, services and products.

Local Age Concerns provide a range of services. Services provided depend on local need and can include day care, lunch clubs, handyperson schemes, crafts and leisure activities, keep fit activities, computer courses and information and advice. Contact your local Age Concern to find out how they can help older people in your community.

Age Concern England
1268 London Road, London SW16 4ER
Helpline: 0800 009966
Switchboard: 020 8765 7200   Fax: 020 8765 7211
Email: ace@ace.org.uk   Website: www.ageconcern.co.uk

Age Concern NI is a voluntary organisation, committed, through campaigning, community development and service provision, to improving the quality of life of all older people and promoting their rights as active, involved and equal citizens.

Age Concern NI provides the following services to older people:

- Residential, day and domiciliary care.
- An Advice Line for older people, their families and carers is available Monday to Friday from 9.30am to 1.00pm on 028 9032 5055.
- A network of 30 local Age Concern groups throughout Northern Ireland. These groups are run by volunteers and offer activities such as luncheon clubs, social outings and computer classes.
- A health promotion programme called 'Actively Ageing Well'. This programme involves older people over 50 in health enhancing activities.

Age Concern NI
3 Lower Crescent, Belfast BT7 INR
Tel: 028 9024 5729   Advice Line: 028 9032 5055
Fax: 028 9023 5479   Email: info@ageconcernni.org

Age Concern Scotland

An independent charity working to help make the lives of older people in Scotland more secure, comfortable, dignified and enjoyable. We support a wide network of older people and older people's groups. We provide information and publications to meet the needs of older people.

Age Concern Scotland
Causewayside House, 160 Causewayside, Edinburgh EH9 1PR
Tel: 0845 833 0200   Fax: 0845 833 0759
Email: enquiries@acscot.org.uk   Website: www.ageconcernscotland.org.uk

Association of Burial Authorities (ABA)

The association was formed in 1993 to fulfil the need for a consumer orientated organisation to coordinate the activities of burial grounds and provide a tangible link between them and the public. It is a not-for-profit company.

The ABA is entirely independent from any other trade or professional association and acts essentially as a national group coordinating plans and actions to achieve the following aims:

- to raise awareness and appreciation of our cemeteries and churchyards as places of commemoration, heritage and amenity value
- to promote the importance of burial grounds as places of remembrance for our communities and the long term care of the bereaved
- to protect and promote the interests of organisations engaged in the management and operation of burial grounds
- to monitor and improve legislation and regulations affecting burial grounds on National and European Union levels.

The Association of Burial Authorities
Waterloo House, 155 Upper Street, London N1 1RA
Tel: 020 7288 2522   Fax: 020 7288 2533
Email: aba@swa-pr.co.uk

ACT – The Association for Children with Life-threatening and Terminal Conditions and their Families

ACT's vision is to achieve the best possible quality of life and care for children and young people with life-threatening or life-limiting conditions and their families.

ACT seeks to influence, coordinate and promote excellence in the provision of care and support for these children and families. To achieve this, ACT will:

- transform and inform government and service commissioners' attitudes to children's palliative care
- lead the development and continued improvement of children's palliative care services through research and publications, education, and effective communication
- empower and support families through provision of information and a national campaigning voice.

ACT is an umbrella organisation whose membership is made up of families, voluntary organisations, statutory services (health, social care and education) and many professional bodies.

ACT, Orchard House
Orchard Lane, Bristol BS1 5DT
Helpline: 0845 108 2201
Tel: 0117 922 1556   Fax: 0117 930 4707
Email: info@act.org.uk   Website: www.act.org.uk

The Befriending Network is a registered charity working with people who are life-threatened or terminally ill and living at home. Its aim is to provide emotional support and improve the quality of life by offering a befriending relationship with community-based volunteers, who are trained and supervised.

Types of support offered by befrienders:

- Weekly meetings to listen, talk and just be with the person.
- Accompanying the person on hospital visits or other trips.
- Providing a link with local health and social services

Please note that the befriender is not a professional or replacement for a nurse, social worker or home help or there to promote any spiritual belief of their own. They are not allowed to benefit financially from the befriending relationship and will not be suffering from a recent stressful loss of their own.

The Befriending Network
24–27 White Lion Street, London N1 9PD
Tel: 020 7689 2443   Fax: 020 7689 2421
Email: info@befriending.net   Website: www.befriending.net

Bereavement Forum London

This website has the contact details for bereavement counselling services in London. It is also the contact point for professionals who care for bereaved people in London and who wish to attend Bereavement Forum London. The website also hosts Bereavement Care Standards, which were produced to promote the development of high standards in bereavement care.

Bereavement Forum London
Website: www.bereavement.org.uk

The Bereavement Register is a service with one simple aim: to reduce the amount of direct mail sent to those who have died. Our names and addresses appear on many databases and mailing files, which means, unfortunately, that we are often bombarded with mail we just don't want. Imagine if that mail is sent to a family member or friend who has recently died. The distress and upset that can cause is immeasurable. Launched in 2000, The Bereavement Register is a service specifically designed to remove from databases and mailing files the names and addresses of people who have died. Those involved with the bereaved and/or in bereavement support can request a supply of leaflets free of charge for distribution to their clients.

The Bereavement Register
The Clock House, Blighs Road, Sevenoaks TN13 1DA
Tel: 01732 460000
Email: info@thebereavementregister.org.uk
Website: www.the-bereavement-register.org.uk

BODY – British Organ Donor Society

BODY provides emotional support and information to families involved in organ donation, especially to donor families; information and support for professionals involved in organ donation; promotes information for the public, to enable informed decisions to be made at the time of donation.

BODY
Balsham, Cambridge CB1 6DL
Tel: 01223 893636
Email: Body@argonet.co.uk   Website: www.argonet.co.uk/body

British Association for Counselling and Psychotherapy (BACP)

BACP is a professional body for Counselling and Psychotherapy. As a membership organisation it has developed an Ethical Framework for Good Practice. Its members are subject to its Professional Standards Procedure. It is a registered charity. BACP has developed individual accreditation schemes for counsellors, trainers and supervisors and has an accreditation scheme for counsellor training courses.

The Association aims to: promote understanding and awareness of counselling; increase the availability of counselling and psychotherapy; maintain and raise standards; provide support for counsellors; supply information and advice; and represent counselling and psychotherapy at a national level.

Details of local counsellors and counselling agencies, and details of how to become a counsellor, are available on request or from the website.

Publications include *Counselling and Psychotherapy* (monthly); *Counselling and Psychotherapy Resources Directory* (for the UK); *Training in Counselling and Psychotherapy Directory*. It maintains a film and video library and publishes books and leaflets.

BACP
BACP House, 35–37 Albert Street, Rugby CV21 2SG
Tel: 0870 443 5252   Fax: 0870 443 5161   Minicom: 0870 443 5162
Email: bacp@bacp.co.uk   Website: www.bacp.co.uk

The Buddhist Hospice Trust is a small registered UK charity that was established in 1986 to offer information and spiritual support to the living, the dying and bereaved from within a Buddhist perspective. It is a totally voluntary organisation that is open to Buddhists of any tradition (or none) and to non-Buddhists who are sympathetic to its aims.

Currently, the BHT has four main projects:

- The Ananda Network – a nationwide network of Buddhist volunteers willing to visit and offer spiritual friendship to those who are seriously ill, dying or bereaved.
- *Raft*, The Journal of the Buddhist Hospice Trust – a biannual journal (published Spring and Autumn) which explores many contemporary bioethical themes from within Buddhist perspectives. It is only available through subscription.
- BHT Publications – occasional booklets, pamphlets and information leaflets on different aspects of death and dying, aimed primarily at health care workers and the general public.
- Seminars, study days and retreats – occasional meetings on all aspects of death, dying and bereavement are frequently held in Central London.

For further information contact:

Dennis Sibley, The Buddhist Hospice Trust
1 Laurel House, Trafalgar Road, Newport, Isle of Wight PO30 1QN
Tel: 01983 526945
Email: dsibley@buddhisthospice.org.uk   Website: www.buddhisthospice.org.uk

Carers UK

Carers UK is the leading campaigning, policy and information organisation for carers. We are a membership organisation, led and set up by carers in 1965 to have a voice and to win the recognition and support that carers deserve. Carers UK continues to make a difference to carers' lives through a range of activities:

- Campaigning for a better deal for carers. Our campaigns are rooted in the experiences of carers, ensuring we speak authoritatively about what needs to change to improve carers' lives.
- Informing carers of their rights and what help is available so that they can make choices about their lives. Carers UK is the leading provider of information to carers. Our free service, CarersLine, receives 50,000 enquiries a year.
- Training and advising professionals who work with carers. Our trainers and consultants are leading experts in their fields. Carers UK provides the latest information on changes to policies and practice affecting carers.
- Working across the UK through our membership and networks of branches and affiliates, Carers UK is in touch with over half a million carers. Carers UK has a devolved structure. Carers Scotland, Carers Wales and Carers Northern Ireland determine priorities in their respective areas and ensure carers' voices are clearly heard by the Scottish Parliament and the Assemblies of Wales and Northern Ireland.

Carers UK
Ruth Pitter House, 20/25 Glasshouse Yard, London EC1A 4JT
Tel: 020 7490 8818   Fax: 020 7490 8824   CarersLine: 0808 808 7777
Email: info@carersuk.org   Website: www.carersuk.org

Chapeltown and Harehills Bereavement Support Group
CHBSG is a voluntary organisation giving free support to any bereaved individual or family, mainly in the Leeds 7 and Leeds 8 areas.

Chapeltown and Harehills Bereavement Support Group
Roscoe Methodist Church, Francis Street, Chapeltown Road, Leeds LS7 4BY
Tel: 0113 266 6816

The Child Bereavement Trust
For professionals – we offer a range of training courses for anyone who comes into contact with bereaved families in the course of their work, such as healthcare professionals, teachers, police officers etc. We also offer telephone support to those professionals caring for a family when a baby or child dies, or when children are bereaved, and resources to inform and support their work in this area.

For families – we offer a listening and signposting service for bereaved families. We keep a database of local and national support, and also produce our own resources for children, young people and adults.

Our interactive website contains a range of information sheets, for both professionals and families, all of which are available to download free of charge. Our website includes a Professionals Discussion Forum, where questions can be asked and best practice shared, and a Families Forum, where bereaved families can share their experiences and lend support to one another.

The Child Bereavement Trust
Aston House, High Street, West Wycombe, High Wycombe, Buckinghamshire HP14 3AG
Information and Support Line: 0845 357 1000
Main Office: 01494 446648   Fax: 01494 440057
Email: enquiries@childbereavement.org.uk   Website: www.childbereavement.org.uk

Child Death Helpline

To lose a child is the most devastating experience any parent has to face. In the UK alone, 16,000 children under 19 die each year. Over 13,000 young adults in their twenties and thirties also die, and grief is no less intense for the surviving parents of an adult child.

We support anyone affected by a child's death, from pre-birth to the death of an adult child, however long ago, and whatever the circumstances. For a parent, their son or daughter will always be their child, irrespective of age. We receive calls and support parents whose child was 30, 40, 50 years old when they died.

We provide support, not only at times of crisis, but also for the ongoing needs of callers over their lifetime. We are open every evening 7.00–10.00 pm and Monday to Friday mornings 10.00 am–1.00 pm, Wednesdays until 4.00 pm.

Child Death Helpline Administration Centre
York House, 37–39 Queen Square, London WCIN 3BH
Tel (admin): 020 7813 8551   Helpline: 0800 282 986   Fax: 020 7813 8516
Email: contact@childdeathhelpline.org   Website: www.childdeathhelpline.org.uk

Citizens Advice

The Citizens Advice Service helps people resolve their legal, money and other problems by providing free information and advice and by influencing policymakers.

For online advice and to find your local CAB see www.adviceguide.org.uk.

Citizens Advice
115–123 Pentonville Road, London N1 9LZ
Tel (admin only): 020 7833 2181

The Compassionate Friends

A nation-wide self help organisation of parents, whose child of any age, including adult, has died from any cause. National telephone helpline, website, email support and personal and group support. We offer a quarterly Newsletter, a postal library and a range of leaflets. This is a befriending, not a counselling, service.

The Compassionate Friends
53 North Street, Bristol BS3 1EN
Tel (office): 0845 120 3785   Helpline: 0845 1282304
Website: www.tcf.org.uk   Email: info@tcf.org.uk

The Cremation Society of Great Britain

The Society, a registered charity, not conducted for profit, was established over 125 years ago in 1874. It is the pioneer of cremation in Great Britain and in 1885 built and operated the very first crematorium in Woking, Surrey. Since the Society's formation, it has worked tirelessly to promote and establish the practice of cremation among all members of the community. It has aided both private enterprise and local authorities in the setting up of new crematoria and has pressed the government departments concerned for developments in the law, so that this rational, safe and dignified method of disposal of the dead might be practised with the least possible restriction.

The Society was responsible for drawing up the forms of certification for cremation and these were later adopted as the basis for the first Cremation Act in 1902. As a direct result of its activities, cremation now accounts for approximately 70 per cent of all funerals in Great Britain.

The Cremation Society of Great Britain
Brecon House (2nd Floor), 16/16a Albion Place, Maidstone, Kent ME14 5DZ
Tel: 01622 688292/3   Fax: 01622 686698
Email: cremsoc@aol.com   Website: www.cremation.org.uk

Crossroads Caring for Carers

Crossroads Caring for Carers has 190 local schemes throughout England and Wales.

Crossroads' core service is the provision of breaks for family and 'informal' carers – including young carers. These are the people whose support and assistance enables adults and children with disabilities, chronic illnesses, learning disabilities and frailty resulting from old age to remain at home amongst family and friends rather than going into long-term hospital, nursing or residential care. Most family carers don't see themselves as that. They are simply doing their family duty to their loved ones, but they themselves need time off to 'recharge their batteries' and enable them to care for longer. Sometimes the breaks we provide are used for essential tasks such as shopping, medical appointments, parent–teacher evenings etc. Ideally, in our view, carers' breaks are for recreation – visiting friends, playing darts, going to the gym, football or theatre. In order to facilitate carers' breaks and support, Crossroads recruits and trains 'Carer Support Workers' who visit the families concerned and 'step into the shoes of the carer', providing personal care, assistance with meals, conversation, assistance with hobbies etc. for the person with care needs.

Historically, the carers served by Crossroads have included many supporting a relative or close friend living with cancer. Sometimes this activity is already funded by Macmillan Cancer Relief. The two organisations are now developing a strategic partnership to build on this work and improve the lives of carers and people living with cancer through the provision of breaks, support and information.

Crossroads Caring for Carers
Central Office, 10 Regent Place, Rugby CV21 2PN
Tel: 01788 573653/0845 450 0350   Fax: 01788 565498
Email: communications@crossroads.org.uk   Website: www.crossroads.org.uk

DEFRA (for burial at sea)

Marine Consents Unit
DEFRA, 328 Whitehall Place West, London
Tel: 0207 270 8659

or contact directly:

1. Newhaven, East Sussex: Tel: 01424 424109/438125

2. Poole, Dorset: Tel: 01202 677539
   Fax: 01202 678598

3. Tyne Dump Site (DEFRA Office NE):
   Tel: 0191 257 4520   Fax: 0191 257 1595
   Email: rod.henderson@defra.gov.uk

European Association for Palliative Care

The EAPC was established in 1988 with 42 founding members. The aim of the EAPC is to promote palliative care and to act as a focus for all of those who work or have an interest in the field of palliative care at the scientific, clinical and social levels.

In 1998 the EAPC was awarded the status of NGO, and was transformed to 'Onlus' (non-profit organisation with social utility).

By 2005 the EAPC counted individual members in 40 countries, with collective members from 32 National Associations in 21 European countries, representing a movement of some 50,000 health care workers and volunteers working or interested in palliative care.

EAPC operates with the following aims:

- Promote the implementation of existing knowledge; train those who at any level are involved with the care of patients and families affected by incurable and advanced disease; and promote study and research.
- Bring together those who study and practise the disciplines involved in the care of patients and families affected by advanced disease (doctors, nurses, social workers, psychologists and volunteers).
- Unify national palliative care organisations and establish an international network for the exchange of information and expertise.
- Address the ethical problems associated with the care of terminally ill patients.

European Association for Palliative Care
EAPC Head Office, Instituto Nazionale dei Tumori, Via Venezian 1, 20133 Milano, Italia
Tel: +39 02 2390 3390   Fax: +39 02 2390 3393
Email: amelia.giordano@institutotumori.mi.it   Website: www.eapcnet.org

The Federation of British Cremation Authorities

Established in 1924, the Federation of British Cremation Authorities includes in its membership 94 per cent of the 250 crematoria operating in Great Britain in 2005. It is the only authority which sets Codes of Practice, monitors standards of operation and offers technical advice on cremation matters. It annually produces valuable statistical information, promotes a training scheme for crematorium technicians and sponsors a national conference. It is consulted by Government Departments and has a reputation as a leading authority on all matters relating to the establishment and management of crematoria and the law and practice of cremation. The Federation publishes advisory handbooks and leaflets as well as *Resurgam*, a quarterly journal.

The Federation of British Cremation Authorities
41 Salisbury Road, Carshalton, Surrey SM5 3HA
Tel/Fax: 020 8669 4521
Email: fbcasec@tiscali.co.uk   Website: www.fbca.org.uk

The Foundation for the Study of Infant Deaths (FSID) is the UK's leading baby charity

to prevent sudden infant deaths and promote baby health. FSID funds research (over £9 million to date); supports families whose baby has died suddenly and unexpectedly; promotes lifesaving information to health professionals and the public.

FSID helped launch the Reduce the Risk campaign which has reduced UK cot death by 75 per cent since its launch in 1991 and has been hailed as one of the most successful health promotion campaigns ever. But still one family a day in the UK suffers the tragedy of cot death, which is why FSID needs more support to continue its lifesaving research.

FSID offers a helpline, 0870 787 0554, available to families, carers and professionals affected by or concerned about sudden unexpected infant death; a wide range of publications and events for parents and health professionals; a network of befrienders to support bereaved families; a phonecard for bereaved families to call the Helpline free of charge; the Care of the Next Infant (CONI) scheme, in partnership with the NHS, to support bereaved families with subsequent babies.

Foundation for the Study of Infant Deaths
Artillery House, 11–19 Artillery Row, London SW1P 1RT
Helpline: 020 7233 2090 (9 am–11 pm Mon–Fri, 6 pm–11 pm Sat–Sun)
Tel: 020 7222 8001   Fax: 020 7222 8002
Email: fsid@sids.org.uk   Website: www.sids.org.uk/fsid

Help the Aged

Help the Aged publishes *Bereavement* (free booklet); *Planning for the End of Life* (£5.00), which discusses health, financial and practical issues that need to be considered in later life; and *Dying in Older Age: Reflections and Experiences from an Older Person's Perspective* (£5.00), which is a summary of the research report *End-of-Life Care* (Help the Aged/The Policy Press, £14.99). P&P charges apply (call 020 7239 1946). The Charity also offers funeral plans (0800 169 1112), through the British-owned provider Golden Charter.

Help the Aged also provides advice on writing a will. For a free Will Information Pack contact the Wills and Legacies Department, Help the Aged, FREEPOST LON 13257, London N1 9BR.

Help the Aged
207–221 Pentonville Road, London N1 9UZ
Tel: 020 7278 1114   Fax: 020 7278 1116
Email: info@helptheaged.org.uk   Website: www.helptheaged.org.uk

Help the Hospices' vision is of a world in which the best possible care is available to all people at the end of life, whatever their circumstances.

Help the Hospices is the national charity that supports the hospice movement and supports over 220 local hospices across the UK. This support is provided through a wide range of services, all aimed at helping hospices provide the very best care for patients and their families. These include training and grants for hospice staff and volunteers, national programmes of advice, information and support, special award programmes to fund new services and the coordination of national fundraising initiatives. We are also involved in supporting services around the world, especially in resource-poor countries. In all that we do, we aim to make a real difference to the care given to patients and their loved ones.

Our core focus is to support the independent, local charities that provide the vast majority of hospice care in the UK. As well as the services mentioned above, we give a national voice to their views and concerns, bringing them to the attention of government, the media and other influential groups and bodies.

Help the Hospices
Hospice House, 34–44 Britannia Street, London WC1X 9JG

Tel: 0870 903 3903 (calls charged at national rates)
Tel: 020 7520 8200   Fax: 020 7278 1021
Email: info@hospiceinformation.info   Website: www.hospiceinformation.info

HM Inspector of Anatomy

The Human Tissue Act 2004 will, from 1 April 2006, replace the Anatomy Act 1984 in England and Wales and the Anatomy Order 1992 in Northern Ireland. In Scotland, separate proposals to amend the Anatomy Act are being considered by the Scottish Parliament. However, the principles for body donation remain unchanged throughout the UK.

Those people who, prior to their death, wish to bequeath their bodies for anatomical examination by dissection for teaching, studying, clinical training or research purposes may continue to do so, provided they make written arrangements prior to their decease. The majority of bodies are used to teach anatomy to medical and dental students. It is also a good idea to make sure that your family and close friends are aware of your wishes.

The Chief Executive
The Human Tissue Authority
Finlaison House, 15–17 Furnival Street, London EC4A 1AB

In Scotland, intending donors should write to:
HM Inspector of Anatomy for Scotland
c/o Health Department, Public Health Division, Scottish Executive
St Andrew's House, Edinburgh EH1 3DG
Tel: 0131 244 2507

Iain Rennie Hospice at Home

Family support has always been an integral part of the care offered by the Iain Rennie Hospice at Home, for the families of patients referred to us. We work both in the pre- and post-bereavement period and are able to offer a range of services. These include: one to one support, social support groups and work with children and young people. In collaboration with two other hospices we run an annual two day workshop for bereaved children from the ages of 5–14 years. We are particularly fortunate to have a Play Specialist working within the team, in addition to a team of trained volunteer bereavement visitors.

We also liaise closely with schools and health care professionals in the area, offering them support and advice when dealing with bereavement issues.

Iain Rennie Hospice at Home
52a Western Road, Tring, Herts HP23 4BB
Tel: 01442 890222   Fax: 01442 891276
Email: info@irhh.org

Inquest

Inquest provides an independent free legal and advice service to bereaved families and friends on the inquest system. It offers specialist advice to lawyers, bereaved people, service agencies, policy makers, the media and the general public on contentious deaths and their investigation.

Inquest, 89–93 Fonthill Road, London N4 3JH
Tel: 020 7263 1111   Fax: 020 7561 0799

Email for general enquiries: inquest@inquest.org.uk
        for media enquiries: communications@inquest.org.uk
Website: www.inquest.org.uk
Inquest is staffed Monday to Friday. We run an answering machine service. Please leave a message and someone will call you back as soon as possible.

The International Cremation Federation

Founded in London in 1937 the International Cremation Federation is an international non-profit organisation devoted to promoting the practice of cremation to the highest standard.

United Nations. In 1996 the International Cremation Federation was granted Consultative Status (Roster) with the Economic and Social Council of the United Nations. The Federation has the ability to contribute to the international cremation movement and work of the United Nations at the highest level. The Federation has accredited representatives at the United Nations headquarters in New York and United Nations offices in both Vienna and Geneva for meetings of ECOSOC.

Aims and objectives. The aims of the Federation defined in its Statutes are: to provide information concerning cremation – the merits, viewed, inter alia, from an hygienic, ethical, economic and aesthetic standpoint; to simplify the process of cremation and to secure a general recognition of this rite; to free cremation from legal restrictions in countries where they still exist; to raise cremation to the same level as interment, including in ecclesiastical circles; to eliminate problems encountered in transporting the ashes of a deceased person from one country to another.

It works towards these objectives by: providing appropriate explanations to members and also by providing explanations to the public and all kinds of organisation concerning the technical procedures and practical experience relating to cremation; implementing agreements between organisations concerning the cremation of deceased members of organisations abroad; promoting cremation with the aid of all available means; holding international cremation congresses and publishing official reports of the transactions of these congresses; negotiating with ecclesiastical and government authorities with the aim of making cremation possible or simplifying it; cooperating with organisations closely associated with cremation. The Secretary-General is Henry J. Keizer.

International Cremation Federation
Van Stolkweg 29a, NL 2585 JN The Hague, The Netherlands
PO Box 80532, NL-2508 GM The Hague, The Netherlands.
Tel: +31(0) 70 351 88 24   Fax: +31(0) 70 351 88 27
Email: keizer@facultatieve.com   Website: www.int-crem-fed.org

IQRA Trust, a Muslim educational charity, provides advice and information about matters relating to Islam, including education and information, radio broadcasting and prisoners' welfare. It aims to promote a greater understanding of Islam among Muslims and non-Muslims alike.

IQRA Trust
3rd Floor, 16 Grosvenor Crescent, London SW1X 7EP
Tel: 020 7838 7987   Fax: 020 7245 6386
Email: info@iqratrust.org   Website: www.iqratrust.org.uk

The Jewish Bereavement Counselling Service offers bereavement counselling to individuals, children and families in north and north-west London and Herts. Confidential counselling and support is provided by trained volunteer counsellors who are professionally supervised. Counsellors visit clients in their own homes and have specific knowledge of the grieving process.

JBCS takes referrals from doctors, social workers, synagogues, schools and hospitals and the service works in partnership with these organisations.

The Jewish Bereavement Counselling Service
8–10 Forty Avenue, Wembley, Middlesex HA9 8JW
Tel: 020 8385 1874 (24 hour answerphone)   Fax: 020 8385 1856
Email: jbcs@jvisit.org.uk   Website: www.jvisit.org.uk

Law Centres Federation

The Law Centres Federation is the umbrella organisation for Law Centres. Law Centres are not-for-profit independent legal advice centres that employ solicitors and caseworkers. Law Centres provide advice and representation to people in their local area, mainly in the areas of social welfare law (such as immigration, employment, housing, welfare benefits and discrimination). The Law Centres Federation can tell people if there is a Law Centre in their area.

Law Centres Federation
Duchess House, 18–19 Warren Street, London W1T 5LR
Tel: 020 7387 8570   Fax: 020 7387 8368
Email: info@lawcentres.org.uk   Website: www.lawcentres.org.uk

Lesbian and Gay Bereavement Project

The Lesbian and Gay Bereavement Project offers a telephone support and advice service for lesbians and gay men bereaved by the death of a partner, or otherwise affected by bereavement. A trained volunteer is on call Monday, Tuesday and Wednesday evenings from 7.00 pm to 10.30 pm on 020 7403 5969. Notes on making a will and a free will form are obtainable for an SAE sent to the Project at the address below.

Lesbian and Gay Bereavement Project
c/o THT Counselling, 111–117 Lancaster Road, London W11 1QT
Tel: 01452 331131   Helpline: 020 7403 5969
Website: www.tht.org.uk

Macmillan Cancer Relief

Macmillan Cancer Relief provides the expert care and emotional support that makes a real difference to people living with cancer. We offer a range of innovative cancer services and are at the heart of improving cancer care throughout the UK. Services include:

- Macmillan health and social care professionals, including nurses, doctors, radiographers, physiotherapists, dieticians and social workers providing information, emotional support, symptom control and pain relief for people living with cancer.
- Information and support services, providing quality information and emotional support to people affected by cancer, delivered locally, or via our Macmillan CancerLine.
- Macmillan Grants and money advice, helping people who are in financial difficulty as a result of their illness.

- Carer support services, offering practical help and emotional support for those caring for someone living with cancer.
- Design and creation of cancer care centres – these healing environments use design principles which have been shown to improve people's response to treatment.
- Self-help and support services, linking people affected by cancer to a network of over 750 groups UK-wide; we also help new groups by providing free information, training and small grants.
- Education, development and support services: educating Macmillan health and social care professionals to keep them at the leading edge of their field, as well as providing information resources to anyone who delivers care to people living with cancer.

Macmillan Cancer Relief
89 Albert Embankment, London SE1 7UQ
Cancerline: 0808 808 2020   Textphone: 0808 808 0121
Tel (general enquiries): 020 7840 7840   Fax: 020 7840 7841
Email: cancerline@macmillan.org.uk   Website: www.macmillan.org.uk

Marie Curie Cancer Care

The charity provides services across the UK. The nursing service gives terminally ill people the choice to be cared for and die in their own home supported by their family.

Our ten hospices provide specialist palliative care to assess and alleviate distressing symptoms, for rehabilitation and for terminal care. The service to patients and their families and carers aims to facilitate care at home if that is the person's choice.

Referrals can be made through the GP and district nurse. Details of how to access all services can be found on the website.

Marie Curie Cancer Care
Head Office, 89 Albert Embankment, London SE1 7TP
Tel: 020 7599 7777   Fax: 020 7599 7788
Website: www.mariecurie.org.uk

Memorials by Artists was founded by Harriet Frazer, three years after the death of her stepdaughter. The experience of searching for, and then finding, a beautiful memorial to her led to the idea of helping others in a similar situation.

Since 1988, Memorials by Artists has overseen the commissioning of many hundreds of unique memorials throughout the British Isles and beyond. Each memorial is individually designed and carved by one of many independent artist-makers, whose work can range from classic simplicity to the lively and innovative.

Memorials by Artists helps people through the often daunting process of finding an artist, commissioning the memorial, and negotiating the rules and regulations governing churchyard or cemetery. A free eight-page illustrated leaflet describes our service and our publications, including the book specifically for babies, children's and young people's memorials. Suitable for parents and all who support the bereaved.

Memorials by Artists
Snape Priory, Snape, Suffolk IP17 1SA
Tel: 01728 688934
Email: enquiries@memorialsbyartists.co.uk
Website: www.memorialsbyartists.co.uk

The Miscarriage Association

Miscarriage can be a very unhappy, frightening and lonely experience. The Miscarriage Association recognises the distress associated with pregnancy loss and strives to make a positive difference to those whom it affects.

A registered charity, we offer support and information for anyone affected by the loss of a baby in pregnancy. We operate a staffed helpline; coordinate a UK-wide network of telephone support contacts and support groups; run conferences for health professionals; provide consultation to health and related organisations on caring for patients who miscarry; and work with the media to raise awareness of the facts and feelings of pregnancy loss.

We will always try to be of help.

The Miscarriage Association
c/o Clayton Hospital, Northgate, Wakefield, West Yorkshire WF1 3JS
Helpline: 01924 200799   Tel (admin):01924 200795
Helpline (Scotland): 0131 334 8883   Fax: 01924 298834
Email: info@miscarriageassociation.org.uk   Website: www.miscarriageassociation.org.uk

Moorfields Eye Hospital Eye Bank

Corneal grafting is a sight-restoring operation whereby healthy corneal tissue is used to replace a diseased cornea to the blind or visually handicapped patient.

Services to the Public: Provide information and support to families who wish to donate eyes for transplantation and research purposes at the time of a loved one's death.

Services to Professionals: Provide transplant tissue, including corneas and sclera, on a patient based distribution scheme. Provide research tissue on ethics committee approved projects aimed at developing new and advanced treatment methods for eye disease.

Moorfields Eye Hospital Eye Bank
162 City Road, London EC1V 2PD
Tel (weekdays): 020 7253 1199   Tel (after hours): 0207 253 3411
Website: www.moorfields.org.uk

National Association of Funeral Directors

The National Association of Funeral Directors is an independent Trade Association with the broadest membership within the profession, including more than 3200 funeral homes nationwide, suppliers to the profession and overseas funeral directing businesses.

Member companies range from small family businesses to Public Limited Companies and Co-operatives, conducting in excess of 500,000 funerals every year.

The Association has been supporting funeral directors and their clients since 1905 and is proud of its traditions and achievements within the profession.

The NAFD's Code of Practice was first established in 1979, and the lion logo is acknowledged as a 'kite mark' of quality assurance, guaranteeing the highest professional standards.

The NAFD takes the lead in education and is responsible for initiating professional development programmes.

The Association represents the profession at all levels of Government in respect of legislation, and campaigns on issues affecting not only funeral directors but also the bereaved. It provides informed opinion on funeral matters to Parliamentarians, Government Agencies and consumer groups.

The National Association of Funeral Directors
618 Warwick Road, Solihull, West Midlands B91 1AA
Tel: 0845 230 1343   Fax: 0121 711 1351
Email: info@nafd.org.uk   Website: www.nafd.org.uk

The National Bereavement Partnership offers a unique service in the provision of information, advice and support to people who have experienced bereavement and professionals working with bereaved people, particularly in the context of post mortem examinations.

We provide training to health care professionals, Coroners and their Officers, voluntary organisations and charities.

We offer support and advice on any issues related to bereavement. We specialise in providing information and advice surrounding the post mortem examination process.

We can assist with the needs of bereaved people whether their loss is recent or some time ago. If we can't help, we can identify other organisations that can provide the advice or support required.

Anyone who needs information, advice and support relating to bereavement can contact us. This includes parents, siblings, grandparents, other relatives, friends, carers and health or related professionals.

The National Bereavement Partnership
Office No. 6, 2 Bear Street, Barnstaple, Devon EX32 7DB
Helpline: 0845 226 7227
Website: www.natbp.org.uk

National Council for Palliative Care (NCPC)

The National Council for Palliative Care is the umbrella organisation for all those who are involved in providing, commissioning and using hospice and palliative care services in England, Wales and Northern Ireland. It promotes the extension and improvement of palliative care services, regardless of diagnosis, in all health and social care settings and across all sectors to government, national and local policy makers.

The National Council runs events and publishes a bi-monthly magazine, an e-mail briefing and regular topical briefing bulletins and publications. Subscribers are supported through an area and country structure providing local meetings, events and ongoing communication with headquarters.

Further information and regular news updates on palliative care can be accessed at www.ncpc.org.uk.

The National Council for Palliative Care
The Fitzpatrick Building, 188–194 York Way, London N7 9AS
Tel: 020 7697 1520   Fax: 020 7697 1530
Email: enquiries@ncpc.org.uk   Website: www.ncpc.org.uk

National Federation of Spiritual Healers (NFSH)

Healing is a natural, gentle, holistic therapy that helps to restore the balance of mind, body and spirit. As well as helping to ease physical discomfort, healing can bring about a sense of calmness and peace that can be of great benefit to terminally ill patients, their families and carers.

NFSH is a registered charity with over 5000 members, some of whom are Medical Practitioners either as Healer or Associate Members.

Healers work alongside the medical profession in hospitals and hospices, and GPs can refer patients to healers. Healing is also widely available at NFSH Healing Centres or in private practice. The charity runs a Healer Referral Service within the UK: 0845 123 2767.

NFSH
Old Manor Farm Studio, Church Street, Sunbury-on-Thames, Middlesex, TW16 6RG
Tel: 01932 783 164   Fax: 01932 779648
Email: office@nfsh.org.uk   Website: www.nfsh.org.uk

Natural Death Centre

The Natural Death Centre is a charitable project launched in Britain in 1991. It aims to support those dying at home and their carers, and to help people arrange inexpensive, family-organised and environmentally friendly funerals. For a complete listing of the UK's natural burial ground sites, plus eco-coffin suppliers, how to organise a funeral with, or without, a funeral director, the law regarding burial on private land etc., please see our publication *The Natural Death Handbook*. We can also provide Advance Healthcare Directives and Advance Funeral Wishes forms.

Natural Death Centre
6 Blackstock Mews, Blackstock Road, London N4 2BT
Tel: 0871 288 2098   Fax: 020 7354 3831
Information line: 07986 034 378
Email: ndc@alberyfoundation.org   Website: www.naturaldeath.org.uk

The Pagan Federation

The Pagan Federation is an international organisation run by volunteers. It was founded in 1971 to provide information and counter misconceptions about Paganism.

The Pagan Federation strives to provide practical and effective help and advice to all members of the public, the media, public bodies and government departments at a personal level. We have a specific department, called Community Services, set up to help people through difficult times, offering support, assistance and advice.

The Pagan Federation
The General Secretary, BM Box 7097, London WC1N 3XX
Information line: 07986 034 378
Email: SECRETARY@paganfed.org   Website: www.paganfed.org

Rationalist Association

The organisation will advise on secular funerals.

Rationalist Association
1 Gower Street, London WC1E 6HD
Tel: 020 7436 1151   Fax: 020 7079 3588
Email: info@newhumanist.org.uk   Website: www.newhumanist.org.uk

RCN Palliative Nursing Forum

With a membership of over 8000 nurses and established for over 20 years, this forum is the voice of palliative nursing in the UK. An integral part of the RCN's professional activity, it provides a forum for nurses engaged in palliative care to improve standards by addressing issues of palliative nursing practice, education, research and management.

Membership is open to RCN members working in palliative care and caring for people in any diagnostic group who require palliative care. The forum publishes a newsletter twice a year, maintains a web page which may be accessed via the RCN website, and holds an annual conference. Membership enquiries should be directed to RCN Direct (24 hour telephone helpline) on 0845 772 6100 or the website (www.rcn.org.uk).

The Royal College of Nursing
20 Cavendish Square, London W1G 0RN
Helpline: 0845 772 6100
Nurse adviser: Celia Manson
Tel (direct): 020 7647 3763   Tel (adviser's secretary): 020 7647 3756
Email: celia.manson@rcn.org.uk   Website: www.rcn.org.uk

RoadPeace – the UK's specialist charity for road crash victims – was set up in 1992 with the first ever helpline dedicated to bereaved and injured road victims. This provides essential information, advice and assistance seven days a week, supported by free literature written from the victims' perspective. Whenever possible, RoadPeace provides escorts to inquests, court hearings and meetings with CPS or MPs.

Long-term support and friendship are offered through mailings, local groups, annual events and many joint acts of remembrance, including:
- Internet memorial
- 'Remember Me' roadside memorials
- World Day of Remembrance for Road Crash Victims
- RoadPeace Wood within National Memorial Arboretum
- National Road Victim Memorial project.

As an advocate for road victims, RoadPeace works with its Lawyers' Group and Associate Parliamentary Group on their behalf.

RoadPeace researches and documents the situation and experiences of road crash victims, produces briefings, responds to relevant consultations and holds regular conferences, lectures and seminars.

RoadPeace offers speakers for relevant conferences and participation in related working parties and projects.

RoadPeace
PO Box 2579, London NW10 3PW
Tel: 020 8838 5102   Helpline: 0845 4500 355   Fax: 020 8838 5103
Email: info@roadpeace.org   Website: www.roadpeace.org

Samaritans was formed in 1953, by Chad Varah, operating from one telephone in London. It is a registered charity, which has 203 branches across the UK and Ireland, which receive 4.8 million contacts a year. These contacts include 2.5 million telephone calls, 90,000 emails (to jo@samaritans.org), face-to-face contact, either at the branches or at festivals, or letters written to PO Box 90 90, Stirling FK8 2SA. The UK helpline number is 08457 90 90 90. (1850 60 90 90 in the Republic of Ireland).

Samaritans is staffed by trained volunteers who are available to give emotional support 24 hours a day, 365 days a year – a unique service anywhere in the world. They respond to the needs of those who contact them in a receptive and not a directive way and without judgement. They offer sympathetic caring and completely confidential support to people who may be feeling unhappy, afraid, worried, desperate, lonely or suicidal. The caller is never deprived of the freedom of self-determination. By enabling people to express their darkest thoughts they try to help them find ways of coming to terms with whatever troubles them and, by befriending them, Samaritans help them through any period of crisis.

Samaritans also work pro-actively on providing 'good' emotional health and reducing stress and anxiety in schools and in the workplace.

Samaritans is not a religious organisation and their service is free of charge for anyone, anytime.

Samaritans volunteers are from all walks of life but are carefully selected and trained for the service they offer. They have 17,000 volunteers but always need more people who are willing to listen to anyone who needs help.

Samaritans General Office
The Upper Mill, Kingston Road, Ewell, Surrey KT17 2AF
UK Helpline: 08457 90 90 90
Tel: 020 8394 8300   Fax: 020 8394 8301
Email: jo@samaritans.org   Website: www.samaritans.org

SAMM National (Support after Murder and Manslaughter)

SAMM is a self-help support group offering understanding and support to families and friends who have been bereaved as a result of murder or manslaughter, through the mutual support of others who have suffered a similar tragedy. SAMM offers telephone support, local voluntary support and training for professionals. We operate a self-referral service allowing anyone and everyone to call us when it is convenient for them.

SAMM National
Cranmer House, 39 Brixton Road, London SW9 6DZ
Tel: 0207 735 3838   Fax: 0207 735 3900
Email: samm@victimsupport.org.uk   Website: www.samm.org.uk

SANDS (Stillbirth and Neonatal Death Society)

In the UK, 16 babies a day are stillborn or die within the first 28 days of life: a devastating bereavement for the parents and for their families and friends.

SANDS offers support and information to parents and families whose baby has died; works with professionals to improve the care bereaved families receive after the death of a baby; and promotes research into the causes of stillbirths and neonatal deaths.

SANDS
28 Portland Place, London W1B 1LY
Helpline: 020 7436 5881
Tel: 020 7436 7940   Fax: 020 7436 3715
Email: support@uk-sands.org   Website: www.uk-sands.org

SSAFA Forces Help (Soldiers, Sailors, Airmen and Families Association)

SSAFA Forces Help is a national charity helping serving and ex-Service men, women and their families in need. We are notified of a serving person's death by the MOD if the serving person had filled out a proforma requesting us to support their family in the event of their death. The MOD, of course, have support agencies, which are the first point of contact for families, Army Welfare Service, Navy Personal Family Service and RAF Social Work Staff. Our In-Service (Community) and Ex-Service (Branch) volunteers will give as much support as they can to families suffering a bereavement, but regrettably they are not trained counsellors and would not undertake such a responsibility. The volunteers would refer a client needing bereavement counselling to the appropriate agency.

SSAFA Forces Help
Confidential Support Line for serving personnel and their families:
Tel: 0800 731 4880   Tel (Mon to Fri): 020 7403 8783
Website: www.ssafa.org.uk

TAMBA (Twins and Multiple Births Association) Bereavement Support Group

The TAMBA BSG is a parent to parent support group and is run by bereaved parents. All BSG coordinators are volunteers and are parents who have lost a child, or children, during a multiple pregnancy or at any stage after birth. None of the coordinators are professionals; they offer a befriending, rather than a counselling, service.

A newsletter is sent twice a year and a parent contact booklet once a year.

TAMBA Bereavement Support Group
2, The Willows, Gardner Road, Guildford, Surrey GU1 4PG
Tel: 0870 770 3305   Fax: 0870 770 3303
Email: enquiries@tamba.org.uk   Website: www.tamba-bsg.org.uk

Tenovus is an expanding and diverse charity, dedicated to improving the lives of people affected by cancer, through high quality research, education, information and support. We have highly trained and experienced Oncology Nurse Specialists, Social Workers, Welfare Rights Officers and Counsellors working directly with people with a cancer diagnosis. We see bereavement support as integral to the care that we provide. Our Social Workers offer sensitive bereavement support in the community to people experiencing loss. We also have trained counsellors, who provide specialist, individual, bereavement counselling. In addition, once a month, we hold a bereavement coffee morning, which provides support and friendship to those who are bereaved.

We cover Porthcawl, Bridgend, Cardiff, Rhondda and Cynon Valley and Merthyr from the Velindre base.

We have a social worker at Ysbty Glan Clwyd in N. Wales, one in Royal Bournemouth and one in the Cancer Centre at Poole. These are hospital based posts.

Tenovus, The Cancer Charity
43 The Parade, Cardiff CF24 3AB
Tel: 029 2048 2000   Fax: 029 2048 4199
Email: post@tenovus.com   Website: www.tenovus.com

Terrence Higgins Trust

THT is the leading HIV and AIDS charity in the UK and the largest in Europe. It was one of the first charities to be set up in response to the HIV epidemic and has been at the forefront of the fight against HIV and AIDS ever since.

The charity was established in 1982, as The Terry Higgins Trust. Terry Higgins was one of the first people in the UK to die with AIDS. A group of his friends wanted to prevent more people having to face the same illness as Terry and named the Trust after him, hoping to personalise and humanise AIDS in a very public way.

Terrence Higgins Trust
52–54 Grays Inn Road, London WC1X 8JU
Tel: 020 7831 0330   Fax: 020 7242 0121
Email: info@tht.org.uk   Website: www.tht.org.uk

Victim Support is the national independent charity for people affected by crime. It provides a free and confidential service, whether or not a crime has been reported and regardless of when it happened. Victim Support has staff and specially trained volunteers who have time to listen and are able to support people bereaved by violent crime. Trained staff and volunteers at affiliated local charities offer information, support and practical help to victims, witnesses, their families and friends. Victim Support provides the Witness Service, based in every criminal court in England and Wales, to offer assistance before, during and after a trial. The national helpline, Victim Supportline (0845 30 30 900), provides information, support and referral to local services. Victim Support works to increase awareness of the effects of crime and to achieve greater recognition of victims' and witnesses' rights.

Victim Support
Cranmer House, 39 Brixton Road, London SW9 6DZ
Tel: 020 7735 9166   Fax: 020 7582 5712
Email: contact@victimsupport.org.uk   Website: www.victimsupport.org

The War Widows Association of Great Britain

The WWA is essentially a pressure group and exists to improve the conditions of War Widows and their dependants in Great Britain. Its work encompasses not only those who have suffered bereavement from the last World War and as a result of more recent conflicts, such as Korea, the Falklands and the Gulf, but also those who have suffered the loss of their husband in peacetime, when his death was attributable to his Service life.

It works with all Government Departments, petitioning for improvement in pensions, the administration of benefits and other issues affecting War Widows. It represents War Widows at national events of remembrance. It maintains close links with all ex-Service organisations and the Service widows' associations.

Through the Association's magazine *Courage* it keeps in touch with all its members and informs them of everything from changes in legislation to national and local events.

The War Widows Association of Great Britain
c/o 48 Pall Mall, London SW1Y 5JY
Tel: 0870 241 1305
Email: info@warwidowsassociation.org.uk   Website: www.warwidowsassociation.org.uk

Winston's Wish – for grieving children and their families.

Winston's Wish supports children and young people in the UK who have been bereaved, to enable them to live with their grief and so to help them grow up to be resilient adults. We actively involve and support the whole family group and other professionals who come into contact with a bereaved child.

We provide a national Helpline, which is staffed by professionals with up-to-date knowledge and experience of supporting bereaved children. Callers include families and carers as well as professionals, such as teachers, who come into contact with bereaved children and young people. It is available Monday–Friday 9 am–5 pm.

Our website is a practical resource and support for bereaved families. Young people can ask questions (answered by one of our team of professionals), post their poems and drawings online, share with other bereaved children and remember the person who has died, by adding a star to the skyscape of memories.

We have a range of publications, activity sheets and other resources for families and children, available online or from our offices.

Winston's Wish
The Clara Burgess Centre, Bayshill Road, Cheltenham GL50 3AW
Helpline: 0845 20 30 40 5   Tel: 01242 515157 Fax: 01242 546187
Email: info@winstonswish.org.uk   Website: www.winstonswish.org.uk

SOURCES OF ADVICE ON FORENSIC PATHOLOGY

From time to time, patients, relatives and professionals may wish to obtain advice on medico-legal aspects of autopsies, arrangements for an independent examination, embalming, organ and tissue retention and other relevant matters. It is also increasingly common for authors, scriptwriters and others concerned with the media to ensure the accuracy of their work. When the first edition of this book was published, forensic pathology was largely an academic discipline, supported by a network of university departments. This is no longer the case; the majority of forensic pathologists now work individually or in small groups, on a commercial basis.

The Home Office has, for many years, maintained a Register of suitably qualified pathologists in England and Wales. The criteria for admission to this list are rigorous, standards are high and a strict code of discipline and practice is enforced. Access to this list is restricted, but advice may be obtained from the Home Office website www.homeoffice.gov.uk.

There are about 30 forensic pathologists serving all the police forces in England and Wales. They come under the remit of the Home Office, which also has responsibility for matters relating to Coroners.

The Home Office's Department of Forensic Medical Sciences – Tel 020 7840 2941 – deals with forensic pathology, clinical forensic medicine, anthropology and its application to human identification.

In Scotland, until recently, there were university departments in Glasgow and Edinburgh; now only the Dundee department remains. Services in these areas are now provided by the Crown Office. The Crown Office and Procurator Fiscal Service is Scotland's independent public prosecution service (similar to the Crown Prosecution Service in England and Wales). It is a Department of the Scottish Executive, led by the Lord Advocate and the Solicitor General for Scotland, who are the legal advisers to the Executive and sit in the Scottish Parliament. Their website is www.crownoffice.gov.uk.

In Northern Ireland, the State Pathologist's Office provides the forensic services.

United Kingdom University Departments of Forensic Pathology and Forensic Medicine

Department of Forensic Medicine
University of Dundee, Dundee DD1 4HN
Tel: 01382 348020   Fax: 01382 348021
Email: d.j.pounder@dundee.ac.uk   Website: www.dundee.ac.uk/forensicmedicine

Forensic Pathology Unit
University of Leicester, Level 3, Robert Kilpatrick Building
Leicester Royal Infirmary, Leicester LE2 7LX
Tel: 0116 252 3221   Fax: 0116 252 3274
Email: wap2@le.ac.uk

Sub-Department of Forensic Pathology
The University of Liverpool
150 Mount Pleasant, Liverpool L69 3GD
Tel: 0151 794 5928   Fax: 0151 794 2060

University of Northumbria at Newcastle
School of Applied and Molecular Sciences
Ellison Building, Newcastle upon Tyne NE1 8ST
Tel: 0191 227 3047   Fax: 0191 227 3519

Wales Institute of Forensic Medicine
Cardiff University College of Medicine,
Heath Park, Cardiff CF14 4XN, Wales
Tel: 029 2074 4830   Fax: 029 2074 5416
Email: rmj@forensicmed.co.uk

Other departments and organisations

Crown Office and Procurator Fiscal
25 Chambers Street, Edinburgh EH1 1LA
Website: www.crownoffice.gov.uk

Forensic Science Service
109 Lambeth Road, London SE1 7LP
Tel: 020 7840 2941   Fax: 020 7840 2946

Forensic Science Service
The Medico-Legal Centre,
Watery Street, Sheffield S3 7ES
Tel: 0114 2738 721   Fax: 0114 2798 942
Email: forensic.path@sheffield.ac.uk

Forensic Science Service
Chief Executive's office/Operational Headquarters/Research
Trident Court, 2920 Solihull Parkway
Birmingham Business Park, Birmingham B37 7YN

Forensic Science Service
Priory House
Gooch Street North, Birmingham B5 6QQ
Website: www.forensic.gov.uk

Home Office Science Policy Unit
Peel Block, 5th Floor
2 Marsham Street, London SW1P 4DF
Tel: 020 7035 3049 or 07801 731004

Royal College of Pathologists
2 Carlton House Terrace
London SW1Y 5AF
Tel: 020 7451 6700   Fax: 020 7451 6701
Email: info@rcpath.org or J.Crane@qub.ac.uk

State Pathologist's Department
Institute of Forensic Medicine
Grosvenor Road, Belfast BT12 6BL
Tel: 028 9024 5597   Fax: 028 9023 7357

For details of UK universities offering undergraduate and postgraduate courses in Forensic medicine and Science, see:
www.fmap.archives.gla.ac.uk/Research%20Guide /Universities_sources.htm

For general information about the Forensic Science Service, see:
 www.bbc.co.uk/crime /fighters/fss.shtml

Other individuals and group practices which have offered to provide information

The Southern Medico-Legal Centre
The Mill House, Winchester Road
Bishops Waltham, Hants SO32 1AH

In other areas we recommend that an approach should be made to the local Coroner's office. They will pass on any appropriate request to one of the locally accredited Home Office pathologists.

APPENDIX C

FURTHER READING

The books and websites listed below have either been consulted during the preparation of this book, or we feel are worthy of further reading. There are now many websites dealing with different aspects of death, dying and religion. Surfing the web by your chosen topic, e.g. Hinduism, will bring you a huge selection of sites. Only a few select websites are given here.

Forensic medicine and law

Bradfield, J.B. (1984) *Green Burial – the D-I-Y Guide to Law and Practice*. London: The Natural Death Centre.

Dimond, B. (1995) *Legal Aspects of Nursing*. Hemel Hempstead: Prentice Hall International (UK).

Dorries, C.P. (2004) *Coroner's Courts: A Guide to Law and Practice*. Oxford: Oxford University Press.

Goff, L.M. (2000) *A Fly for the Prosecution. How Insect Evidence Helps Solve Crimes*. Cambridge, MA: Harvard University Press.

Grubb, A. and Kennedy, I. (1994) *Medical Law: Text With Materials*. London: Butterworths.

Isser, N.K. and Schwartz, L.L. (2000) *Endangered Children: Neonaticide, Infanticide and Filicide*. Boca Raton, FL: CRC Press LLC.

Knight, B. and Saukko, P. (2004) *Knight's Forensic Pathology*, 3rd edn. London: Arnold.

Kohner, N. (1992) *A Dignified Ending: Recommendations for Good Practice in the Disposal of the Bodies and Remains of Babies Born Dead Before the Legal Age of Viability*. London: SANDS.

Montgomery, J. (1997) *Health Care Law*. Oxford: Oxford University Press.

Olshaker, J.S., Jackson, M.C. and Smock, W.S. (eds) (2001) *Forensic Emergency Medicine*. London: Lippincott Williams and Wilkins.

Polson, C.J. and Marshal, T.K. (1974) *The Disposal of the Dead*, 3rd edn. London: English Universities Press.

Richardson, R. (1989) *Death, Dissection and the Destitute*. London: Pelican Books.

Robertson, B. and Vignaux, G.A. (1995) *Interpreting Evidence. Evaluating Forensic Science in the Courtroom*. Chichester: John Wiley.

Saunders, K.C. (2001) *The Medical Detectives: A Study of Forensic Pathologists*. London: Middlesex University Press.

Smale, D.A. (2002) *Davies' Law of Burial, Cremation and Exhumation*. Crayford: Shaw.

Thomas, L., Friedman, D. and Christian, L. (2002) *Inquests – A Practitioners Guide*. London: LAG Education and Service Trust.

Weinrich, S. and Speyer, S. (eds) (2002) *The Natural Death Handbook*. London: Rider.

Pathology and transplantation

Dolinak, D., Matshes, E. and Lew, E. (2005) *Forensic Pathology*. New York: Elsevier.

Knight, B. and Saukko, P. (2004) *Knight's Forensic Pathology*, 3rd edn. London: Arnold.

Payne-James, J., Busuttil, A. and Smock, W. (eds) (2003) *Forensic Medicine: Clinical and Pathological Aspects*. London: Greenwich Medical Media.

Polson, C.J., Gee, D.J. and Knight, B. (1985) *The Essentials of Forensic Medicine*, 4th edn. London: Pergamon.

Virchow, R. (1876) *Post Mortem Examinations*. London: Churchill.

Youngner, S.J., Anderson, M.W., Schapiro, R. (eds) (2003) *Transplanting Human Tissue: Ethics, Policy and Practice*. Oxford: Oxford University Press.

Palliative care

Cathcart, F. (1994) *Booklet 1. Understanding Death and Dying: Your Feelings*. Worcester: British Institute of Learning Disabilities (BILD).

Cathcart, F. (1994) *Booklet 2. Understanding Death and Dying: A Guide for Families and Friends*. Worcester: British Institute of Learning Disabilities (BILD).

Cathcart, F. (1994) *Booklet 3. Understanding Death and Dying: A Guide for Carers and Other Professionals*. Worcester: British Institute of Learning Disabilities (BILD).

Clark, D. and Have, H.T. (eds) (2002) *The Ethics of Palliative Care: European Perspectives*. Buckingham: Open University Press.

Doyle, D., Hanks, G., Cherney, N.I., Calman, K. (eds) (2004) *Oxford Textbook of Palliative Medicine*, 3rd edn. Oxford: Oxford University Press.

Ellershaw, J. and Wilkinson, S. (2003) *Care of the Dying: A Pathway to Excellence*. Oxford: Oxford University Press.

Fisch, M.J. and Bruera, E. (eds) (2003) *Handbook of Advanced Cancer Care*. Cambridge: Cambridge University Press.

Glasgow Palliative Care Information Network: www.palliativecareglasgow.info

Henley, A. (1987) *Good Practice in Hospital Care for Dying Patients*. Project Paper No 61, 2nd edn. London: King Edward's Hospital Fund for London.

Jones, A. (2004) *Positive Approaches to Palliative Care*. Worcester: British Institute of Learning Disabilities (BILD).

Lawton, J. (2001) *The Dying Process: Experiences of Patients in Palliative Care*. London: Routledge.

Macmillan Cancer Relief (2003) *Macmillan Gold Standards Framework Programme*. www.macmillan.org.uk or www.modern.nhs.uk/cancer

McHaffie, H.E. in association with Fowlie, P.W. *et al.* (2001) *Crucial Decisions at the Beginning of Life: Parents' Experience of Treatment Withdrawal from Infants*. Abingdon: Radcliffe Medical Press.

NHS Executive (1997) *Patients Who Die in Hospital*. HSG (97) 4.

Robbins, J. and Moscrop, J. (eds) (1995) *Caring for the Dying Patient and the Family*, 3rd edn. London: Chapman and Hall/Cheltenham: Stanley Thornes.

Saunders, C. and Baines, B. (1989) *Living with Dying: The Management of Terminal Disease*, 2nd edn. Oxford: Oxford University Press.

Sheldon, F. (1997) *Psychosocial Palliative Care: Good Practice in the Care of the Dying and Bereaved*. Cheltenham: Stanley Thornes.

Snyder, L. and Quill, T.F. (eds) (2001) *Physician's Guide to End-of-Life Care*. Philadelphia: American College of Physicians, American Society of Internal Medicine.

Sofaer, B. (1998) *Pain: Principles, Practice and Patients*, 3rd edn. Cheltenham: Stanley Thornes.

Staton, J., Shuy, R. and Byock, I. (2001) *A Few Months to Live: Different Paths to Life's End*. Georgetown: Georgetown University Press.

Trent Palliative Care Studies Group: www.sheffield-palliative.org.uk

Medico-legal issues at the end of life

American Heart Association in Collaboration with the International Liaison Committee on Resuscitation (ILCOR) (2000) 'Guidelines 2000 for Cardiopulmonary Resuscitation and Emergency Cardiovascular Care – An International Consensus on Science.' *Resuscitation 46*, 1–448.

American Heart Association (2005) *Highlights of the History of Cardiopulmonary Resuscitation*. Website of the American Heart Association: www.americanheart.org

Colquhoun, M. and Martineau, E. (2000) *The Legal Status of Those who Attempt Resuscitation*. Resuscitation Council (UK).

Dunstan, G.R. and Lachmann, P.J. (eds) (1996) 'Euthanasia: death, dying and the medical duty.' *British Medical Bulletin 52*, 2. London: Published for the British Council by the Royal Society of Medicine Press.

European Resuscitation Council (1998) 'The 1998 European Resuscitation Council Guidelines for Adult Advanced Life Support.' In L. Bossaert, (ed) *European Resuscitation Council Guidelines for Resuscitation*. Amsterdam: Elsevier.

Exit produces several books relating to death, dying and euthanasia. See their website at: www.euthanasia.cc

Finch, J. (1994) *Speller's Law Relating to Hospitals*, 7th edn. London: Chapman and Hall.

General Medical Council (2002) *Withholding and Withdrawing Life Prolonging Treatments: Good Practice in Decision-Making*. London: GMC.

General Medical Council (2004) *Confidentiality: Protecting and Providing Information*. London: GMC.

Hendrick, J. (2000) *Law and Ethics in Nursing and Health Care*. Cheltenham: Stanley Thornes.

Humphry, D. (1991) *Final Exit. The Practicalities of Self-Deliverance and Assisted Suicide for the Dying*. Oregon, USA: The Hemlock Society.

Jennett, B. (2003) *The Vegetative State. Medical Facts, Ethical and Legal Dilemmas*. Cambridge: Cambridge University Press.

Kemp, N.D.A. (2002) *Merciful Release: The History of the British Euthanasia Movement*. Manchester: Manchester University Press.

Keown, J. (2003) *Euthanasia, Ethics and Public Policy: An Argument Against Legalisation*. Cambridge: Cambridge University Press.

Kudenchuk, P.J., Cobb, L.A., Copass, M.K., Cummins, R.O., Doherty, A.M., Fahrenbruch, C.E. *et al.* (1999) 'Amiodarone for resuscitation after out-of-hospital cardiac arrest due to ventricular fibrillation.' *New England Journal of Medicine 341*, 871–878.

Kushner, T.K. and Thomasma, D.C. (eds) (2001) *Ward Ethics. Dilemmas for Medical Students and Doctors in Training*. Cambridge: Cambridge University Press.

Magnusson, R.S. (2002) *Angels of Death: Exploring the Euthanasia Underground*. Yale: Yale University Press.

Murray, R. (1997) *Ethical Dilemmas in Healthcare: A Practical Approach Through Medical Humanities*. Cheltenham: Stanley Thornes.

Quill, T.E. (1996) *A Midwife Through the Dying Process*. Baltimore: Johns Hopkins University Press.

The Patient's Association in collaboration with the British Medical Association (1996) *Advance Statements about Future Medical Treatment. A Guide for Patients*. London: The Patient's Association.

Bereavement

Alderson, P. (ed) (2003) *Saying Goodbye to Your Baby: A Guide for Parents Whose Baby Dies Around the Time of Birth*. London: SANDS.

Cutcliffe, J.R. (2004) *The Inspiration of Hope in Bereavement Counselling*. London: Jessica Kingsley Publishers.

Dickenson, D., Johnson, M. and Katz, J. (eds) (2000) *Death, Dying and Bereavement*. London: The Open University in association with Sage Publishing.

Kohner, N. (undated) *After the Death or Stillbirth of Your Baby: What Has to be Done?* London: SANDS.

Ministry of Defence (2004) *Guidance in Bereavement. Help and Guidance for Families of Servicemen or Women Who Die Whilst on Service*. April 2004, MOD.

Monroe, B. and Oliviere, D. (eds) (2004) *Death, Dying and Social Differences*. Oxford: Oxford University Press.

Parks, C.M., Laungani, P. and Young, B. (1997) *Death and Bereavement Across Cultures*. London: Routledge.

Rees, D. (2001) *Death and Bereavement. The Psychological, Religious and Cultural Interfaces*, 2nd edn. London: Whurr Publishers.

Rosen, M. and Blake, Q. (2004) *Michael Rosen's Sad Book*. London: Walker Books.

SANDS publishes a variety of useful leaflets including: *Mainly for fathers; About the other children; For family and friends – how you can help; The loss of your grandchild; The next pregnancy: guidance for parents; Sexual problems following a stillbirth; Support for you when your baby dies*.

Spall, B. and Callis, S. (1997) *Loss, Bereavement and Grief: A Guide to Effective Caring*. Cheltenham: Stanley Thornes.

Stillbirth and Neonatal Death Society (1995) *Pregnancy Loss and the Death of a Baby. Guidelines for Professionals*, 2nd edn. London: SANDS.

Infection control

Bakhshi, S.S. (2001) 'Code of Practice for funeral workers: managing infection risk and body bagging.' *Communicable Disease and Public Health 4*, 4, 283–287.

Department of Health/NHS Estates (2004) 34335 *The NHS Healthcare Cleaning Manual*. London: DoH. Also available on www.dh.gov.uk

Department of Health (2004) *Towards Cleaner Hospitals and Lower Rates of Infection. A Summary of Action*. London: DoH.

General Medical Council (1997 but undated) *Serious Communicable Diseases*. London: GMC.

Healing, T.D., Hoffman, P.N. and Young, S.E.J. (1995) 'The infection hazards of human cadavers.' *CDR Review Communicable Disease Report 5*, 5, RR61–73.

Health and Safety Executive (1998) *Five Steps to Risk Assessment*. Leaflet INDG 163 (rev 1). London: HSE Books.

Health and Safety Executive (1999) *Safe Disposal of Clinical Waste*, 2nd edn. London: HSE Books.

Health and Safety Executive (2002) *Control of Substances Hazardous to Health. The Control of Substances Hazardous to Health Regulations 2002. Approved Code of Practice and Guidance* L5, 4th edn. London: HSE Books.

Infection Control Nurses Association (2002) *Hand Decontamination Guidelines*. London: ICNA.

Lawrence, J. and May, D. (2003) *Infection Control in the Community*. Edinburgh: Elsevier Science/Churchill Livingstone.

Meers, P., McPherson, M. and Sedgwick, J. (1997) *Infection Control in Health Care*, 2nd edn. Cheltenham: Stanley Thornes.

NHS Executive (2000) *The Management and Control of Hospital Infection. Action for the NHS for the Management and Control of Infection in Hospitals in England.* HSC 2000/002.

US Armed Forces and the American Registry of Pathology have a website for Severe Acute Respiratory Syndrome (SARS). www.afip.org/Departments/Pulmonary/SARS/02.html

Cultural and religious

Barrett, L. (1977) *The Rastafarians: The Dreadlocks of Jamaica.* London: Heinemann.

Cashmore, E. (1979) *Rastaman: The Rastafarian Movement in England.* London: Allen and Unwin.

Cohn-Sherbok, D. (1993) *The Jewish Faith.* London: Society for Promoting Christian Knowledge.

Firth, S. (1999) *Dying, Death and Bereavement in a British Hindu Community.* Leuven: Peeters.

Gatrad, A.R. and Sheikh, A. (2000) *Caring for Muslim Patients.* Abingdon: Radcliffe Medical Press.

Henley, A. and Schott, J. (1999) *Culture, Religion and Patient Care in a Multi-Ethnic Society. A Handbook for Professionals.* London: Age Concern England.

Hoffer, B. and Honna, N. (eds) (1986) *An English Dictionary of Japanese Culture.* Tokyo: Yuhikaku Publishing.

Japan Travel Bureau (1994) *Japanese Family and Culture.* Japan: Japan Travel Bureau.

Japan Travel Bureau (1996) *Living Japanese Style.* Japan: Japan Travel Bureau.

Lamm, M. (1969) *The Jewish Way of Death and Mourning.* New York: Jonathan David Publishers.

Langley, M. (1993) *World Religions.* Oxford: Lion Publishing.

Mackintosh, J., Bhopal, R., Unwin, N., Ahmad, N. (1999) *Step by Step Guide to Epidemiological Health Needs Assessment for Ethnic Minority Groups.* Newcastle: University of Newcastle.

Neuberger, J. (2003) *Caring for Dying People of Different Faiths.* Abingdon: Radcliffe Medical Press.

Nolan, P. (undated, accessed March 2006) 'Rastafarians and Ganja.' At: www.rism.org/isg/dlp/ganja/analyses/nolan.html

Peel, R. (1987) *Spiritual Healing in a Scientific Age.* New York: Harper and Row.

Pepper, M. (1989) *The Pan Dictionary of Religious Quotations.* London: Pan Books.

Philips, A.A.B. (2001) *Funeral Rites in Islam.* Kuala Lumpur: A. S. Noordeen.

Qureshi, B. (1994) *Transcultural Medicine: Dealing with Patients from Different Cultures,* 2nd edn. Lancaster: Kluwer Academic Publishers.

Rabinowicz, Rabbi H. (1969) *A Guide to Life – Jewish Laws and Customs of Mourning,* 2nd edn. London: Jewish Chronicle Publications.

Sambhi, P.S. (1989) *Sikhism.* World Religions Series. Cheltenham: Stanley Thornes.

Snelling, J. (1987) *The Buddhist Handbook. A Complete Guide to Teaching and Practice.* London: Rider, an imprint of Ebury Press.

Warrier, S. and Walshe, J.G. (2001) *Dates and Meanings of Religious and other Multi-Ethnic Festivals, 2002–2005.* Slough: Foulsham.

Weller, P. (ed) (1997) *Religions in the UK. A Multifaith Directory.* Derby: University of Derby.

General interest

British Medical Journal (2003) What is a good death? *British Medical Journal 327.* [The entire journal is filled with numerous articles which discuss many aspects of death and dying.]

Catlett, E. (2002) *When Someone Dies. Things You Need to Know and Do.* Kingswood: Elliot Right Way Books.

Center to Advance Palliative Care (New York): www.capc.org

Department for Work and Pensions (updated annually) *What to Do After a Death in England and Wales. A Guide to What You Must Do and the Help You Can Get*. D49, Department for Work and Pensions.

The Encyclopaedia Britannica CD (2004) [remains a wonderful source of information about religious and cultural matters]. Rugeley: Focus Multimedia.

Harris, P. (2000) *What to Do When Someone Dies*. London: Which? Ltd.

Hinnels, J.R. (ed) (1984) *The Penguin Dictionary of Religions*. Harmondsworth: Penguin Books.

Howarth, G. and Leaman, O. (eds) (2001) *The Encyclopaedia of Death and Dying*. Abingdon: Routledge.

Jupp, P.C. and Gittings, C. (eds) (2000) *Death in England. An Illustrated History*. Manchester: Manchester University Press.

Karmi, G. (1996) *The Ethnic Health Handbook: A Factfile for Health Care Professionals*. London: Blackwell Science.

Lynne, J. and Harrold, J. (1999) *Handbook for Mortals. Guidance for People Facing Serious Illness*. Oxford: Oxford University Press.

Mann, J. (1992) *Murder, Magic and Medicine*. Oxford: Oxford University Press.

Mason, J.K. (1962) *Human Life and Medical Practice*. London: Butterworth.

Mitford, J. (1980) *The American Way of Death*. London: Quartet Books.

Nuland, S. (1993) *How We Die*. London: Chatto and Windus.

Richardson, R. (1989) *Death Dissection and the Destitute*. London: Pelican.

Spiers, J. (1996) *Who Owns Our Bodies? Making Moral Choices in Health Care*. Abingdon: Radcliffe Medical Press.

Spitzer, J. (2003) *Caring for Jewish Patients*. Abingdon: Radcliffe Medical Press.

Willson, J.W. (1991) *Funerals Without God. A Practical Guide to Non-Religious Funerals*. New York: Published for the British Humanist Association by Prometheus Books.

Subject Index

abortion 80
  Chinese attitudes to 300
  Japanese attitudes to 307
  religious objection to 221,
    225, 234, 239, 244,
    248, 253, 259, 277,
    282–3, 289, 293
accidental death 59, 67
Advanced Directives 167–9
Advisory Committee on
  Dangerous Pathogens
  199, 206
African-Caribbeans 246–9
  and death 247–8
  Methodism 228
AIDS *see* HIV/AIDS
Alder Hey inquiry 93–4
alternative medicine
  and Christian Science 242,
    243
  and Rastafarianism 251
anaesthetics 60
analgesics 153–5
anatomical dissection 129–30
  certificate 117
Anatomy Act
  (1832) 122, 132
  (1984) 123, 125, 129
Anatomy, HM Inspector of
  123, 129, 325
Anatomy, Licensed Teacher of
  130
Anglican Church 219–22
  cemeteries 106–7
  and death 220–2
anointing 220
anthrax 210
antibiotic resistant organisms
  202–4
Arches Court of Canterbury
  107
Armed Forces 52–3
ashes, scattering of 119, 284
assault 189

autopsy
  academic 41, 92
  Coroner's 95
  decline in 91
  disaster victims 139–40
  history of 89–90
  on infants 63, 86
  and infection 205–6
  reasons for 91–2
  religious objections to 258,
    276, 293
  and suspicious deaths 63,
    97–8
  techniques of 95–8
  virtual 91
  see also organ/tissue
    retention

Bahá'i Faith 268–71
  and death 269–71
Bahá'i National Office 271
Bahá'u'lláh 268
baptism 218, 219–20, 223,
  231–2, 237, 243
  Sikh 285
Baptist Church 227
bereavement 191–5
  and child death 192–3
  and covert relationships
    193–4
  and disasters 138, 193
  and infectious disease 211
  and Last Offices 188–9
bereavement counselling
  194–5
  terminal care staff 156, 157
bereavement counsellors 188
Bhagavad Gita 281
Bible 229, 241, 242, 243,
  250–1
Births and Deaths Registration
  Act
  (1836) 38
  (1874) 39
  (1926) 79, 81
  (1953) 49, 61, 78
Bland, Tony 163–4
blood
  and Jehovah's Witnesses
    229–30
  standard infection control
    precautions 201

blood transfusion
  alternatives to 230–1
  religious objections to 230,
    233, 253, 293
body bags 204, 205
body fluids, infection control
  precautions 201
body snatching 90
Book of Mormon 236
Book of Remembrance 35
brainstem death 127–8
British Medical Association
  (BMA) 115, 162, 168
Brodrick Committee 58
brucellosis 210
Buddhism 264–7
  and death 265–7
Buddhist Hospice Trust 267
burial 105–6
  Christian 106–7
  and disinterment *see*
    exhumation
  garden 109
  'green' 108–9
  Jewish 262
  Muslim 277–8
  registration of 108
  at sea 35, 110
  vault 27
  woodland 109–10
Burial Acts 105–6, 133
burial clubs 26

cancer 149–50, 151
cardiac pacemakers 112, 187
cardio-pulmonary resuscitation
  (CPR) 169–72
carers' organisations 319–20,
  322
caste system 280
Casualty Identification Bureau
  142
Catholicism 223–6
cemeteries 105–7
  Local Authority 34, 35
  maintenance of 35
  municipal 105–6, 107
  private 107
certification/forms
  Coroner's 32–3, 61, 63–4
  for cremation 113–18
  'out of England' 36, 62
  see also Medical Certificate

Chevra Kadisha 260–1
children
    consent 161
    death and bereavement
        192–3
    dying 156
    see also infants
Children Act (1989) 161
Chinese 296–302
    and death 298–302
Christian Sacraments 218,
    223–4, 228, 237–8, 243
Christian Science 241–5
    and death 243–5
    and healing 242, 243
Christianity 217–18
    free churches 227–49
    Last Offices of 182–90
    Roman Catholicism 223–6
Church of England see
    Anglican Church
Church of Jesus Christ of
    Latter Day Saints see
    Mormon Church
Church of Scotland 228
churches, burial in 106
churchyards 34, 106–7
Civil Aviation Acts 52
Civil Partnership Act (2004)
    313–14
Code of Practice for the
    Prevention of Infection in
    Clinical Laboratories and
    Post Mortem Rooms
    (Howie Code) 199, 206,
    209
common grave 34
Common Law 61, 106
communicable disease see
    infectious disease
community care, HIV infection
    207
confidentiality 160–1
consecrated ground 34, 107
consent
    incapacity to give 161–2
    minors 161
    permanent/persistent
        vegetative state (PVS)
        162–7
    to autopsy and retention of
        material 62–4, 92–3, 94,
        124–6

Consultant for Communicable
    Disease Control 197
Coppett's Wood Hospital 200
corneal donation 189–90, 329
Coroner
    autopsy 95
    and decision to end life 31
    disaster investigation
        139–40
    history of 56–8
    and inquests 66–75
    order, exhumation 134
    and organ donation 128–9
    referral to 44–5, 51–2
Coroners' Act
    (1887) 39, 57
    (1988) 66, 71, 134
Coroners' (Amendment) Act
    (1926) 39, 57, 58, 94
Coroner's certificates 61, 63–4
Coroner's forms 63–4, 118
Coroner's Office 58–9, 63, 64
Coroner's Rules 57, 58, 62–3,
    66, 70, 124, 126
cot death see Sudden Infant
    Death Syndrome (SIDS)
counselling
    HIV/AIDS 312
    see also bereavement
        counselling
County Coroners' Act (1860)
    57
CPR see cardio-pulmonary
    resuscitation
cremation 27, 112–20
    arrangements for 119
    ashes 119, 284
    Buddhist 266–7
    certification/forms 113–18
    Hindu 283–4
    history and principles
        112–13
    infectious diseases and 206
    legal requirements for
        113–17
    legislation 113
    and pacemakers 112, 187
    popularity of 113
    religious prohibition of 113
    Sikh 289
    stillborn infants and fetal
        remains 118–19

Cremation Acts 27, 113, 117
Cremation Regulations,
    England (1930) 198
Cremation Society 27
Creutzfeldt–Jakob disease 209
Crown Prosecution Service 57
cytomegalovirus 207

Dangerous Pathogens Advisory
    Group 199, 206
death
    accidental 59, 67
    cause of see specific causes
    changes following 104
    diagnosis of 28–9
    helping organisations
        315–36
    medico-legal requirements
        160–81
    signs of 29
    suspicious 59, 63, 97–8
death certificate 44, 45
    see also Medical Certificate
        of Cause of Death
        (MCCD)
DEFRA (Department for
    Environment, Food and
    Rural Affairs) 110,
    112–13
Department of Health (DoH)
    94, 98, 197
    palliative care guidelines
        148–51
Department of Health and
    Social Security (DHSS)
    148–9, 150
Department of Social Security
    (DSS) Social Fund 34
diet, religious 224, 252, 256,
    273–4, 280–1, 286
disasters 137–43
    care of the bereaved 193
    definition 137
    facilities required 140–2
    identification of victims
        138, 140, 141, 142
    pathologist role 139–40
    planning for 138–9
disinfection 201
    and terminal cleaning
        204–5
disinterment see exhumation

disposal
  by exposure 294
  in special circumstances
    50–1
  see also burial; cremation
Disused Burial Grounds
    (Amendment) Act (1981)
    133
doctors
  and autopsy 41–4
  and cremation 115–17
  death records see entries
    beginning Medical
    Certificate
  general practitioners 152,
    153
  unregistered 39
donation of body see medical
    research; organ donation
drowning 59
drug abuse 60, 67
drug therapy see anaesthetics;
    analgesics
dying
  care of the see palliative care
  children 156
  diagnosis 155–6
  and religious ritual 225,
    256–7, 265–6, 274,
    281, 287

Eastern Orthodox Churches
    227
embalming 104–5
emergency services 61, 138,
    139
enteric infections 210
environmental health 197
epidemics 198
Eucharist 218, 237
  see also Holy Communion;
    Memorial, the
euthanasia 175–6
  Chinese attitudes 300
  Japanese attitudes 306
  religious objection to 225,
    234, 239, 245, 248,
    253, 259–60, 270, 277,
    288–9, 293
executors 33, 49, 102, 103
exhumation 132–6
  by order of Coroner 134

health and safety 136
history of 132–3
practice of 134–6
under Home Office
    authority 133, 134,
    135–6
export of bodies 36
exposure, disposal by 294
extreme unction 225

family
  autopsy and tissue retention
    64–5
  bereaved see bereavement
  of disaster victims 193
  funeral responsibilities of
    33, 102, 103
  infection and 211
  Last Offices and 182
  organ donation and 125,
    128–9
  registration of death by 49,
    51–2
  and terminally ill 157–8
family doctors see general
    practitioners
Family Law Reform Act (1969)
    161
Federation of British
    Cremation Authorities
    323
fetal remains, cremation
    118–19
Forensic Medical Examiner
    (FME) 139
forensic pathology/medicine
    95–6, 337–9
Foundation for the Study of
    Infant Deaths 323–4
friendly societies 26
Funding of Hospices and Similar
    Organisations 149
funeral directors 33–4, 102,
    103
  and cremation 119
  and infection 34, 102, 204
funerals
  African-Caribbean 248–9,
    253
  Bahá'i 270–1
  Buddhist 266–7
  Chinese 300–2

Christian denominational
    222, 226, 228, 234,
    239–40, 245
  development of UK practice
    26–7, 102
  for disaster victims 138
  financial responsibility for
    34
  Hindu 283–4
  Japanese 307–8
  Jewish 262
  Muslim 277–8
  planning of 103
  Sikh 289–90
  for stillbirths 221
  Zoroastrian 294–5

Gay Bereavement Project 327
General Medical Council
    30–1, 129, 168
general practitioners 152, 153
graves 34–5
  common 34
gravestones 35
graveyards 26
grief 191–2
  see also bereavement;
    bereavement counselling
Gurdwara 289, 290
Guru Gobind Singh 285, 286
Guru Granth Sahib 285, 287,
    288, 290
Guru Nanak 285, 288

halal ritual 273, 276
hands, washing of 200
health care professionals
  and AIDS 206–7
  and infection 196, 204
  Last Offices 182
  and terminal care 152–3,
    156, 157
  see also doctors
Health and Safety at Work Act
    (1974) 98, 107
health and safety, exhumation
    136
helping organisations 315–36
hepatitis B 206
Hillsborough football stadium
    disaster 138

Hinduism 279–84
  and death 281–4
  diet 280–1
HIV/AIDS 310–14
  and death 313
  infection risk 206–7
HM Inspector of Anatomy
  123, 129, 325
Holy Communion 223–4, 243
  see also Eucharist; Memorial,
  the
home deaths 103
Home Office 74
  exhumation 133, 134,
  135–6
Home Office pathologists 95
homicide see unlawful killing
homosexuality 313–14
hospice staff 156, 157
hospices 152
  Buddhist 267
  children's 156
hospitals
  and autopsy 41, 91, 92
  death in 60, 183–4
  infection control in 200–2,
  204–5
  Last Offices in 182, 183–90
  NHS 92, 94
  palliative care in 152–3,
  158
Howie Code (Code of Practice
  for the Prevention of
  Infection in Clinical
  Laboratories and Post
  Mortem Rooms) 199,
  206, 209
human immunodeficiency virus
  see HIV/AIDS
Human Organ Transplants Act
  (1989) 122, 123, 126,
  129
Human Rights Act (1998)
  177–8
Human Tissue Act (1961)
  123–5, 126, 129–30
Human Tissue Authority (HTA)
  125

identification
  bracelets 99, 186–7
  disaster victims 138, 140,
  141, 142

infectious disease 204
Independent Mental Capacity
  Advocate (IMCA) 179
industrial accidents 59, 66
industrial disease 59, 67
Infant Life Preservation Act
  (1929) 78
infanticide 26, 79
infants
  autopsy 63, 86
  death and bereavement 192
  see also children
infection control 196–213
infection risk
  exhumation 136
  resuscitation 173
infection routes 196
infectious disease 60
  autopsy 205–6
  bereaved contacts 211
  classification of organisms
  199
  legal aspects 197–8
  mortuary practice 205
  notifiable 197
  place of treatment 200
  specific diseases 206–11
  Standard Infection Control
  Precautions 200–2,
  204–5
  stillbirth 211
inquests 66–75
Inspector of Anatomy, HM
  123, 129, 325
International Cremation
  Federation 326
Islam 272–8
  and death 274–8
  dietary laws of 273–4

Japanese 303–9
  and death 304–8
Jehovah's Witnesses 229–35
  and blood 229–31, 232–3
  and death 233–4
Jewish community 254–63
  and burial 262
  and death 256–62
Judaism
  dietary laws 256
  Orthodox 259, 260
juries 66–70

Kegworth air crash 138
Kensal Green Cemetery Act
  (1832) 105
kidney donors 129
kosher diet 256
kyphoscoliosis 185

laboratory workers 199
Last Offices 182–90
  Hindu 281–2
  infectious diseases and 204
  Jewish 257
  Muslim 277
  routine 183–8
  Sikh 287
  and unnatural death 189
  see also laying out
laying out
  limited 189
  see also Last Offices
Legal Aid Act (1974) 71
Legionnaire's disease 199
leptospirosis 210
Licensed Teacher of Anatomy
  130
life support
  and discontinuation 29–30
  and organ donation 175
Living Wills 167–9
Local Authorities 33–4
  and infectious diseases
  197–8
  'Proper Officers' 197–8
Local Authorities Cemeteries
  Order 107
Local Government Act (1972)
  107
Lockerbie disaster 138
Lutheran Church 227

Macmillan Cancer Relief 151,
  328
Macmillan nurses 152
manslaughter see unlawful
  killing
mausolea 27
Medical Certificate of Cause of
  Death (MCCD) 40–1
  accuracy of 41–4, 45
  and Coroner 61, 62
  format of 42–3
Medical Certificate of Stillbirth
  81–3

medical education 129–30
medical negligence 71
Medical Officer for
    Environmental Health
    (MOEH) 197
medical practitioners see
    doctors
medical referee (for cremation)
    116–17
medical research, donation of
    body for 129–30, 259,
    276, 293
medical schools 130
Memorial, the 232
    see also Eucharist; Holy
        Communion
meningitis 208
Mental Capacity Act (2005)
    167, 168, 178–80
Methicillin Resistance
    Staphylococcus Aureus
    (MRSA) 202–4, 211
Methodism 227, 228
military service 52–3
Millais, John 27
Ministry of Defence 52
miscarriage 329
missing persons 53–4
Moorfield's Eye Hospital 329
Mormon Church 236–40
    and death 238–40
mortuaries
    design and administration
        98–100
    for disasters 140
    documentation 99–100
    staff and infection 199,
        204, 205, 207
mosques 36, 272
mourning
    Jewish ritual 262
    see also bereavement
MRSA 202–4, 211
Muhammad, Prophet 272
murder see unlawful killing
Muslim community see Islam

National Association of Funeral
    Directors 329
National Health Service (NHS)
    92, 94
negligence 70–1

neonatal death 53, 83–6
Newcastle General Infirmary
    200
non-conformist churches
    227–49
Northern Ireland 54
notifiable diseases 197
nurses see health care
    professionals
nursing homes, Christian
    Science 242

Offences Against the Person
    Act (1861) 78
organ donation 127–8
    and coroner 128–9
    and life support 175
    religious objection to 248
organ donors
    live 129
    selection 127–8
organ transplant
    donation and 121–32
    history 122
    religious objections to
        233–4, 253, 293, 305
    transplant coordinator 129
organ/tissue retention
    Alder Hey inquiry 93–4
    consent 62–4, 92–3, 124–6
    and cremation 117–18
    objections to 64–6
Orthodox Judaism 259, 260
'out of England' certificate 36,
    62

pace makers 112, 187
PACE (Police and Criminal
    Evidence Act 1984) 86
pain control 153–5, 177
palliative care
    care of friends and family
        157–8
    delivery 151–3
    Department of Health
        guidelines 148–51
    quality in 157–8
    symptom control 153–5
palliative care teams 152–3
    counselling 156, 157
Parochial Registers Act (1812)
    108

Parsees see Zoroastrianism
pathogens, classification of 199
pathological autopsy 90
pathologists
    disaster investigation by
        139–40
    and infection 204
    and organ donation 128
    specialised 63
Patients Dying in Hospital
    (DHSS) 148–9, 150
Pentecostal Churches 246, 249
perinatal death 80, 83–6
permanent vegetative state
    (PVS) 162–7
persistent vegetative state (PVS)
    30–1, 162–7
poisoning 60, 173
police 61, 139
police custody deaths 60
Poor Law Act (1834) 38
post mortem see autopsy
pregnancy 79
prenatal testing 79
Price, Dr William 27
prison deaths 60
Procurator Fiscal 71–2
    disaster investigation 140
Prophet Muhammad 272
protective clothing 202
Public Health (Control of
    Diseases) Act (1984) 150,
    197
Public Health (Infectious
    Disease) Regulations
    (1988) 197
putrefaction 104

Quakers see Society of Friends
Qur'an 277, 278

rabies 208
Ramadan fast 274
Ras Tafari 250
Rastafarianism 250–3
    and alternative medicine
        251
    and death 252, 253
Register of cremations 117
Registrar of Births, Marriages
    and Deaths 38, 39, 40,
    44–5, 47–8

Registrar General 38, 44–5, 48, 51–2
Registration of Births, Marriages and Deaths Regulations (1968) 44–5
Registration of Burials Act (1864) 109
Registration of death 38
    at sea, or overseas (HM Forces) 52–3
    and Coroner 44–5, 51–2
    by family 49, 51–2
    history of 28, 47–8
    responsibility for 49
    without reference to Coroner 49–50
relatives see family
religious emblems, Last Offices 186
reportable deaths 59–61
resuscitation 169–75
    CPR 169–72
    'do not resuscitate' 173–4
    legal status of those who attempt 174–5
    risks to rescuer 172–3
Resuscitation Council 169
rigor mortis 104, 183
road traffic accidents 66
Roman Catholicism 223–6
Royal College of Nursing 168
Royal College of Pathologists 62, 63, 87, 94, 95
Royal College of Physicians 166

St Paul's Cathedral 106
Sabbath observance 255
Sacraments, Christian 218, 223–4, 228, 237–8, 243
Salvation Army 227
sanitisation see embalming
SARS (Severe Acute Respiratory Syndrome) 210–211
Science and Health with Key to the Scriptures 241, 242, 243
Scotland
    assisted suicide 176–7
    death registration in 54
    exhumation 135–6
    living wills 167–8

Scottish legal system 71–2
septicaemia 207–8
Seventh Day Adventists 227
Severe Acute Respiratory Syndrome (SARS) 210–11
Shipman, Harold 73, 75–6
shrouds 187
SIDS (Sudden Infant Death Syndrome) 81, 86–7
Sikhism 285–90
    baptism 285
    and death 287–90
    diet 286
Social Services departments 152
Society of Friends 227
Standard Infection Control Precautions 200–2
stillbirth 80
    certification and registration 81, 82, 83
    funeral 221
    and infection 211
Stillbirth and Neonatal Death Society (SANDS) 79, 83
sudden death 59, 61
Sudden Infant Death Syndrome (SIDS) 81, 86–7
Sudden Unexpected Death in Infancy (SUDI) 80–2, 86–7
suicide 67, 176
    assisted 176–7
    Chinese attitudes to 300
    Japanese attitudes to 305–6
    religious attitudes to 226, 234, 239, 245, 248, 253, 259–60, 266, 270, 277, 283, 288, 293, 300
Suicide Act (1961) 106, 176
suspicious deaths 59, 63, 97–8
symptom control, palliative care 153–5

TB (tuberculosis) 210
teaching hospitals 45
Terminal Care (Health Circular) 149
terminal cleaning 204–5
terminal illness see palliative care

terminal sedation 177
Thompson, Sir Henry 27
tissue retention see organ/tissue retention
Torah, the 254
Town and Country Planning Act (1990) 133
Towers of Silence 294
transplant coordinator 129
transport accidents 66
Trollope, Anthony 27
tuberculosis (TB) 210

undertakers see funeral directors
unlawful killing 51, 66, 67
Unrelated Human Live Transplant Regulating Authority (ULTRA) 129

vault inhumation 27
vegetarianism 280–1, 286
violent death 189
viral haemorrhagic fevers 208
virtual autopsy 91
voluntary workers 139
vultures 294

washing of hands 200
Wells, Spencer 27
Westminster Abbey 106
wills see Living Wills
women
    Hindu 280
    Muslim 273
    Orthodox Jewish 255
    Rastafarian 251, 252
    Sikh 286

Zeebrugge Ferry sinking 138
Zoroaster 291
Zoroastrian Trust Funds of Europe 295
Zoroastrianism 291–5
    and death 292–5
    and disposal by exposure 294

Author Index

Akabayashi, A. 306
Alexander, R.T. 86
Andrew, N. 209
Ardagh, M. 169

Beckwith, R.E. 81
Bergman, A.B. 81
Bissett, R.A.L. 91
Blackmore, M.A. 200
Bradfield, J.B. 109
Buck, N. 92
Busuttil, A. 138
Byles, J. 132

Cameron, D. 306
Camps, B.S. 211
Chadwick, E. 26
Charlton, C.A.R. 28–9
Chen, A.W.Y. 138
Christensen, H. 134
Coleman, P. 59

Day, A. 59
DeBard, M.L. 169
Devlin, H.B. 92
Donaldson, O. 137
Dorries, C.P. 28
Dyer, C. 129

Easton, G. 138
Edwards, A. 137
Elkins, A.P. 25
Emmerson, A.M. 203
Enright, D.J. 28
Eustace, S.J. 91

Faugier, J. 182
Favero, M.S. 200
Fong, C.L. 297
Forrest, A.R.W. 58

Garner, J.S. 200
Gavaghan, C. 176
Giarelli, A. 305
Gittings, C. 25, 27

Hanzlick, R. 105
Hartley, D.H. 127
Haslam, F. 90
Healing, T.D. 211
Hinnels, J. 279
Hoffman, P.N. 211
Hogan, J. 86
Humphrey, D. 176

Inglis, B.A. 89
Irwin, M. 169

Jones, A. 194
Jupp, P.C. 25, 27

Kerrie, P.K. 298
Knight, B. 61, 104
Kwong, L. 298

Lawrence, J. 200, 201
Leadbeater, S. 61
Littman, K. 251
Lunn, J.N. 92

McDermott, M.B. 92
Marshall, T.K. 25, 26, 27, 294
Milroy, C.M. 58
Moore, W. 90
Morrison, D. 203
Motohashi, Y. 305

Nash, T.P. 154
Nelson, E. 91
Nudeshima, J. 303–4, 305, 308
Nurmikko, T.J. 154

O'Grady, G. 90, 91

Pallis, C. 127
Polson, C.J. 25, 26, 27, 294
Pounder, D.J. 58, 134

Radisch, D. 86
Rae, C.O. 81
Redfearn, H.C. 41, 65, 89, 92, 93
Richardson, R. 89–90
Robinson, W.S. 206

Saukko, P. 104

Smale, D.A. 47, 106, 108, 113, 132, 133
Stanford, P. 223
Start, R.D. 59
Steel, J. 135
Steentoft, A. 134
Stone, E. 71

Takao, M. 305
Tom-Johnson, C. 193
Tuffs, A. 89

Underwood, J.C.E. 90

Valera, J. 230
Virchow, R. 90

Wade, E. 137
Whitwell, H.L. 58
Wiles, J.R. 154
Wilson, K. 209
Wise, J. 305
Wise, S. 90
Worm, K. 134

Young, S.E.J. 211